HIMALAYAN 'PEOPLE'S WAR'

MICHAEL HUTT

editor

Himalayan 'People's War'

Nepal's Maoist Rebellion

HURST & COMPANY, LONDON

First published in the United Kingdom by
C. Hurst & Co. (Publishers) Ltd,
38 King Street, London WC2E 8JZ
© 2004 Michael Hutt and contributors
All rights reserved.

The right of the editor and contributors to be
identified as the authors of this work has been asserted
by them in accordance with the Copyright, Designs and
Patents Act, 1988.

A Cataloguing-in-Publication data record for this book is
available from the British Library.

Printed in India

ISBNs
1–85065–721–1 *casebound*
1–85065–722–X *paperback*

CONTENTS

Part III. GEOPOLITICAL AND COMPARATIVE PERSPECTIVES

Part IV. AFTERWORDS

Part V. APPENDIXES

THE CONTRIBUTORS

KRISHNA HACHHETHU is Reader in Political Science at the Centre for Nepal and Asian Studies (CNAS), Tribhuvan University. His publications include *Party Building in Nepal: Organization, Leadership and People* and *Leadership in Nepal* (co-authored with Lok Raj Baval and Hari Sharma, 2001). He is currently working on a book entitled *Nepal: Democracy, Pluralism and the State*.

MICHAEL HUTT is Reader in Nepali and Himalayan Studies at the School of Oriental and African Studies in the University of London. His publications on the subject of modern Nepali language and literature include: *Himalayan Voices: An Introduction to Modern Nepali Literature* (1991), *Modern Literary Nepali: An Introductory Reader* (1994), *Teach Yourself Nepali* (2000), *Devkota's* Muna-Madan: *Translation and Analysis* (1996). He has edited a book on Nepali political culture: *Nepal in the Nineties: Versions of the Past, Visions of the Future* (1994). *Nepal: A Guide to the Art and Architecture of the Kathmandu Valley* (1994) reflects his interest in art and architecture. He is also the author of numerous articles in a range of academic journals. His most recent publication is *Unbecoming Citizens: Culture, Nationhood, and the Flight of Refugees from Bhutan* (2003).

MARIE LECOMTE-TILOUINE is a social anthropologist attached to the CNRS (Centre Nationale de la Recerche Scientifique). Her most recent publications in English include 'The Enigmatic Pig' (*Studies in Nepali History and Society* 5, 1, 2000), 'The History of the Messianic and Rebel King Lakhan Thapa' in *Resistance and the State: Nepalese Experiences*, edited by David N. Gellner (2003) and *Ethnic Revival and Religious Turmoil: Identities and Representations in the Himalayas* (ed. with Pascale Dollfus, 2003). She is currently heading a programme on the history and culture of the Khas of the Western Himalaya.

PRATYOUSH ONTA is a historian. He is the convenor of the Centre for Social Research and Development in Kathmandu. He was also

vii

the convenor of Martin Chautari from 1996 to 2003. Among other books, he has co-edited *Sthaniya radio* (Local Radio) (2002) and *Mediako antarvastu* (Media Contents) (2002) and edited *Ksetriya media* (Regional Media) (2002), all of which analyse and document media activity in Nepal. He is currently working on a study of radio in Nepal.

JUDITH PETTIGREW is a senior lecturer at the University of Central Lancashire and a research associate at the University of Cambridge. Her most recent publications include 'Guns, Kinship and Fear: Maoists among the Tamu-mai (Gurungs)' in *Resistance and the State: Nepalese Experiences*, edited by David N. Gellner (2003) and 'Healing Here, There and In-Between: A Tamu Shaman's Experiences of International Landscapes' (with Y. Tamu) in *New Approaches to Medical Archaeology and Medical Anthropology*, edited by G. Carr and P. Baker (2002). She is presently writing a book on the impact of the Maoist insurgency on rural civilians.

JOANNA PFAFF-CZARNECKA is Professor in Social Anthropology at the University of Bielefeld, Germany. From 1996 until 1998 she was president of the Swiss Society of Social Anthropology. Her recent publications include the co-edited volumes *Ethnic Futures: The State* and *Identity Politics in Asia* (1999) and *Rituale heute. Theorien, Kontroversen, Entwürfe* (Rituals Today: Theories, Controversies, Designs) (1999). She is currently working on the democratisation process at the sub-national level in Nepal and on the incorporation of religious minorities in Central Europe.

DINESH PRASAIN has an MA in Sociology from Tribhuvan University. He is volunteering as the President of the national peace network, Collective Campaign for Peace (COCAP).

PHILIPPE RAMIREZ is a researcher at the CNRS (Centre Nationale de la Recerche Scientifique). His works have dealt mainly with the political anthropology of rural Nepal. His publications include *De la disparition des chefs. une anthropologie politique népalaise* (On the Disappearance of Headmen: A Nepalese Anthropology) (2000) and *Resunga, the Mountain of the Horned Sage* (2000).

HARI ROKA, a left activist, has completed an MPhil dissertation in political economy at Jawaharlal Nehru University in New Delhi, and is working towards a PhD. He contributes articles of political analysis on a regular basis to Nepali journals, notably *Himal Khabarpatrika*.

SAUBHAGYA SHAH is an assistant professor in the Department of Sociology/Anthropology, Tribhuvan University. His most recent publications include 'From Evil State to Civil Society' in *State of Nepal*, edited by Kanak Mani Dixit and Ramachandran Shastri (2002) and 'Service to Servitude: Domestication of Household Labor in Nepal' in *Home and Hegemony: Identity Politics in Asian Domestic Service*, edited by Kathleen Adams and Sara Dickey (2000). He is currently working on his PhD dissertation on state, social movements and international development at the Department of Anthropology, Harvard University.

MANDIRA SHARMA holds an L.L.M in International Human Rights law and has been working as a human rights defender for the last ten years. As Executive Director of Advocacy Forum, a national NGO, she has been visiting different places in Nepal to document cases of human rights violations and to offer legal aid to victims. She is also researching the incidence of illegal detention and torture in Nepali police custody.

SUDHEER SHARMA is a leading journalist in Nepal who has contributed many pioneering articles on the Maoist movement to journals such as *Himal Khabarpatrika* and *Mulyankan*. These articles are based on extensive travels to Maoist-dominated areas, and in-depth interviews. He is currently the Assistant Editor of the fortnightly news magazine *Nepal*.

SARA SHNEIDERMAN is conducting PhD research in Anthropology at Cornell University in Ithaca, New York, under a National Science Foundation Fellowship. Her dissertation focuses on ethnic, religious, and political identity among the Thangmi, a largely undocumented ethnic community resident in the Himalayan borderlands of Nepal, Tibet and India. Her publications include 'Embodied Ancestors: Territory and the Body in Thangmi Death Rituals' in *Territory and Identity in Tibet and the Himalayas*, edited by K. Buffetrille and K. Diemberger (2001) and a forthcoming article in the *Himalayan Research Bulletin* entitled 'Violent Histories and Political Consciousness: Reflections on Nepal's Maoist movement from Piskar Village'.

DEEPAK THAPA is a freelance journalist and book editor based in Kathmandu. Besides having authored two in-depth articles on the Maoist movement in *Himal South Asian*, a monthly journal, he is the editor of *Understanding the Maoist Movement of Nepal* and author of *A Kingdom Under Siege: Nepal's Maoist Insurgency, 1996 to 2003* (both published in 2003).

MARK TURIN divides his time between the Anthropology Departments at Cambridge and Cornell. He runs the Digital Himalaya Project (*www.digitalhimalaya.com*) and is a regular contributor to the *Nepali Times* and *Contributions to Nepalese Studies*. He recently co-edited *Themes in Himalayan Languages and Linguistics*, which is jointly published by the South Asia Institute of Heidelberg and Tribhuvan University, Kathmandu. He continues to work on ethnolinguistic issues in the Himalayan region.

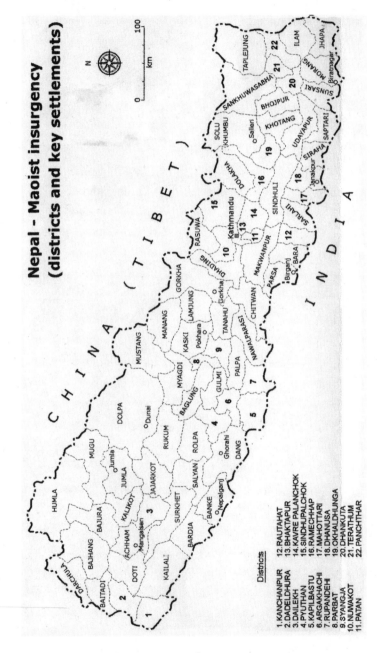

Nepal - Maoist insurgency (districts and key settlements)

Districts

1. KANCHANPUR
2. DADELDHURA
3. DAILEKH
4. PYUTHAN
5. KAPILBASTU
6. ARGAKHACHI
7. RUPANDEHI
8. PARBAT
9. SYANGJA
10. NUWAKOT
11. PATAN
12. RAUTAHAT
13. BHAKTAPUR
14. KAVRE PALANCHOK
15. SINDHUPALCHOK
16. RAMECHHAP
17. MAHOTTARI
18. DHANUSA
19. OKHALDHUNGA
20. DHANKUTA
21. TERATHUM
22. PANCHTHAR

INTRODUCTION

MONARCHY, DEMOCRACY
AND MAOISM IN NEPAL*

Michael Hutt

It is not unusual for a faraway tourist destination to be described as a 'land of contrasts'. Certainly this is one of the clichés that has regularly been pressed into service by those who have sought to attract dollar-carrying guests to Nepal: their brochures and guidebooks have regularly contrasted the steamy jungle resorts with the rarefied atmosphere of the high snowpeaks, and the modern urban bustle of Kathmandu with the 'traditional' ways of the kingdom's remoter ethnic communities. However, there are many other contrasts and contradictions that do not figure in tourist literature: between the constitutional definition of Nepal as a Hindu state and the presence of significant religious minorities; between its status as a multi-party democracy under a constitutional monarchy and the long term presence of a well-entrenched communist movement; between its status as a unitary state with one official state language and the presence within its borders of scores of different ethnic groups speaking dozens of different languages; between its status as one of the most aided 'developing' nations on earth and the impoverishment and marginalisation of a large chunk of its population; and between its

* Thanks are due to the Research Committee of the School of Oriental and African Studies and the Society for South Asian Studies for funding the conference upon which this book is based. The British Embassy in Kathmandu, and especially Mr Andrew Mitchell, played an extremely helpful role in facilitating travel arrangements for four colleagues from Nepal, and the British High Commission in New Delhi for a fifth. I must add a word of personal thanks to Heather Naylor and Raechel Leigh Carter for their help with the conference and the preliminary editorial work. All of us who have contributed to this volume also owe an enormous debt of thanks to Bela Malik, our tireless copy editor, who saved us from ourselves on innumerable occasions. Many thanks to Rhoderick Chalmers for his efficient preparation of the index to this book.

1

reputation as a land of peace and the ruthless violence of the struggles for power that have taken place at several junctures in its history. They suggest that the outside world still understands Nepal imperfectly, and they explain why it is that the emergence in Nepal of a violent Maoist insurgency during the late 1990s met with bewilderment and incomprehension even among many of those who claimed to know the country well. Such a development cannot be explained satisfactorily outside its specific context: it possesses its own historical depth and its own socio-cultural environment.

This book is intended to provide some of that contextual detail, without which one is not really able to explain why the people of Nepal had to experience their beautiful country being torn apart by civil war.

HISTORICAL PRELUDE

The Shah kings, of whom the first seized the throne of the tiny hill kingdom of Gorkha in the mid-sixteenth century, are generally credited with having created the modern nation-state now known as Nepal. This development took place during the second half of the eighteenth century when Prithvi Narayan Shah overran most of the other petty states of the central and eastern Himalaya in a campaign of military conquest, and incorporated them into his own territory. The Gorkhali expansion ended in 1816 after a series of battles with the armed forces of the British East India Company, and thirty years later the Shah kings' power was eclipsed by a courtly family which adopted the title of 'Rana'. The Ranas pursued a programme of Hinduisation which systematised the incorporation of Nepal's many disparate ethno-linguistic groups into a national hierarchy of castes and ethnic groups headed by the Khas (later called Chetri) and Bahuns (Brahmins) of the Gorkhali élite. Between 1846 and 1951, the Rana regime achieved an accommodation with the British that suited both sides, but which strengthened the traditional order in Nepal against the forces of change unleashed by British rule in India. The extractive nature of the Nepali state thus remained very deeply ingrained, and the ruling élite continued to regard the mass of the population as revenue-producing subjects rather than citizens with rights. Over the course of these 105 years, the Shahs and Ranas intermarried on a regular basis, and their genealogies became closely intertwined.

The first Nepali political party, the Praja Parishad, was established in Kathmandu in 1936 and was sternly suppressed. Therefore, its successors, the Nepali Congress Party and the Communist Party of Nepal, which though splintered still constitute the two main party political camps, were formed not in Nepal but in India, during the 1940s. In 1951 the Rana regime was overthrown by a coalition which included the Shah king, Tribhuvan, the political parties, and disgruntled factions of the Rana élite; Nehru's government in India also played an important role as broker of the subsequent political settlement. Eight years later, the Nepali Congress gained a majority in Nepal's first general elections, but in December 1960 King Mahendra, who had succeeded his father in 1955, used the emergency powers granted by the Constitution to dismiss the Congress government, on the pretext that it had failed to maintain law and order and was endangering the sovereignty of Nepal. Mahendra asserted that multi-party parliamentary democracy was an alien system that was unsuited to the circumstances of Nepal, and in 1962 a new Constitution was promulgated which enshrined a new political dispensation, the Panchayat system. This was designed to provide a veneer of democratic participation and electoral accountability, while the king retained ultimate power and party political activity was banned.

The political parties continued to operate underground, proliferating all the while. As education spread and levels of political consciousness rose during the 1960s and '70s, opposition to the Panchayat system grew—partly because of its increasing exclusivity and unaccountability, partly because it was patently failing to deliver the 'development' (*bikas*) that had become one of its watchwords, and partly also because of the manner in which, latterly, it tried to suppress dissent, even among adherents of the system. Anti-Panchayat movements were led by the banned parties in 1979 and 1985: the first, spearheaded by student activists, led to a National Referendum, conducted in 1980, which was deemed to have provided the system with a renewed mandate; the second, which was planned as a peaceful movement of civil disobedience, was called off when bombs exploded at several locations in Kathmandu.

Finally, in April 1990, the Panchayat system was dismantled in the wake of a people's movement (*jan andolan*) for democracy and human rights led by the Nepali Congress and a United Left Front

4 *Michael Hutt*

consisting of seven communist parties. This movement was formally launched in February, against the background of worsening economic conditions brought on by a dispute over trade and transit agreements between the governments of India and Nepal, and although the agitation remained largely confined to urban areas it quickly drew in the professional classes. The Panchayat system was replaced by a bicameral parliament, a new democratic constitution was promulgated in November 1990, and the palace was deemed to have surrendered its powers and acquiesced to a purely constitutional role.[1]

The Nepali Congress Party has been the dominant political party since the restoration of multi-party democracy: it won a majority in the first general elections held under the new dispensation, in 1991, but the government collapsed in 1994 due to internal divisions within the party. Fresh elections produced a hung parliament, and the Nepal Communist Party (Unified Marxist-Leninist; hereafter 'UML'), the largest single party, attempted to run a minority government, but this fell after less than a year in power. Between 1995 and 1999, some half dozen different coalitions came to power, involving some very unlikely bedfellows, and the popular perception quickly spread that the political parties were interested only in clinging to power, and that their leaders were taking every opportunity to feather their nests before they were ousted by the next incongruous coalition (Dhruba Kumar 2000). In the 1999 general elections the Nepali Congress party was returned to power with a parliamentary majority, partly because the UML had split and the left vote was divided.

THE MAOIST INSURGENCY

After 1990, many of the parties situated at the extreme left of the political spectrum resorted to extra-parliamentary tactics such as street demonstrations and *bandhs* (shutdowns of businesses and vehicular traffic enforced with threats of violence) to press their demands. However, they also established political front organisations to contest elections, most notably the United People's Front (Samyukta Jan Morcha), which managed to win nine seats in the

---

[1] For an analysis of the 1990 people's movement (*jan andolan*) see Hoftun et al. (1999), and for a collection of essays on the political change see Hutt (1994).

1991 general elections, making it the third largest party in parliament. Its stronghold was in the mid-western hill districts of Rukum and Rolpa, where three contiguous UPF constituencies interrupted a great swathe of Congress-controlled constituencies.[2] After 1991, the UPF and its supporters were subjected to repeated abuses of power by officials belonging to the ruling Nepali Congress in these areas, with the result that the Nepali Congress, and the police force that did its bidding, came to be widely hated there.

The United People's Front split into two factions in 1994: the one that was recognised by the Electoral Commission fielded forty candidates in the 1994 general election but failed to win a single seat. In February 1996, having renamed itself the Communist Party of Nepal (Maoist), the unrecognised faction announced that, because the Congress-led coalition government had failed to respond to a list of forty demands submitted by the UPF, it had launched a people's war (*jan yuddha*).[3] The forty-point demand was for an end to the intrusion into Nepal and domination of foreign elements; for a secular state free of all discrimination and oppression with the monarchy stripped of its privileges; and for a wider range of welfare provisions and social and economic reforms (see Appendix A for a full list).

The Maoist leaders laid plans for a protracted war, during which they would recruit, train and equip an army, establish 'base areas' (*adhar ilaka*) in rural hill districts from which all state bodies and institutions would be banished, and gradually encircle the towns and cities. Their main tactics were the concerted political indoctrination of villagers in the areas they controlled, armed attacks on govern-

---

[2] Whelpton (1994: 79). Nepal is divided for administrative purposes into 14 zones, comprising a total of 75 districts.

[3] The editor of a volume such as this has some difficult stylistic choices to make. For instance, the Maoist leadership describes its military actions as a people's war (in English) or *jan yuddha* (in Nepali). Naturally, most of the chapters in this book are peppered with references to this campaign, and it is necessary to settle on a consistent form of usage. People's War (upper case initials, without quotes) might suggest that contributors to the volume have accepted that the campaign is or was being waged genuinely on behalf of and with the universal support of 'the people', which is debatable. On the other hand, repeated usage of the form 'people's war' (lower case initials, in quotes) might suggest that contributors are highly sceptical of the legitimacy of the campaign. This book is not intended either to dismiss legitimate grievances or to produce validating arguments for a violent insurgency: instead, it aims to analyse and clarify the underlying causes of the conflict. We have therefore settled on the following usages: people's war, *jan yuddha*, people's government, *jan sarkar*, and so on.

ment officials and police posts in those areas, the replacement of state institutions by 'pro-people' bodies, and the eventual establishment of a *jan sarkar* (people's government) in each district under their control. The government's response, when it realised, belatedly, that the situation in certain districts was spinning out of its control, was to try to crack down with repressive security measures, but its inability to deploy the Royal Nepalese Army and its use of poorly-trained, inadequately-equipped police personnel meant that many innocent lives were lost and allegations of human rights abuses multiplied (Amnesty International 1997). Subsequently, the government softened its response and attempted to initiate a political dialogue with the Maoists, but progress on this front was hampered by divergences of opinion within the Nepali Congress Party, and between it and its various coalition partners, on how best to handle the crisis. The government's approach remained muddled and contradictory, with prisoner releases and negotiations one month and police actions the next.

The killing by the Maoists of fourteen police personnel at Dunai, the district headquarters of the inaccessible district of Dolpa, on 25 September 2000, marked a turning point in the conflict. The level of violence escalated quickly: for instance, more than seventy police personnel were killed in different places over a five-day period in April 2001. By mid-2001, the Maoists had gained almost total control of five mid-western hill districts, where they were busy establishing local *jan sarkar*s, and their cadres were active almost everywhere else. The people's war and the state's response to it had so far led to the deaths of nearly 2,000 people.

THE ROYAL MASSACRE

On the night of Friday 1 June 2001, King Birendra and the whole of his immediate family were either killed or fatally injured by gunfire while they were attending their customary monthly gathering at the Narayanhiti Palace in Kathmandu. Of the twenty-one guests, Birendra, his wife, Aishwarya, their younger son Nirajan, and their only daughter Shruti, were all pronounced dead at the Birendra Military Hospital shortly after the incident. Their other son, Crown Prince Dipendra (who was proclaimed king even as he lay in a coma) was declared dead on 4 June. Five other relatives also died of gun-shot wounds, including Dhirendra Shah, one of King Birendra's two younger brothers. Prince Gyanendra, the only surviving brother, was crowned king on 4 June.

In the absence of any substantive explanation, rumours spread rapidly in the immediate aftermath of the massacre. The situation was not helped by the fact that the palace, now bereft of the monarch and his immediate successors, retreated behind its traditional veil of secrecy, although a story was leaking out about Crown Prince Dipendra running amok with firearms and then shooting himself through the head. Conspiracy theories multiplied, fuelled by suspi-cions that Gyanendra, perceived as the chief beneficiary of the massa-cre, might have had some hand in planning it, and by the widespread public unpopularity of his son, who was widely believed to have been implicated in some well-known drunk-driving incidents, of which at least one had led to a fatality. Demonstrators who ventured out on to city streets found that they were being fired upon by police, and for several days the capital was placed under a curfew.

Immediately after he had been crowned, Gyanendra announced that a high-level commission would carry out an investigation of the massacre. In the event, the commission consisted of the Chief Justice and the Speaker of Parliament (a member of the ruling Nepali Congress Party) and after a week a 196-page report was released, consisting mainly of verbatim transcripts of interviews with eyewit-nesses. These all related how Crown Prince Dipendra had gunned down his parents, siblings, and other relatives. Eyewitnesses stated that he had consumed a quantity of whiskey, cannabis and another unidentified narcotic that evening, and it emerged that he had for some time been at loggerheads with his family (and particularly Queen Aishwarya) over the choice of a marriage partner. However, the report contained a number of contradictions and left many ques-tions unanswered. Many Nepalis (possibly a majority of the popula-tion) remained unconvinced. Even those who accepted the version of events recorded in the official report argued that more details should be made public:

...distasteful events related to Kathmandu royalty have historically been swept under the feudal carpet, with society having to move along with a less-than-complete version of events. This cannot be so in the present age, nor is it in the interest of the country, but that is indeed what is happening (Dixit 2002a: 70).

Those who viewed the royal massacre as the outcome of a political conspiracy tended to hold out little hope for the survival of either the monarchy or Nepal's democratic system. In their view, the Maoist insurgency could only draw strength from such a cataclysmic event. Prominent among those who held this view was the leading Nepali Maoist ideologue Baburam Bhattarai, under whose byline a piece appeared in the Nepali-language daily *Kantipur* on 6 June (Bhattarai 2001a). Referring back to the Kot massacre of 1846, in which Jang Bahadur Kunwar engineered the deaths of most of his political rivals, inaugurating the Ranas' century of autocratic rule, Bhattarai alleged that the massacre was the result of a conspiracy involving the Indian Research and Analysis Wing (RAW) and unnamed 'imperialist forces', which was intended to replace a patriotic king with one who would do India's bidding. He praised the role that had been played by certain members of the Shah dynasty in the preservation of Nepal's sovereignty and independence, and claimed that the Maoists and Birendra had been thinking along similar lines on many questions of national importance. His essay ended with an implicit call to the army to mutiny against the 'puppet of expansionism born inside the palace', and to side instead with the 'patriotic sons of Mother Nepal who had been born in huts'.[4]

It was alleged soon after the royal massacre that Birendra had been becoming more politically active in recent years (Hachhethu 2001: 11–12). He was said to have sent various party leaders advice, messages and warnings on numerous occasions, and to have met with many of them individually. It was also known that the palace had lines of communication open to the Maoists, and that this lay behind Baburam Bhattarai's claims to a certain commonality of views, and also explained the king's reluctance to deploy the army. Krishna Hachhethu argues that the Nepali monarchy had been operating 'semi-constitutionally' since 1990, and in the aftermath of the massacre he and many other political analysts suggested that there was now a need to amend the 1990 Constitution, partly in order that royal

[4] The editor and publishers of *Kantipur* were arrested shortly after Bhattarai's article appeared in their newspaper, and charged with treason. They were released after ten days, and the case against them was later dropped.

affairs could be subjected to a measure of scrutiny, and partly to bring the Royal Nepalese Army fully under the control of parliament.

Many analysts predicted that the monarchy would now become more active than before, and that this would weaken democracy. It was generally believed that various members of the royal family had become politically active in an 'underground gang' (*bhumigat giroh*) after Birendra's announcement of a national referendum on the future of the Panchayat system in 1979. It was also widely believed that all of the royals except Birendra himself had been opposed to the political reforms of 1990.

Others argued that Nepal's constitutional monarchy and parliamentary democracy would weather the storm, and those who held this view were heartened by the new king's early public statement of his commitment to the democratic dispensation. However, although the institution of the monarchy remained capable of generating loyalty among the general population, Birendra's legal successor began his reign from a very weak position, and questions were raised about whether his son would ever be acceptable to the Nepali people as his successor. The fact that Paras was not granted the title of 'Crown Prince' immediately, and that the title was bestowed upon him during the autumn festival of Dasain, when most newspapers were not published and the politically volatile university campuses were empty, reflected an awareness of public anxieties on the part of the palace.

ABDUCTIONS AND NEGOTIATIONS

During the second week of July 2001, the Maoists attacked six police posts and in the course of these actions abducted approximately seventy policemen from their headquarters at Holeri in the district of Rolpa. At this point the prime minister, Girija Prasad Koirala, ordered that the army should be deployed to release them. Soldiers were flown into the area, and Nepali newspapers reported that they had surrounded the Maoists, but in fact there then occurred a kind of stand off, with neither of the two sides engaging the other in combat. Soon afterwards, it emerged that senior army staff had refused to send their soldiers into action, at which point Koirala tendered his resignation.

This bizarre series of events reflected severe tensions between the elected government and the palace over the question of who actually controlled the Royal Nepalese Army. Although the army had been stationed in Maoist-affected areas for some years (and many observers alleged that the army could have come to the rescue of the police at Dunai if it had been so ordered), it had not yet engaged militarily with the Maoists at all. Article 118 of the 1990 Constitution provides for the king to 'operate and use' the Royal Nepalese Army 'on the recommendation of the National Defence Council'. This consists of the prime minister (as chairman), the defence minister, and the commander-in-chief. According to Article 119, the king is the supreme commander of the Royal Nepalese Army, and he appoints the commander-in-chief on the recommendation of the prime minister (Dhungel et al. 1998). However, Nepali military culture, dominated as it is at senior level by Ranas and Thapas, is traditionally royalist and suspicious of politicians, a feature that would remain unaffected by any constitutional amendment, at least in the short term. Koirala had failed to bend the army to his will, and he had to go.

On 19 July 2001, Koirala was replaced by Sher Bahadur Deuba, who had already served once as prime minister from September 1995 to March 1997. Deuba had also been in charge of the efforts to promote dialogue with the Maoists that had been initiated under Koirala's predecessor, Krishna Prasad Bhattarai, in 1999. The Maoists attacked a police post in Bajura, killing seventeen, on 20 July, but three days later their leadership agreed to 'postpone' offensive actions and enter into talks with the government. It suddenly became respectable for elected politicians to talk with the Maoist leadership, and it emerged that several of these leaders, including the supreme leader Pushpa Kamal Dahal, alias 'Prachanda', were actually residing not in Nepal, but in India, where they met opposition politicians in mid-August.

Three rounds of talks were conducted between five government negotiators and three mid-ranking Maoist leaders in August, September and November 2001. The Maoists put three core political demands on the table: these were for an interim government, the election of a constituent assembly to draft a new Constitution, and the redesignation of Nepal as a republican state. The government made concessions by scrapping a controversial set of public security regulations it had introduced in June and releasing sixty-eight Maoist detainees, and the Maoist side responded by dropping its demand for a republican state. However, the talks ground to a halt after the

Maoists' final demand, for a constituent assembly, was rejected, and on 21 November Prachanda declared that there was no longer any point in continuing the talks. The Maoist leadership announced the establishment of a Joint Revolutionary People's Council headed by Baburam Bhattarai, and on 23 November attacks were launched in Surkhet, Dang, Syangja and other parts of the country. For the very first time, the Maoists attacked the Royal Nepalese Army, at its base in Gorahi in Dang. The Nepali press reported that fourteen soldiers and twenty-three policemen were killed and that a total of Rs 225 million was looted from banks. The Maoists also captured and made off with a very large quantity of arms and ammunition. Two days later, on 25 November 2001, Maoists attacked the army again, this time at Salleri in the eastern district of Solu, killing twenty-seven policemen, a chief district officer and four soldiers, but also sustaining heavy casualties themselves.

THE STATE OF EMERGENCY

On 26 November 2001 the king declared a National State of Emergency (see Appendix B for the text of the prime minister's address to the nation). Taking its cue from the American-led 'war against terror' launched in the wake of the 11 September attacks on New York and Washington, the Nepali government promulgated the TADO (Terrorist and Disruptive Activities [Control and Punishment] Ordinance), declared the Maoists to be terrorists, and deployed the Royal Nepalese Army to fight against them.[5] The king invoked Clause 1 of Article 115 of the 1990 Constitution[6] to suspend sub-clauses (a), (b) and (d) of Article 12 (Clause 2) which guarantee freedom of thought and expression, peaceful assembly, and movement, respectively; sub-clause 1 of Article 13, which outlaws censorship of reading material, and Articles 15, 16, 17, 22 and 23, which provide rights against preventive detention, to information, to property, to privacy, and to constitutional remedy, respectively. Guidelines were also issued to news-

---

[5] The Nepali Maoists had already been designated as 'terrorists' by Jaswant Singh, the Indian foreign minister, several days earlier.

[6] This reads: 'If a grave emergency arises in regard to the sovereignty or integrity of the Kingdom of Nepal or the security of any part thereof, whether by war, external aggression, armed rebellion or extreme economic disarray, His Majesty may by Proclamation, declare or order a State of Emergency in respect of the whole of the Kingdom of Nepal or of any specified part thereof.'

paper publishers on what they could and could not report. All political parties voiced their support for the three-month emergency, which was renewed on 22 February 2002 with majority support in parliament, and again, more controversially, on 27 May the same year.

The casualty figures announced by the ministry of defence mounted dramatically: the official death toll during the first three-month period of the emergency was 1,045 (including 769 Maoists and 229 members of the security forces), and by June 2002 this had risen to 2,850 Maoists, 335 police, 148 soldiers and 194 civilians. The Nepali press, now cowed and self-censoring, reproduced defence ministry announcements of the number of 'Maoists' killed during 'encounters' with the security forces on a daily basis. This continuous violence erupted at regular intervals into massacres, with reports of scores and sometimes hundreds of fatalities. However, serious doubt began to be cast on the way in which the casualty figures were presented: many analysts believed they were being inflated in favour of the army. A retired Indian general described the June 2002 figures as 'not a very credible statistic' and argued that to gain a more accurate picture the government's casualties should be doubled and Maoist casualties halved. He also alleged that the Royal Nepalese Army was not only shooting to kill, but also shooting first, and argued that putting a price on the heads of Maoists leaders, as the government had recently done, was 'not the done thing' (Mehta 2002: 4–5). Grave concerns also began to be expressed in the Nepali media about the apparently indiscriminate manner of the army operation[7] and about the treatment of Nepali journalists (especially those regarded by the army as Maoist sympathisers), one of whom is widely believed to have died in custody in May 2002.[8] A report published by Amnesty International at the end of 2002 underlined these concerns very emphatically (Amnesty International 2002a).

The prediction that democratic politics would be marginalised and that the palace and the Royal Nepalese Army would play an increasing role in the wake of the royal massacre appeared to conspiracy

---

[7] Dixit (2002a) and Mainali (2002). The latter article is based on the reporter's visit to a village in Dhading from which 17 young men had recently gone to work as construction labourers on a new airstrip in Kalikot. All had been killed by the army in a massacre of 35 people during anti-Maoist actions.

[8] See the Nepal postings on the Reporters sans Frontieres website (*www.rsf.fr*), particularly that of 15 October 2002: 'Nepal: The Death in Detention of Journalist Krishna Sen and a Regime's Lies'.

theorists to be becoming true in dramatic fashion. In May 2002, Deuba agreed to a second extension of the emergency and the king immediately dissolved the House of Representatives on his advice. This led to a dramatic deepening of the rift that already existed within the Nepali Congress, between supporters of G. P. Koirala, the party's president, and the prime minister. The Koirala faction filed a writ petition in the Supreme Court against the dissolution of parliament, and in due course it announced that Deuba had been expelled from the Nepali Congress for failing to consult the party on matters of vital importance. Deuba responded by summoning a party convention and expelling Koirala in turn. The Electoral Commission was charged with deciding which faction should be recognised as the legitimate Nepali Congress Party and granted the party's election symbol, the tree.

Shortly after the dissolution of parliament, it was announced that general elections to the House of Representatives would be conducted on 13 November 2002. However, this promise was regarded with scepticism from the outset, especially as in mid-August it was decided that the security situation was such that it would not be possible to conduct local elections, and that local government institutions would be handed over to appointed bureaucrats. The five-year terms of elected local bodies (village development committees and district development committees) had expired in mid-July 2002, and many had argued that they should simply be extended for a year, in the hope that conditions would improve. How, they asked, could the Deuba government (led by a prime minister who appeared to have been expelled from his own party) insist on the one hand that general elections would certainly take place while arguing on the other that, because of the security situation, local elections could not?

The Supreme Court took two months to rule that the dissolution of the House of Representatives had not been illegal, while the Electoral Commission dithered for three months before announcing that the faction of the Nepali Congress led by G. P. Koirala would be registered, while Deuba's faction would not. Deuba was therefore obliged to establish a new party, the Nepali Congress (Democratic), which he registered on 22 September. On 29 September, a meeting of the leaders of the six biggest political parties recommended postponing the elections for a further six months, i.e. until April 2003, and on 3 October a meeting of the cabinet took this further, authorising Deuba to request the king to use Article 127 of the 1990

Constitution to defer the polls until 19 November 2003. Deuba's re-commendation to the king provided the catalyst for the most dramatic royal intervention in Nepali politics since King Mahendra dismissed the Nepali Congress government in 1960. On 4 October 2002, having consulted widely, the king invoked Article 127 and announced that Deuba had been relieved of his duties because of his inability to con-duct general elections within the prescribed timeframe, that the cabi-net had been dissolved, and that the general elections had been postponed. While he undertook to exercise executive powers until new arrangements were made, Gyanendra also restated his commit-ment to constitutional monarchy and multi-party democracy and announced that a new council of ministers would be formed within five days. He asked the political parties to forward nominations of people with 'clean images' who would not be standing in the next general elections (see Appendix C for the text of the king's address to the nation). The Maoists had achieved one of their objectives: very little now stood between them and the king.

Thus, after October 2002 the government of Nepal consisted of a small cabinet of ministers handpicked by the palace. Although the holding of general elections and the re-establishment of the House of Representatives was this government's ultimate stated aim, this appeared a remote prospect at the time of writing, and there are many (particularly in the parliamentary parties) who question its sin-cerity. The king chose to appoint Lokendra Bahadur Chand, a leader of the pro-palace Rastriya Prajatantra Party (RPP) who had already headed a government under the Panchayat system, as his first prime minister. Chand resigned at the end of May in the face of an agitation raised by five parties including the UML and G. P. Koirala's Nepali Congress. He was replaced not by the leader of the CPN (UML), as had been recommended by the parties, but by yet another erstwhile Panchayat prime minister and RPP leader, Surya Bahadur Thapa.

The period 29 January to 27 August 2003 represents one of the most extraordinary periods of Nepal's extraordinary political history. On the first of these two dates, a second ceasefire was declared: the Maoists had been calling for this for some time, but the govern-ment's agreement to it was largely unexpected, and seems to have been the result of intensive negotiations behind the scenes, in which a retired army officer, Narayan Singh Pun, played a leading role. The government agreed to remove the 'terrorist' tag from the CPN (Maoist) and its leadership (with, significantly, the sole exception of the supreme leader, Prachanda) emerged into the daylight. They gave press conferences in Kathmandu, addressed rallies and public meetings all over the country, and even opened a liaison office in the capital. Soon talks got underway and the prospect of the Maoist leadership being re-integrated into the political mainstream inched a little closer—though the fear remained that if such a development occurred it would not necessarily quell the rebellion in the Maoists' rural heartlands.

However, as this book goes to press in October 2003, Nepal is undergoing the agonies of another period of sustained violence. This commenced after the collapse of a third session of peace talks at the end of August. Once again, the Maoists' demand for elections to be held for a constituent assembly that would draft a new Constitution had proved the main sticking point. Although this political issue was the ostensible reason for the walkout, it had been clear that the ceasefire was about to break down for several days. Maoist cadres in the countryside had recently killed police personnel in several scattered incidents, and had also abducted political opponents and engaged in financial extortion. They even appear to have attempted to assassinate the ex-prime minister, Sher Bahadur Deuba, as he was passing through Kailali district. On 17 August, the very day that the negotiations were set to begin, seventeen or nineteen 'Maoists' were killed by the army during an 'encounter' in Ramechhap district. This was by far the highest number of killings in a single day since the ceasefire. Amnesty International alleged that those who died were victims of summary executions, and the report of the National Human Rights Commission's investigation into the matter reached a similar conclusion, though the army has defended its action robustly. These and other killings of alleged Maoists were the second reason cited by Prachanda for his party's abandonment of the negotiation process.

Outside the talks, as mentioned earlier, the five parties had been engaged since April in a 'movement' intended to reverse the king's move of 4 October 2002. The Maoists had attempted to draw the parties closer to them, but there was only limited support among the parties for the Maoists' main political demand—a constituent assembly. To date, the parties have resisted all calls to cease their agitation and join the government in its efforts to 'protect democracy and national sovereignty'.

The king, whose public popularity had been much lower than any of his predecessors', gained credibility when the ceasefire was declared. With its collapse, the palace again finds itself facing political opposition on two fronts: from the mainstream parties as they contest the constitutionality of the government, and the Maoists, whose ultimate aim is a republican state.

The resumption of conflict again raises the spectre of overt foreign intervention in Nepal. One of the factors that brought both the government and the Maoists to the negotiating table in January 2003 was the increasingly active interest being taken not just by India but also by the USA and the UK: the need to preserve the sovereignty of Nepal provided them with common ground. But both sides used the cessation of hostilities as an opportunity to rearm and regroup, and the Royal Nepalese Army received arms and training from several foreign donors, including the US government. Increased US involvement in Nepal is a matter of concern not just for the Maoists but also for the Indian government. Thus, the king could not take Indian support wholly for granted. Indeed, Indian perspectives on Nepal's political travails are complex and nuanced. The Indian government's response has alternated between covert support for the CPN (Maoist) and the peremptory extradition of certain of its members to Nepal. Meanwhile, civil society groups have raised a hue and cry over matters such as the banning of Indian Nepali organisations deemed sympathetic to the Maoists. The 'Indian angle' of the affair is a crucial one, which deserves much greater attention.

The Maoist leadership described its withdrawal from the talks as 'temporary'. But it clearly considers now that the onus is on the government to come up with an agenda that includes its main political demands. While the government went further than it has ever gone to address the socio-economic problems that make it possible for the Maoists to garner support in rural areas, with promises to ensure the representation of women, lower castes and minorities in the legislature, the Maoists dismissed the changes it proposed as 'cosmetic'. The CPN (Maoist) is committed to a 'systemic' change which significantly reduces the power and influence of the royal palace and removes the army from its control. It sees the drafting of a new Constitution by elected people's representatives as a non-negotiable precondition for such change. It also argues that feudal rulers do not hand over power in negotiated compromises, but have to be forced to do so. Since the end of the 2003 ceasefire, the Maoists have assassinated several public figures in the capital, and renewed their military campaign in rural areas. Once again, the Nepali newspaper headlines record that the Royal Nepalese Army is killing people described as 'Maoists' almost every day.

'ONE COUNTRY, TWO REGIMES'

Nepali society is profoundly unequal. Average income in Kathmandu is five times higher than income in the mid-western districts that have become the Maoist heartland, and there are poorer districts still. The majority of Nepal's people are excluded from most avenues of personal advancement and many sources of justice for reasons of ethnicity, caste, gender, social class and regional origin. The country is also extremely Kathmandu-centric, and the fact that the Maoist insurgency was not properly addressed by the government until it had assumed massive proportions can be explained at least partly in terms of the ruling élite not having any political nerve endings in the districts that were most affected by it. Nepali party politics since the mid-1990s has been short-termist, and parties have often used the people's war as a stick with which to beat their rivals. Many politicians have used their positions to form what Joanna Pfaff-Czarnecka (this volume) describes as 'distributional coalitions' in order to enrich themselves, and forces with a longstanding antipathy towards multi-party democracy have been biding their time. For most Nepalis, democracy since 1990 has been a game played by politicians at the centre which has brought the people very few rewards. As one Nepali author puts it:

People, intoxicated with the idea of power that was corrupted but not hereditary, were taking turns in playing an opaque game. Power to corrupt. Power to demand kickbacks, allocate tenders, appropriate public resources, demand donations for campaigns. The power to never have to be accountable. It had been nine years of freedom, nine years during which the roads had become a little more crowded, women had become more fashionable. There were five times as many cars in the city, and the communists had shaved off their beards (Joshi 2002: 134–5).

One day in July 2001 I went to eat lunch in a Kathmandu restaurant. As I waited for my snack to arrive I flicked through the latest issue of the *Himal Khabarpatrika*. Each issue of this fortnightly magazine features a photograph selected from the Nepali press for its impact or topicality, and this particular issue contained a photograph of the body of a young woman named Parvati Davadi lying dead in a pool of

18 Michael Hutt

blood on the verandah of her village home. Beside her body sat her brother-in-law, cradling her two-month-old daughter.[9] According to the caption, she had been killed by Maoist gunfire in the early morning. The waiter arrived with my meal as I stared at this horrifying picture, and he picked the magazine up from the table. He read the caption and then he angrily declared, 'The Maoists didn't do this. The Maoists don't do things like that. The police probably did it.' On top of this unwillingness to believe the worst of them, the Maoists enjoyed widespread support for much of their social agenda, despite abhorrence of their use of fear and intimidation to achieve their objectives. They were also able to recruit easily from among Nepal's massive generation of literate but under-educated youth, both male and female (see Mandira Sharma and Dinesh Prasain, this volume). In areas under their control they abolished the usurious rates charged by the local moneylenders who have been the villains of Nepali village societies since time immemorial. They harnessed the long-standing resentment of many minority ethnic communities to their cause, and outlawed the teaching of Sanskrit, a symbol of Bahun domination, in schools. They established local people's courts, which dispensed justice without the need for bribes, and outlawed the payment of the huge dowries which had often crippled poorer families. To begin with, they employed an anti-India rhetoric which pandered to the ordinary Nepali's ambivalent attitude to and inherent distrust of the southern neighbour, and later pleased women's groups by outlawing the sale of alcohol in several districts. They courted public favour by forcing the private schools which capitalise on the dreadful condition of Nepal's national education system to lower their fees, though latterly this favour was squandered as their campaign became vicious and vandalistic. The Maoists are undoubtedly feared, and the efficiency of their village-level systems of intelligence-gathering, targeted coercion and punishment provide ample grounds for this. However, the arbitrary and brutal nature of the police actions in the early stages brought the CPN (Maoist) many recruits, and the deteriorating human rights record of the Royal Nepalese Army, due in some measure to poor intelligence and also to a prevailing climate of impunity, will probably bring it more.

Two reports published in *Himal Khabarpatrika* (15–29 June 2002) painted a vivid picture of life in Rukum and Jajarkot, where villagers

[9] *Himal Khabarpatrika* 11 (7), 16–30 July 2001, p. 5.

were caught between the Maoists and the security forces. There, the security forces were in control only of the bazaar towns that form the district headquarters, which were all under dusk to dawn curfews, while the Maoists controlled the movement of people and goods on most routes through the hills. The facilities destroyed by the Maoists included an airstrip, a bank, and a private school. Two hydropower plants had been shut down, so there was no electricity, nor was there any telephone system. The local police were never called upon, no cases were ever brought to the local courts, teachers were cowed and terrorised, many religious observances had been banned or curtailed, and all foreign NGOs had either left or were leaving. It really was a case of two regimes, in which villagers had to choose between support, acquiescence, opposition, or flight—and none supported the government as wholeheartedly as *some* supported the Maoists. Even if the militaristic manifestation of the Maoist rebellion can be quelled by the Royal Nepalese Army with the help of its foreign backers (to date, assistance has been either provided or promised by the governments of the United States, the United Kingdom, India and Belgium), the multifarious angers it both exploits and articulates will continue to smoulder. If such angers are not to find new avenues and vehicles, their root causes will have to be addressed.

THE LONDON CONFERENCE AND THIS BOOK

Most of the papers upon which the chapters of this book are based were presented at a conference at the School of Oriental and African Studies in London on 2–3 November 2001, just weeks before the declaration of the emergency. The principal aim of the book is to explain why it is that in the twenty-first century, with communism supposedly discredited throughout the world, a death in a Nepali village home can be blamed on a revolutionary Maoist movement, and to provide an objective analysis of the factors that led to the wider agony such a death reflects (see also Gellner 2003).

The chapters of this volume vary greatly in terms of their themes, approaches, methodologies and styles. It is hoped that by its very diversity the book will encourage discussion and enhance understanding from a variety of disciplinary and professional perspectives. Of course, much ground remains to be covered before a comprehensive understanding of a contemporary movement such as this can be achieved, and this volume makes no claim to completeness or finality. It is especially difficult to study a movement that is mostly underground and that allows the world only selective glimpses of itself. The movement has forced all thinkers and activists to adopt one position or another in respect of it, which makes it all the more difficult to achieve true objectivity. The conference and this volume were thought of as a way of bringing together differing views and analyses. Other volumes have already been produced on the same subject, and doubtless there are more in the pipeline.[10]

The first three chapters set the Maoist movement in its historical context. Deepak Thapa traces the ancestry of today's Communist Party of Nepal (Maoist) right back to the early days of party political activism in Nepal, Sudheer Sharma explains how the insurgency developed and was organised, and Krishna Hachhethu examines the state's responses to it up to late 2001. We then turn to an assessment of the ground from which the insurgency sprang and its reception by various groups within Nepali society. Sara Shneiderman and Mark Turin describe how the movement impinged upon and was received in the context of one particular hill area. Marie Lecomte-Tilouine examines the Maoists' utilisation of the grievances of minority ethnic groups, in this case the Magar, Pratyoush Onta takes a critical look at the 'duplicitous' relationship between the Maoists and the Kathmandu intelligentsia, and Mandira Sharma and Dinesh Prasain explore and explain the high level of women's involvement in the insurgency. Next is a broader perspective on the Maoist phenomenon: Joanna Pfaff-Czarnecka identifies the shortcomings of the post-1990 democratic set-up as one factor, particularly at local level, where she argues a great deal of further research is required. Saubhagya Shah looks at it in the context of India's geopolitical domination of Nepal, while Philippe Ramirez compares it with Maoist insurgencies elsewhere in the world. In the concluding section, Hari Roka reflects on the political implications of recent changes since the deployment of the army, and finally Judith Pettigrew provides a firsthand account of conditions in the hills of west Nepal.

[10] Karki and Seddon (2003) is, as the title suggests, a compilation of perspectives from the left on the Maoist movement and Deepak Thapa (2003) is a reader, comprising a collection of writings dating from before the movement was formally launched right up to the recent past.

Part I. The Political Context

RADICALISM AND THE EMERGENCE OF THE MAOISTS

Deepak Thapa

Since its founding in Calcutta in 1949, the Communist Party of Nepal has had a chequered history. The past five decades have seen it through many ups and downs, personality clashes, splits, reunions, mergers and subsumptions, and at present the mainstream left is represented by the Communist Party of Nepal (Unified Marxist-Leninist) together with at least half a dozen others that veer further to the left. Outside this grouping stands the Communist Party of Nepal (Maoist), with an ideological stance that is farthest left.

This chapter provides a concise view of the strains of radicalism that have appeared with regularity among the various communist parties of Nepal, and which ultimately culminated in the rise of the Maoists in 1995. It draws both on published texts and on personal interviews with some of the protagonists.

ORIGINS

Going back in history to seek the germination of leftist ideals in Nepal, we find that the well-known humanist, Jai Prithvi Bahadur Singh, had fallen under the influence of Marxist thought long before the Calcutta meeting that established Nepal's communist party. In this sense, Singh was arguably the first Nepali to be exposed to Marxist thought. Due to differences with his father-in-law, the powerful Rana prime minister, Chandra Shamsher, Jai Prithvi Bahadur Singh went

Deepak Thapa

into self-imposed exile in India (Surendra K. C. 1999/2000: 36),[1] but Chandra Shamsher could not ignore the changes that were sweeping the world. His founding of Trichandra College in 1918, the abolition of *sati* in 1919, and the abolition of slavery five years later, are believed to have resulted from Singh's humanitarian movement as well as an appreciation of the import of the Bolshevik revolution (ibid.).

The next milestone in the development of the country's communist movement came in 1947 during the famous strike by workers at the Biratnagar jute and cloth mills. According to B. P. Koirala (2001: 39), this marked the first appearance of the communists in Nepal, with Man Mohan Adhikari, who had earlier joined the Communist Party of India, taking the lead among communist workers. There are two views on the leadership of this strike: the 1949 manifesto of the Communist Party of Nepal claimed that it was led by the trade union headed by Man Mohan Adhikari (Rawal 1990/1, Appendix 2), while B. P. Koirala (2001: 39) states that the 'movement was led by Girija [Prasad Koirala]'.

Whatever the truth may be, it is certain that the Biratnagar strike at least included the first communist activity on Nepali soil. There is also no denying that the Nepali Congress played an instrumental part in fostering political activism in Nepal. The founder of the Communist Party of Nepal (CPN), Pushpa Lal Shrestha, himself began his political career with the Nepali National Congress, for which he worked as its office secretary.[2] However, he was soon disillusioned with the way the party functioned and he left it to set up a communist party apparatus. By April 1949, Pushpa Lal had translated the *Communist Manifesto* into Nepali, and in September 1949 he launched the Communist Party of Nepal. Anirudha Gupta explains the background to the birth of the party:

By 1947, when India became free, some India-trained Communists were reported to have become active in certain parts of Nepal in organising revolts and strikes among peasants and workers.[3] Though these Communists

---

[1] Surendra K. C. cites Madan Mani Dixit's 1984/5 article, which claims that Singh was in touch with the firebrand M. N. Roy, one of the founders of the Communist Party of India, that he later travelled to Europe, and that in 1921 he even attempted to visit Moscow, in order to meet Lenin.

[2] The Nepali National Congress merged with the Nepal Democratic Congress to form the Nepali Congress party in April 1950.

[3] This seems to be a reference to the Biratnagar strike.

were working on purely individual initiative, it seems that among a section of the Nepalese youth, then studying in India, a conviction was growing that only communist methods were suitable in the Nepalese conditions to solve her outstanding political, social and economic problems. Inspired by the Indian Communists, these young intellectuals soon came to believe that a class struggle in Nepal was imminent and that some foreign 'imperialist' powers were conspiring with the Ranas to convert their country into a military base. Following the tactical line of the Indian Communist Party about the 'collaborationist' character of India's national leadership, they also feared that the free Government of India was harbouring expansionist schemes in Nepal (Gupta 1993: 199–200).

The communists did not make their position clear during the armed uprising against the Rana regime (ibid.: 201). While Rawal states that armed groups were active as a Mukti Fauj (Liberation Army) in the east, centre and west, he admits that some communists believed that the revolt had been launched to 'arrest the rise of communism' (Rawal 1990/1: 33–4).[4] According to Gupta (1993: 201), the communists explained their vacillating position 'by saying that the revolt had no political significance at all'. Nevertheless, the CPN denounced the Delhi Agreement between the Nepali Congress, King Tribhuvan and the Ranas, calling it a 'betrayal' of the revolution (Rawal 1990/1: 34).[5]

The communists adopted a strongly anti-Congress position in the immediate post-Rana period. They considered the Nepali Congress to be 'a 'stooge' of the Indian government and called upon all 'progressive forces' to form a broad 'People's Front to fight it' (Gupta 1993: 201).[6] Accordingly, a National People's United Front was formed with like-minded others, and the Front declared in its November 1951 manifesto that the Nepali Congress was the 'Nehru government's toy' (Surendra K. C. 1999/2000: 92):

Pointing out that more than 75 percent of Nepal's commercial and industrial enterprises were in Indian hands, the manifesto declared that India was trying to prevent Nepal from becoming friendly towards China. Stressing its admiration for the Soviet Union and China, the Front openly condemned

---

[4] Rawal cites Pushpa Lal Shrestha (1974). All translations from Nepali texts are my own.

[5] Rawal refers to *Notes on the Communist Movement in Nepal* by 'Mohan Dhwoj Gurung', a pseudonym adopted by Pushpa Lal Shrestha.

[6] Gupta mentions *May Divash ko Avasarma Kamyunist Party ko Ghosanapatra* (Manifesto of the Communist Party on the Occasion of May Day), 1951.

the 'expansionist war-mongering camp of America and Britain' (Gupta 1993: 202).[7]

The United Front was able to oppose the then Rana-Congress government by calling strikes and organising processions. During one of these a school student was killed, and the incident brought the coalition government to an end in November (Surendra K. C. 1999/2000: 92). Buoyed by what it perceived as its success, the Front believed it could replace the 'bourgeois-cum-feudal Government' with a 'People's Democracy' (Gupta 1993: 202). However, in January 1952, following a day-long revolt by the Raksha Dal (the para-military force created largely out of men from the Mukti Sena, the Nepali Congress's fighting force against the Ranas) for which the CPN tried to claim responsibility, the party was banned for attempting to take advantage of the situation (Shaha 1996: 275). The ban was to last until April 1956.

Meanwhile, the CPN's senior leaders had begun to jostle for positions of power. Not long after the Ranas had been ousted, the politburo removed Pushpa Lal as general secretary and replaced him with Man Mohan Adhikari. Surendra K. C. (1999/2000: 172) calls that event 'the beginning of the never-ending leadership struggle within the party', a description that would apply equally to all of the other factions that branched out of the mother party.

THE SPLITS BEGIN

The CPN's first convention was held in secret in Patan in January 1954. Apart from confirming Man Mohan Adhikari as general secretary, it reiterated its opposition to the Delhi Agreement (Rawal 1990/1: 38). Further, it 'adopted the resolution upholding "continuous struggle" against "feudalist" regime and advocating replacement of the monarchy by a republic formed by an elected Constituent Assembly' (Baral 1977: 82). However, the convention failed to agree on the question of whether any future revolution should be led by the peasant-worker class, and this led to the emergence of ideological

[7] On the CPN's alignment with the Praja Parishad, Lok Raj Baral (1977: 35) comments: 'Ideologically, the NCP [CPN] was inarticulate in a variety of ways. This was apparent when it aligned with the Praja Parishad in 1951 for the formation of the National People's United Front which adhered to the "people's democracy".'

differences between 'revisionists' and 'revolutionaries' (Surendra K. C. 1999/2000: 173).[8]

The schism widened further in April 1956, when, in order to gain political legitimacy, the party leadership changed its uncompromising stance on the monarchy and issued a statement accepting the king as the country's constitutional head. Although that statement provided the Tanka Prasad Acharya government with an excuse to lift the ban on the CPN, it marked the beginning of the process of division and the entry of the idea of 'rightist tendencies' within the party (ibid.: 104).[9]

Four months after the ban on the party had been lifted, Man Mohan Adhikari left Nepal for China, where he remained for medical treatment. Keshar Jung Rayamajhi took over as acting general secretary, and differences of opinion on the question of the monarchy began to take precedence over the party's professed aim of fostering a Marxist revolution in Nepal (ibid.: 153). The radicals, led by Pushpa Lal, had opposed the pro-king statement 'as an inexcusable compromise with the basic tenets of the party ideology' (Baral 1977: 82) and there was further polarisation between the faction that favoured cooperation with other democratic forces and the one that was for 'an adventurist and fighting policy' (Gupta 1993: 204). This divergence of opinion went to such an extreme that the North Gandak regional committee of the party had broken off relations with the central committee by 1956 (Rawal 1990/1: 44), while within the politburo a group under D. P. Adhikari advocated following the Chinese example of peasant uprising to establish a 'people's government' (Gupta 1993: 205).[10]

The CPN's second convention was held in Kathmandu in June 1957 in a bid to reconcile these ideological differences. This convention

---

[8] Eventually, the 'revisionists' would be led by Keshar Jung Rayamajhi and the 'revolutionaries' by Pushpa Lal (Rawal 1990/1: 42).

[9] The ban was lifted just before King Mahendra's coronation, and this is seen as a tactical move: the guests were to include representatives of the Soviet and Chinese communist parties, to whom it would have been embarrassing to have had to explain that the CPN was outlawed. It was also believed that there was a distinct possibility that the party would cause disruption during the coronation. Thus, the CPN's statement and the subsequent lifting of the ban on it represented a compromise.

[10] Gupta goes on to say: 'From this time onward, it also appears that a faction began to work as a nucleus of the pro-Chinese elements in the Nepal Communist Party. It was owing to the instigation of this group that several agrarian riots took place in Eastern Terai during the summer of 1957.'

proved to be a highly controversial affair, in that the various person-alities involved seemed to have their own interpretations of what actually took place (Surendra K. C. 1999/2000: 176, Rawal 1990/1: 45), and no agreement could be reached on the party's future prog-ramme. The draft thesis *'Parti Karyakramma Parivartan Kina'* (Why the Party Programme Needs to be Amended) prepared by the five-member politburo (with Pushpa Lal dissenting) was rejected by the convention (Rawal 1990/1: 44).[11] Surendra K. C. states (1999/2000: 176) that the only item that was finally adopted was the concise slo-gan coined by Pushpa Lal during the meeting itself: '...while retain-ing intact the call for a republic, the present struggle will be for a constituent assembly'. The convention also elected Rayamajhi as the CPN's general secretary. According to Surendra K. C., one of the most significant results of the convention was that, although the leadership was seized by Rayamajhi, the resolution it adopted had been authored by Pushpa Lal (ibid.), whereas the usual practice everywhere is for the one whose resolution is adopted to be elevated to the leadership.[12]

On 1 February 1958, King Mahendra announced general elections to parliament. Up to this point, the CPN's position had been that any election should be held first to a constituent assembly, as per Mahendra's father, King Tribhuvan's proclamation of 18 February 1951. This was a view that it held in common with the Nepali Con-gress. In fact, a joint statement issued by the CPN, the Nepali Congress and the Nepali National Congress[13] on 10 July 1957 had declared: 'So long as the country's resurgent-reactionary forces are getting stronger all the democratic forces should unite and the basis of such a unity should be the election of a sovereign constituent assembly'

[11] According to Gupta (1993: 206), the thesis 'condemned the adventurist policy of "permanent revolution" as suicidal, described the demand for nationalising land with-out taking due interest of the middle peasants as a "left-wing mistake", and put for-ward a programme of forming a united front with the Nepali Congress'.

[12] In a personal interview with this writer on 18 April 2001, Shyam Shrestha, editor of *Mulyankan* monthly and a former member of the Fourth Convention, explained this contradiction. He said that, although Pushpa Lal was the organiser, the ideologue and the one with fresh ideas, he was not very successful when it came to dealing with party cadres. That was why he repeatedly failed to secure the post of general secretary, los-ing out first to Man Mohan Adhikari, then to Keshar Jang Rayamajhi, and finally to Tulsi Lal Amatya.

[13] This party was a splinter group from the larger Nepali National Congress, which merged with the Nepal Democratic Congress to form the Nepali Congress.

(Surendra K. C. 1999/2000: 111). But the meeting of the CPN central committee held after the 1 February announcement decided to take part in the election even as it registered a protest at the fact that it was not designed to elect a constituent assembly (ibid.: 112). According to Lok Raj Baral, 'As the Central Committee of the party was dominated by the moderates, it decided to fight the election on practical grounds as opposed to Pushpa Lal's hardline attitude towards the election' (Baral 1977: 83).

The CPN performed miserably in the 1959 elections, winning only four of the forty-seven parliamentary seats it contested,[14] but its attitude towards the Nepali Congress government remained just as confrontational as before (Surendra K. C. 1999/2000: 130 ff.), even though it was rent by internal dissension (Baral 1977: 83). There was also growing criticism of Rayamajhi, who was blamed for the party's ignominious electoral performance (Rawal 1990/1: 51). Things finally came to a head following the royal takeover of 15 December 1960. While Rayamajhi, who was in Moscow to attend a conference, welcomed the king's dissolution of parliament as a 'progressive' step, Pushpa Lal distributed a circular in the name of the politburo which demanded an end to 'military terror' and called for a conference of all parliamentary parties (ibid.: 52). After Rayamajhi's return in January 1961, the CPN released a statement calling for the 'release of political detenus, lifting of the ban on political activities, and guarantee of fundamental rights' but remained silent on the question of the dissolved parliament (Baral 1977: 83). According to Baral, 'Since then it was apparent that the communists were broadly divided into two factions: (1) the pro-Peking faction consisting, among others, of Pushpa Lal Shrestha, Man Mohan Adhikari and Tulsi Lal Amatya; and (2) the pro-Moscow faction led by Keshar Jang Rayamajhi' (ibid.).[15]

In March 1961, the CPN organised a conference in Darbhanga, India. After a month of heated debate, voting took place on the three major 'political lines':

1. Establishment of parliamentary democracy. This line supported constitutional monarchy and guided democracy and was proposed

[14] Gupta (1993: 207) attributes the party's election failures mainly to a 'lack of clarity in its programme and policies'.

[15] Apart from internal differences, this divergence also followed the growing Sino-Soviet rift, which was reflected in the Communist Party of India, and which in turn affected the CPN.

by Rayamajhi. It received seventeen out of a possible fifty-four
votes as well as majority support from the central committee.
2. Restoration of the erstwhile parliament. This line, proposed by
   Pushpa Lal, favoured joint action with the Nepali Congress and
   received six votes.
3. Election of a constituent assembly. This line opposed both constitutional monarchy and joint action with the Nepali Congress, and
   received 28 votes. It was proposed by Mohan Bikram Singh, who
   was the only central committee member to vote in its favour (Rawal
   1990/1: 53).[16]

The Darbhanga Plenum, however, decided to ignore the majority
decision to press for a constituent assembly and adopted Rayamajhi's proposal as its immediate policy (ibid.: 54).[17] Then, in May 1961,
Rayamajhi declared that he was in favour of a civil disobedience
movement for the restoration of fundamental rights, but that any
such movement would not aim to overthrow the monarchy (Baral
1977: 84, quoting the *Motherland*, 20 May 1961). In April 1962, the
anti-Rayamajhi group within the CPN held the third convention in
Varanasi. Rayamajhi and four others were expelled from the party
for supporting King Mahendra's 'undemocratic' action—but this was
only a formality, because in effect the party had already split verti-
cally.[18] Again, three 'political lines' were presented to the party con-

[16] Rawal says that although the figures vary from source to source, the end result is
the same.
[17] Rawal quotes from p. 67 of the monograph written by 'Ananda Bahadur Chetri'
(a pseudonym used by Mohan Bikram Singh) entitled *Gaddar Pushpa Lal* (Traitor
Pushpa Lal). Elsewhere (1990/1: 109, fn 53), Rawal reports that in a personal interview in 1985, Rayamajhi said that the votes were split as follows: 25 for Mohan
Bikram, 19 for his side and 4 for Pushpa Lal. However, because Mohan Bikram's proposal would have meant an armed uprising, which was against the spirit of the resolution adopted by the second convention, his own proposal was given precedence,
though this was on the understanding that Mohan Bikram would be allowed to introduce his proposal at the third convention.
[18] The Rayamajhi faction of the CPN held its own third convention in 1966 and
advocated a united front with the Nepali Congress. The meeting also denounced
Pushpa Lal Shrestha and Tulsi Lal Amatya as 'extremists'. After this, the split between
the two sides became final with the Rayamajhi group adopting a 'peaceful path' within
the country and supporting the Soviet Union internationally, while the other faction
chose the path of Mao Zedong Thought and agrarian revolution (Rawal 1990/1: 63).

vention—Pushpa Lal's, Mohan Bikram's and newly elected general secretary Tulsi Lal Amatya's proposal for a 'Supreme Sovereign Parliament'. Amatya's proposal received a majority of the votes, but because it had not been approved unanimously, the idea of 'national democracy' was mooted (Rawal 1990/1: 59), in opposition to Pushpa Lal's idea of 'people's democracy' (Baral 1977: 84).

As well as reconstituting the central committee, the third convention also formed a National Council, which passed a resolution to the effect that the Panchayat system was sustaining a 'military dictatorship', and that the 'highly exploitative' feudal system was destined to collapse. But Pushpa Lal adopted a more extreme position, because the resolution did not include his model of democracy (ibid.: 85). The differences between Pushpa Lal and Tulsi Lal continued to widen after the third convention. In May 1968, Pushpa Lal and his associates held a meeting at Gorakhpur in India and announced the formation of a separate party, with Pushpa Lal as general secretary. Among the objectives of the new party was 'to identify feudalism and imperialism as the chief enemy and act accordingly and to build a disciplined revolutionary party that will work mainly among peasants' (Rawal 1990/1: 69).[19]

The fortunes of Pushpa Lal's new party turned out to differ little from those of the party he had originally helped to found: various factions had split off from it by the time of his death in 1978 (Rawal 1990/1: 70 ff.). In terms of political ideology too, Pushpa Lal seems to have floundered. Baral (1977: 89) refers to him as an 'extremist Maoist' in one place,[20] while elsewhere he records that after parting company with Tulsi Lal, Pushpa Lal 'adopted a two-front strategy which by and large was in keeping with Rayamajhi's line, at least in letter if not in principle, and encouraged his followers within Nepal to infiltrate into panchayats and Class Organisations' (Baral 1977: 86).

[19] In a personal interview given to this writer on 9 June 2001, Amik Sherchan, chairman of the United People's Front, said that he and his colleagues had repeatedly entreated Pushpa Lal not to set up a new party while so many of the CPN's leaders were still in jail.

[20] Baral narrates that Man Mohan Adhikari 'dissociated himself from the extremist faction led by Pushpa Lal' after his release from jail in 1968. He describes both groups as 'Maoist factions of the NCP' and claims that neither of them was dominant (1977: 88, 89).

THE FOURTH CONVENTION

The division in the leadership of the CPN was reflected at the lower levels of the party as well, and various local units began to operate independently. Although they were ostensibly branch organisations of the CPN, in the absence of a central command structure their activities were uncoordinated.[21] The very existence of the party had come into question when its jailed leaders decided they had to get out of jail (ibid.: 73).[22] Man Mohan Adhikari and Sambhu Ram Shrestha were released in 1968, following their issuing a statement agreeing to assist and support the king without reservation (ibid.: 73),[23] and in December 1971, after Mohan Bikram Singh's release, a 'central nucleus' was set up to prepare for the formation of a central party by tying together the various strands of the communist movement.[24] The central nucleus also tried to negotiate with Pushpa Lal in order to include him in the new grouping as well, but it was unsuccessful because on the one hand Pushpa Lal proposed that everyone else should be subsumed within his party, and on the other he was in favour of cooperating with the Nepali Congress against the Panchayat system.[25]

Soon, however, differences arose within the central nucleus. According to the Mohan Bikram faction, this was due to disagreement on the party's policy towards China and Mao Zedong Thought, while

---

[21] Interview with Shyam Shrestha (18 April 2001). Shrestha says that one of the many reasons for this situation of flux was that while many of these local units could not accept Pushpa Lal as their leader, those whom they considered their leaders were in jail.

[22] Rawal cites a personal interview with Man Mohan Adhikari. Among the other leaders were Sambhu Ram Shrestha, Mohan Bikram Singh and Nirmal Lama. Rawal claims that their action was precipitated by a statement made by the acting president of the Nepali Congress, Subarna Shamsher Rana, in May 1968, in which he hinted at the danger of communism and pledged support to the king.

[23] Rawal quotes Ghimire (1980).

[24] According to Shyam Shrestha, the key figures of the central nucleus were Man Mohan Adhikari, Mohan Bikram Singh, Nirmal Lama and Sambhu Ram Shrestha. The other members of the central nucleus are mentioned in Rawal (1990/1: 73).

[25] Interview with Shyam Shrestha (18 April 2001). The latter clause led to Mohan Bikram Singh's famous denunciation of Pushpa Lal as 'Traitor Pushpa Lal'. Rawal (1990/1: 74) quotes Bharat Mohan Adhikari as saying in a personal interview that the unity talks failed because Sambhu Ram Shrestha proposed dismantling Pushpa Lal's party.

Man Mohan Adhikari blamed it on 'pro-king elements' who were opposed to the idea of a constituent assembly. The Mohan Bikram group, which included Nirmal Lama, moved ahead and held the 'fourth convention' of their faction of the CPN in September 1974 in India (ibid.: 74).[26]

Their faction, with Mohan Bikram Singh as its general secretary, came to be known as the CPN (Fourth Convention or 'Fourth Congress') and was to emerge as the strongest communist grouping of the following decade.[27] The Fourth Convention adopted a hard-line position, in that it advocated 'armed revolution'. However, this revolution was not to take place in isolation from the people, but would carry them along in a mass uprising. Later, at the Nationwide District Secretaries' Conference held in 1979, the proposal made by the new general secretary, Nirmal Lama, for 'training guerrillas, proletarianising party cadre, creating separate base areas, taking action against local cheats, and initiating an agrarian uprising' was adopted. Accordingly, some actions were taken, but these came to a halt with the king's announcement in May 1979 of a national referendum, to be held the following year.[28] The choice before the people was the Panchayat system with 'suitable reforms' and a multi-party system of government.

In response to the king's proclamation, the Fourth Convention issued a call asking all left parties to achieve 'working unity' in demanding that the referendum be free and fair, and it joined all the major communist parties in an agitation for the fulfilment of five preconditions for taking part in the referendum.[29] Nirmal Lama was thus able to bring about such an understanding among the divided left, but he had to face criticism within his own party for accepting a

[26] The Man Mohan group established its own party in 1979, but this too was riven with dissension. In 1987, it united with Pushpa Lal's rump CPN and emerged as the CPN (Marxist).

[27] Interview with Shyam Shrestha, 18 April 2001.

[28] Ibid. Mohan Bikram had by this time been indicted because of various allegations about his personal life and was facing disciplinary action, and Nirmal Lama had taken over as general secretary. But this was also to prove the beginning of factionalism within the Fourth Convention.

[29] Interviews with Amik Sherchan (9 June 2001) and Shyam Shrestha (18 April 2001). According to Hoftun et al. (1999: 92), although their demands were not met, the communist parties in general campaigned for a parliamentary system.

Deepak Thapa

referendum proposed by the king, and he was forced to quit as general secretary.[30]

Factionalism within the party had reached an advanced stage by this time. After the referendum and the still-disputed victory for a Panchayat system, which now recognised adult franchise for direct elections to the national legislature,[31] Nirmal Lama was in favour of using the opportunity to penetrate the Panchayat bodies, while Mohan Bikram wanted to continue to boycott elections.[32] Finally, in 1983, the Fourth Convention split into the Nirmal Lama and Mohan Bikram factions, and each began calling the other 'police agents', 'pro-Panchayat, pro-Nepali Congress elements' and 'ambitious and conspiratorial' (ibid.: 76–7).

THE JHAPA MOVEMENT

While the central nucleus mentioned above was still being organised, an actual communist uprising took place in the south-eastern district of Jhapa. This was inspired by a violent Maoist uprising led by extremists within the Communist Party of India (Marxist) which broke out in 1967 in the Naxalbari region of North Bengal, just across the border (Nayar 1977),[33] and was also influenced by the ongoing Cul-

[30] According to Amik Sherchan, Lama resigned under pressure from a faction within the party, including Mohan Bikram, that was in favour of boycotting the referendum. The new leadership later realised that not voting at all meant indirectly supporting the Panchayat system, and ultimately it went along with what Lama had originally proposed. Shyam Shrestha's opinion is that Lama had to resign because he had advocated united action with the Nepali Congress, which Mohan Bikram described as a 'rightist view'.

[31] Before 1980, the apex legislature was elected by an electoral college which was formed through a rather complex process. The people voted only for the village or town panchayat, i.e. the first tier of local government. Representatives from these bodies formed the district assembly, which in turn elected a district panchayat. The district panchayats together formed the zonal assembly, which elected the members of the Rastriya Panchayat, the national legislature. The king nominated a few Rastriya Panchayat members as well. There were some amendments to this system made in 1975, but the fact was that people did not vote directly for the national legislature.

[32] Interviews with Amik Sherchan and Shyam Shrestha. Shrestha also says that Mohan Bikram had a dictatorial attitude within the party. He would brook no dissent and would immediately suspect conspiracies behind differences of opinion. In the end, according to Shrestha, Mohan Bikram was just in a hurry to split from the party and would not listen to pleas for debate within it.

[33] Originally known as the Naxalites, this group later formed the Communist Party of India (Marxist-Leninist) in 1969 (Nayar 1977: 319).

tural Revolution in China (Rawal 1990/1: 80). The Jhapa rebellion was initiated by a decision taken by the Jhapa District Committee of the East Kosi Coordination Committee on 22 April 1971. The East Kosi Coordination Committee was nominally under Man Mohan Adhikari[34] and had been functioning independently since 1965. After Man Mohan's release from jail in 1968, intra-party differences on 'capturing state power' became more acute, and later the Jhapa District Committee decided to go ahead on its own. In May 1971, its campaign to eliminate 'class enemies' began.

According to one of the leaders of the Jhapa movement, Radha Krishna Mainali, 'The situation of exploitation by feudal elements was such that our movement could not but be violent.'[35] However, their action turned out to be no more than a romantic adventure and was soon suppressed by the government. A sum total of seven 'class enemies' had been killed by the time the movement came to an end.

Mainali recalls that the leaders of the Jhapa movement had indeed sought to work together with the central nucleus, but neither Mohan Bikram nor Nirmal Lama showed any inclination to cooperate. The young 'Jhapalis' (as those involved in the uprising have since been known) were looking for a mature leadership, but were disappointed by the attitude of those in the central nucleus. The Jhapalis later came out strongly against other communist groups, calling them 're-visionist traitorous groups' (ibid.: 81). For its part, the Fourth Convention condemned the Jhapa movement from the outset, declaring, 'While we support the spirit and sacrifice shown in the struggle against class enemies, the terrorist tactics adopted...cannot be called Marxism-Leninism. This is a form of semi-anarchy' (Singh 1994/5: 156). Pushpa Lal's comment was: 'The assassination of individuals will not topple the Panchayat system' (Rawal 1990/1: 82). (According to the pro-Maoist Nepal National Intellectuals Association [Nepal Rastriya Buddhijibi Sangathan] [1997/8: 10], the Jhapa movement was 'a historic revolt which encouraged all communist revolutionaries to understand the Maoist viewpoint on the question of power and struggle...But even though they were right in the main, they could not develop it into a people's war.')

The Jhapa District Committee found itself under attack, both from the government and from others within the left movement. In

---

[34] Interview with Radha Krishna Mainali, 16 April 2001.
[35] Ibid.

June 1974 it called for coordination among all 'communist revolutionaries or groups', and in June 1975 it held a conference involving
representatives from various districts, and formed the All Nepal Communist Coordination Committee (Rawal 1990/1: 83). Mohan Bikram
reacted to the formation of this new alliance with the comment, 'The
resolution of the so-called coordination committee says, "Traitor
Mohan Bikram is moving ahead by holding the fourth convention."
Since they were worried about the possibility of the Fourth Convention emerging as a true Marxist-Leninist party, they held their conference and formed the so-called coordination committee' (Singh
1994/5: 159).

Over the course of the years, other localised movements joined
the Coordination Committee, until in December 1978 the CPN
(Marxist-Leninist) was established at a national conference. The
process of subsuming smaller groups into the CPN (ML) continued
unabated until the 1990 people's movement, by which time it had
become the largest communist organisation in the country.[36]

THE CPN (MAOIST)

Most of the CPN (Maoist) leaders trace their political roots back to
the CPN (Fourth Convention).[37] Following the split between Nirmal
Lama and Mohan Bikram Singh, the latter established his own party,
the CPN (Masal), in November 1983, while Lama held a national
conference of his group a month later and formalised the split
(Rawal 1990/1: 78).[38] In 1984, Masal became one of the founding

---

[36] According to Shyam Shrestha, the CPN (ML) was the main beneficiary of the
splits within the Fourth Convention, because these provoked the exodus of a large
number of party workers into its ranks. Hoftun et al. (1999: 91–2) describe the Fourth
Convention and the CPN (ML) that arose from the Jhapali movement as the two most
radical communist groupings in the run-up to the 1980 referendum, and go on to say
that by 1986 the CPN (ML) had replaced the Fourth Convention as the most dynamic
left force (ibid.: 106) and that by 1990 it had become 'the Leftist group with the most
effective network of cadres' (ibid.: 116).

[37] Prachanda joined the party in 1977 (2034 v.s.), while Baburam Bhattarai 'came
into contact' with the CPN (Fourth Convention) in 1980 (2037 v.s.) through Nirmal
Lama (interview with Amik Sherchan).

[38] Prachanda, Baburam Bhattarai and Mohan Baidya went with Mohan Bikram.
The Nepal National Intellectuals Organisation (1997: 11) describes Lama's faction as
'rightist'.

members of the Revolutionary Internationalist Movement (RIM), a worldwide grouping of Maoist parties.[39]

In 1985, after its fifth convention, Masal split further into CPN (Mashal) and CPN (Masal), with the breakaway party led by Mohan Baidya.[40] Under Mohan Baidya, the CPN (Mashal) is believed to have adopted the doctrine of armed movement in the hope of a mass uprising. The so-called 'Sector Incident' of 1986, in which King Tribhuvan's statue at Tripureshwor in Kathmandu was blackened and some police posts were attacked, was a part of that strategy. But by these very actions the party had to relinquish its secrecy, and the central committee deemed that to be a mistake. Mohan Baidya was replaced by Prachanda as general secretary (CPN [UML] 2001).[41]

As the 1990 people's movement approached and the United Left Front was formed by, among others, CPN (ML) and the Fourth Convention, Masal and Mashal teamed up with a number of smaller groups to form the United National People's Movement to fight against the Panchayat system.[42] With the re-instatement of democracy, the more hard-line of the left parties, i.e. Mashal, Masal, the Fourth Convention and others, pressed unsuccessfully for the formation of a constituent assembly, which would write a 'people's constitution' (Maharjan 2000: 116).

Baburam Bhattarai had stayed behind with Mohan Bikram during the Masal-Mashal split, but as the 1991 parliamentary elections approached and Mohan Bikram decided that the party should boycott the elections, he too broke away from the rebel CPN (Masal) (CPN

---

[39] Masal was 'expelled' from RIM in 1996, and the CPN (Maoist) is now the only party from Nepal in the RIM.

[40] Amik Sherchan told me that the reasons behind the split were 'technical' (he declined to elaborate on this) rather than ideological, while Shyam Shrestha says that it was a conspiracy hatched by Mohan Baidya and Prachanda since they knew that as long as Mohan Bikram remained in the party they would never be able to become its top leaders. The Nepal National Intellectuals Association says that the fifth convention concluded that neither Mohan Bikram's viewpoint nor his character was proper.

[41] The report says that Prachanda initially seemed disposed to conduct a struggle within the Constitution, but later emphasised people's war.

[42] According to both Amik Sherchan and Shyam Shrestha, one of the reasons why the CPN (Mashal) led by Mohan Bikram and the CPN (Masal) led by Prachanda could not be accommodated within the United Left Front was Sahana Pradhan's objection to working together with those who had called her party leader, Pushpa Lal (who was also her husband), a traitor.

[UML] 2001). In November 1990, four parties, including the Fourth Convention, Mashal and Bhattarai's Masal, merged to form the Communist Party of Nepal (Unity Centre) during what has been called the 'Unity Congress'. Prachanda was chosen as the general secretary of the new party. The Congress accepted 'Mao-Tse Tung Thought as the third, new and better phase of Marxism-Leninism and itself as Maoism' and passed the resolution to initiate a 'people's war to bring about a new democratic revolution in Nepal'.[43]

For the 1991 elections, the Unity Centre floated the United People's Front (UPF) with Baburam Bhattarai as its coordinator. The UPF won nine of the seventy seats it contested and emerged as the third largest party in parliament. Differences soon arose within the Unity Centre between Nirmal Lama and Prachanda over whether the time was ripe for an armed uprising. Lama was opposed to the idea, while Prachanda insisted that was what had been agreed upon at the Unity Congress.[44] In 1994, the party split, producing one Unity Centre led by Prachanda and another by Nirmal Lama.[45] Accordingly, the UPF was also divided, with Baburam Bhattarai heading the one that was allied to Prachanda, and Niranjan Govinda Vaidya (one of the founders of the original CPN in 1949) leading the one close to Lama.

In March 1995, Prachanda's Unity Centre held its 'Third Plenum', during which it foreswore elections[46] and decided to take up arms. It was at this point that the CPN (Unity Centre) was renamed the Communist Party of Nepal (Maoist). In September, the 'Plan for the Historic Initiation of the People's War' adopted by the Central Committee of the Party stated that it

…would be based on the lessons of Marxism-Leninism-Maoism regarding revolutionary violence. On the occasion of formulation of the plan for initiation of the process that will unfold as protracted people's war based on the

---

[43] Nepal National Intellectuals Association (1997: 12). According to Shyam Shrestha, the resolution was rammed through by Prachanda's group without debate since it already had the majority on its side.

[44] Interview with Amik Sherchan.

[45] According to Shyam Shrestha, Nirmal Lama and the others were not permitted to have their say in the party, and left as a result.

[46] On the insistence of the Revolutionary Internationalist Movement, according to Shyam Shrestha.

strategy of encircling the city from the countryside according to the specificities of our country, the Party once again reiterates its eternal commitment to the theory of people's war developed by Mao as the universal and
invincible Marxist theory of war (*Worker*, June 1996).

On 13 February 1996, the CPN (Maoist) struck in six districts. The
people's war had begun.

THE MAOIST MOVEMENT

AN EVOLUTIONARY PERSPECTIVE*

Sudheer Sharma

Prior to 1995, few people were aware that the Communist Party of Nepal (Maoist) was one of the dozens of communist parties that existed in Nepal.[1] Press releases issued by the Maoist leader Prachanda (a.k.a. Pushpa Kamal Dahal) were largely ignored by the media; even when his statements were printed, they did not enjoy a wide readership. By late 2001, things had changed to such an extent that each and every word that came from Prachanda attracted a tremendous amount of interest and speculation amongst all sections of Nepali society.

When the forty-point demand (see Appendix A) was put forward by the Maoist leader Baburam Bhattarai on 4 February 1996, it was totally ignored by the prime minister of the day, Sher Bahadur Deuba, who opted to go on an official visit to India instead of responding to it. However, during his second period of tenure as prime minister, the biggest challenge Deuba faced was the successful negotiation of a peace settlement with the Maoists. This change in the government's attitude to the Maoists was an indication of the importance and effectiveness of the people's war over the previous six years. The sparks of revolt that first appeared in Rolpa, Rukum, Gorkha and Sindhuli districts had grown into a raging conflagration that was threatening to scorch the entire country. With a handful of exceptions, the people's war had spread to almost all of Nepal's seventy-five districts, affecting every sector of the nation.

---

* Translated from Nepali by Jyoti Thapa.

[1] This chapter is written from the perspective of early November 2001, and therefore does not take developments that occurred after that date into account.

MAOIST ORGANISATION

Within six years of starting an armed insurgency, the CPN (Maoist) had managed to establish itself as a formidable alternative political force. An effective two-pronged strategy consisting of both political and military programmes was responsible for its phenomenal success. It also embraced Mao Zedong's principle that the party, the people's army and a united front are the three weapons for a people's revolution: while the party itself was involved in spreading the party's ideology as well as formulating policies related to the people's war, the people's army was responsible for attacking 'enemies' and defending the areas under its control. The third arm of the people's war, the united front, consolidated friendly forces with a view to creating the prerequisites for the proposed people's government.

THE PARTY

The organisational structure of the CPN (Maoist) has the standing committee at its top with the politburo, central committee, regional bureaus, sub-regional bureaus, district committees, area committees, and cell committees beneath it. According to Maoist sources, the central committee that was formed after the amendment to the party constitution at the party's second national conference in February 2001 comprised fifty-five members. However, despite its size, its authority was less extensive than before. The politburo and standing committee formulate most of the political and strategic policies. At the time of writing, the standing committee, with fewer than ten members, has been the most decisive body in the party. When the relevant committees have been unable to hold meetings, the chairman, Prachanda, has taken all the decisions. There is also a central advisory body of between nine and eleven members, made up of the heads of frontal organisations.

The CPN (Maoist) has five regional bureaus (eastern, central, Kathmandu valley, western, and international department) under its central committee. The eastern bureau looks after Mechi, Koshi, Sagarmatha and Janakpur zones, as well as some parts of the eastern districts of Bagmati and Narayani zones; the central bureau is responsible for most parts of Narayani, Bagmati, Gandaki, Lumbini and Dhaulagiri zones; and the western bureau takes responsibility for

Rapti, Bheri, Karnali, Seti and Mahakali zones (CPN [UML] 2001/2). Various sub-regional bureaus and, in some places, even special sub-regional bureaus, were formed under the regional bureaus. The international department is responsible for, among other things, organising Nepalis outside the country, maintaining international relations and contacts, collecting money, buying weapons and arranging for guerrilla training. Representatives of the international department are active in various Indian cities, as well as in London, Brussels and Berlin.

At the time of writing, not much was known about the command and control structure of the CPN (Maoist). Both the party and most of its leaders were underground. Certain leaders were above ground, but they were publicly active under different guises and concealed their association with the party. Apart from those stationed in the field, most of the Maoist leaders generally lived in safe urban areas with most leaders of the core group living in Kathmandu. A few of them lived in India as well. In this context, densely-populated urban areas were much safer for the Maoist leaders than jungles and villages.

THE PEOPLE'S ARMY

The most powerful arm of the CPN (Maoist) is the 5,000-odd guerrillas who are known to the Maoists as the people's army. Total authority regarding the mobilisation of the people's army rests with the central military commission, which is presided over by the party chairman, Prachanda. There are also regional, sub-regional and district-level military commissions.

Each army unit is under the dual control of the military commander and the political commissar. At the lowest level of the guerrilla forces (these are the ones who wear military fatigues) is the squad, comprising nine to eleven members. Above the squad are, in ascending order, the platoon, the company and the battalion. Maoist strategists have plans to develop the people's army to regimental and brigade strength in the future. In addition to the army, there are thousands in the people's militia. The militiamen and women do not wear uniforms and they carry muzzle-loaders, unlike those in the people's army, who are generally equipped with .303s. Unlike the guerrilla squads, the militia does not have to take part in guerrilla activities very regularly, and it only provides support when it is needed. Militias are formed and mobilised by village people's committees. The Maoists have a policy of including female members in their armed units, to the extent that this is possible. Women have become squad commanders and are also active in platoons, companies and battalions. In some places, separate women-only guerrilla squads have been formed (Yami and Bhattarai 2000/1: 66).

When the Maoists began their war, they did not have an organised armed wing. With limited weapons at their disposal, they had formed fighting groups, security groups and volunteer groups in some places. According to Comrade Neperu, a platoon commander in Rolpa, the people's army was developed only after the government began its Kilo Sierra Two operation in 1998.[2] He held the view that the training ground for communist guerrillas is the battlefield itself. Nonetheless, special training is provided in the base areas of the mid-west region. Selected guerrillas are on occasion sent for advanced training outside the country, mainly to Andhra Pradesh and Jharkhand in India, where the Communist Party of India (ML-People's War) is active.

A UNITED FRONT

The United People's Front was dissolved in February 2000 after the CPN (Maoist) concluded that it could not play the role of the grand united front it had envisaged. After that, using a similar concept, the CPN (Maoist) formed joint people's committees which existed in parallel with the local government bodies. This led to the creation of numerous ward, village, area and district level people's committees, which were publicly proclaimed as people's governments. By November 2001, district people's governments had been formed in twenty-one districts. The Maoists' long-term plan was to establish a central people's government.

With the aim of creating a grand united front, the CPN (Maoist) has also formed around a dozen ethnic and regional fronts such as the Magarant National Liberation Front, the Tamuwan National Liberation Front, the Tharuwan National Liberation Front, the Tamang National Liberation Front, the Thami Liberation Front, the Majhi

---

[2] Interview with Comrade Neperu, Rolpa, September 2001.

Liberation Front, the Madhesi National Liberation Front, Newa Khala, the Nepal Dalit Liberation Front, and the Karnali Regional Liberation Front. In 2001, the Limbuwan National Liberation Front and Khambuwan National Front were merged to form a new organisation, called the Kirat National Liberation Front. The Ethnic and Regional Fronts Coordination Committee coordinated the activities of these fronts.

At the same time, the CPN (Maoist) established numerous organisations involving various classes of society in order to create public opinion in support of its campaign through activities above ground. According to one study, the Maoists have more than twenty frontal organisations (*Maobadi samasya...*2000/1: 12). Although these include at least a dozen working class organisations, their role in the Maoist movement does not appear momentous; nor does the role of the peasants' organisation appear to be very significant. The Maoist strategy of influencing the urban professional classes through its intellectuals' front does not seem very successful either. On the other hand, the All Nepal National Free Students' Union (Revolutionary) and the All Nepal Women's Association (Revolutionary) have played an effective role in their own areas. The main Maoist-aligned organisations active in India are the All India Nepali Unity Society, the All India Nepali Students' Association, the All India Nepali Youth Association, and the All India Nepali Ethnic Society.

MAOIST AREAS

Because of the success of the CPN (Maoist) in spreading its influence country-wide in addition to achieving complete control over some areas, it has earned itself a prominent position in Nepal's political arena. In the mid-western districts of Rolpa, Rukum, Jajarkot, Salyan, Pyuthan and Kalikot, the government's presence is limited to the district headquarters, with the remainder of each district under the control of the Maoists. The home ministry has classified these districts as 'Sensitive Class A'. Further government classification places nine districts (Dolakha, Ramechhap, Sindhuli, Kavre, Sindhupalchok, Gorkha, Dang, Surkhet and Achham) in 'Sensitive Class B' and seventeen (Khotang, Okhaldhunga, Udaypur, Makwanpur, Lalitpur, Nuwakot, Dhading, Tanahun, Lamjung, Parbat, Baglung, Gulmi,

Arghakhachi, Bardiya, Dailekh, Jumla and Dolpa) into 'Sensitive Class C'. However, in view of the meteoric rise in the influence of the Maoist movement, even home ministry officials admit that this classification has become obsolete.

As mentioned, the Maoists have announced people's governments in twenty-one districts (Rolpa, Rukum, Jajarkot, Salyan, Gorkha, Dhading, Tanahun, Dailekh, Parbat, Dolakha, Sindhupalchok, Palpa, Lamjung, Sankhuwasabha, Terhathum, Sindhuli, Ramechhap, Gulmi, Jumla-Kalikot, Kalikot-Achham-Bajura and Rasuwa-Nuwakot). However, Pyuthan, classified by the government as 'Class A', as well as the 'Class B' districts of Dang, Kavre and Surkhet, have not seen the formation of people's governments.

The CPN (Maoist) has divided the areas under its influence into three categories. The areas under their complete control are known as 'principal' base areas. Areas adjoining base areas are known as 'secondary areas' or 'guerrilla areas', and control of these areas shifts back and forth between the guerrillas and the government (Bhattarai 1998/9: 99). Cities such as Kathmandu have been designated as 'propaganda areas'. Maoists use the capital as a location for meetings, contacts, and the dissemination of information and publicity. In Kathmandu, the main object of Maoist activity is publicity; hence they avoid engaging in acts that might invite a major reaction from the government.

CONDITIONS IN MAOIST AREAS

As soon as a truce was reached with the government, the Maoists expended a lot of energy on trying to expand their sphere of influence in the capital, in the tarai, and in the eastern region, and met with some limited success in their endeavour. However, if the government decides to mobilise the army, this influence could drop back to zero. In such a scenario, the only districts which would have the wherewithal to keep the people's war alive would be the mid-western districts of Rolpa, Rukum, Jajarkot, Salyan, Pyuthan and Kalikot. These districts can be accurately described as the epicentre of the Maoist movement, because here the Maoist presence is much stronger than the government's (which is limited to district headquarters alone, as mentioned earlier). The Chief District Officers and the Deputy

Superintendents of Police (these are the district police chiefs) who are posted to these district headquarters can be described as 'ambassadors' of the Kathmandu government to the 'Maoist nation'.

Managing to rid the villages of the police and the administration is truly a huge strategic achievement for the Maoist movement. In order to solidify its defensive position and to counteract the various defeats it has suffered in the guerrilla war, the government has started to amalgamate police posts. An unfortunate outcome of this move has been that the police force has been weakened to the point where it cannot realistically counter any attacks by the Maoists. The district of Rolpa provides a good example of the shrinking police force. The number of police posts has shrunk to only two from a former total of thirty-nine. Similarly, Rukum has seen a decrease from twenty-three police posts to two.

In the rural countryside, the onus of maintaining the presence of the state has fallen upon schools, health posts, agricultural offices and post offices. The only reason these institutions are allowed to function is that they are not seen as hindrances to the Maoist movement. The fate of village development committees (VDCs) has been similar to that of police posts, and most VDC office-bearers have been evicted from the villages. Some of these expelled VDC personnel operate out of the district headquarters. In the villages, the only non-Maoist political workers are those who have surrendered to the Maoists. Everyone else has had to take refuge, either in the district headquarters or in Kathmandu.

In the recent past, the Royal Nepalese Army (RNA) has become increasingly active in the Maoist areas. After the Maoist attack on Dunai, the headquarters of Dolpa, in September 2000, the army was deployed in the capital towns of sixteen districts. The Maoists attacked the army itself when it attempted to free sixty-nine members of the police force who were abducted from Holeri in Rolpa in July 2001. A change of government in the immediate aftermath of this incident as well as the ceasefire declaration between the government and the CPN (Maoist) has averted any confrontation between the RNA and the Maoists for the time being. However, the possibility of such a confrontation appears even more probable in the future.

The Integrated Internal Security and Development Programme (IISDP) has legitimised the increase in RNA activities in the Maoist areas. Army companies (each approximately 150 strong) have been deployed in every parliamentary constituency of Rolpa, Rukum, Salyan, Jajarkot and Pyuthan districts. The operational base of the IISDP, located at Libang in Rolpa, is under the command of a lieutenant-colonel. The RNA has adopted Gorkha district as a model for the implementation of the IISDP.

The police force was not able to elicit the sympathy and support of the general public because of its own excesses in the past. That is probably the reason why the army is attempting to win the public's trust from the very beginning with gestures such as establishing health camps in villages. As far back as 1999, the army had allocated a special budget for a road to be constructed from Salyan to Rukum's district headquarters, Musikot, as a special public relations stratagem. The army has also been guarding fifty-six telephone and eight radio towers against possible Maoist attack since February 1998. While the setting up of army camps in villages under Maoist control (for the implementation of the IISDP) has not resulted in any direct confrontation between the army and the rebel force, the Maoists do find themselves in a tight corner because of the army's presence.

THE PEOPLE'S GOVERNMENTS

Over a span of six years, the Maoists converted some places into base areas, defining the formation of base areas as 'the establishment of people's government by nullifying the presence of reactionary government rule'. To that end, the Maoists set up various people's committees at the ward, village, area and district levels. These people's governments are formed through elections based on class representation. Guerrillas, *janajatis*, Dalits, intellectuals, women, business people, and so on, are all given representation. However, 'feudalists' and 'comprador and bureaucratic capitalists' are not allowed to either elect or be elected to people's governments. The 'Directive for Local New People's Government' promulgated by the CPN (Maoist) has divided the operation of Maoist government into political, economic and socio-cultural components:

Political component. By rendering the present central government's local bodies, i.e. VDCs and DDCs, virtually useless, and by displacing police posts from villages, the Maoists first created a power vacuum. Then they started forming people's committees to establish people's governments.

Economic component. The Maoists are attempting to make their people's governments economically self-sustainable. They are trying to replace banks and 'small farmer development programmes' with their own economic programmes. For instance, the Jaljala Financial Co-operative Fund established in Rolpa by the Maoists in 1999 has been providing banking services to the residents. It gives eight per cent interest on deposits and charges fifteen per cent interest on loans. In some cases, the tillers' rights have been established by capturing land belonging to 'feudal' landlords in order to run communes. Several village people's committees even issue land registration papers and collect taxes. This is probably the reason why government tax collection is nil in Maoist-affected areas. The Maoists collect periodic as well as seasonal taxes from everyone—from bureaucrats and traders to woodcutters and graziers.

Socio-cultural component. The Maoists declare that they are building a new culture. Culture in fact is an important aspect of mobilisation, where elements of existing cultures are incorporated into mobilisation strategies that are themselves varied in different contexts. In Maoist areas, festivals such as Dasain and Tihar have dwindled in importance in comparison to Martyrs' Day, a day to honour the memory of the cadres who have fallen in the course of the people's war. The families of the 'martyrs' engage in holding memorial services rather than traditional funeral rites. Instead of customary weddings, people now stand on a stage for 'people's weddings' whilst pledging their commitment to the Prachanda Path. Levels of alcoholism, gambling and crime have been significantly reduced in villages. The practices of teaching Sanskrit and singing the national anthem in schools have also ended. Instead of the songs one hears in the rest of the country, revolutionary songs are much more popular. There has been an unprecedented increase in the local people's capacity for study and analysis. Awareness among females has also reached a high level. Most people regard journalists as lacking in credibility. Radio Nepal is perceived as an institution totally lacking in veracity. However, people do listen to Radio Nepal more than any other radio station, and then analyse what they hear from their own perspective. The BBC Nepali Service enjoys the highest credibility.

The Maoists have also established a parallel judicial system in which people's courts hear cases and pass judgements and sentences. The directive for people's committees has divided crime into three categories—simple, heinous, and tending towards heinousness. The punishment the Maoists mete out can include anything from being sent to labour camps to fines to execution.

LATENT DISSATISFACTION

Although the Maoists have been very successful in the formation of their armed forces, they are now facing the challenge of keeping the armed cadres under strict control. The militia and guerrillas seem to be lacking in discipline. Instead of ideas leading the guns, guns appear to be showing the way to ideas. The victims are the general public who initially welcomed the rebels as a welcome alternative to police excesses, but the distinction between the rebels and the police they displaced is becoming blurred. In remote mid-western villages where most people lead a hand-to-mouth existence, having to provide shelter and food for ten or twelve Maoist rebels has become an inordinately tough burden, but no one dares raise a voice in protest, for fear of inviting 'people's action'. The memory of a CPN (UML) worker being killed because of his refusal to feed the Maoists is all too fresh.

Ram Prasad, a priest from Jajarkot, lost his life in a similarly unnecessary fashion. When a son of his who was a Maoist activist surrendered to the police with his rifle, the rebels immediately abducted him. They demanded payment of Rs 200,000 in compensation for the rifle his son had handed over to the police. As Ram Prasad did not have the wherewithal to produce the payment, he remained in Maoist custody and later died.[3]

Since the emphasis seems to be on increasing the sheer number of people's warriors rather than on their quality, the CPN (Maoist) is experiencing problems in administering the rebel forces. Rebels under the age of twenty, who make up a large proportion of the people's army, are undisciplined and immature. Age itself is not a factor, since even the RNA recruits are teenagers. The lack of discipline is more a reflection of the training and command system. There are

[3] *Himal Khabarpatrika*, 14–28 March 2001.

many who enlist in the people's army due to the lure of the uniform and the gun. Some are made to enlist. There are stray cases of individuals being drawn into the fighting force more for their physical capacities than for their ideological orientation. The lack of discipline is even more evident amongst the militia, who are issued with guns after an orientation programme that lasts a mere week. This can be explained in part by the speed of recruitment and lack of adequate briefing; the nature of the Maoists' expansion in Nepal is a contributory factor. In the Chinese case, there was a highly centralised command, and physically the Maoists were concentrated. In Nepal, on the other hand, the encirclement is different: the base areas are spread out. The geographical distribution of the Maoists can result in a district committee not having much idea of what the armed wing in its district is up to. Even within the army, the lowest level activities can tend to be autonomous of higher command. In a telephone conversation with Madhav Kumar Nepal, general secretary of CPN (UML) in October 2001, the Maoist leader Baburam Bhattarai admitted that his militia had strayed beyond the party's control.

Similarly, the people's committees were established rapidly during the truce period and problems often ensued. An incident in which a member of the people's committee in Nuwakot became involved in an alleged case of the sexual abuse of a child (actually his own niece) gained wide-scale notoriety. Even though the individual was subsequently dismissed from the committee and punished, the damage had been done.

The punishments handed out by people's courts sometimes appear whimsical and based on personal motives. For this reason many people have been forced to flee from their villages when they have been unable to pay fines ordered by the Maoists. Village people's committees determine the prices shops are allowed to charge for their merchandise, so that the shops cannot make any profit. When villagers sell their produce to the 'reactionary government' (i.e., the district headquarters), they are required to pay a tax of ten per cent of their earnings. Bureaucrats and teachers working in Maoist areas have to suffer endless 'fund-raising', and are required to give one day's salary every month to the Maoists. One has to procure the permission of the people's government in order to travel. People may be dissatisfied with the way the Maoists operate but no one dares risk opposing them. The CPN (Maoist) has itself admitted to being permeated by deviant tendencies. In the words of Prachanda, 'The abundance of economic and physical materials that has accompanied the success of the people's war may have an adverse effect on the simple and hard-working proletariat way of life' (CPN [Maoist] 2000/1: 53).

ANALYSING THE GOVERNMENT'S FAILURE

A week after the CPN (Maoist) declared the people's war, the then home minister, Khum Bahadur Khadka, declared 'I am confident that we will be able to bring the present activities under control within four or five days.'[4] Interestingly, after an interval of six years he was enjoying his second tenure as home minister and the Maoist movement had grown much more intense.

After the commencement of the Maoist insurgency, the local elections held in 1997 showed the future of the people's war. Because the Maoists had decided to boycott the elections, no elections were held in eighty-three VDCs in Rolpa, Rukum, Salyan and Jajarkot. The power vacuum thus created allowed the Maoists a chance to practise running a people's government for four months. Prachanda said, 'Organising activities such as communal labour and agriculture, the building of roads, bridges, memorials to martyrs, land registration, the sale and purchase of land, security, people's culture, people's courts and operating schools became the initial exercise of the new people's government. For the first time in their lives, people in these areas got to enjoy becoming masters of their own destiny' (Prachanda 1998/9b: 3).

But that period came to an end. Because of its failure to hold the local elections and the proximity of general elections, the government decided to adopt harsh measures to control the growth of Maoist influence. An offensive, code-named Operation Kilo Sierra Two, was launched against the Maoists in eighteen districts from May 1998 to May 1999. Within a period of a year, almost 500 people lost their lives at the hands of the police. Among the casualties, innocents far outnumbered Maoist rebels, and this benefited the Maoists. In

---

[4] Interview in the weekly *Deshantar*, 25 February 1996.

the wake of the police excesses, many people were driven by the motive of revenge into the rebel camp and the number of Maoists saw a phenomenal increase.

Because Operation Kilo Sierra Two continued until the eve of the parliamentary elections of May 1999, the Maoists avoided incurring any more losses (which would have been the consequence if they had tried to disrupt the elections) by merely announcing their boycott of the elections. Because the new election saw the formation of a new government under Krishna Prasad Bhattarai (considered more liberal than Girija Prasad Koirala), the Maoists got enough breathing space to pick up the pieces of what was left of their party. Before Koirala was reinstated as prime minister in March 2000, the Maoists were busy consolidating their power even as they were engaged in discussions about talks with the government.

From the end of 1999, the Maoists adopted an offensive stance, rather than their earlier defensive one. Their first offensive was the attack on the police force base in Mahatgaon in Rukum on 22 September 1999. The rebels managed to kill seven policemen and abduct the Deputy Superintendent of Police (DSP), Thule Rai. Over the next two years the impression was created that the people's war was actually a war between the Maoists and the police. Between 1996 and late 2001, more than 500 policemen were killed, among them a Senior Superintendent of Police (SSP), a DSP and eight inspectors.

The main objective of the Maoists' attacks on the police was to capture arms and to displace police posts, and in this they were successful. In the aftermath of Maoist strikes, the police tended to relocate police posts instead of counter-attacking. The police began to lose almost every battle against the Maoists. The move to amalgamate police posts accelerated even more after the attack on Dunai in September 2000. Because of the shortsightedness of their own policies, the 50,000-strong police force was brought to its knees by a ragtag rebel force of merely 5,000 within six years.

The Nepal Police has always claimed that a shortage of modern weapons and a lack of counter-insurgency training are the main reasons for its inability to fight the rebels. When they realised that the procurement of modern weapons was not possible, the police headquarters suggested to the government as far back as 1999 that the army should be deployed in Rolpa, Rukum, Salyan, Jajarkot, Pyuthan

and Kalikot districts. The issue of army mobilisation, however, remained in limbo, due to the long-standing tussle vis-à-vis the army
between the government and the royal palace.

MAOIST METHODS

On the basis of the experience of the Chinese revolution, the Nepali
Maoists have divided the process of their people's war into three
phases: strategic defence, strategic balance and strategic offence.
The Maoist movement has now (November 2001) reached the end of
the strategic defence phase and the second phase of strategic balance
is being prepared. When the rebel forces become as strong as the
government's security forces, that phase is defined as 'strategic balance' in Maoist terms. In the third phase 'strategic offence', the rebel
force becomes stronger than the government force and the rebel
forces capture central governance. To achieve that end, the CPN
(Maoist) has implemented the following plans.

First Plan. The first plan, which lasted for a month following the
commencement of the people's war, carried the slogan: 'Let us move
ahead on the path of the people's war to establish the new people's
democratic state by destroying the reactionary state'. During the
plan, more than 6,000 'people's actions' were carried out, which
included publicity (80 per cent), destruction (15 per cent) and other
activities (5 per cent) (Nepal National Intellectuals' Association
1997: 28). The Maoist party concluded that despite some weaknesses
the first plan was successful.

Second Plan. This plan lasted from March 1996 to June 1997, and its
main slogan was to 'develop the people's war in an organised way'.
The second plan also included the strong action of 'eliminating
selected enemies' (Prachanda 1996/7: 27), in accordance with which
the Maoists started a series of killings. Two policemen were the first
casualties in an ambush by the Maoists in Tak VDC of Rukum on 6
May 1996. During the second plan, the Maoists succeeded in capturing weapons and developing guerrilla zones.

Third Plan. The third plan lasted for a year from June 1997 with the
slogan of 'raising the development of guerrilla warfare to new heights'.
The underlying objective of the plan was to make the Maoist

guerrillas capable of fighting the RNA. Later incidents, however, showed that the people's army had not yet become capable of this. During the third plan, the Maoists also carried out a programme of boycotting local elections and, later, of forcing elected representatives to resign from their posts. This consequently led to a political vacuum in a couple of districts, where the Maoists began to exercise their people's rule to a limited extent. The Maoists also declared the existence of their Central Military Commission on 13 February 1998. As the Maoists intensified their activities, the government launched Kilo Sierra Two.

Fourth Plan. With the slogan 'Let's embark on the great path of creating base areas', the fourth plan of the Maoist movement commenced on 27 October 1998. That night, the Maoists carried out unprecedented co-ordinated attacks in many places in a 'country-wide blow'. At a time when the state was engaged in brutal repression, it had become necessary for the CPN (Maoist) to bring forth a programme that was more advanced than previous ones. The Maoists also succeeded in organising a rally in New Delhi in February 1998 under the banner of the 'Solidarity Forum to Support the People's War in Nepal', which in turn involved six Indian organisations.

Fifth Plan. The fifth plan began in August 1999, and was also related to the creation of base areas. The slogan of this plan was 'Let's move further ahead on the great path of creating base areas'. The killing by the police of a CPN (Maoist) politburo member, Suresh Wagle, in Gorkha on 8 September was a severe blow to the party during this period. Following this, the Maoists demonstrated their strength by carrying out simultaneous attacks in twenty-five districts on the night of 22 September and by organising for the first time on its own initiative a Nepal Bandh on 7 October. An influential central leader, Yan Prasad Gautam (Comrade Alok), was expelled from the party in a purification campaign during the fifth plan.

Sixth Plan. The sixth plan was carried out during the transitional period between the fifth plan and the second national conference, i.e. from July 2000 to February 2001. The slogan of the plan was to 'Raise to new heights the guerrilla war and the people's resistance struggle'. The sixth plan has special significance in the history of the people's war, given that it was during this period that the attack on Dunai was carried out.

Having completed its six war plans, the CPN (Maoist) organised its second national conference in February 2001. The conference was a turning point, at which the Maoists expanded their policies and plans beyond the narrow confines of the people's war. Current policies were reviewed and revised to the extent that the party completely changed its direction to embrace what is now known as 'Prachanda Path'.

PRACHANDA PATH

Just as the policy of 'people's multi-party democracy' introduced by Madan Bhandari, the late general secretary of CPN (UML), brought Bhandari's party into the fold of parliamentary democracy, the 'Prachanda Path' could provide an avenue for the CPN (Maoist) to escape becoming mired in communist fundamentalism. By passing the political document presented by Prachanda entitled 'The Great Leap Forward: The Inevitable Necessity of History', the Maoist conference gave its ideological assent to the Prachanda Path.

Keeping in mind the new changes the world is experiencing, none of the proletarian revolutions of the past was deemed to be as appropriate as Prachanda Path for the Nepali context. Prachanda Path assumes a kind of revolution that would be a fusion of the Chinese model of protracted people's war strategy (to expand from villages to towns) and the Russian model of general armed insurrection. Hence, the Maoists now (November 2001) have the slogan 'Let us consolidate and expand our base areas and move forwards towards a people's government in the centre' (CPN [Maoist] 2001b).

The aim of Prachanda Path is to use the people's war in order to expand the Maoists' base areas in villages, and to use these as a platform from which to invoke a people's revolt at the centre, in order to overthrow the government. In a centralised political atmosphere like Nepal's, nothing that happens in the countryside carries the same weight as any movement that takes place in Kathmandu. There are ample precedents that demonstrate the importance of affecting Kathmandu before any political change is possible. That is probably the reason why the Maoists have adopted the policy of people's revolt. But so far they do not have a strong enough organisational base in the capital to allow them to push through an effective and final people's revolt. One aspect of their mobilisation in urban areas, mostly among an already politicised segment in Kathmandu, has been their raising the flag of patriotism, especially by voicing an anti-India rhetoric on issues that have been a part of the political agenda of left parties for a while now.

When the movement reaches a certain point, the Maoists plan to announce an alternative central government. The proposed government, which is to be known as the 'Organisational Committee of the New People's Government', will be formed not after the revolution is a *fait accompli* but to actually engineer the revolution. In October 2001 Prachanda unveiled the party's plans to announce a central people's government if and when the talks with the government failed.[5] The Maoists have also created around fifteen central departments in the form of a shadow cabinet.

TALKS: THE LAST HOPE

From a war strategy point of view, the present talks between the government and the Maoists are the product of a new balance of power.[6] In the present context, Maoists have been able to form their base areas in some districts but have been unable to take control of the district headquarters. They might have formed people's governments in some districts, but the time is not yet ripe for them to announce a central people's government. The talks have been initiated at just such a crucial juncture.

The unprecedented expansion and achievements of the Maoist movement have been attained at an unimaginable pace (even by the admission of Maoist leaders themselves) and have proved to be difficult for the party to manage. Therefore, they are looking for a political outlet. Similarly, as a resolution of the Maoist issue has risen to the top of the government's political agenda, it too is pushing for talks.

Despite the failure of all the talks in the past, the incentive for a fresh round of talks between the government and the Maoists was provided by the Holeri (Rolpa) incident in July 2001. After they abducted sixty-nine policemen, the Maoists inadvertently found

[5] Interview with Prachanda in the monthly *Sambhavana*, October 2001.
[6] Editor's note: these talks broke down on 23 November 2001 (see the introduction to this volume).

themselves on the brink of a confrontation with the army. The Maoists reacted by throwing the ball of talks into the government's court. This could indicate that they may not yet be capable of taking on the army, despite their claims. In the meantime, events took a dramatic turn after Sher Bahadur Deuba became prime minister for the second time. Deuba announced a ceasefire and called upon Prachanda to reciprocate, which he did.

Until the second round of talks, in September 2001, there was a general feeling that the Maoist wind had managed to blow across the entire country. During that period, they organised mass meetings in order to present their views to town-dwellers. They started preparing for a mass meeting on 21 September in Kathmandu with hundreds of thousands of people expected to turn up. However, the Maoists were not impervious to the international wave against terrorism brought about by the 11 September attacks on American cities. Even though the Maoists had always enjoyed recognition as a political force, the changing circumstances presented a fresh danger that they might face isolation by being branded as a terrorist force. At about the same time, people themselves started raising protests against the terror and extortion of the Maoist activists. In such a domestic and international atmosphere, the government was able to prevent the much-publicised Maoist meeting from taking place.

After their analysis of the royal palace massacre of 1 June 2001 proved erroneous, many of the Maoists' actions proved counterproductive for their cause. Their premise that it was possible to keep alive the anger that initially provided the impetus for the protests against the royal palace massacre turned out to be a mistake. The Maoists claimed that the massacre was a conspiracy involving India, the United States and even the new king, Gyanendra, but were not able to provide any evidence to substantiate these claims. Their desire that the general anger of the populace should lead to a revolt in the army's ranks, and their efforts and entreaties to create that situation, all met with failure.

On the other hand, China did not support the Maoists against King Gyanendra, as the Maoists had hoped. In view of the geopolitical situation of Nepal, the Maoists have identified the support of either India or China as a prerequisite for the realisation of their goal. Because targeting India is an integral part of their movement,

the Maoists have made a conscious effort to improve their relations
with China.

The Maoists' declaration that Nepal had become a republic after
the palace massacre failed to garner the support of either communist
China or the various communist parties within Nepal. The CPN (Unity
Centre) was the only party that supported the Maoist proposal for
'the formation of an interim government, a new Constitution and the
institutional development of a republican state'. The rest of the communist parties rejected the Maoist line, primarily because of the 'republic' issue, with the result that apart from the CPN (Maoist) and
the CPN (Unity Centre), all the communist parties sided with the
government.

The new atmosphere created by the royal palace incident has
pushed the Maoists into a very difficult corner. In the past, disagreement between the royal palace and the government regarding the
deployment of the army had given the Maoists reason to be confident that the army would not be used against them. According to
claims made by the Maoists, King Birendra was in direct contact with
them.[7]

The Maoists calculated that their previous relationship with the
royal palace would not continue with King Gyanendra in charge,
hence their demand for a republic. Whether they are debating a new
Constitution in talks with the government or (in the event of the talks
failing) coming face to face with the army, it is certain that the war
will now be between the Maoists and the king. In order for the talks
to be successful, either the Maoists will have to compromise on their
insistence on a new Constitution, or else a part of the Maoists' demands will have to be met by the government. Otherwise, no agreement can be reached.

There are voices within the Maoist party that say that in the present imbroglio some agreement should be reached, even if the government only agrees to revise the present Constitution. However,
there is also a strong lobby of those who believe that they have to go
back to war if the talks fail. At the same time, the Maoist cadres in
the base areas have also threatened open revolt if there is any compromise on the issue of a republic. For its part, the government is
hoping to prolong this state of flux in the hope that differences within

---

[7] Baburam Bhattarai, writing in the daily *Rajdhani*, 29 June 2001 (15 Asadh 2058 v.s.).

the CPN (Maoist) will lead to a rift in the party and that one side can be brought over, while the other can be marginalised and destroyed.

The experience of liberal-style democracy over the past ten years has proved that there is plenty of room to improve the system: this has been recognised even by those within it. The amendment of the Constitution is also one of the major demands of the main opposition party, the CPN (UML). If the government is ready to accommodate the Maoists in an interim government and begin the process of major constitutional amendment to the satisfaction of the latter, even as the debate on a republican Nepal continues, it will be easier for the Maoists to enter the mainstream.

APPENDIX

ORGANISATIONAL STRUCTURE OF CPN (MAOIST)[8]

Party	People's Army	United Front
standing committee | politburo | central committee | regional bureaus (five in total) | sub-regional bureaus (or 'special sub-regional bureaus') | district committees | area committees | cell committees	central military commission | regional military commissions | sub-regional military commissions | district military commissions *Included in this are* temporary battalion | companies | platoons | squads (separate people's militias also exist under joint village people's committees)	joint people's district committees | joint people's area committees | joint people's village committees | joint people's ward committees

[8] This structure was changed after the ceasefire broke in November 2001. As of June 2003 three commands have been formed under the central committee. The domain of these commands includes both the military and political organisational structures. The establishment of a people's liberation army was announced, within which brigade-level formations have been made. In the united front, a central-level people's government has been created.

THE NEPALI STATE AND THE MAOIST INSURGENCY, 1996–2001

Krishna Hachhethu

The Maoist insurgency in Nepal has been viewed from several different perspectives.[1] Some see it as a consequence of failed development, others view it as an ethnic uprising, and many attribute it to bad governance. If the Maoist development is considered to be solely an outcome of the problems of poverty and unemployment, the possibility of its upward movement to the point where it takes over state authority cannot be denied. But this approach seems insufficient to answer two questions: Why did the Maoist's people's war begin from Rolpa, and not from some other area where conditions were worse? Why are none of the districts of Nepal's far-western region (the most underdeveloped area) included in the list of those twenty-five districts in which the Maoists have formed their own district governments, or *jan sarkars*? If the Maoist insurgency is viewed mainly as a rebellion against the exclusion of ethnic groups and the Dalit community, the possibility of a Maoist takeover is very unlikely. Moreover, how can this view account for the fact that out of a total of 608 persons killed by the Maoists up to October 2001, 37.33 per cent belonged to non-Bahun and non-Chetri/Thakuri castes?[2]

The perceptions of the Maoist issue which overemphasise economic and/or ethnic factors seem to be informed by the forty-point demand of the United People's Front (UPF-Baburam Bhattarai faction) that was submitted to the government on 13 February 1996, a few days before the Maoists began their armed action. This list of demands is an auxiliary item: it is an agenda provided for public consumption, rather like an election manifesto. It is designed to be used

---

[1] This chapter is written from the perspective of early November 2001, and therefore does not take political developments that occurred after that date into account.

[2] This figure is taken from Maharjan (2001).

as an instrument (a) to neutralise pro-establishment forces, and particularly urban dwellers, opinion-makers, civil society, and articulate sections of the masses; and (b) to cultivate and mobilise rural inhabitants and poor and marginalised sections of society to achieve the Maoists' goals. These are proclaimed to be the overthrow of the present polity, based on multi-party parliamentary democracy and constitutional monarchy, through armed revolution, and its replacement with a new political system known as New People's Democracy. The Maoists' key agenda items during their negotiations with the government—an interim government, a new Constitution, and a republican state—reveal the real crux of the issue. As another point of reference, it should be noted that the Maoist people's war started at a time when the Nepali state was heading towards instability and crisis owing to the unholy alliances, both in nature and purpose, that were being struck between various parliamentary parties. Of course, the Maoist insurgency has its own multiple dynamic, and this includes social, ethnic and economic issues, but it is basically an ideological and political offensive against the present political system of the country. This chapter confines itself to an analysis of how the state has tried to contain the Maoist insurgency through security measures as well as negotiation. Table 1 presents the various strategies the state adopted to deal with the Maoists' violent people's war between early 1996 and late 2001.

The chapter is organised in four sections. The first section deals with the state's withdrawal from the insurgency area, creating a conducive environment for the Maoists to have their own territory. The second section focuses on why the government's attempts to reinstate the state failed, and the third on the state's peace offensive. The final section suggests that the election of a constituent assembly would be the best means of managing the Maoist insurgency.

STATE WITHDRAWAL

From one perspective, the Maoist insurgency in its mid-western stronghold areas can be seen as a renewal of an old confrontation between the Thakuri Raj and the radical left. The Thakuris (descendants of the rulers of the old principalities) and their clients had long dominated this area, and the nature of their rule at local level was

Krishna Hachhethu

Table 1 STATE REACTIONS TO MAOIST VIOLENCE

Strategies	*Features*
Non-military security measures	1. Operation Romeo (November–December 1995): conducted by a total of 317 police resulting in the arrest of 339 suspects and legal action against 172 Maoists. 2. General law and order treatment: 91 persons killed by police and 38 by Maoists. 3. Failed attempt to introduce an anti-terrorist law. 4. Kilo Sierra Two Operation and Jungle Search Operation, (1998–1999). Number of casualties: 662 Maoists and 216 police. 5. Integrated Security Programme (December 1999-November 2000): (a) a collective political campaign against Maoists; (b) development package including programmes entitled 'B. P. Koirala with the Poor', 'Ganesh Man Singh Peace Campaign', 'Women's Employment', 'Youth Self-Employment'; and (c) administrative security measures. 6. Establishment of armed police force; Silent Kilo Sierra Three Operation, Delta Operation, and Chakrabyuha Operation (2000 to May 2001): 219 Maoist casualties, 338 police casualties.
Security measures with military involvement, with or without a development package	1. Initial deployment of army in 17 'Maoist-affected' districts (September–October 2000): a decision to extend to six more districts was reportedly consented to by the king in October 2001. 2. Integrated Development Programme of Rs 190 million to five 'severely Maoist-affected' districts (Rolpa, Rukum, Salyan, Kalikot and Jajarkot) involving the combined efforts of army, police, bureaucracy, people's elected representatives and party workers (November 2000 to March 2001). 3. Special Security Plan in six Maoist stronghold districts (Rukum, Rolpa, Salyan, Pyuthan, Jajarkot and Kalikot) to be implemented in three phases: mobilisation of 6829 army and 1977 police in phase one, reduction of army numbers to 3832 and increase of police numbers to 4083 in phase two, and replacement of army by 6829 armed police force along with 1977 general police in phrase three. 4. Integrated Internal Security and Development Programme (initiated May 2001): mobilisation of army in seven 'severely Maoist-affected' districts along with the allocation of a Rs 70 million development budget. 5. Mobilisation of army at Holeri in Rolpa district on 13 July 2001.
Peace offensive	1. Ceasefire declared on 23 July 2001. 2. Declaration of whereabouts of detained Maoists and release of previously-arrested Maoist leaders and workers. 3. Negotiations, beginning on 30 August 2001.

repressive. This was in accord with the authoritarian regime at the centre during the partyless Panchayat system (1962–90). Even after the restoration of democracy in 1990, the former Panchas survived, reviving their power base under a new guise by responding to the Nepali Congress's policy of incorporating the traditional social and political élites in its scheme of party building during the early 1990s. However, the sense of popular empowerment that spread after the successful 1990 *jan andolan* introduced a new power against the traditional forces. Both the CPN (UML) and the CPN (Maoist, formerly the UPF) emerged as the most influential left forces in the people's fight against various forms of the Thakuri Raj in this region. The equation among the left forces has changed in favour of the CPN (Maoist) as a consequence of the UML's movement from the left towards the centre, while the Congress Party is constantly heading towards the right from the centre in the political spectrum of the country. The local Thakuri-centrist alliance in the mainstream parties has never been strong under the democratic set-up, and it deteriorated during the period of hung parliament (November 1994 to May 1999). Because politics was concentrated at the centre in the game of government making and unmaking, the parliamentary parties grossly ignored the need for party building at the grassroots level. This was the most appropriate time for the CPN (Maoist) to create its own space and territory for a long drawn-out people's war.

Starting from the initial period, when the Maoists staged a rehearsal of the people's war in Rolpa district in October–November 1995, the government treated it as a law and order problem. Police suppression during 'Operation Romeo' culminated in mass arrests and legal actions against hundreds of suspected 'law violators'. From the day the Maoists formerly inaugurated their violent actions by attacking police stations in Rolpa, Rukum and Sindhuli on 13 February 1996, the government responded with police repression. Against the Maoists' murder of thirty-eight persons in the first two years of the people's war, the police killed ninety-one persons and arrested several suspected 'terrorists'. Due to the courts' decisions to release most of the arrested rebels, the government felt a serious need for an anti-terrorist law, but failed to get this endorsed by parliament. Despite the government's efforts to check the insurgency, Maoist activities rapidly expanded to other parts of the country. One part of

62   *Krishna Hachhethu*

the reason for this was the government's failure to diagnose the problem properly, and as a consequence its response to the Maoists became the subject of bitter criticism from the people and political forces. The government's treatment of the Maoist issue as a law and order problem contradicted the parties' perceptions and prescriptions, as well as the task forces' recommendations for the resolution of the problem.

Table 2 PARTIES' PRESCRIPTIONS FOR THE RESOLUTION OF THE
MAOIST PROBLEM

	Perceived nature of problem	*Recommendations*
NC	Terrorist activities dressed up as political activism	1. Constitutional amendment, local self-governance, peaceful elections, democratisation of constitutional bodies, legislation against corruption, legislation to regulate parties. 2. Search for ways of peaceful negotiation with Maoists. 3. Strengthen bureaucratic mechanisms, mobilise all security-related structures, disarm Maoists, set up an all-party security committee at district level to counter violence and terrorist activities. 4. Common political campaign by all parties. 5. Initiate state campaign against exploitation and for development in Maoist-affected areas.
UML*	Political problem with terrorist activities	1. Prepare for negotiation and create conducive environment, be flexible except on multi-party system, fundamental rights, territorial and national integrity, caste/ethnic harmony. 2. Build national consensus, wage political and ideological campaign against violence. 3. Strengthen civil and armed police with impartiality. 4. Reforms in political, economic, social, judicial, human rights, foreign policy and other areas, special programme of service and development for remote areas. 5. Amend Constitution.

Table 4.2 continued…

...Table 4.2 continued

CPN, Marxist-Leninist (ML)	Ultra-left political problem	1. Relief measures for the people. 2. Ethnic autonomy at local level. 3. Progressive economic measures. 4. Change in foreign policy. 5. Introduce proportional electoral system. 6. *Am mafi* (general amnesty) to all arrested Maoists. 7. Campaign against corruption.
United People's Front (UPF)	Political problem	1. Amendment of Constitution. 2. Radical transformation of Nepali society. 3. Correct misdeeds of ruling parties. 4. Government to abide by Constitution. 5. Progressive and nationalist measures in social and economic sectors.
Nepal Workers and Peasants Party (NWPP)	Anarchism	Peaceful resolution through negotiation.
United National Front (UNF)	Political problem	Peaceful resolution through negotiation.
Rashtriya Prajatantra Party (RPP)	Political problem	Integrated programme to address multi-dynamics of Maoist issue.

* Adapted from the abstract of a UML report on the situation of Maoist and state violence and terror, prepared by a task force under the convenorship of Jhal Nath Khanal.

Instead of giving specific policy inputs to counter the insurgency, most political parties put forward a vague mixture of their own general agendas and their recommendations for the resolution of the Maoist problem. Sifting through the pages of the left parties' positions, as submitted to the Deuba Commission, one can easily see that these documents are overly concerned with condemning the Congress government's mishandling of the Maoist issue. The RPP also seemed preoccupied with its oppositional role while giving a single-sentence suggestion—'to formulate an integrated programme'—to address the manifold issues raised by the Maoist movement. The Deuba Commission's highly populist report is also largely conditioned by the Congress Party's internal conflicts, as manifested in its

Table 3 TASK FORCE RECOMMENDATIONS FOR THE
RESOLUTION OF THE MAOIST PROBLEM

Task forces	*Recommendations*

Dhami Commission	1. Dialogue be considered as the first initiative:
	  a. Offer pardons to Maoist leaders and workers, assure the release of those arrested step by step, offer rehabilitation to victims.
	  b. Constitute an all-party negotiation team, attempt to prolong negotiations.
	2. Coercive measures:
	  a. Undertake special security measures, capture Maoist arsenals and disarm them as soon as possible, arrest leaders and workers, expand conservation areas (under military jurisdiction), making jungles occupied by Maoists a special target, hold elections in areas where they were previously postponed.
	  b. Build national consensus, launch political campaign branding Maoists as terrorists.
	  c. Bring ethnic groups into the mainstream, undertake social and economic reform measures against exploitation and unemployment.
	  d. Speed up infrastructure building and development in Maoist-affected areas.

Deuba Commission	1. Negotiation, relief to victims. 2. Build national consensus. 3. Decentralisation, good governance, cultivate external relations, reform judicial system. 4. Promote and protect ethnic groups' own local cultures and religious harmony, empower women. 5. Socio-economic development centred on the poor. 6. Special development packages for affected areas. 7. Grant military jurisdiction to Maoist-occupied jungles. 8. Strengthen intelligence office and reorient police.

dissidents' demand for the resignation of G. P. Koirala from one of
the two posts—prime minister and party president—he then occupied. Koirala's handling of the issue, bypassing Sher Bahadur Deuba,
was another point of controversy. The Congress Party's recommendations and the Dhami Commission report both agree on the need
for negotiations with the Maoists, but both seem pessimistic and so
recommend that the government should use coercive measures as an
alternative option. Some points that the parties' recommendations

and task force reports have in common are: (1) the state's capacity to manage internal conflict should be strengthened; (2) social and economic development policies should be formulated to target problems of poverty, exploitation and unemployment; (3) marginalised sections of society should be brought into the mainstream; (4) development incentives should be given to the 'Maoist-affected' areas; (5) the Maoist insurgency should be considered as a political problem; (6) negotiation should be pursued as a means for the peaceful solution of a violent conflict; and (7) a national consensus should be built.

These recommendations could become meaningful if the mainstream parties can develop a common approach in dealing with the Maoists' violent activities. Consensus building in Nepal is a very difficult task, because one of the dominant characteristics of Nepali politics is the polarisation of the Congress and communist camps. Except for an artificial division created in the Nepali Congress after April 2000 between the soft- and hard-liners vis-à-vis the Maoists, Congress leaders and workers have preferred to deal with the problem from a position of strength. This means first crushing the insurgency and then sitting down at the negotiating table. The communists have taken a different position. Small non-conformist communist parties, i.e. the UNF, UPF, NWPP, have some differences with the Maoists, but they do not object either to the Maoists' goals or to the violent means they have adopted. Their only objection is to its timing: according to them, the situation is not yet ripe for armed revolution. Their opposition limits itself to condemning Maoist activities as 'extremist adventurism'. The UML, the main opposition party, has also presented itself as a leftist party rather than a conformist party in its response to the Maoist problem. The UML sometimes calls the Maoists a 'friendly force', but when its cadres became victims of the so-called people's war, it roundly condemned them. The UML has constantly opposed the government's counter-insurgency policies and strategies, irrespective of the merits of the issue.

Political polarisation between the Congress Party and the communists in general has been evident since the beginning of the Maoist movement. Two separate reports, prepared by members of parliament after their visit to Rolpa district during the Operation Romeo period, clearly indicated such a division. The Congress MPs described events in Rolpa as 'terrorist activities', whereas the left MPs called it 'a political confrontation between the Nepali Congress and the UPF'. This approach had long worked in keeping the UML clear of the violent confrontations between the Congress government and Maoist guerrillas, despite the UML's denunciation of the Maoists' goal and activities. Among the party cadres killed by Maoist guerrillas up to July 2000, the number of Congress workers was 136, followed by 22 from the UML, 19 from the RPP and 1 from Mashal.[3] The UML's own study team, led by Jhal Nath Khanal, also found that during the initial phase of their violent actions the Maoists targeted only Congress workers (CPN [UML] 2001/2). The UML also tried to utilise the situation created by the Maoists to cut its immediate electoral rival, the Nepali Congress, down to size. On the eve of the 1997 local elections, the then UML-dominated coalition government led by the RPP leader Lokendra Bahadur Chand did not merely take a soft line on the Maoists (see Adhikari 1999), it was also reported that the UML had donated Rs 800,000 to them (Maharjan 2000: 178). Once the election result had gone in favour of the UML, it took a U-turn in its dealings with the Maoists. Following the recommendations of the Dhami Commission, the government decided to take resolute action against them. Its failed attempt to introduce an anti-terrorism bill was one more piece of evidence. But, once the UML had been ousted from power in October 1997, it revived its original position of opposing the next government's efforts to counter the insurgency. To highlight the inconsistency of the UML's and its splinter group CPN (ML)'s policy towards the Maoists, one could refer here to the fact that they constituted the junior partner in the G. P. Koirala-led coalition government during 1998–9, when the government's offensive against the Maoists went to the extent of the police killing a total of 662 persons. The government's offensive has continued, in one way or another, at least in plan (for example, the constitution of an armed police force, the deployment of the army) since the Nepali Congress formed a majority government after the 1999 general elections. The CPN (UML) and CPN (ML) have continuously criticised any plan for the government to use force against the Maoists.

---

[3] Text of the Nepali Congress's recommendations to resolve the Maoist problem, submitted to the Deuba Commission, September 2000.

In retrospect, all communist parties have had their own limitations when it comes to countering the Maoists. In Nepal, the word 'left' or 'communist' is more closely associated with certain popular slogans and radical programmes than with the exclusive identity of a particular party. To be left or communist, in the Nepali understanding, means to speak for *gans, bas, kapas* ('food, shelter and clothing') for the poor, to advocate radical and revolutionary change, to be anti-India, and, above all, to stand for absolute economic equality even at the cost of political liberty. Thus, a person could be a voter for the UML at election time as well as a worker for the CPN (Maoist) in the insurgency period. This explains why the UML and other communist parties are constantly pleading for the Maoist conflict to be resolved through non-violent means. This, in turn, contributes to making public opinion favour a peaceful resolution.

The results of an opinion survey conducted in 2001 showed that the Nepali people were in favour of 'talks between the government and the Maoists' (Himal Association 2001). Many believed that the Maoist problem was political, but mixed up with terrorist activity. The Deuba Commission went so far as to describe the Maoist insurgency as 'an expression of people's dissatisfaction through violence...the Maoist problem is the outcome of defects in managing and handling statecraft and political instability caused by frequent changes of government, and the existing social discrimination, unemployment and economic development'.[4] There is a big gap between public perceptions and the government's policy vis-à-vis the Maoist problem. Political instability, frequent changes of government, the politicisation and division of the police, the erosion of ideology, the decrease in the credibility of political parties and their leaders: all of these account for the state's abandonment of the Maoists' stronghold areas.

While they were launching the people's war, the Maoists adopted a uniform plan of action in different places: first, they disarmed the local people by seizing their weapons, and then they killed certain individuals (whom they accused of being local thugs, exploiters or informants) in a public display in broad daylight. The strategy seems to have been to create fear and terror rather than to take the lives of many people. Their next targets were banks, non-government

[4] Ibid.

organisations (NGOs) and international NGOs (INGOs). Their planned attacks on police stations began, and their violent activities were designed to lead to the establishment of their own governments at local level. Starting with the formation of the Maoists' own government at village and area level from late 1998, the party has rapidly intensified such activities to the extent of forming its own district-level governments in twenty-five districts. The people's representatives in locally-elected bodies, and the political parties' local cadres, most of whom belonged to either the Nepali Congress or the RPP, fled to the district headquarters for security. The activities of NGOs and INGOs were scaled down, and several offices were shut. The number of police stations was reduced in the Maoist areas. The absence of any nominations for forty-one village development committees (VDCs) in addition to the postponement of elections in sixty-two VDCs in the Maoist stronghold areas during the 1997 local elections showed that some parts of the country were beyond the state's control. Some other reports from 1999 and 2000 also indicated the state's withdrawal from Maoist-controlled areas:

Among the 43 VDCs in Rukum, only six have chairpersons residing in their respective village.[5]

Among the 26 police posts in Rukum, only eleven have been retained.[6]

The number of cases registered in the Rolpa District Court for nine months (from July 1998 to April 1999) was only 28 against its previous record of having court cases [*sic*] at least 30–35 per month.[7]

ATTEMPTS TO REINSTATE THE STATE

Reinstating the state in guerrilla-controlled areas obviously requires the use of force. On the pretext of the May 1999 general election, the government exerted massive force in the form of the Kilo Sierra Two and Jungle Search operations. The government reinstated police in three police posts in Jajarkot, twenty-seven in Rukum and twenty-three in Salyan. But this proved to be a short-term plan, intended merely to ensure that general elections were conducted in the Maoist hinterlands, because the police were recalled after the elections.

---

[5] *Kathmandu Post*, 10 March 2000.

[6] *Kathmandu Post*, 11 March 2000.

[7] *Himal Khabarpatrika*, 15–30 April 1999.

A new dimension was added to the government's plans to reinstate the state when the Integrated Security Programme (ISP) was inaugurated in December 1999 by the Nepali Congress government under Prime Minister Krishna Prasad Bhattarai. This programme was a departure from the previous strategy of taking only security measures, and it provided a mixture of security measures, political campaigns and development packages to counter the Maoist insurgency. This approach was maintained by the G. P. Koirala government that followed, but under different names: first as the Integrated Development Programme (IDP) and later as the Integrated Internal Security and Development Programme (IISDP). Unlike the original ISP, these two programmes included a military component and were targeted on specific Maoist-controlled areas: Rolpa, Rukum, Salyan, Kalikot, Jajarkot, Gorkha and Pyuthan.

The question of mobilising the army against the Maoists has long been a controversial issue. Every government after 1997, i.e. the coalition governments led by Lokendra Bahadur Chand, Surya Bahadur Thapa and G. P. Koirala, made attempts to mobilise the army, but the army has all along shown a reluctance to be involved, apparently on technical grounds, i.e. logistics, resources, mandate and so on. Initially, the Nepali Congress was hesitant to mobilise the military for three main reasons. First, there was the legacy of history: the late King Mahendra had used the army to stage a coup in 1960 against the then Congress government and multi-party system. Second, the army is not under the control of the civilian government. The present Constitution has a separate provision for mobilising the army: the National Defence Council, consisting of the prime minister, defence minister and chief of army staff, can recommend it, but the king takes the final decision. Third, there are some other ambiguous clauses in the Constitution relating to the dissolution of parliament and the declaration of an emergency on which the palace can manoeuvre against the elected government. Despite his formal status as a constitutional monarch, the king has preventive powers to block government decisions on critical issues. A retrogressive trend because of royal interventions in state affairs has been observed.[8]

Moreover, the Nepali Congress has long been suspicious of the palace's intentions behind the Maoists' ever-increasing threat to

---

[8] See Hachhethu (2000) for detailed accounts of political retrogression.

parliamentary democracy. Its senior-most leaders have publicly hinted that they suspect that the palace may have played some role in sabotaging anti-Maoist operations.[9] Even the opposition leader, Madhav Kumar Nepal, has speculated that the palace may be using the Maoists against multi-party democracy.[10] That the palace had had its own separate dealings with the Maoists was disclosed when a report was published of a meeting between Maoist leaders and Ramesh Nath Pandey, one of the king's nominees to the upper house of parliament. The claim made by the Maoist leaders Prachanda and Baburam Bhattarai that they had an _aghoshit karyagat ekta_ (undeclared working alliance) with the late King Birendra has not yet been contradicted by the palace. They said, 'The late king was not in favour of PM Koirala's plan to mobilise the army against the People's War.'[11] All of this suggests that the democratic forces need first to win over the palace before they can make any gains in their battle against the Maoists.

Partly because of the Congress Party's suspicion of the army, and partly because of the palace's opposition to army mobilisation, the government searched for other coercive measures. It set up an armed security force to combat 'terrorists' and increased police expenditure by 100 per cent for arms purchases and new recruitment. The original idea was to construct a joint military and police force, but the army's refusal to be a part of this proposed paramilitary force led to it being reduced to an armed police force. Before the armed police force personnel could be trained and equipped, the Maoist insurgency took a new direction, with the attacks escalating from isolated assassinations of rural-based party workers to regular assaults on the police. From December 2000, the CPN (Maoist) began to form its own district level governments. In the absence of a minimal security environment, the government's announcement of political campaigns and the distribution of development packages in the Maoist-affected areas was confined to paper. The Maoists' constant victories in their battles against the state's security forces are evident from the casualty figures from this period. The battles took a new turn after Maoist guerrillas seized Dunai, the headquarters of Dolpa

[9] _Kantipur_, 28 June 2001; _Rajdhani_, 7 September 2001.
[10] _Kantipur_, 3 September 2001.
[11] _Kathmandu Post_, 4 June 2001.

district, on 24 September 2000, and killed fourteen policemen. The Dunai incident led the government to review the situation, and it concluded that controlling the Maoists was beyond the capacity of the police. Thus, the government decided to use its last security option: the army.

The question of military mobilisation has brought about conflict and contradictions between the elected government on the one hand and the palace and the army on the other. A number of Nepali Congress leaders, including the then home minister, Govinda Raj Joshi, accused the army of obstructing the equipping of the armed police force, and of non-cooperation with the government's plans to counter the insurgency.[12] The army chief countered this by blaming the politicians and insisting that an all-party consensus was a precondition for military mobilisation. The demand for an all-party consensus has been repeated time and again, even after the National Defence Council's decision to use the army in the frontline for the purposes of the IISDP received the formal consent of the king. The army's rigid disobedience of the government was in fact a manifestation of the role played by the palace. Soon after the king had given his consent to the IISDP, he also made various other suggestions, e.g. to identify the Maoist problem as terrorism or insurgency, to grant general amnesty to the Maoists, to mainstream the Maoists, and to reach an all-party consensus. These were at odds with the spirit of the IISDP.[13] Although the conflict between the army and the government continued, the army was used after the Dunai incident, but its involvement was limited to small-scale deployment in seventeen districts in the Maoist strongholds. The army mobilisation following the IISDP was confined to social and economic activities, and did not involve combating the guerrillas. Now [November 2001] the army seems to be active, but its concern is exclusively confined to countering the Maoists' republican agenda. The army has deliberately and consciously maintained its distance from the elected government and multi-party parliamentary democracy, as if its primary duty is only to protect the palace.

Leaving aside the failure of the police and the non-cooperation of the army, the government led by G. P. Koirala was very ineffective in

---

[12] *Nepal Press Digest*, 25 September 2001.
[13] *Space Time*, 17 May 2001.

addressing the other political problems that undermined the state's ability to counter the Maoist insurgency. Koirala's influence in his own party, the Nepali Congress, declined considerably. Soon after he succeeded K. P. Bhattarai as prime minister, demands for his resignation began to bring the internal conflict within the Congress sharply into focus. The Koirala government's relations with other parliamentary parties were so bad that the opposition parties boycotted the entire nineteenth winter session of parliament. Meanwhile, the stigma of being accused of corruption by the Commission for the Investigation of Abuse of Authority in connection with the leasing of a plane from an Austrian company, Lauda, damaged Koirala's credibility. The Koirala government was alienated from opponents within its own party, from opposition parties, from civil society, from the palace, and from the army. Koirala was eventually forced to resign on 18 July 2001 after the army betrayed him by disobeying the government's decision to act against the Maoist guerrillas who took about seventy policemen hostage on 12 July at Holeri in Rolpa district.

A PEACE OFFENSIVE

Relations between the state and the Maoists suddenly, though not unexpectedly, took a new direction, from armed conflict to peaceful negotiation, from the day Sher Bahadur Deuba succeeded Girija Prasad Koirala as prime minister on 22 July 2001. The last two rounds of negotiations have been devoted to an exchange of views on the Maoist agenda. Table 4 summarises the positions of the two negotiating parties.

The table shows two distinct features of the Maoist-government negotiation. First, the Maoists made an upward revision of the demands which relate to the nature of the polity. Before the palace massacre on 1 June 2001 the Maoists' ideological stand on the need for a republican system had been confined to rhetoric, but since that event it has constantly pleaded for the abolition of the monarchy. The government and the major parliamentary parties have strongly defended the present system, arguing that there can be no compromise on constitutional monarchy and multi-party democracy. So the government and the Maoists are negotiating on non-negotiable

Table 4 NEGOTIATION AGENDAS AND POSITIONS OF GOVERNMENT AND MAOISTS

	Upward revision of Maoist agendas			Government's position
	40-point demand	Pre-palace massacre	Post-palace massacre	
Government	–	Interim government.	Dissolution of the present government and parliament and constitution of an interim government.	Possible but within the present Constitution.
Constitution	New Constitution drawn up by people's elected representatives.	Changes to present Constitution.	New Constitution drawn up by people's elected representatives.	Amendment to the present Constitution except for its four fundamental principles.
Monarchy	Abolish all rights and privileges of king and royal family members.	–	Institutionalisation of republican set-up.	No compromise on constitutional monarchy.

Table 4 continued…

...Table 4 continued

	40-point demand	Demands for negotiation	Government's position
For excluded groups	1. Equal inheritance/property rights 2. Abolition of caste discrimination and untouchability 3. Equal status for all languages 4. Ethnic autonomy 5. A secular state.	Retained demands 1, 2, 4, and 5.	1. Prohibition of caste-based social discrimination 2. Constitution of a national commission for the welfare of Dalits 3. Legislation to end gender discrimination, including equal inheritance/property rights 4. Legislation to promote the interests of ethnic groups 5. Special action plan for excluded groups.
Development	1. Radical land reforms, confiscating the lands of landlords and distributing them to the landless 2. Job guarantees and stipends for the unemployed 3. Promotion of the interests of labourers 4. Land and shelter for landless people (*sukumbasi*) 5. Waiving of loan debts for poor peasants 6. Provision of basic services to the people 7. Free education and health services and an end to commercialisation in these areas	Retained demands 1, 3, 7, and 8. Added: 1. 70 % budget allocation for rural development 2. Public probe into royal massacre 3. Progressive tax system.	1. Land reform to lower ceiling on landholdings 2. Legislation against corruption 3. Land and shelter for former bonded labourers (*kamaiyas*) 4. Land to landless people.

Table 4 continued...

...Table 4 continued

	8. Services to the handicapped 9. Decentralisation 10. Prohibition of commissions and corruption 11. Promotion of small and cottage industries.	
Nationalism	1. Abrogation of 1950 treaty and other unequal treaties with India 2. Nullification of Mahakali treaty 3. Nullification of Tanakpur treaty 4. Control of open border 5. An end to Gurkha recruitment 6. Introduction of work permit system 7. Checking of foreign monopoly in trade, industry and other sectors 8. Checking of Indian cultural encroachment 9. Checking of imperialist penetration through NGOs and INGOs.	Retained demands 1, 2, 4, 6, 7 and 9. Added demand relating to safeguards for Nepalis residing abroad. For negotiation.

issues. Second: at the time of writing they had not started a dialogue on points relating to the mainstreaming of marginal sections of society, to development, or to foreign affairs: these are points on which they could reach a consensus. So there are no strong grounds for optimism regarding a peaceful resolution of the Maoist insurgency. Baral (2001) has rightly pointed out four constraints on the negotiations: constitutional rigidity, the failure of the Nepali state to show its resilience and strength, the government's weak bargaining position, and the fact that the Maoists were winning the psychological battle.

Now the situation, which could have an impact on the negotiations, is developing in favour of the government. Unlike in the past, when the Maoists took advantage of internal conflicts and contradictions between the ruling and opposition parties, and between the government and the palace, the mainstream political forces have come together after the change of prime minister. The political forces are polarised into two camps: Maoist and anti-Maoist. This is because over the past two years [2000–01], the Maoist insurgency has been developing to the extent that the palace and the mainstream communist parties, the UML in particular, have also felt a serious threat to their own future. After the royal massacre, the Maoists actively offended the monarchy by portraying King Gyanendra and his son Paras as demons. This, in turn, brings the palace and the government closer to each other vis-à-vis the Maoists. It seems that the new king and the new prime minister (Sher Bahadur Deuba) have a good rapport and this obviously implies that there is scope for a new sort of relationship to develop between the government and the army. Besides, King Gyanendra's constant efforts to establish a rapport with the leaders of the legal communist parties naturally reduce the Maoists' ability to neutralise the leftist forces in their fight against the government and the palace. The Maoists' efforts to construct a loose left coalition in support of their demands for a republican system and elections to a constituent assembly are now rejected by the UML and many other small communist parties, thus isolating the Maoists further.

Recently, the UML has come out aggressively against the Maoists, because the Maoists' plan to expand their territory by constituting their own government at village, area, and district levels has naturally had an adverse effect on the UML's influence and support base. Table 5 demonstrates that the greatest loser in the Maoists' campaign to constitute their own government at local level is the UML.

Table 5 PARTIES' POSITIONS IN DISTRICTS UNDER THE MAOIST
JAN SARKAR

	Districts under Maoist jan sarkar	Ruling party of District Development Committee (DDC)	Elected MPs from
1.	Rolpa	UML	NC × 2
2.	Rukum	NC	NC, UML
3.	Salyan	UML	UML, RPP
4.	Jajarkot	UML	RPP, UML
5.	Kalikot	RPP	UML
6.	Jumla	UML	UML
7.	Dailekh	UML	UML, NC
8.	Humla	NC	UML
9.	Gorkha	NC	NC × 3
10.	Dhading	UML	RPP, NC, UML
11.	Lamjung	UML	NC × 2
12.	Tanahu	UML	NC × 2, UML
13.	Parbat	UML	NC, UML
14.	Gulmi	UML	UML × 3
15.	Palpa	UML	UML × 3
16.	Argha Khanchi	UML	UNF, UML
17.	Sindhuli	UML	UML × 2, UPF
18.	Dolakha	UML	UML, NC
19.	Ramechhap	UML	UML, NC
20.	Sindhupalchok	UML	NC, UML.RPP
21.	Kabhre	UML	UML × 2, NC × 2
22.	Sankhuwa Sabha	UML	NC, UML
23.	Terhathum	UML	UML
24.	Nuwakot	UML	NC × 2, UML
25.	Rasuwa	UML	NC

In fact, the palace, the Nepali Congress and the UML share a common threat perception, and this brings them together on a single agenda: countering the Maoist insurgency, preferably through non-violent means. The 'global war against terrorism' which began after the attacks on the Pentagon and the World Trade Centre on 11 September 2001, followed by India's announcement that it would assist Nepal in its efforts to counter 'Maoist terrorism' and the deployment of the Indian army along the border with Nepal, all indicate a favourable external environment. Besides this, some new developments (e.g. constant consultation among the parliamentary parties, the army's signal that it might get involved against the Maoist guerrillas, people's strong protests against the local Maoist cadres in Parsa district, differences and divisions among the Maoist leaders, the loss of the party's command over the armed guerrillas and so on) all contribute to strengthening the government's position vis-à-vis the Maoists. Although the present situation appears to favour the establishment, however, there has been no improvement so substantial that it leads one to believe that the state has turned back from its ongoing journey towards decay. If the situation changes in the future, the state may well return to its defensive position vis-à-vis the Maoist insurgency.

The relationship between the Maoists and the state is becoming more complicated, because a number of actors with conflicting interests are becoming involved, either directly or indirectly, in the negotiation process. At one extreme, the Maoists are exerting pressure for radical changes such as the establishment of a republican system and the election of a constituent assembly. To achieve its objective of bringing the Maoists into mainstream politics, the government cannot go beyond an amendment to the present Constitution. Its ability to respond with radical changes to the present Constitution is also limited by the palace's ostensible assertiveness. King Gyanendra is perceived as more active and aggressive than his late brother. His allegation that the parties and leaders have 'violated the Constitution', along with his remark that he would not be 'a silent spectator' despite the limitations of a constitutional monarch, have been taken as indications of political reaction. In contrast, opinion favouring a republican set-up has increased since Gyanendra became king. Thus, of all the measures that are available to resolve the Maoist problem and the other political problems of Nepal, elections to a constituent assembly seem to be a plausible way out. This could provide the Maoists with an acceptable political solution. For the stability of the constitutional monarchy too, this could be an opportunity to regain legitimacy in the changed context.

Part II. The Maoists and the People

THE PATH TO *JAN SARKAR* IN DOLAKHA DISTRICT

TOWARDS AN ETHNOGRAPHY OF THE MAOIST MOVEMENT*

Sara Shneiderman and Mark Turin

CONTEXT: THE ESTABLISHMENT OF A JAN SARKAR

On 23 July 2001 (8 Saun 2058), the same day that Sher Bahadur Deuba was sworn in as prime minister, the Communist Party of Nepal (Maoist) proclaimed the formation of its *jan sarkar,* or people's government, in Dolakha district of central-eastern Nepal. The announcement was made during a mass meeting in the village of Rankedanda in Sailungeshwor Village Development Committee (VDC), near the well-known pilgrimage site of Sailung. Between 10,000 and 15,000 people are reported to have attended the ceremony (Popham 2001, Anon. 2001b).

We suggest that this meeting and the resulting proclamation are mileposts by which the development of the Maoist movement in Dolakha may be measured, and that alongside their immediate practical consequences, these events possessed powerful symbolic value. By providing an ethnographic approach that complements the predominantly political and historical analyses of the movement that

* We thank all of the participants of the November 2001 conference at SOAS on the Maoist movement, in particular Michael Hutt and Ben Campbell. George van Driem, David Holmberg, Alan Macfarlane, and the participants in the Himalayan Studies seminar at Cornell University in the fall of 2001 provided valuable comments and helpful criticism.

have been advanced to date, we examine how the Maoist activities that led up to the ultimate proclamation of the *jan sarkar* in Dolakha were portrayed in the press and understood at the village level. Our primary objective is to focus on issues of motivation by exploring how and why Dolakha villagers became involved with, and formulated opinions about, the Maoist movement at this juncture in its historical development. Further, by looking closely at the situation in Dolakha, a more recent front in the people's war, we shed light on the development and maturation of Maoist rhetoric as the movement travelled east. Finally, we hope that the questions we pose will serve as a starting point for a more complete ethnography of the Maoist movement in Nepal that is both attentive to local particularities and firmly grounded in the emerging anthropological discourse on political violence.

Several features of the Dolakha proclamation are worth noting at the outset. First, while Dolakha was the eighth district in Nepal in which a Maoist *jan sarkar* was established, it was the first district outside the Maoists' western stronghold to provide sufficient support for the Maoists to proclaim their own government with confidence. Second, the ethnic composition of the seventeen-member committee of the people's government of Dolakha, which included at least one member from every ethnic group found in the district, highlighted the Maoists' appeal to and acknowledgement of ethnic diversity (Anon. 2001b). Third, the large number of villagers reported to have attended the meeting confirms our observations regarding the extensive grassroots support which Maoist units enjoyed at the time in many areas of Dolakha, a fact frequently ignored by the local and national government, as well as the media. Finally, in Nepali press reports on the proclamation of the Dolakha *jan sarkar,* much was made of the fact that a foreign journalist and photographer had been invited to attend the meeting at Rankedanda. Their presence resulted in a full-colour feature in the *Sunday Review* section of the well-respected British broadsheet newspaper the *Independent* on 12 August 2001. Entitled 'Mao's Children', the article brought the Dolakha proclamation into the international limelight (Popham 2001). We suggest that the presence of a western news team at such a politically and symbolically significant event offers a glimpse into the Maoists' position vis-à-vis foreigners and the outside world at the time.

However, the establishment of the people's government was only one in a continuum of important events in the region, and was soon overshadowed by the State of Emergency declared by Sher Bahadur Deuba's government on 26 November 2001. The deployment of Royal Nepalese Army troops soon after the declaration of the emergency radically altered the local and national situation. Most notably for our purposes, the emergency reportedly prompted at least 263 Maoist supporters in Dolakha, including members of the *jan sarkar* discussed here, to surrender.[1] For these reasons, our discussion here is consciously presented as a period piece constructed within the framework of local assumptions that were current up to September 2001. With the exception of a few essential notes, we do not address more recent developments in Dolakha, nor have we revised our argument to reflect them. We have chosen to let this piece stand as a historical document of a certain phase of the movement, the particulars of which, as manifested in Dolakha, offer an insight into the larger workings of the Maoist movement.

OUTLINE AND METHODOLOGY

This chapter contains three interconnected narratives, each of which presents a different perspective on the development of the Maoist movement in Dolakha. We first offer a chronology of Maoist activities in the district up to September 2001 as they were reported in print media, both Nepali and Western. In the detailed list of 'newsworthy' incidents from the region, a rough outline of events emerges. A bottom-up local narrative follows, pieced together from informal discussions and more structured interviews conducted between 1998 and 2001 with villagers living in areas of Maoist activity throughout the valleys of Dolakha. At certain points, this narrative corroborates the events described in the press, but at times it also contradicts and challenges them.

Interspersed with extracts from interviews, we offer our own perspective on and analysis of events during the time that we were resident in the Dolakha region between 1998 and 2001. By the summer

---

[1] *Kathmandu Post*, 7 December 2001. Due to the restrictions imposed on the press by the Terrorist and Destructive Activities (Control and Punishment) Ordinance (TADO) of 26 November 2001, newspaper articles after that date must be treated with a greater degree of scepticism than before. We ask readers to bear in mind that the accuracy of this report may be questionable.

of 2000, we had a good vantage point from which to observe the movements of Maoist activists, their ever-widening sphere of influence, and the growth of village-level support for their actions. Our privileged position in this unlikely arena had two causes: the geographical location of our field site, and the type of work in which we were engaged. The village in which we were living happened to be situated along a 'final frontier' of sorts, both for the Maoist units active in the area and for the police and local administration.[2] While the Maoists had concentrated their earlier efforts in the more inaccessible (and often poorer) valleys of Dolakha, by mid-2000 they were moving their 'propaganda' and 'education' campaigns to villages closer to the bazaar town of Dolakha and the neighbouring district headquarters, Charikot, both of which were less than a day's walk from our location. On the other hand, the Charikot-based district administration had by this point withdrawn from playing an active role in all but the nearest villages. We were living and working in one of a number of villages through which the battle lines were drawn: the government was still in control but the Maoists were closing in. It is in this context that we gained an unusual view of the practical and ideological conflicts that affected many aspects of local life.

The second factor, which facilitated our residence in an otherwise tense area, was our line of work. Unlike many of the other foreigners (both Western and Asian) who were active in the area, we were neither managing an NGO development project nor engaged in a business enterprise. We were conducting anthropological and linguistic research with the Thangmi ethnic community, many of whom were either overt Maoist supporters or implicitly sympathetic to their cause. While other foreigners were asked to leave, some more forcefully than others, we received a steady stream of signs that we were welcome to stay and could continue working as before.

In short, the coincidence of two factors, geographical and professional, created an environment which permitted us to continue with our research projects with the tacit support of both authorities: the local government and the Maoist commanders. In retrospect, and after discussions with a number of colleagues, we realised that we had witnessed an important moment in the unfolding history of both the Dolakha region and the Maoist movement.

---

[2] For reasons of confidentiality and security, we have chosen not to cite the name of the village in which we resided or the names of individuals with whom we worked.

ETHNOGRAPHIES OF VIOLENCE

We did not explicitly set out to document the Maoist movement. Rather, it became an inescapable presence within our 'normal' work, requiring increased attention as a feature of the social world we were researching. In this way, we differ from ethnographers who intentionally work in conflict zones around the world. Such researchers consider the challenge of accurately representing the social causes and effects of violence to be a central feature of their work (Nordstrom and Martin 1992, Nordstrom and Robben 1995, Sluka 2000). Yet many of the insights resulting from their work are relevant to the Nepali situation we describe. Following Carolyn Nordstrom and Antonius Robben's general call for an even-handed, particularising ethnographic approach which examines the everyday aspects of local conflict situations (1995), we emphasise the need for a full ethnography of political violence in Nepal. This is by no means an unproblematic proposition:

Researching and writing about violence will never be a simple endeavor. The subject is fraught with assumptions, presuppositions, and contradictions. Like power, violence is essentially contested: everyone knows it exists, but no one agrees on what actually constitutes the phenomenon. Vested interests, personal history, ideological loyalties, propaganda, and a dearth of firsthand information ensure that many 'definitions' of violence are powerful fictions and negotiated half-truths (Nordstrom and Robben 1995: 5).

Despite, or perhaps even because of, its complexity, we must acknowledge violence as a valid category of analysis, whose contradictions demand careful attention rather than condemnation and dismissal. Maintaining this analytical focus is challenging, but remains essential if we wish to identify the deeper causes of violence and understand its effects on local lives.

In Nepal, we are confronted by the additional difficulty of our 'regional ethnography traditions' (Fardon 1990), which have largely focused on the more traditional anthropological domains of 'religion' and 'culture' rather than on government, civil society and political change.[3] Historically, the prevailing tendency of ethnography in Nepal

---

[3] 'At its simplest then, the regional tradition influences the entry of the "working" ethnographer into a "field" imaginatively charted by others' (Fardon 1990: 24–5).

has been to describe small-scale village-based communities at the expense of examining state structures. This may preclude us from easily understanding the roots of the current situation, and may lead us to believe that ethnographies of conflict do not fit legitimately within Nepal's established anthropological persona. However, as Joanna Pfaff-Czarnecka argues elsewhere in this volume, we need to expand our field of research to new domains in order to grasp the particularities of the situation more thoroughly.

We are, however, just at the beginning. To use a term coined by Frank Pieke to refer to his own unexpected study of the 1989 Tiananmen Square massacre in Beijing, our own account of the Maoist movement in Dolakha is a sort of 'accidental anthropology' (Pieke 1995). Our local relationships and the site of our work were predetermined by our previous residence in the area, and our perspective on the unfolding political situation was shaped by our ongoing fieldwork there. Given our existing allegiances and interests, we can present only one aspect of a multi-faceted story, echoing Pieke's assertion: 'I cannot but write from the perspective of the people with whom I experienced it. I simply do not have the ethnographic experience and empathy to do equal justice to the perspectives of, for instance, the communist party leadership or the student activists' (Pieke 1995: 78). In our case, we cannot do justice to the perspectives of government officials, police and diverse groups of villagers with whom we did not have close relationships. Rather than misrepresenting such groups with inadequate information, we have chosen to present only the perspectives of those with whom we did closely experience this uncertain time. We hope that this chapter may open the way for further studies, which build on as well as challenge what we present here.

A CHRONOLOGY OF PRINT MEDIA REPORTS
ON MAOIST ACTIVITY IN DOLAKHA

Journalists covering Dolakha district are situated comparatively close to the capital, and the examples cited here demonstrate that

---

Fardon argues that specific modes of ethnographic practice have been developed as normative in each world region, and that the structures of academic life make it difficult to break out of such patterns.

Dolakha is anything but remote. It should therefore come as no surprise that a fair amount of local news from Dolakha makes it back to the national dailies printed and circulated in Kathmandu. With a few key exceptions, we have focused on the English-language press. This choice was motivated by reasons of accessibility and space, and a thorough analysis of Nepali-language sources would add much to the preliminary conclusions reached here.

The full list of news clippings is presented in a tabular form to facilitate comparison, and can be found in the appendix to this chapter. However, we do not regard these clippings as a foolproof technique for collecting factual information on Maoist activities. In most cases, the reports are several stages removed from the incidents that they describe. There are plenty of opportunities for withholding or embellishing information, starting with villagers who report an incident to the authorities, who in turn release the information to the press and are likely to have a vested interest in portraying their own involvement in a positive light, to the journalist filing the report, and finally to the editorial desk of the paper, the latter not being free of political affiliation. Thus, actual events on the ground are likely to have been quite different to the short reports on them that reach the papers. In addition, the list is not a complete collection of news reports about Maoist activities in Dolakha during this period, but rather a representative sample shaped by the dates of our own travels and access to print media. However, the reports are of interest in that they show how the rising conflict was reported to the rest of the country. Referring the reader to the appendix for the full list of news clippings, we note only a few general issues here.

First, a range of terminology is used to refer to the Maoists in the articles cited. The earliest reports labelled Maoists as 'terrorists' and 'insurgents', while in later articles these highly pejorative terms give way to somewhat less negative labels such as 'rebels', 'guerrillas', and 'activists', implying that these were people fighting for a cause. Since the emergency declaration of 26 November 2001, however, the Maoists have been officially declared 'terrorists', and this has become the only acceptable term. On a related note, government forces were first referred to as 'security personnel' and only more recently as 'police'. The choice of the former term, both vague and euphemistic, may have been motivated by a desire to avoid presenting the police, and thus the government whom they represented, as engaged in physical

combat with a little known and poorly understood adversary. We
have come a long way from the early descriptions of 'security personnel [who] fired in self defense' (19 June 1998) when we read about
'shell-shocked villagers...still trying to come to terms with the police
atrocity' and 'recent indiscriminate police firing' (13 March 2000).
Again, such reports disappeared after the emergency was declared.

Another intriguing element is the access of foreign reporters to
Maoist camps in Dolakha and Sindhupalchok. Reporters returned
from their sojourns with Maoists bearing glossy colour photos and
first-hand accounts of consciousness-raising activities. In 2000, foreign journalists with a brief to cover the Maoist movement in Nepal
began to be guided towards Dolakha and Sindhupalchok rather than
to western Nepal. One simple explanation for this is the accessibility
of these central districts, but another factor may have been the Maoist leadership's desire to present Dolakha as a successful arena of
operations, a model Maoist stronghold.

After the activities surrounding the anniversary of the people's
war in February 2000, which included the looting of a bus full of Polish tourists and the burning down of a cargo helicopter in Jiri, the
press took a greater interest. We may surmise that the media interest
paralleled a growing realisation in Kathmandu that the movement
was no longer contained in the so-called remote western regions, but
that Dolakha and other central eastern districts had become active
fronts in the people's war. It took just three months from the killing
of a policeman (3 December 1999), described as the 'first such incident in the central hill district since the insurgency began nearly four
years ago' for Dolakha to be declared 'a Maoist hotbed' by the
Kathmandu Post on 13 March 2000. Unfortunately for the government, this realisation came too late for it to catch up with the reality
on the ground: just over a year later, Dolakha had been transformed
from a 'hotbed' to a region with a fledgling Maoist government.[4]

THE VILLAGE PERSPECTIVE

The following narrative is based on a combination of informal discussions and more structured interviews held between 1998 and 2001

[4] Indicating a further stage in Dolakha's development as a central site of the movement, a post-emergency article stated that 'Dolakha is a major Maoist hub in the central region' (*Kathmandu Post*, 7 December 2001).

with a young man from a village in Dolakha. Some interviews were also conducted in group environments, so details were contributed from multiple sources. Although this is not a representative sample of Dolakha's population, we have only included statements which we heard frequently enough from different people for us to consider them to be generally-held sentiments in the communities in which we worked, rather than individual predilections and grievances. It should be noted that the views represented are those of relatively impoverished members of the Thangmi ethnic community,[5] and may differ from those held by members of other ethnic, caste, or class backgrounds. The Thangmi were one of the primary groups targeted by the Maoists in Dolakha as a potential source of support and recruits, and were well-represented in the *jan sarkar* (two members out of seventeen belonged to this ethnic group, which was a disproportionately large number considering their relatively small population).[6] As discussed earlier, an in-depth ethnographic study of the movement's causes and effects which represents multiple viewpoints from various social backgrounds is sorely needed, and we hope that such a study may be possible in the future. These interview extracts have been minimally edited for purposes of confidentiality and clarity. We offer analysis and supplementary information from our own experiences after each short citation, in the understanding that we provide a commentary on the sentiments felt by a substantial group of individuals in the village, not an endorsement thereof.

The Origin and Objectives of the Maoist Movement

'In Nepal, democracy has only come to people in the towns and district headquarters and then only to those with loud voices. In the villages and remote

[5] The Nepali name for this ethnic group and their language is 'Thami', a Sanskritised term which the Thangmi themselves are eager to shake off. Culturally-active members of the Thangmi community request that they be referred to as 'Thangmi' rather than 'Thami'.

[6] The Thangmi have a history of resistance to landowners and the state that long predates the advent of the current movement, and have suffered state-perpetrated violence in return. The so-called 'Piskar Massacre' of 1984 is the most notable example of this: tenant farmers in the Thangmi village of Piskar, Sindhupalchok, protested against their work conditions and were shot by police, an action which produced two well-known Thangmi 'martyrs'. This history may have both piqued the Maoists' interest in the Thangmi and also influenced the positive predisposition of certain Thangmi individuals towards the movement. Shneiderman (2003) discusses the relationship between the Piskar Massacre and the Maoist movement in depth.

areas, people have no idea what democracy is or how it should feel. How can they know? But the villagers do know one thing for certain: at present there is a real problem all over the country—the Maoists. The people from the towns probably don't even know exactly what the Maoists are, or what they believe in. Even though it eventually reached the villages, the people's movement[7] was something that started in Kathmandu and spread outwards. But the Maoist movement is exactly the opposite: it started in the villages. The villagers now know what the democracy movement must have felt like, since we are seeing and living another such movement in our villages and inside our own homes. There is a Nepali proverb: *"gaun nabanikana desh banna sakdaina"* (without building the village, the country cannot be built). All politicians make use of this saying, but none have acted upon it. In contrast, the Maoists have worked according to this rule.'

The citation outlines two central beliefs which we heard reiterated by villagers throughout Dolakha: first, that the people's movement of 1990 passed them by and had little noticeable effect at the village level; and, second, that the Maoist movement was the precise inverse of this. Within the Maoist movement, according to local rhetoric at the time, villagers felt that they were empowered agents shaping and creating their country's destiny, not passive spectators watching from the political sidelines (which is how they felt in 1990). These villagers viewed their participation in the movement—whether explicit or implicit—as their contribution to the body politic, and as a cause for some pride on their part. In turn, this had a positive impact on their self-image as people who possessed the ability to play a role on the national stage. There was also a clear feeling that the Maoist uprising was a natural conclusion of, and development from, the earlier democratic movement.

These common perceptions in Dolakha contrast with the relationship of Kham Magar villagers to the Maoist movement, as described by Anne de Sales, who frames her discussion around a series of questions, including: 'How have rural people reacted to the campaigns of politicization originating in the towns? How is it that they have found themselves involved in, and how have they allowed themselves to be dragged into, fatal combat?' (de Sales 2000: 41). Although it is important to note that de Sales describes an earlier stage of the uprising, not to mention a different locale, the situation in Dolakha requires a different understanding of villagers' *perceived* agency within the

---

[7] The *jan andolan* or people's movement of 1990 is also often referred to in English as the 'movement for the restoration of democracy'.

movement. Whether or not the people's war was in reality a movement from periphery to centre, and whether or not villagers were
genuinely empowered, the Maoists succeeded in portraying their
movement as village-based. In our understanding, many of those
who joined the Maoists in Dolakha did so out of an active desire to
be involved in a struggle they saw as their own, rather than out of a
passive willingness to be dragged into a struggle that originated
externally. The shift in motivation from the situation described by de
Sales may well be due to the fact that Dolakha villagers were joining
at a later historical stage: by the time the Maoist movement expanded into Dolakha, it was a nationally-known entity. As we shall
see below, the villagers were already familiar with the Maoists' activities elsewhere in the country when they arrived in the Dolakha
region, and had many reasons to believe that the Maoist agenda in
some ways matched their own pragmatic one.

'In 2053 v.s. [1996/7], we heard that Maoists were starting to break into the
houses of wealthy people, tax collectors and moneylenders, stealing their
money and property and distributing it to the poor. What amazing news, we
had never heard anything like that before! I was also happy when I heard this
rumour, but I was afraid that this struggle would end badly. But I put those
thoughts aside when I heard the wonderful news about sharing out the
wealth of the rich landowners. The Maoists had even burnt all the papers
and accounts kept in some banks... We heard that the Maoists were breaking the arms and legs of moneylenders and tax collectors in the west of the
country and were taking control of villages. How amazing!'

The above paragraph may be best understood in the context of the
exploitation which Thangmi, Tamang, and other groups in central and
eastern districts such as Dolakha have long faced (see Holmberg,
March and Tamang 1999). Historically a Newar-ruled kingdom that
served as an important entrepôt for the Kathmandu-Lhasa trade,
Dolakha was incorporated into the nascent Nepali state by Prithvi
Narayan Shah in 1754. Over the next 250 years, the area was settled
by favourites of first the Shah dynasty, and then the Ranas. Many
families in the area still view the actions of high-caste Hindu immigrants who engaged in questionable practices of moneylending and
land appropriation as essential parts of a local history of oppression.
Interest rates of up to sixty per cent per annum on private monetary
loans remain common in the Dolakha area today for those who do
not have collateral for bank loans. A deep-seated sense of injustice

and anger has resulted from these practices. That the Maoists were said to be attacking the well-established vested interest of usury, and then distributing the spoils to poor villagers seemed, from a local perspective, quite literally unbelievable and wonderful. The enthusiasm felt for the incineration of written records is best understood in the context of the moneylending practices described above: loan documents and tax records epitomise the historical exploitation of illiterate and poor villagers whose naïve thumb-prints on such documents often had consequences beyond their control. It is important to note that this sense of excitement was not an anarchic celebration of the end of state control, but rather an expression of satisfaction at the symbolic destruction of unchecked local corruption, the victims of which were the illiterate poor. As Holmberg et al. state, '...contemporary movements are intentional social action in direct continuity with the past of the nation-state which for groups like the Tamang is a past of exploitation and denial...' (1999: 61). Such grievances existed long before the arrival of the Maoists, but with their promises of a Robin Hood-style redistribution of wealth the Maoists were in a strong position to gain support by taking advantage of existing frustrations.

From Demons to Humans

'In 2052–3 v.s. [1995/7], when we heard about the Maoists on the radio or read about them in the newspaper, we were terribly afraid of them. There were stories about people wearing headbands with a star, about guns, and of shooting people. We thought they were perhaps monsters, totally different people with wild hair and strange habits.'

The above sentiment echoes a widely-held pre-contact fear about the form and shape of the Maoists. In some cases, they were described as powerful local spirits with magical powers to blend into the jungle and become invisible (see Pettigrew 2003). Against the background of widespread condemnation and even demonisation of the Maoists by the national press and local political leaders, it comes as little surprise that in the village imagination they were conceived of as political demons, neither fully human nor animal. One individual even described them as 'political *ban manche*' (forest-dwelling wild men). This impression would slowly change when villagers in Dolakha came into contact with Maoists active in their district.

'Then we heard that Maoists were in the general region, and could be recognised by the red star on their caps. They were walking through villages and coming to schools, giving out orders and directions for how things should be run. They prohibited the singing of national school songs that praised the king. These young men and women, wearing caps with red stars...came to schools and told teachers to stop teaching useless subjects, and to teach new disciplines of everlasting use. The Maoists told schoolteachers to reduce the monthly fees, and to stop teaching Sanskrit. We were very happy to hear about all this.'

The above description illustrates the important first step in the humanisation of the Maoists. Coming from kin and close friends in other villages, the information received about Maoist activities was accepted as trusted hearsay. In this way, feelings of fear and trepidation were gradually replaced by cautious expectation.

'After hearing about Maoists elsewhere in the region for so long, about two years ago, in early 2056 v.s. [mid-1999], they began arriving in our village. At first only a few people came, in civil dress, but then ten to twelve people would come, and finally forty-five people came in full guerrilla dress, sometime in 2057 v.s. [2000/1]. Only then did we realise that the Maoists were just normal people. Perhaps they had more motivation or spirit, but physically they were just like us.'

The final stage in the humanisation of the Maoists came when villagers actually met them face-to-face, and realised that—apart from their heightened motivation and devotion to a cause—there was little that separated them from other villagers. We should not underestimate the importance of this process for engendering support at the village level: the Maoists had transformed from unknown and dangerous beings far from Dolakha to motivated and powerful humans meeting villagers in their own homes. Many villagers spoke of their sense of incredulity that such brave and powerful individuals should come to speak with them, ask them for their opinions on weighty issues, and address them with respect. This last element of the equation is crucial: villagers expected to be frightened into submission when the Maoists finally came, but instead they were addressed humanely and respectfully by people who seemed to understand the predicament of their lives. A logical extension of such experiences is a sense of empowerment. As one man put it, 'If the Maoists are like us, does that also mean that we are like them?'

Motivations for Joining the Maoists

'Slowly the villagers began to accept the Maoists, and lost their initial fear. Then people began to join. In the village, there are three categories of people who join the Maoists. The first are those who understand the ideology and join because they genuinely agree with the cause. The second are those who don't fully understand the ideology, but join because a brother or friend has joined and they don't want to be left out. The third are those who join out of fear, regardless of their ideological beliefs.'

A noticeable absence in the above account of possible motivations for joining the Maoists is any reference to the resolution of existing intra-village conflicts, a motivation which previous studies have identified as central in village level support for the movement. Both de Sales (2000) and Pettigrew (2003) describe how Maoists either became 'intermediaries' for existing clan disputes, or manipulated ancestral conflicts and the logic of kinship and identity to gain support. Although these may have been contributing factors in the Dolakha situation, we believe that Maoist tactics and village reactions both underwent a shift in this newer theatre of the people's war. Gaining the upper hand in pre-existing disputes did not seem to be a primary motivation for joining the Maoists in Dolakha. Individuals did, however, join the Maoists in reaction to conflicts that had arisen since the movement began, and in particular to seek revenge for police violence. The Maoists' earlier willingness to be used as intermediaries in existing local conflicts may have been a pragmatic strategy to gain support at an earlier stage in the struggle, but by the time they reached Dolakha such tactics were no longer necessary. Most villagers in Dolakha had heard about Maoist policies of agrarian reform and economic reorganisation, were aware of their successes in other areas of the country, and joined because the revolutionary ideas in some way spoke to their own experience of exploitation. Although the desire to be treated with respect (and even fear) by others, the yearning for a purpose beyond the limited horizons of village life, and the desire for personal power all remain part of the complex web of motivation, these personal desires must be understood within the framework of the practical ideology that was successfully promoted by the Maoists at the village level.

The issue remains of those who joined in imitation of others, or out of fear. According to villagers, some recruits did not understand the issues themselves, and simply followed those who had joined for ideological reasons. Concerning those who joined out of fear, it is not clear whether they were afraid of what the Maoists would do to them if they did not join or what the police would do to them if they did. Or were they afraid of what might happen if they were caught in between? All of these are possibilities, but the fact that such individuals often chose to join the Maoists rather than simply maintaining the status quo suggests that joining was a strategic choice which anticipated positive results.

'About two years ago, at the beginning of all this, a Bahun was run out of his house in a nearby village. The Maoists took all of his stored grain and belongings and distributed them to others. The man was known to have exploited others in the Panchayat era. After this event, he abandoned his house and fled. Around the same time, there was an Indian Christian missionary in another village, and the same thing happened to him. One of our family friends actually received a plate from the Maoists which came from the looted house.'

Here it may be useful to differentiate between the theoretical ideology advanced by the Maoist leadership at a national level, and the practical ideology employed at the village level. Although villagers may have remained unaware of the political complexities of the movement's national goals, let alone its international and historical context, they were attracted by events such as the ones described above. Grassroots redistribution of wealth lent credence to the Maoists' more abstract promises of political power for those who had previously remained excluded. In our experience, while many villagers had never heard of Mao Zedong or the results of Maoism in China, when they were asked what the Maoists stood for they immediately answered 'reclaiming our land' or 'bringing the exploiters to justice'. These objectives were explicitly articulated at the local level in a way that may not have been the case at earlier stages of the movement (see de Sales 2000: 65). Many villagers were willing to accept this practical ideology at face value, feeling that they had little to lose. Moreover, they found the Maoists more convincing than any other political party, and were willing to give them a chance.

On the Police

'The strangest thing is that the Maoists are fighting with the police. The police are also just commoners, and the Maoists' real fight is with the government. But I also remember the bad things the police did after democracy. If they were called to break up a fight, they would support the side of whoever gave them more *raksi* [home-brewed alcohol], meat and money. Attacking those thieving police is one thing, but attacking young innocent policemen, who were just children then, is another. But you know, those young men should know better than to join the police at a time like this. When the Maoists first began killing large numbers of police, people were shocked. But this is how the Maoists' numbers grew: when the police killed one Maoist, five more people from among his family and friends would join, then they would kill more police. And in that way, their numbers multiplied quickly. People are not scared if they hear that many police have been killed. They have become numb to the numbers. They used to feel frightened if two or five people were killed, but then they became used to that. Then they heard about ten or twenty people being killed, and became used to that. Now even if forty or fifty are killed, no one thinks much of it. This is because it is largely police who are killed and villagers don't have much sympathy for them anymore. If villagers were being killed it might feel different.'

This articulates the well-attested antipathy towards the police in rural areas (see Thapa 2001). Although villagers felt sorry for young men who joined the police before the Maoist movement took off and who unwittingly became targets, they had little sympathy for those who had joined more recently, or for the police as a defined group. Few people viewed the police as a security force working to protect them, seeing them instead as a symbol of corruption and exploitation. As shown above, the Maoists managed to manipulate police violence in their favour by providing an easy mode of revenge for the family members of those villagers who lost their lives at the hands of the police.

THE MYTH OF THE MAOIST COMMANDER

'If people inform the police of Maoist activities, the Maoists then kill those informants. There was an example of this in Dolakha just after the Maoists arrived, in 2054 v.s. [1997/8]. Maoists went to a Tamang house and asked for snacks. The Tamang man went out secretly to call the police, who then came and arrested two Maoists. One of these was a commander named Rit Bahadur Khadka, who was not from Dolakha. The other was a local Thangmi, who was terribly beaten by the police at their office in Charikot. Khadka was already famous as a Maoist commander, so he was treated more leniently. He was brought to Kathmandu for sentencing, but he escaped from jail. The rumour is that he was taken to Bir Hospital for treatment while in jail, and he went to the toilet and escaped out the window. In the meantime, the Tamang man who had informed on them had got a job as a security guard at a hydropower project. There was some suspicion that he had received this job through police connections. After Khadka escaped from jail, either he or his followers killed the Tamang man. After hearing about this example, others were afraid to inform.'

The incidents described here match up with those reported on 21 January 1998 and 12 September 1999 in the media chronology of events. That these incidents were reported in roughly the same manner by both the newspapers and the villagers suggests that they were indeed important moments in the development of the Maoist movement in Dolakha. From the villagers' account, it becomes clear that the events described above were crucial in developing the local myth of Rit Bahadur Khadka. Until his death in an 'encounter' with security forces in the summer of 2002, Khadka remained the chief commander of the Maoist forces in Dolakha, and was responsible for announcing the formation of the Dolakha *jan sarkar.* Khadka was viewed with a mixture of awe and fear, and was a focal point for discussions of what a Maoist government would really be like. Villagers cited his return to Dolakha after his imprisonment as evidence of his genuine devotion to, and concern for, the people of the district.

However, it was not clear why there was so little fear of Maoist intimidation, even after the Maoists' violent practices and taste for retribution became common knowledge. Perhaps ongoing police brutality together with the history of oppression in Dolakha during the Rana and Panchayat eras caused villagers to expect violence as an inevitable feature of political change. Although the Maoists were indeed dangerous, they were often perceived as the more conscientious aggressor: the villagers saw their violence as motivated by a supposedly positive ideology for political change. The police, on the other hand, were seen to be using violence to defend an unequal status quo. It was precisely this dynamic which secured the Maoists a large part of their support as the violence increased. Despite the Maoists' brutality, and the potential for far worse, as has been historically demonstrated in China and Cambodia, villagers already felt that they were suffering from more subtle, yet equally deadly, state-sanctioned violence. This may explain in part why villagers inured themselves to Maoist violence and accepted it as an inevitable part of the move towards a better political future.[8]

---

[8] Nordstrom and Martin provide a useful analysis of this type of 'structural violence' and the difficulties inherent in studying it: 'expanded definitions of violence have been

A Turning Point

'At Mainapokhari just a few months ago [April 2001], five police and three Maoists were killed. One of the Maoists was a Thangmi from Sindhupalchok. The police brought the corpses to Charikot for a post-mortem, and also made them available for public viewing. This was perhaps to frighten the villagers. The police buried the Maoists a little way out of Charikot. They didn't give them a proper funeral or call their families. Villagers found this upsetting.'

This description corresponds to the event reported in the newspapers on 3 April 2001. The confrontation was part of a larger nationwide offensive in which thirty policemen were killed at Rukumkot on the same day. Since the numbers of dead in Rukumkot were much higher than those in Dolakha, most media attention focused on what was dubbed the 'Rukumkot massacre', and the Dolakha events were relegated to the end of reports. While from the national perspective '...meanwhile in Dolakha...' (*Kathmandu Post*, 3 April 2001) was an apt way to describe these events, in Dolakha itself the confrontation was seminal in the transformation of the region from 'Maoist hotbed' to *jan sarkar*.

The confrontation at Mainapokhari was the first time that Dolakha saw multiple police deaths in the style that had previously been limited to western regions. Many residents of the area cited this as the moment they realised that the Maoists were in *de facto* control of most of the district. Furthermore, many people who had previously sat on the sidelines now felt compelled to join the Maoist forces or make sympathetic gestures towards them. This was for two primary reasons. First, the Mainapokhari incident indicated to villagers that the Maoists were gaining in confidence and strength, and those who had been wondering whether it might be prudent to join had their question answered. Second, many villagers viewed the police handling of the event with distaste and resentment. Although the intention was to scare potential Maoist recruits by publicly displaying dead bodies, this move had the opposite effect. Particularly because one of the dead was a member of their own ethnic group, Thangmi villagers felt indignation that the deceased Maoists were not accorded the

---

useful in giving a voice to systems of violence no less powerful by virtue of their intangibility. They clearly demonstrate that violence enacted is but a small part of violence lived' (1992: 8).

dignity of a funeral ritual, and that their families were not notified. The insensitivity of the police in this incident worked to weaken earlier reservations about joining the Maoists or offering them support.

Cultural Forms of Maoist Activity

'Last year in Magh 2057 v.s. [January–February 2001], the Maoists staged a fake wedding procession through the hills. Starting somewhere near their northern stronghold of Lapilang, an entire procession was put together including the bridegroom, musicians and porters to carry the bridegroom's sedan chair. In full Bahun style, the wedding procession approached the police post in Charikot. There were perhaps thirty participants altogether. The police had no idea that they were Maoists, and complimented them on their dancing and music! The procession continued to Phasku, out of Charikot on the way to Sailung. Once they reached Phasku, they gave up the wedding disguise and changed into their guerrilla uniforms. In Phasku, another group was waiting to meet them, who had come with guns and other necessary equipment. Then a large mass meeting was held in Phasku. The purpose was to make fun of the police and show us how witty they [the Maoists] were, as well as how brazen they could be.'

If this account is true—and we have reason to believe that the basic storyline is factual—it shows how the Maoists appropriated cultural symbols to their own ends. These were not necessarily ethnic symbols alone, although that was part of their strategy, but overarching cultural forms such as a Hindu wedding procession. By using this familiar cover as their camouflage, the Maoists were able to travel directly through the district headquarters, taunt the police, and move on to their mass meeting without arousing suspicion. When villagers described this event, they underscored how it demonstrated the Maoists' respect for local traditions and sense of humour, in stark contrast to the inhumane actions of the police. Villagers were also impressed by the strength and confidence implicit in such a display of subterfuge.

Furthermore, this is a fitting example of the Maoists' strategic use of local practices to generate goodwill. Although the theoretical disjunction between Maoist ideology and the rhetoric of cultural and religious identity is well-documented (see Ramirez 1997, de Sales 2000), within the framework of the practical ideology implemented locally, neither the Maoists nor the villagers appeared to be concerned about this possible contradiction. As seen in the photographs accompanying the news reports about the announcement of the

Dolakha *jan sarkar*, which show dance troupes in 'traditional' dress wearing Maoist headbands, 'cultural' performances at mass meetings played an important role in maintaining the Maoists' populist façade. We were present at Thangmi festivals organised by local cultural committees at which Maoists donned their headbands half-way through the event to make their allegiance known. They did not, however, make speeches or promote their cause in any other obvious way. Their actions were perceived as tacit support for indigenous culture. This manner of action—supporting local events without explicitly taking advantage of them for their own purposes—added to the Maoists' popularity.

Maoists at School

'Sometime last year, the Maoists stopped the schools from collecting a monthly fee. The villagers were happy with this change. This year [2000/1], the schools were closed down by the Maoists, because the teachers had not done as the Maoists had asked. The schools were closed for a week. Although I had liked the Maoists' earlier demands and ideas, I could not support this action. I didn't mind when they closed all of those boarding schools, which were sprouting like mushrooms. Only the children of wealthy people study in those schools. But while the closure of the government schools might have been good for the Maoist plan, it most certainly didn't help the villagers.'

As reported on 11 February 2000, the Maoists had on a number of occasions closed schools throughout the district for days or weeks at a time. Villagers who were otherwise largely sympathetic to the Maoists did not support this policy. Education was seen as the main opportunity for children to escape a life of poverty, and villagers did not accept that closing schools was a necessary feature of the movement. Although there was a general distrust of boarding schools due to their perceived exacerbation of inequalities between rich and poor, and villagers were supportive when these were shut down by the Maoists, the closure of government schools was seen as an attack on the very same impoverished people for whom the Maoists claimed to be fighting. Villagers did not easily appreciate the Maoist drive for 're-education', and failed to see why government education and support for the Maoists were incompatible.

This account also highlights the Maoists' use of schools as a primary forum for the dissemination of their ideology among young people, and as a recruiting centre for new members. From the early days of the Maoist presence in Dolakha, school grounds were used as preferred locations for meetings.[9] Many villagers saw a large group of armed Maoists for the first time in late 1999, when the activists called a meeting at the local secondary school, and one member from each household was required to attend. At the close of the meeting, a Maoist flag was planted in the schoolyard, and threats were given to anybody who dared take it down. One of the primary Maoist operatives in the area was a young Thangmi man from a Maoist stronghold elsewhere in the district who claimed to be taking tuition for his School Leaving Certificate (SLC) exam at the secondary school in the village. He was a very affable individual, and after he had gained the confidence of many students he proceeded to promote Maoist ideology among them. The reaction to his proselytising was mixed. He introduced Maoist songs into the school curriculum, a move that the teachers apparently felt compelled to support, and soon village children were singing 'I used to carry books with these hands, but now I carry a gun. What good is education when we can fight the people's war?' While some parents were noticeably upset by these developments, others were in awe of their children, who had the privilege of being in close contact with the Maoists, yet were not perceived to be in direct danger due to the relative security of their status as schoolchildren. In this manner, children became a crucial source of information on the movement for their parents. Overall, Maoist directives and related news were filtered through the school, either via the operative mentioned above, or by groups of Maoists in 'civil dress' who routinely visited the school in attempts to garner support among the students.

Preliminary Forms of Government

'In each village development committee, the Maoists are now establishing what they call an *adhar ilaka*, which is their local government. There they organise everything from land deeds to the mediation of disputes. They have also instructed locals not to pay government taxes. They tried to establish an

---

[9] This fits the well-attested model of schools as sites of resistance in Nepal, as described by Skinner and Holland. In their analysis, 'school participants—teachers and students—were often struggling to turn the schools from a site of state control to a site of opposition not only to the state, but also to systems of caste and gender privilege hegemonic in the society' (Skinner and Holland 1996: 273).

adhar ilaka in our VDC a year ago, and put up a signboard announcing that it had been established, but the police found out and forty policemen came to take the board down. Now, they have begun to establish one in the adjacent VDC. Last year, the Maoists also announced that they would build four gates to mark their *adhar ilaka* within Dolakha: in Lapilang, Gumu Khola, Kalinchok, and Phasku, but these have not yet been constructed.'

Adhar ilaka can be translated as 'base area'. This form of Maoist administration was established in a number of areas before the district-wide *jan sarkar* was announced, and gave villagers the first flavour of what a Maoist government might be like. For the most part, villagers from nearby *adhar ilaka*s seemed to treat them as a valid form of local government, and reported that they functioned more successfully in local interests than the national government had in recent memory. Now, rather than having to travel to Charikot or even Kathmandu, a dispute could be mediated at the local level through the so-called *jan adalat*, or people's court.

Attitudes Towards Development and Foreigners

'In VDCs where they have established *adhar ilaka*s, the Maoists have stated that development offices with foreign connections cannot stay. This is not because they are explicitly against development, but rather because they have seen how corrupt most of these organisations are. Usually only fifty per cent or less of their money actually goes towards development, the rest goes into people's pockets. The Maoists say that if they saw one hundred per cent of the funds going directly to local development, they would consider letting the offices stay.'

The Maoist attitude towards development expressed above is corroborated by our observations of Maoist behaviour towards us and other foreigners. As mentioned earlier, several groups of non-Nepalis, both Western and Asian, were engaged in development work when the Maoists first established themselves in the region. Most of these groups were eventually forced to leave, on the basis of the rhetoric described above. Although we have no evidence that any of these outfits was as corrupt as the Maoists assumed most foreign-funded projects to be, the development-oriented objectives of these projects were enough to incriminate them in the eyes of the Maoists. We were told by villagers that another reason behind their expulsion was that the Maoists were averse to other forms of social action, which they feared might interfere with their plan for social revolution. However, some locally based Nepali NGOs were allowed to continue working in the area, and reports from other parts of the country also suggest that the merits of such projects were evaluated on a case-by-case basis. Organisations that genuinely appeared to be working for the welfare of the poor were given special dispensation to remain active in the area.

In addition to development workers, foreign residents and researchers, we began to see a new kind of foreigner implicated in the Maoist movement in 2001—journalists. The Maoists invited foreign journalists from mainstream publications to cover the movement. They were carefully escorted into Maoist-controlled areas, usually in Sindhupalchok or Dolakha, and invited to take photos and speak with cadres. This seemed to herald a new phase in the development of Maoist attitudes towards the outside world, an opportunistic *modus operandi*: foreigners who threatened the cause were expelled, while those who might prove helpful were welcomed. This may explain, in part, why we were allowed to stay; we may have unwittingly aided the Maoist agenda by working within a largely poor, disenfranchised ethnic community and documenting unwritten histories of exploitation. Although we were not aware of it at the time, such activities may well have played into the rhetorical strategies of Maoist practical ideology.

'Last week, on 8 Saun 2058 v.s. [23 July 2001], the Maoists declared their government. They named Rit Bahadur Khadka as their leader, the same man who escaped from the hospital some time ago.[10] One of our hopes is that if the Maoists come to power, development will start originating in the villages instead of having to be brought in from outside. If the new Maoist government succeeds, this could be one benefit. The people have already lost faith in all of the political parties: each one has made promises and failed. People are willing to give the Maoist government a chance. They are the only ones who have not yet let us down.'

CONCLUSIONS

Let us return for a moment to the proclamation of the *jan sarkar* with which we began. Having reviewed reports of events that occurred in Dolakha, and analysed the village perspective on them, we can now

---

[10] As mentioned above, Rit Bahadur Khadka was killed in a summer 2002 'encounter' with the security forces.

consider some of the conditions that made Dolakha a logical choice for the Maoists' first publicly-declared eastern base.

When reviewing the Maoists' manipulation of ethnic and caste/ class concerns, one might argue that Dolakha's ethnic composition was a key factor in its choice as a Maoist base. Unlike other areas where one ethnic group predominates, such as the Tamu-mai (Gurung) in Lamjung or the Sherpa in Solu-Khumbu, Dolakha is a patchwork of many ethnic communities and caste groups—Tamang, Newar, Thangmi, Sherpa, Jirel, Magar, Sunuwar and Gurung (listed in order of declining population size)—concentrated in disparate locales. No other ethnic community has a population density comparable to the approximately 80,000-strong Bahun-Chetris. However, when taken together, the various minority ethnic and low-caste groups of Dolakha comprise an almost equivalent population totalling over 75,000.[11] This may have been the ideal demographic situation for the Maoist movement to gain local support: a number of susceptible communities, none of which was sufficiently networked with other communities to resist Maoist influence, yet which, if converted to the cause, could together form a substantial bedrock of support. The Thangmi and Tamang populations of Dolakha in particular occupy a similar position to the Kham Magar described by de Sales: they have suffered exploitation at the hands of high-caste Hindu landowners, yet lack a solid cultural and political organisation of their own. They were consequently strong candidates for joining the Maoist cause. It is revealing that the two Maoist strongholds within Dolakha district emerged in the predominantly Thangmi and Tamang areas of Lapilang and Sailung respectively, indicating that the Maoists did indeed succeed in targeting and receiving support from these two ethnic populations.[12]

In examining the situation closely, however, more subtle distinctions must be drawn between the Maoists' selective appropriation of ethnic symbols on the one hand and their use of caste/class distinctions

[11] These statistics are compiled from the 1991 National Census (Central Bureau of Statistics 1999).

[12] The large Newar population of Dolakha has not featured prominently in the movement to date. Concentrated in the semi-urban areas around Dolakha bazaar and Charikot, the Newars remain largely outside the rural sphere of Maoist influence. Furthermore, their strong community and ethnic organisations make them less drawn to Maoist ideology, and they are, for the most part, in a higher economic stratum than either the Thangmi or Tamang.

on the other. While the Maoists were quick to adopt cultural forms ranging from the traditional wedding procession to the contemporary 'cultural programme', they did not promise ethnic autonomy to any group in Dolakha in the manner that de Sales describes for the Kham Magar. Rather, the Maoists promised full participation in a multi-ethnic republic to those who were previously disenfranchised, with the expectation that those who joined would eventually put aside their ethnic claims in the interest of the overarching class struggle. This shift in strategy may have been due to the increased drawing power of Maoist ideology itself, which was refined and recast in local terms while it was being established in Dolakha. The practical ideology which appealed to so many villagers was based on a rhetoric of agrarian reform, land redistribution and economic empowerment, and not of ethnic struggle. However, those who have been disenfranchised in rural Nepal are in many instances ethnic minorities, so the two objectives are often conflated. In other words, although the Maoists made use of ethnic symbols for their own ends in their initial campaign to gain support, this appears to have been a pragmatic move employed during an earlier phase of the struggle. The long-term strategy appeared to be moving beyond ethnicity as an organising paradigm in order to achieve the ideological goal of a Maoist republic.

The large number of attendees reported at the Rankedanda mass meeting demonstrates the widespread appeal of the Maoist movement in Dolakha in July 2001. Even if we opt for the lower estimate of 10,000 people present, as reported in the *Independent*, the figure represents approximately five per cent of the total population of the district. While fear and intimidation are known to be Maoist tools, it is unlikely that upwards of 10,000 people would walk for hours and gather purely out of fear. We argue that the practical ideology advanced by the Maoists at the village level compelled local people to join what they perceived to be a social movement which promised concrete improvements in their own living conditions. The initial enthusiasm for the movement in Dolakha was based on an expectation of positive social change. It remains to be seen whether villagers will at a later date feel that they have been let down, once again, by empty political promises. If and when this happens, the dynamics of the movement may change substantially.[13]

[13] The curtailment of civil liberties under the TADO and the shift in power dynamics after the army deployment may have precipitated this process of disillusionment.

Finally, we return to the symbolic importance of the Western journalist's presence at the Rankedanda meeting. As he reported, 'despite the presence of 20 Nepalese journalists, no reports appeared in Kathmandu's English language newspapers' (Popham 2001: 18). Yet his own report publicised the event to a far wider audience than the *Kathmandu Post* could ever reach. Perhaps by accident, perhaps by design, Dolakha became a microcosm representing pre-emergency Maoist Nepal to the outside world. It is our hope that this discussion has shed some light on the complex set of events that made it so.

APPENDIX

NEWS CLIPPINGS ABOUT DOLAKHA 1998–2001

Each clipping begins with details of the date of publication, the source of information and the village or area under discussion. Irregularities in spelling, grammar and punctuation have been retained, and apart from cuts indicated by ellipses, the articles are presented as printed.

21 January 1998   US State Department website   Bhimeswor municipality, Dolakha

'Residents of Bhimeswor Municipality-4 have handed over to the police two armed Maoists who were quarrelling with the fish sellers over the purchase of fish. The two alleged Maoists, Rit Bahadur Khadka of Dolakha and Bhuval Dhami of Sindhupalchok, had suddenly brandished their weapons to threaten the people selling fish on the bank of the Tama Koshi. Villagers gathered immediately, nabbed the two and handed them over to the police. According to Deputy Superintendent of Police Jit Bahadur Pun, both were active participants of Maoist movement. Police have seized grenades, a six-round revolver, cartridges, gunpowder, fuse wire, binocular, explosives and Maoist books from them.'

19–20 June 1998   US State Department website   Namdu VDC, Dolakha

'On June 19–20, a Maoist activist was killed in encounters with security personnel in the Namdu VDC of Dolakha district.'

19 June 1998   US State Department website   Namdu VDC, Dolakha

'One terrorist was killed when security personnel fired in self defense after they came under sudden attack of a gang of about 12 terrorists armed with muzzle loaders and country made pistols in Namdu VDC on June 19. According to the spokesman of the Home Ministry, one policeman was injured in the incident. Security personnel have recovered one muzzle loader, one country made pistol, one khukuri and some explosives from the site.'

27 October, 1998   US State Department website   Charikot, Dolakha

'One person was seriously injured when explosives contained in his bag that he was carrying exploded at Tikhatal, about a kilometer from the district headquarters of Charikot. Kumar Pandey, 22, has been sent to Kathmandu for medical treatment after preliminary check-ups at the Gaurishankar General Hospital. Pandey told the Kathmandu Post that the bag had been given to him by one Himal, believed to be a Maoist activist from Sindhupalchowk, who was supposed to see him, a few kilometers ahead on the route.'

22 November 1998   US State Department website   Dolakha

'Two Maoist insurgents have been shot dead in an encounter with police on the banks of the Tamakoshi river in Dolakha district. Police said, the encounter took place on the night of November 22 when suspected Maoists fired shots at a police patrol. Two Maoists died on the spot when police returned fire. The bodies have not yet been found. Police said, they recovered a small cache of weapons and propaganda material from the site of the incident.'

16 January 1999   Kathmandu Post   Phasku VDC, Dolakha

'*Maoists hack one to death* In another incident in Dolakha, a group of Maoists hacked Chakra Bahadur Budathoki aka Bharat at his house in Phasku VDC. He was attacked from the back on his neck with a khukuri by the insurgents after they brought him to the ground floor of the house.'

2 February 1999   Kathmandu Post   Mailapokhari bazaar, Dolakha

'*ICIMOD office vandalised* Armed Maoist insurgents set alight office furniture, equipments and motorbike belonging to the ICIMOD field office near Mailapokhari bazaar here Tuesday night, causing loss of property worth about Rs 2 million, police sources said. A group of about 18 insurgents, wielding pistols and khukuris entered the ICIMOD field office around 10 in the night threatening the only junior staff with his life if he cried for help. Then they took out all the articles from the office including a computer and documents and set them alight. The verandah of the office building was partially destroyed by fire. The insurgents could not set the building on fire as the police reached the spot and resorted to blank firing, causing the insurgents to flee the area.'

29 April 1999   *Kathmandu Post*   *Dolakha*

'*UML workers attack NC activist* Former District Development Committee president of Dolakha Uddhav Raj Kafle who was elected from the Nepali Congress (NC) has been hospitalized following an attack which he alleged was spearheaded by the CPN (UML) district committee chief...'

12 September 1999   *US State Department website*   *Pawari VDC, Dolakha*

'Maoist rebels on September 12 killed a man who had helped police arrest a rebel commander about two years back, police said. Mitra Bahadur Tamang's body was recovered on September 12 in the Thulopakhar jungle, at Pawari VDC, according to the district police office. Tamang's hands were tied and his body left hung to a tree.'

22 September 1999   US State Department website   Charikot, Dolakha

'Two pipe bombs planted by the Maoist insurgents went off at 8:45 on the night of September 22 near the Charikot police office in Dolakha. The bombs were planted 200 metres away from the police office.'

3 December 1999   *Kathmandu Post*   *Mehul, Dolakha*

'*Maoists, cop killed in bank raid* Three persons—one police personnel and two Maoists—were killed when a group of Maoist insurgents clashed with police in Mehul, Dolkha on Wednesday night, in what has been described as first such incident in the central hill district since the insurgency began nearly four years ago...a group of armed insurgents attacked...with bullets, pipe and grenade bombs, while beleaguering the police post and the bank from all sides...'

7 February 2000   *Kathmandu Post*   *Khare VDC, Dolakha*

(Front-page photo) *caption*: 'A house used by a foreigner in the remote village of Khare, Dolakha district, after it was set on fire by the NCP-Maoist activists last month.'

9 February 2000   *Rising Nepal*   *Mali VDC, Dolakha*

'*Armed group loots goods from trekkers* An armed group of about 15 looted a video camera and some still cameras from Polish trekkers and Rs. 10,000 from the Nepalese accompanying them at Mali VDC in Dolkha district on Feb. 7, according to the district police office. The Polish nationals, who were 15 in number, were together with five Nepalese fellow trekkers leaving for Panchpokhari of Ramechhap from Jiri Bazaar. Police suspect that the looters were Maoists.'

11 February 2000   *Kathmandu Post*   *Dolakha*

'*SLC test exams in Dolakha deferred* Authorities here have been forced to postpone the district level School Leaving Certificate (SLC) test examinations following warnings from the underground Maoist rebels to close all educational institutions to mark the fifth anniversary of people's war...According to school teachers here, Maoist activists have sent letters to the schools appealing them to "support for our cause by closing down your institutions on the War's anniversary day".'

12 February 2000   *Kathmandu Post*   *Jiri, Dolakha*

'*Helicopter damaged in arson attack* A private airline-operated cargo helicopter was completely destroyed in an arson attack here during the early hours today, police officials said...About 10 armed arsonists first held the four people guarding the helicopter at gun point, sprayed kerosene and set it on fire...Police suspect Maoist rebels operating in the hills of Jiri to be responsible for the attack.'

21 February 2000   *Kathmandu Post*   *Jyaku VDC, Dolakha*

'*Maoist killed in clash with police* One Maoist was killed and the next one wounded when Dolakha district police patrol and the so-called Maoist gang exchanged fire near Jyaku VDC in Dolakha district on Friday. According to the district police, police found two revolvers, two pipe bombs, four grenades and revolver parts, some bags and documents after the incident...'

13 March 2000   *Kathmandu Post*   *Jiri, Dolakha*

'*Villagers shell-shocked* Days after police fired randomly at a school building in Shyama VDC, two hours away from here, shell-shocked villagers are still trying to come to terms with the police atrocity. Police suspect that the teachers of Garjung Dhunga Higher Secondary School had given shelter to Maoist insurgents. Dolakha is a Maoist hotbed. Some 30 policemen entered the teachers' quarter Tuesday afternoon and opened fire...Fortunately for the teachers, they managed to hide themselves under the cot amid the volley of bullets.'

17 March 2000   *Kathmandu Post*   *Dolakha*

'*Teachers against police fire in Dolakha* Local teachers have called on all the school authorities here to close their institutions on March 29 to protest recent indiscriminate police firing in Garjandhunga secondary school...The teachers, caught in cross fire between the Maoists and the police forces, have voiced concern for their safety stating that the dangerous climate has made it difficult for them to do their job.'

8 April 2000   *Kathmandu Post*   *Namdu VDC, Dolakha*

'*Maoist related incidents reported* Police today detonated the ambush laid by Maoist rebels in Namdu VDC of Jiri-Kathmandu highway. Police had narrowly escaped last month in a similar ambush laid by the insurgents in the same area. Police suspect that the ambush was laid for the bandh yesterday but was unsuccessful because of the strict vigilance.'

20 May 2000   *Kathmandu Post*   *Gumu Khola, Dolakha*

'...Meanwhile, in Dolakha a team of police battled with Maoist rebels for two hours in a remote village today. They hauled a large quantity of ammunition after the rebels fled the scene, Central Regional Police Office Hetauda, said...It all started with the rebels firing indiscriminately at the police team from their jungle hide-outs at around 4:30 pm Friday...'

22 May 2000   *Kathmandu Post*   *Charikot, Dolakha*

'*VDCs sans Secretaries* Seventeen Village Development Committees (VDCs) out of the total 51 VDCs in Dolakha district do not have the VDC Secretary at present. The posts of the VDC Secretaries had fallen vacant after those posted earlier have been transferred and the concerned ministry has not filled up those vacancies yet.'

1 August 2000   *Kathmandu Post*   *Chhetrapa VDC, Dolakha*

'A group of armed Maoists looted official documents from Chhetrapa VDC office near Mainapokhari bazar, 33 km away from the district headquarters yesterday. The group of 24 Maoist insurgents, who were carrying guns and pistols, stormed into the office and took away all official documents including stacks of land tax receipts...'

2 October 2000   *Nepalnews.com*   *Jiri, Dolakha*

'*Maoists rob bank in Jiri* Maoist insurgents robbed a commercial bank in a broad day light in Jiri, about 200 kilometers east of Kathmandu, and fled with 300 thousands rupees on Monday. According to police, a group of rebels entered into the branch office of Nepal Bank Ltd in Jiri, Dolkha at about 11:30 am Monday and fled with all cash and kind. The bank had kept minimum amount of cash due to the fear of the Maoist attack. Insurgents also took away arms and ammunition from the security guards of the bank.'

3 April 2001   *Kathmandu Post*   *Mainapokhari, Dolakha*

'*Rebel hits kill 35 policemen, Two dozen more abducted...*five policemen and three Maoist rebels have been killed in Mainapokhari village in Dolkha district 154 km east of Kathmandu. Around 20 policemen have been wounded in the assault...In the Mainapokhari attack in Dolakha, our correspondent Ishwari Neupane reported that rebels started attacking the local police post at around 3 o'clock in the morning. The rebels surrounded the police post, 34 kilometers from the district headquarters Charikot, from three sides and started firing and throwing socket and pipe bombs. The assault lasted for two and half-hours till 5:30 am.'

8 April 2001   *Observer*   *Chautara*

Maoists lay siege to Nepal article about Maoists in Sindhupalcok, with colour photo of 'Maoist guerrillas' near Chautara.

15 April 2001   *Kathmandu Post*   *Sundrawati, Dolakha*

'*Solve Maoist problem through talks: Nepal* CPN-UML general secretary Madhav Kumar Nepal inaugurated the new building of Kalika

Secondary School Sundrawati today...The CPN-UML leader spoke of the need to resolve the Maoist problem through talks, adding that army mobilization is not a solution to the problem.'

16 April 2001   *Kathmandu Post*   *Singri, Dolakha*

'Yet another report from Dolakha says that the Maoists burned down the police building at Singri bazar, which the policemen had deserted five days earlier due to fear of a Maoist attack.'

18 June 2001   *Newsweek*   *Piskar, Dolakha*

Nepal's Maoist Threat 2-page spread in the international news magazine, with details and photographs from the predominantly Thangmi (Thami) VDC of Piskar in Sindhupalchok, located close to the Dolakha border.

19 July 2001   *Kathmandu Post*   *Charikot, Dolakha*

'*Dolakha festival in the offing* Dolakha festival is to be organised on October 1, 2 and 3 under the joint auspices of the Nepal Tourism Board and Dolakha Tourism and Cultural Promotion Committee. The objective of the festival is to bring to light the natural, religious and cultural aspects of Dolakha district and attract domestic and foreign tourists.'

24 July 2001   Jana Bhavana National Daily   Rankedanda, Dolakha

'*Yasari ghoshana gariyo jilla jan sarkar*' Nepali language article detailing the announcement of the *jan sarkar*, and including excerpts from the speeches given by local commanders Rit Bahadur Khadka and Comrade Kanchan. The presence of a foreign journalist is also mentioned.

25 July 2001   *Space Time Dainik*   *Dolakha*

'*Asthako asha, chuvachut ta hatnaiparcha*' Nepali language article discussing the role of female rebels in the movement in general, and in the proceedings of the announcement of the Dolakha *jan sarkar* in particular. Once again, the foreign journalist is mentioned.

26 July 2001   *Kathmandu Post*   *Rankedanda, Dolakha*

'*A glimpse of a cultural program organized by CPN (Maoist) in Ranke Danda, Dolakha, Sunday. The underground rebels had organized the program to mark the start of the "People's Government".'* Caption accompanies colour photo of Maoist dancers in 'traditional' dress.

12 August 2001   Independent Sunday Review   Sailungeshwor, Dolakha

'*Mao's Children: Nepal Year Zero* First it endured the massacre of its royal family; now Nepal faces the prospect of a Maoist revolution. As the rebels seized control of yet another province, they invited one Western journalist to meet their leaders.'

19 September 2001   Kathmandu Post   Dolakha

'*UML to launch counter Maoist move in Dolakha* The district council meeting of the Communist Party of Nepal (Unified Marxist-Leninist) CPN-UML has decided to launch an ideological campaign in the district against the Maoist extortion and atrocities. "The Maoists themselves will be responsible for the activities which contradict with the people's expectations. We request them to immediately stop such anti-people move," stated a press statement issued after the conclusion of the council's two-day meet on Tuesday. The meeting of the council also asked the underground party to open offices of the various Village Development Committees and allow the elected representatives to carry out their daily administration. Out of the total 51 VDCs in the district, Maoists have forcibly closed down the offices of 41 VDC offices…The council meet also condemned the Maoists for forcibly closing down all private schools and disrupting the education activities of public schools.'

ETHNIC DEMANDS WITHIN MAOISM

QUESTIONS OF MAGAR TERRITORIAL AUTONOMY, NATIONALITY AND CLASS*

Marie Lecomte-Tilouine

'*Une idée ne peut être jugée par aucun des crimes que l'on commet en son nom, elle ne saurait être trouvée dans aucun des modèles qu'elle inspire.*'[1]

It has become a commonplace to associate the Maoist guerrillas in Nepal with the Magar ethnic group. However, the relationship between the Maoists' ideology and actions and the Magar organisations and their ethnic demands has not been dealt with in depth until now.[2] Here I shall examine both the references to ethnic minorities (focusing on the Magars) that can be found in Maoist writings and the references to Maoism that appear in Magar ethnic and ethno-Marxist literature.[3] My focus introduces a bias, because it does not represent all the opinions present within the group, nor even probably the opinion that is most widely-held. Indeed, Magars are extremely numerous in the Nepali police and army among whom especially the policemen, along with their families, have been targeted by the Maoists and are thus opposed to their movement. Many of them have fled to the tarai and are afraid to return to their native villages. Also, a large number of villagers, especially women, are

---

* I warmly thank my *bhai*, Chitre Bahadur Dogami Gharti, who sent me many documents for this article, as well as Deepak Thapa, who was discussant for an earlier draft of this paper which was presented at the London conference.

[1] 'An idea cannot be judged by any of the crimes perpetrated in its name, it cannot be found in any of the models it inspires.' Romain Gary's cynical sentence refers to communism (Gary 1979).

[2] For a discussion of identity and territoriality with regard to the Kham Magars' participation in the people's war see de Sales (2000). See also Lecomte-Tilouine (2000) for an examination of Magar ethnic (and somehow revolutionary) literature relating to a Magar rebel of the 19th century.

[3] In Nepal, ethnic minorities are a sizeable proportion of the total population.

tired of the present political agitation, and confess their nostalgia for
the Panchayat era and yearn for peace. Though the opinions of policemen and women tend not to get published because they are deemed
conformist, they can be found in several Magar journals published by
the Magars of Rolpa.[4]

As is well known, a quickening of ethnic feeling in Nepal preceded
the Maoist movement between 1990 and 1995. This took a particularly strong inflection during 1993, enhanced by the fact that this year
was declared the 'Year of Indigenous Peoples' by the United Nations.
One indication of the importance of the ethnic revival among the
Magars is given by the large number of Magar ethnic journals—more
than thirty titles, according to a list published in *Lapha* 18/19 (1999).[5]
Despite the increasing awareness of ethnic identity inside the Magar
group and the growing importance of their demands, since 1996 the
news media have focused on the Maoist movement. The Magars' eth-
nic revival has been eclipsed by it or associated with it, to the point that
Gore Bahadur Khapangi, leader of the Nepal Magar Association
(Sangh), felt the need to declare publicly in December 1998 that there
was no relationship between the Magar Association and the Maoists.
Despite this declaration, let us examine the basis upon which the
Magars and their ethnic activities might be associated with Maoism.

One obvious link between the Magar ethnic movement and the
Maoist guerrillas is the composition of the population in Rolpa, the

[4] See, for instance, *Konja Marum* or *San* or the anonymous (and note that it is anonymous) article in *Janajati Manch* (III, 3: 23), 'Di. Es. Pi. Thule Rai maobadibata
mukta' ('D. S. P. Thule Rai Freed from the Maoists').

[5] According to Suresh Ale Magar (1993/4), the Magars organised their first meeting
in 1955 at Mahottari, and the Association for the Reform of Magar Society was created that same year by Giri Prasad Budhathoki, in order to unify the Magars and
to eliminate their bad customs (*kuriti, kusamskar*). According to D. B. Rana Magar
(1995/6), the first Magar meeting took place in 1957 in the village of Kulang (Tanahun). This same year the 'Great Magar Conference' was held in Bharse (Gulmi), during which the Association for the Reform of Magar Society (Magar Samaj Sudhar
Sangh) was created (Licchavi Magar 1993/4). Led by Giri Prasad Budhathoki, a high
ranking military man, and then by his son, who was the minister of tourism, the
Magars of Bharse, a prosperous village of soldiers, were the first to publish books in
Nepali about their village and their clans. After an apparently long interruption of
Magar activities, the 'Langhali family' was created in 1971 in Kathmandu. Finally, in
1992, the Nepal Langhali Sangh became the Nepal Magar Association (Nepal Magar
Sangh) and the association became more active, publishing several journals and
organising an annual conference.

cradle of the people's war. The numerous Magar casualties on both sides of this war[6] and the arrest of some prominent figures of Magar ethnic activism are further indications. These latter include the poet Jit Bahadur Sinjali Magar, an active defender of Magar culture and language who became a Maoist and went underground, and at the time of writing was still wanted by the authorities (S. Lungeli Magar 1997/8), and Suresh Ale Magar, the general secretary of the Great Janajati Mahasangh, who has repeatedly been arrested and accused of Maoist activities.[7] Finally, on the ideological side, there are common aspects in both movements, including the belief that violence is the only possible means of liberation for oppressed groups.

ETHNIC MINORITIES IN MAOIST DISCOURSE

In the forty-point ultimatum presented to the government by Baburam Bhattarai before the initiation of the people's war in February 1996, the Maoist movement seems to have gathered in most of the popular grievances. The demand contains something for all marginalised sections: the poor, women, Dalits, and *janajati*. Point twenty is particularly significant for the *janajati*: 'All kinds of exploitation and

[6] According to the list of people killed by police and Maoists between 13 February 1996 and 25 August 1998 published by the Human Rights Internet (*www.hri.ca*), of the 205 persons killed by the police a maximum of 76 may have been Magars (i.e. I have counted in those named Rana, Thapa, Gharti and Roka, although these could equally well be Chetris). Forty-nine of the 205 were inhabitants of Rolpa and 37 of Rukum. Of the 89 persons killed by the Maoists, 35 may have been Magars, and 30 were inhabitants of Rolpa and 24 of Rukum, indicating a higher concentration of Maoist violence, compared with police violence, in these two districts during this period. The majority of victims bore high caste names, whereas low caste victims were apparently very rare (only six of the 205 killed by the police, and only five of the 89 killed by the Maoists), showing that their participation in this political conflict may be less important than is commonly asserted.

[7] Suresh Ale Magar spoke at the 'Historic Delhi Rally' on 13 December 1998, under the banner 'Solidarity Forum to Support the People's War in Nepal' (*Worker* 5). In May 2001, *People's Review* published an extract from the weekly *Janadharana* of 5 May, which described him as the coordinator of the 'Racial and Regional Front', which was close to the Maoists. Detained between October 1999 and 29 February 2000, Suresh Ale Magar was never issued with a detention order or taken to court for trial (*www.freemedia.at*). He was previously an active member of Magar ethnic associations, the Langhali Parivar and the Langhali Parivar Sangh, the Nepal Janajati Sangh, and the Akhil Nepal Janajati Sangh, as well as an adviser to several Magar and other ethnic journals.

prejudice based on caste should be ended. In areas *having a majority* of one ethnic group, that group should have autonomy over that area' (emphasis added). While the elimination of discrimination is advocated only with reference to caste (and apparently minimising only its effects, i.e. exploitation and prejudice, but since castes are by definition status groups, one wonders whether 'castes' can survive in the absence of prejudice), the specificity of the ethnic group is on the other hand not only recognised but even reinforced by this promise of territorial autonomy. However we should note that the word 'majority' has a well-known double meaning: if point twenty is referring not to a relative majority but to an absolute majority, then very few groups would be given territorial autonomy. The incorporation of ethnic demands in the Maoists' agenda can obviously be seen as one aspect of their avowed tactic of 'discerning and utilising contradictions within the enemy camp' because one of the major contradictions noticed by the Maoists at the beginning of the people's war was that 'in recent years the contradictions of the state with the oppressed nationalities have sharpened further'.[8]

In an interview published in February 2000, the Maoist leader Prachanda also stated that he had 'solved' the question of 'nationalities' by 'autonomy'. He revealed the presence of numerous Magars in his army and reiterated commonly-held stereotypes about this group.[9] When the Maoist journalist Li Onesto, his interviewer, asked, 'What is the material basis for the revolution being more advanced in the west [of Nepal]? Is the question of the oppressed nationalities a big factor?' Prachanda answered 'Yes', and identified two related factors to explain this situation. First, the ruling class neglected the west, because it was inhabited mainly by oppressed nationalities. He then added that western Nepal had kept a kind of autonomy, because it had been annexed by the Gorkhalis at a late stage of their

---

[8] 'One Year of People's War in Nepal', *Revolutionary Worker*, 911, 15 June 1997.

[9] However, Baburam Bhattarai apparently rejected this association with the Magars, and distanced himself from it: 'The phobia of "guerrilla war" is haunting the reactionary ruling classes of Nepal for quite some time. That is why they have been projecting the poor, illiterate peasants of tribal Kham Magar stock of Rolpa as prospective "guerrillas" through their T.V. channels. Had that been true, ninety percent of the poor and toiling population of Nepal could be branded as prospective "guerrillas"' (interview with Dr Baburam Bhattarai, *Independent*, Kathmandu, 13–19 December 1995, p. 41 [posted on *www.maoism.org*]).

campaign, and concluded, 'those areas were not totally captured'. Another assertion made by Prachanda was that among the 'Chinese-looking oppressed minorities of the West' (clearly the Magars, although they are not named), 'there is less feudal tradition, there is a kind of democracy, of primitive democracy'.

This idea is important because it shows how Prachanda seemed to consider Magars as natural potential Maoists because of the 'primitive democracy' which prevailed among them. Other Maoist leaders went further in their references to the Magars' 'primitive communism'. For instance, Anuman (*sic*), a member of the central committee of the Magarot (*sic*) Liberation Front, said in an interview with Li Onesto, 'In Magar society, there is a primitive kind of communistic/collective way of living'. Onesto quotes him in her 'Magar Liberation' article (1999), which she begins with the following general consideration: 'In fact, the strong unity between the struggle of the oppressed Magar people and the revolution is one of the reasons these districts have become strongholds of the People's War.' So, if we combine these views, the primitive democratic and communistic Magar group is engaged in a struggle that finds resonance in the Maoist movement, and their common enemy is 'the oppressor'. For a reader familiar with Magar ethnic literature, 'the oppressor' is the Bahun and his long history of cultural (including linguistic and religious) domination of the ethnic minorities. Now, brahmanocracy (*bahunvad*) prevails in the central committee of the CPN (Maoist) just as much as it does in other parties; therefore we should examine who 'the oppressors' are for the ultra-leftist Magar ethnic activists, and how they combine the views of the two movements. For the time being, let us simply say that if Magars joined the Maoists it would be to get rid of oppression and to fight for Magar autonomy, which is what the leaders had promised them.[10]

Before examining the Magar project of autonomy and its connection with the people's war, it should be noted here that the CPN (Maoist)'s position on nationalities was severely criticised by its Indian counterparts during an international seminar on the nationality

---

[10] In fact, this is not sufficient as an explanation for the Magars' support for the CPN (Maoist) in particular, because there are other parties which advocate regional autonomy. For instance, the CPN (Masal) also advocates local autonomy (*sthaniya svayatta*), but for all the *jati*s, not only the *janajati*s (S. P. Thapa, 1999: 20).

question organised by the All-India People's Resistance Forum[11] in February 1996. The author of a report on this seminar examines two papers given by Hisila Yami,[12] and the position of the CPN (Maoist) is criticised by the Indian revolutionary author thus: 'As can be readily understood the CPN (M) rejects the right of secession of the oppressed nationalities of Nepal and substitutes in its place a demand for "autonomy"...The logic given by the CPN (M) for rejecting the right to secession for the oppressed nationalities of Nepal is that they are: "keeping in view the low level of development of the nationalities".' This position is described as a 'throwback to the view projected in the period of the Second International' and it is therefore asserted that 'the views of the AIPRF [All-India People's Resistance Forum]...stand far in advance'.[13]

While the revolutionary organisations discuss amongst themselves who may be granted secession, autonomy or self-determination on the basis of their 'development' (see footnote 13), the principal members of the secessionist MLF (Magarant Liberation Front; Magarant Mukti Morcha), do not seem to have a precise idea of what they would do if they were granted the autonomy they demand. This absence of a detailed programme may indicate that the project is not yet mature or realistic enough for it to be publicised, or that it is deliberately being kept secret.

[11] 'Report on the International Seminar on the Nationality Question' (*www.revolutionarydemocracy.org*).

[12] Yami is the president of the All Nepal Women's Association (Revolutionary) and the wife of the Maoist leader Baburam Bhattarai.

[13] The AIPRF states that the right of secession is a 'democratic right of national self-determination'. This concerns a first category of nationalities: the Kashmiris, the Assamese, the Manipuris, Nagas and Mizos, defined as 'those nationalities which, historically, have never been a part of India and were territorially annexed to the Indian Union'. A second category includes the 'relatively developed nationalities' whose bourgeoisie is in conflict with the central state; the third category embraces movements for statehood in regions characterised by uneven capitalist development (such as Uttarakhand). The nationalities that fall into these two categories should get autonomy. The AIPRF is afraid that the nationalities will not believe them because of what happened to the Tibetans and the Mongolians in China, and concludes, 'The professions of the AIPRF shall only be taken seriously if they demarcate their positions from those of the CPC and Mao Zedong just as vigorously as they have distanced themselves from the positions of the CPI and CPI (M).' By contrast, the Nepali *janajatis* never mention recent Chinese history in a critical way.

BETWEEN THE TWO MAGARANT LIBERATION FRONTS

Prachanda informed Li Onesto that numerous ethnic associations had been born from the people's war and were merely branches of the Maoist organisation. These included the Magar National Liberation Front, the Tarai National Front and the Newa Khala.[14] The link between the Magarant Liberation Front (MLF) and the Maoists was further underlined by Narendra Buda, who told Li Onesto that the MLF 'openly promotes the People's War' and 'agrees with the Maoist position and demands to participate in the revolutionary united front'.

The attentive reader will have noticed a slight difference between the names of the two Magar liberation organisations mentioned above. The first contains the word 'National', while the second does not. The two fronts are not usually clearly differentiated when they are mentioned. The Magarant Liberation Front seems to be the older of the two, and is described by its founder, Hit Bahadur Thapa Magar (1999), as 'a common political platform for all the Magars of different political ideologies so as to converge [unite] the opinions for the creation of a Magar homeland—Magarant'. It was created in 1991, long before the initiation of the people's war, but did not gain any real popularity until 1993. Indeed, an article published in February of that year[15] refers to the 'as yet unknown "Magarant Liberation Front"', which has in a recent appeal demanded the recognition by the government of a 'Magarant' state comprising the twelve districts of Tanahun, Syangja, Parvat, Myagdi, Baglung, Gulmi, Palpa, Argha-Khanci, Pyuthan, Rolpa, Rukum and Salyan. This declaration was timed to coincide with the 'Year of Indigenous Peoples'. In this first appeal, it was said that within the Magarant state 'all communities would be treated equally, irrespective of their caste and creed', but the Front's chairman, Hit Bahadur Thapa Magar, warned that if the state was not created, 'we will fight for separation'.

In fact, the map of Magarant, comprising the twelve districts listed above, had already appeared on the cover of the first issue of *Lapha*,

14. 'Many organisations among the oppressed nationalities developed after the initiation [of the people's war], like the Magar National Liberation Front' ('Red Flag Flying on the Roof of the World'). Prachanda probably meant the Magarant National Liberation Front.

15. M. R. Josse, '"Magarant" State Demanded By Liberation Front', *Independent*, Kathmandu, 17 February 1993.

dated August–October 1992. This issue did not include any article relating to Magarant, but its editorial strongly underlined the importance of the territory: 'we the sons of the earth, earth imbued by the blood, the sweat and the tears of our ancestors, which is dearer to us than our lives…' This map was reproduced in the second issue of the same journal without further comment, but a letter to the editors about the map published in issue 1 appeared in issue 2. This argued that the territory should be extended to include Dolpa, Jajarkot, Surkhet, Dang, Nawalparasi and Gorkha. The very same map was reproduced once again in issue 3, along with an article on the demand for an autonomous province of Magarant which mentioned a publication by Hit Bahadur Thapa Magar dated January 1993. Hit Bahadur was presented as the *adhyaksha* (chairman) of the MLF in this third issue of *Lapha*, and again in the same journal in 1998.[16] One reference to ethnic liberation fronts in 1991[17] may allude to the MLF. Although Hit Bahadur's MLF was not mentioned in the newspapers until 1993, in his preface to Hit Bahadur's book, *Magarant Itihas*, published in 1994, Gopal Khambu wrote, 'I met H. B. Thapa at the meeting of the editors' forum two years ago…And one year before [our meeting], my friend had created the Magarant Liberation Front.' From this, we can conclude that the organisation was created

[16] Hit Bahadur Thapa Magar also published *An Introduction to Kham Magaranti Language* in 1993. The foreword to this book is signed by Lok Bahadur Thapa Magar, who later founded the Magarant *National* Liberation Front. Hit Bahadur thanks him as one of several friends who have helped him with his book. The text on the back cover, attributed to Pradip Thapa, provides more detail on the book's author. Born in 1961 (2018 v.s.) in Rolpa district, he studied English and journalism in India. Back in Nepal, he published articles in *Connection, Kathmandu Review* and *Spotlight* and edited the English weekly *Outcry*. In 1993 he is described as a member of the Nepal Editors' Forum and of the central committee of the Nepal Magar Sangh, and he is said to be fighting for the provincial autonomy of the historical territory of the Magars. Hit Bahadur Thapa Magar is the editor of *Pracin Nepalko itihasma Magar asakharu*, a booklet written by Jayabahadur Hitan Magar and Pradip Thapa Magar, and published by Sorathi Prakashan, Magarant. On the back cover, the MLF's slogan reads: 'Let us protect the soil of the Magarant for the development of the Magaranti language, script, culture, religion and history.'

[17] On the establishment of the United People's Front in 1991, the *Revolutionary Worker* records, 'Enthusiastic responses to the People's War from different Organisations for the Liberation of Nationalities and from prominent individuals has brightened the prospects of building such a front' ('One year of People's War in Nepal' *Revolutionary Worker*, 911, 15 June 1997).

in 1991. In his book, Hit Bahadur specifies, 'The goal of the MLF is to establish an autonomous Magarant government, invested with every right except those relating to the army, foreign relations and money.' He urges Magar intellectuals to adopt a clear conduct regarding autonomy and states that it is precisely the writings of these intellectuals, namely Gore Bahadur Khapangi, Suresh Ale Magar, M. S. Thapa and Jayabahadur Hitan, which led him to create the MLF. He further adds that in the absence of such a programme, 'they would have wasted their time'. More than a mere project of regional autonomy, Hit Bahadur's programme is a real decolonisation: 'Just as the socialist leader Mao Zedong has chased away the Japanese from China, and the democrat Mahatma Gandhi the British from India, now the autochthonous Magar must utter this slogan: "Hindus, leave the Magarant".'

In 1993, Hit Bahadur and Lok Bahadur Thapa Magar were both members of the Nepal Magar Sangh and apparently good friends. Both of them were members of the advisory board of *Lapha* at its creation. But Hit Bahadur did not last long: he is not mentioned from issue 6 (1993) onward, whereas Lok Bahadur has remained in this position to date. As a matter of fact, after 1993 *Lapha* remained silent on the Magarant question until issue 18/19, published in 1999. We may suspect that a split occurred between two factions among the Magar activists, which would explain these six years of silence.

In issue 18/19 an excerpt from a text[18] about Magarant was published without comment. It reproduced a map of the Magarant territory, which included twenty-one districts, (namely Dailekh, Surkhet, Jajarkot, Salyan, Rukum, Dolpa, Rolpa, Pyuthan, Dang, Argha-Khanci, Kapilavastu, Gulmi, Baglung, Myagdi, Parbat, Syangja, Palpa, Rupandehi, Nawalparasi, Tanahun and Gorkha) as well as twenty-two demands from the Magarant Liberation Front. These included the replacement of the 1990 Constitution with a federal constitution: Magarant would be one of the nations within this federation. In this new state, only those of Magar or indigenous blood would be granted membership and the right to vote. Only one party—the MLF— would be allowed within it, and 'only Magars would be allowed to

---

[18] 'The Question of Magar Homeland Magarant', *Lapha*, 18/19, 1999, pp. 17–19. The author of this text, which I have not yet been able to consult, is not given and may be Hit Bahadur Thapa Magar.

function as leaders of any political party[19] within the state... all non-Magars and non-indigenous outsiders should leave the Magarant Nation (State) for the good of all.' Against the background of this very uncompromising programme, point 18 reads ironically: 'We demand the abolition of international and national racial, economic and political imperialism in Nepal.' Two major questions arise from a reading of this text. First, after six years of silence on the question of Magarant, one wonders why *Lapha* published this very radical text. Was it a sign that old companions had been reincorporated within the group at a time when radicalism seemed to pay dividends because of its popularity, or was it a kind of scarecrow intended to frighten off moderate readers? And why did the editors of this journal choose to present the view of Hit Bahadur's Magarant Liberation Front to coincide precisely with the publication by Lok Bahadur, the founder of a rival organisation and a member of the editorial board of the journal, of a book in which he presented his own views on Magarant?

The Magarant National Liberation Front (MNLF) published Lok Bahadur Thapa Magar's book in 1999/2000.[20] The author's point of view was radically Marxist, the method was historical materialism, and the thinkers quoted were Stalin, Lenin, Marx and Mao. A fresco of the different stages in the history of Magarant shows a first period when property and borders were unknown, and during which the Magar group, described as a 'primitive ethnic group' (*adim jati*) was formed. The second step is marked by the introduction of shifting agriculture, hunting and fishing. The Magars are presented as still very attached to this stage, as shown by their present slash and burn practices in the Mahabharat hills and their keen taste for hunting

[19] Despite the statement that immediately precedes this, the possibility that parties other than the MLF might exist is already envisaged in this programme, as is clear from the use of 'any'. In any case, this point would disqualify the actual political leaders of the Maoist movement, who are not Magars.

[20] Beside this book, this author wrote several articles on the autonomy of Magarant, but they do not contain important additional information. The Magarant National Liberation Front published another book by Lok Bahadur Thapa Magar (1999/2000a), who was the secretary of the Nepal Magar Sangh central committee from its creation in 1991 and an adviser to Magar journals such as *Lapha, Kanung Lam* and *Janajati Manch*. In 1992 and 1993, Lok Bahadur published several articles on the Magar language, and had already identified regional autonomy as one tool with which to counter the linguistic domination and unification of Nepal.

and fishing (Thapa Magar 1999/2000a: 2–3). A third stage is characterised by the domestication of animals and the development of villages. At this time the Magarant was formed: it was not ruled by a
single chief but by several headmen and it was divided into two regions, the Bahra (twelve) Magarant in the east and the Athara (eighteen) Magarant in the west (ibid.: 8). Then the cunning Aryans fled
from India, invaded Magarant and Sanskritised the Magars (ibid.: 4).
People of high caste took the good lands and forced the Magars to
cultivate the steep slopes and live in the heights. In order to control
them more easily, some of the Magars were given the high positions
of *mukhiya* (headman) and *pujari* (priest) (ibid.: 20).

Lok Bahadur continues his analysis on the basis of statistics from
the 1991 national census. He notes that the Magar population exceeded 50,000 individuals in eight districts (namely, in descending
order of importance: Palpa, Rolpa, Nawalparasi, Tanahun, Baglung,
Syangja, Gulmi and Pyuthan) where a total of 42.5 per cent of the
Magar population lived (ibid.: 24). Despite the large number of Magars
living in the plains, the 'project' is to leave the plain, and 'take' only
the mountainous region (ibid.: 25). The author then correlates the
Magar population data with linguistic data and shows that many
more Magars speak their language in the east (Morang 72 per cent,
Tanahun 66, Sindhuli 65, Nawalparasi 62, Syangja 61, and Palpa 55 per
cent) than in the west (in this region, except in Rolpa where 19 per cent
of the Magar population declare themselves to be Magar-speaking,
the percentages are indeed very low: Pyuthan 3.45, Rukum 0.94,
Gulmi 0.64, Myagdi 0.24, and so on.) The author logically concluded
from these statistics that Kham[21] was disappearing, unlike Magaranti.

Using a combination of historical, linguistic and statistical elements, the author draws a map of Magarant, confessing that it is not
an easy task because the Magars are so scattered. This is why he

---

[21] Despite the small number of Kham speakers, the government realised that it was
important to reach them: 'In what is seen as a strategic move on part of [*sic*] the government, the state-owned Radio Nepal has started airing news in two more local languages, Doteli and Kham Magar, beginning Friday. With this, the number of
languages in which programmes are being broadcast has reached 17…While transmission in Doteli will target the audiences in far-western Nepal, the Kham Magar language transmission will target ethnic Magar community residing in Maoist-affected
mid-western hills. Reports say, hundreds of youths belonging to Magar community
have been recruited by the underground party to serve in their "People's Army"'
(*Daily News*, 24 June 2000).

distinguishes between several different Magarant territories: two main regions (the Kali Gandaki Autonomous Region in the east and the Rapti Dhaulagiri Autonomous Region in the west) as well as several other autonomous areas. Each of the two main regions covers six districts (Palpa, Syangja, Navalparasi, Tanahun, Parvat and Gorkha in the east; Rolpa, Rukum, Pyuthan, Gulmi, Baglung, Myagdi in the west). This territorial balance is striking and may be designed to ensure good relations between the two groups. The geographical and human characteristics of each region are then enumerated by the author, who insists that the best irrigated lands of the numerous valleys of the eastern region belong to the high castes, although he does not say what will happen to them after the creation of Magarant (ibid.: 53). He notes in passing that the contrasting settlements of the Magars (dense villages on the middle slopes) and the high castes (scattered villages in the valley bottoms) are related for the former to the primitive stage and for the latter to the stage of slavery, leaving readers free to draw their own conclusions (ibid.: 54). He advocates a return to self-sufficiency: this is to include the exploitation of local mines and the cultivation of cotton, in order to get rid of Indian imperialism (ibid.: 57).

When he turns to the characteristics of the western region, Lok Bahadur Thapa Magar clearly reveals his sympathy for the Maoists. This territory is described as 'backward and remote', but as having experienced important changes since the initiation of the people's war:

In the districts of Rolpa and Rukum, old superstitions and conventions [*purano andhavishvas, rurhivadi*], and bad customs [*kuriti ra kupratha*] have been suppressed. The banning of alcoholic drink, of dice and card games, of violent marriages has brought a great change. Having abandoned the old traditions, culture and customs which were useless [*purana kam nalagne ritithiti, parampara ra samskriti*], a popular, scientific and modern [*janavadi, vaigyanik, adhunik*] culture has developed.

It seems that the author distinguishes between a bad and a good deculturation: these are, respectively, Hinduisation and Maoisation. As a matter of fact, the latter is especially good for the backward and remote territory of the west, whereas the preservation of the original culture seems to be more of an imperative in the eastern part.

The creation of the smaller autonomous regions is presented as a less urgent matter: '*It would be possible* to create autonomous *ilaka* [areas], like Tarakot in Dolpa and Udayapur' (ibid.: 73; emphasis added).[22] According to the author, it might be possible to create autonomous villages, and even hamlets. However, nothing is said about the fate of the non-Magar population of Magarant, and the book is not very informative about the practical conditions under which it would be possible to create the autonomous territory.[23] On the other hand, the political views of the author clearly show his dual inspiration, which is also true of the other ultra-leftist Magar activists. The official political parties and their leaders are all described as oppressors and exploiters of the people (ibid.: 30).[24] Alongside this very common opinion, it is interesting to see that the author also condemns those among the Magars who have internalised the logic of the parties (ibid.: 31). Lok Bahadur Thapa Magar seems to be caught between two fires: on the one hand, he expresses that it is very painful for him to see Magars having the same discourse as *bahunvadi*s (ibid.: 32), thus revealing his very sensitive *jati* identity, but on the other hand he criticises those who think only in terms of *jati*— which is a surprising declaration in a book intended to promote ethnic autonomy.

This trend, the author adds, is important within the Nepal Magar Sangh, whose members are nationalists. Lok Bahadur expresses it clearly: 'The Magars are exploited by the "high Hindus", but *janajati*s may also exploit the others, or Magars other Magars.' He thus seems to advocate solidarity between exploited persons within the same *jati* in a way that combines class and ethnicity as factors. In his view, one *jati* can contain two classes: the oppressor and the oppressed.

[22] The creation of these two autonomous *ilaka* reflects the symbolic importance they possess for Magar ethnic activists. The Magars of Dolpa, although amounting to only 3,000 persons in the 1991 census, are mentioned frequently in the ethnic literature because of their 'named language', Kaike (declared as their mother-tongue by fewer than ten individuals in the 1991 census), and the fact that they are Buddhists. Kaike is always presented as one of the three Magar languages, and some go as far as asking for radio news to be broadcast in Kaike. As for the district of Udayapur, Lok Bahadur Thapa Magar describes it as a 'model' because 80 % of its Magar population declared their language to be Magar in 1991.

[23] However, we learn that the territory will be independent in all matters except currency, army and foreign relations (p. 44), exactly as already stated by Hit Bahadur Thapa Magar.

[24] He adds (p. 37): 'All the parties made a tail [*puchar*] or a weapon of the Magar *jati*.'

If we compare this programme with Hit Bahadur's, we can first say that it is more ambiguous, because nothing is said about the fate of the non-Magar inhabitants of Magarant, whereas it is clear to Hit Bahadur that they should be expelled. In fact, this position does not fit with the 'unity of the oppressed' advocated by Lok Bahadur. Neither does Lok Bahadur say what the fate of the exploiters, and particularly of the Magar exploiters, will be if Magarant is created. Another difference between the programmes of these two liberation fronts concerns the territorial basis of the autonomous Magar country: while Hit Bahadur sees it as a unique territory which would unite different groups of Magar, Lok Bahadur advocates the formation of two distinct territories which would reinforce the differences between the western Magars, who are speakers of the Kham language, and the eastern Magars, who speak Magaranti dialects. This is an important difference. Indeed, in political terms, both fronts seem to be revolutionary and close or affiliated to the Maoists, and their main ideological difference seems to concern the notion of territory, and thereby their conception of the Magar group. In the only article I have found that deals with the two Magarant liberation fronts (Vijaya Ale Magar 1999/2000), this aspect is underlined and deplored. The author first defends the 'neutral' position of the Nepal Magar Sangh, which is described as 'based on blood relations' and which therefore cannot and should not have any party political engagement. The author explains that if the Magars are in fact divided regarding national politics, all of them share the same blood and their main concern is a common one: the search for a politics which would put an end to their oppression and exploitation. For the author, the answer is the creation of an autonomous territory, which is the goal of the Magarant Liberation Front. This latter organisation would have 'fraternal relations' with the Nepal Magar Sangh. But the author deplores the existence of two Magarant liberation fronts, the first led by Hit Bahadur Thapa Magar, the Magarant Mukti Morcha (MLF) and the other by Lok Bahadur Thapa Magar, the Magarant Rastriya Mukti Morcha (MNLF). The first is probably more active in Dang, the second in various districts of the Gandaki, Rapti and Dhaulagiri zones. The MNLF is likely to be stronger than the MLF, from an organisational point of view. Despite the author's pleas to the two fronts to unite now or remain ineffectual, their distinct territorial base certainly reveals the temporary nature of the regrouping of the various Magar organisations within the frame of the Nepal Magar Sangh. If this split occurred within the context of the Maoist guerrilla movement then, interestingly, it was apparently over the question of territory and not because of any political divergence.

Whatever the relations may be between the two fronts, and despite the vagueness of their programmes, we note that the Magarant Liberation Front[25] became a more tangible reality on the occasion of the creation of and elections to the Rolpa 21 Village Development Committee (VDC) people's local government which were held in April 2001 and whose results were announced in May. Indeed, the nineteen-member committee in charge of local government was headed by Santosh Budha, a Magar member of the CPN (Maoist) central committee, but also included representative(s?) of the MLF (Ujir Magar 2001). Although this is not specified, it is probably the *National* Front to which reference is being made here. Indeed, if the written production of the two fronts does not show their differences clearly, oral interviews with Magars from Dang indicate that only the National Front is affiliated with the Maoists and promotes violent action. A person who attended a meeting of the Magarant National Liberation Front in Dang in summer 2001 described it in these terms:

'The meeting was held in a private house. In one room, several Dalits were gathered. The Magars occupied another room. Akash, a Magar area commander, addressed the audiences in both rooms, one after the other. He told us about the creation of Magarant, and told us that we should fight for it with the Maoist forces. He asked us if we had bullets since they did have not enough of them.'

About the Magarant Liberation Front, this person reported:

'Hit Bahadur says he does not want to fight with the Maoists, he says: "Let them fight and lose, afterwards I will create Magarant." He is less popular among the Magars of Dang, because he is considered a normal person. ['What do you mean by normal?'] 'I mean that he does not advocate that people should fight, so people are not attracted by him.'

---

[25] Information on the membership of the Magarant Liberation Front is scarce: a certain Ramesh Thapa Magar of the 'Magarat Freedom Front' participated in a programme organised by the Research Centre for Indigenous and Ethnic Issues on 2 January 2000 in Biratnagar (*Rising Nepal*, 3 January 2000). He also wrote an introduction to Lok Bahadur Thapa Magar (1999/2000b). Suresh Ale Magar is presented as the *adhyaksa* of the MLF in *Janadesh*, 2 October 2001.

Although I focus here on the Magarant liberation fronts, in fact several similar fronts are sympathetic or related to the Maoists and approve of their actions. For instance, in February 1999 it was reported that 'The decision of Maoists to actively boycott the polls, has been welcomed by different ethnic parties like Khambuwan Freedom Front, Limbuwan Freedom Front, Tamang Ghedung Association, Magarat Freedom Front, etc.'[26] And from the UML's point of view, 'Their daydream is to build up a federation of ethnic states (*rajya*) by creating a state for each of the Nepalese groups' (Communist Party of Nepal [UML] 2001). Besides, several regional liberation fronts[27] support the CPN (Maoist) in the same manner.

THE VIEWS OF MAGAR ACTIVISTS AND INTELLECTUALS

In 1999, several articles were written by Magars which dealt with their group's relationship with Maoism. Two by Surendra Thapa Magar are notable. In an article entitled 'Maoist Popular War and the Magars' (1999: 5–6) he compares Maoism with a disease (*rog*). He then attributes the significant participation of the Magars in the people's war to their oppression, and seems to be afraid of the new image that the Magar group may project: 'the autochthonous Magar group *is still* frank [*sojho*] and loyal [*imandar*]' (emphasis added). For this author, the Maoists have utilised the Magars' oppressed status to provide impetus for the people's war by demanding self-government for the *janajati*s. This, says the author, must be considered as 'a *trick* by the Maoists'. This war is in fact a war against the Magars, who are the main victims of both sides. Popular tribunals punish them with amputations. The other side kills them or puts them in jail. He proposes that the government should take action for the rights of the *janajati*s, in order to put an end to the people's war. In a later issue of the same journal, the same author's views seem to have changed slightly (S. Thapa Magar 2000: 5–6). He writes that people resort to the Maoists for justice, because the governmental institu-

---

[26] *Spotlight*, 12–18 February, 1999, p. 30, excerpt from *Nepalipatra*, 5 February.

[27] Among them, the Karnali Liberation Front published a booklet on its programme in 1992 (Lal Bahadur 1992/3). Its objective is the restoration and autonomy of King Bali's territories: Mugu, Humla, Dolpo, Jumla, Kalikot and a part of Bajura. It is worthy of note that this apparently Khas liberation front has chosen a territorial label for itself.

tions are corrupt: 'Whenever someone suffers injustice he does not go to the governmental court of justice anymore. He takes refuge in the Maoists. Why?...[Because] justice is expensive.' Moreover, the police oppress the people, and so 'the only way to get free from all these injustices is the Maoist People's War'. If the police continue to kill innocent people in ignominious ways, 'we too may turn into Maoists'.

These two contrasting discourses from the same author are quoted not as an example of a specific person's intellectual evolution, but to show a clear example of a rather general state of indecision among Magars and other *janajati*s, over the choice between two possible bases of grouping for action: ethnicity and class. This hesitation parallels the apparent pendulum movement among some Magars (and others) between condemning and supporting the Maoists, depending on the context.

B. K. Rana (2001b) seems to fish in the same troubled waters. For him,[28] it is not fitting to apply the government's label of 'terrorists' to the Maoists, because the present ruling party also wielded arms in the past.[29] Thus, he does not distinguish between different kinds of revolts, i.e. against an oligarchy or against a democracy.[30] For him, the Magars are portrayed as villains in the pages of history and have remained deprived of all opportunities to serve the country. 'On being insulted by the "government officials" the Magars of Rolpa started a rebellion. Then Maoist leaders went to command them [and] exploited the situation' (ibid.). He considers, as do many other Magar ethnic activists, that the Maoists 'are "using" Magars as King Prithvi Narayan Shah "used" Magars to unify a number of principalities'.[31]

[28] B. K. Rana wrote a book on the history of the Magars of Gorkha as well as several articles, some of which are collected in Rana (1999/2000).
[29] Some Nepali commentators often treat different kinds of rebellions alike. See, for instance, B. Kaucha Magar (1998/9), who compares the suppression of Lakhan Thapa's rebellion with the Maoist rebellion.
[30] The same remark may be made about the very interesting article written by Deepak Thapa (2001) who reminds the Maoists in his conclusion that revolutions do not generate democracies. It would perhaps be more appropriate to remark that it is dangerous to import an ideology and apply it to a democracy when the ideology is one that was constructed long ago in reaction to very different systems, and which led to atrocities and injustice in its turn.
[31] See, for instance, the concerns of an intellectual of the Magar Association Hong Kong 'over Magars who live in the West of Nepal entering into jungles for violence

On the other hand, however, he seems to think that the Maoists also serve the Magars' cause: 'They are campaigning against "compulsory Sanskrit education" in schools and we support this. They also seem prepared to offer autonomy to the indigenous peoples. It is also fine, however, we do not know how they are going to do so.'[32] Despite his doubts about the modalities under which autonomy may be set up by the Maoists, and perhaps about what final share the Magars will get if the Maoists succeed, it is obvious from his last remark that this author sees support coming from the people's war.[33] This question of the reciprocal support between the Maoists and the *janajati*s is presented in a reverse way by Chitra K. Tiwari (n.d.): 'more and more persons from *janajati* people…are joining the ranks of Maoist insurgency in the hope that they will be "emancipated" from the "clutches" of BCN [i.e. Bahun-Chetri-Newar]…it is not clear whether these *janajati*s will remain loyal to Maoist cause in the aftermath of the success of Maoist "People's War".'

Thus, both Surendra Thapa Magar and B. K. Rana oscillate between the concern that ethnicity is being exploited by the Maoists and the feeling that the Maoists are helping realise a quest, though the pace is fast and should be more under *janajati* control. This is even true of the leader of the Nepal Magar Sangh, Gore Bahadur Khapangi, according to S. Pradhan (1999): 'Some fear the Maoists could link up with the disgruntled ethnic minorities. Gore Bahadur Khapangi, a low caste leader [*sic*] of a minority group, recently denied links with the Maoists. But under further questioning, he admitted to being ideologically close to them.'

We have seen that B. K. Rana suggests that the Magars were used in the people's war in the same way that they were used during the

---

after being confused by enticement of the clever men' or the same parallel drawn by B. K. Rana between the use of the Magars by Prithvi Narayan and the Maoists: 'It is a strange coincidence that the hotbed of the present insurgency is centred in the erstwhile state of Magrat…, once part of the Gurkha kingdom ruled by King Prithvinarayan Shah. He too, waged a war against Kathmandu and united Nepal' (Mehta: 2000).

[32] Interestingly, these last sentences do not appear in a very similar article by B. K. Rana published simultaneously in *Kathmandu Post* (2001a).

[33] Other ethnic liberation fronts advance the same considerations. Thus, Bir Nemwang, president of the Limbuwan Liberation Front said: 'If they [the Maoists] support our cause (for autonomy) we thank them. But we have no relations with them' (*Samakalin*, 4 February, quoted in *Spotlight*, 12–18 February 1999).

unification of Nepal: as good warriors forming an army behind non-Magar leaders, for a final purpose which is foreign to them. This analogy is also frequently found, but in a positive version, in Maoist writings: 'When leading his expedition to extend his kingdom, Prithvi Narayan Shah went ahead by establishing local power in the villages and finally encircled the city, a strategy which appears to be the same as the Maoist tactic' (Yami 1997/8: 32). It seems in fact that Yami is describing the Maoists' tactics rather than Prithvi Narayan's, but her article shows that his unification is a model for the Maoist leaders who have apparently based their future success on this famous strategic and military triumph. They have also used it for their own legitimacy, and they present themselves as the continuation of the Shah dynasty—two allusions which are certainly not lost on the Magars, who see in the military operations of the unification of Nepal their major contribution to the history of Nepal.

For the non-revolutionary Magar thinkers, nationality or *jati* is the more appropriate basis of group formation. Thus, when asked if it is more legitimate to think in terms of nationality or class, the leader of the Nepal Magar Sangh, Gore Bahadur Khapangi (1996/7: 26), answers that the *jati* is more ancient than class, and that the liberation of class would not solve the specific problems of the Magars in terms of their culture, language and religion. Viewing the group as a set of people sharing the same blood, culture, language and religion may well lead to the idea of autonomy. In their writings, the Magars often present themselves as refugees in their own land, and compare themselves to endangered species. They ask that their 'original' culture and language should receive the same protection from the government as wild animals or plants,[34] which, as a matter of fact, benefit from the seventeen per cent of Nepali territory which consists of restricted areas.[35] This very naturalistic view of a cultural group, with not its physical but its cultural existence perceived as threatened, clearly reveals the nature of the *jati*.

Opposed to this stress on the *jati* grouping, which is by far the most common view among the Magars and others, the Maoist ideologues describe their society as formed of classes, and in the main they distinguish only two: the oppressors, and the oppressed. It is difficult to

[34] For an expression of this commonly-held view, see S. Thapa Magar (1999?: 26).
[35] I am grateful to Joëlle Smadja for this statistical information.

determine from their writings whether they are referring to economic or social classes, since both views are commonly found. Moreover, the problem of the transposition of a class model onto the Nepali caste system is not resolved, since, for instance, poor Bahuns are often ranked among the oppressed class despite their high status, as well as people from 'backward and remote regions', whatever their local position and relations with their neighbours might be. For the Maoist thinkers, the fact that Nepali society is composed of classes is first of all a postulate, an axiom, a reality which is not discussed, as can be seen for instance in the first sentences of a press communiqué written by Prachanda (1998/9a): 'the great process of the People's War is based on the following scientific principle: "In a class-divided society, everything is an illusion except state power".'

Let us now examine why some Magars have chosen the communist path instead of the ethnic one, apparently to achieve the same goals as those who believe in *jati*-based action: getting rid of oppression and exploitation, and preserving their culture and dignity. In the writings of the Maoist and Magar activist Suresh Ale Magar, both ethnic and economic factors are highlighted in the reasoning that communism helps the poor in both sectors (see Suresh Ale Magar 1997/8, S. Thapa Magar 1999: 26). More frequently, the reason why the Magars are told to join the CPN (Maoist) is to avoid communalism, which is considered as a great sin across the whole political spectrum.[36] This idea has been internalised by some Magars, and notably by the communists. Thus, for instance, following tautological reasoning, Balkrishna Kaucha Magar (2000/1) claims that only the Marxists should express the grievances of the ethnic movement, because the Magars should not yield to communalism, which is severely condemned by the Marxist thinkers as the 'most risky fighting'. 'This is why only Marxism can solve the ethnic problems.'

Resham Sris Magar (2000/1) expresses similar views: if all the members of a caste or an ethnic group oppose all the members of another, then a movement shall be called communalist. But, in fact, the exploiters on both sides do cooperate, and communalist movements thus always protect and help the exploiters. So the exploited among the *janajati* must all join together and ask for self-determination,

---

[36] For some examples, a discussion of the condemnation of ethnic communalism by the government, and some Magar answers to it, see Lecomte-Tilouine (2002).

which alone can bring them equality. Now this is the aim of the Maoists, who have understood that the only means of reaching this self-
determination is autonomy. Lok Bahadur Thapa Magar (1999/2000b:
7) goes further. For him, the need for a separate ethnic state (*rajya*)
depends on the form of exploitation and oppression. If there were
neither exploitation nor oppression, the right to self-determination
and to territorial autonomy would be meaningless. He remarks that
while exploitation and oppression exist all over Nepal, among high
caste groups this is economic, whereas the *janajati*s are oppressed in
cultural, economical and religious terms (ibid.: 9). This is why ethnic
demands are included within class struggle. For him, it is erroneous
to support ethnic demands while fighting the notion of class, as does
the Rastriya Janamukti Party, i.e. 'the circle of M. S. Thapa'. For this
party, created by the leader of the Nepal Magar Sangh, the fight for
granting of territorial autonomy would result in the destruction of
Nepal, and it is therefore a communalist fight. 'It is ridiculous,' asserts
Lok Bahadur Thapa Magar, 'that those who work for the liberation
of their *jati* oppose the right to self-determination' (ibid.: 47). In
short, he asks: given the two types of ethnic movements, which kind
should be opposed and which should be supported? Stalin and
Marx provide the answer: the reactionary and imperialist movements
should be opposed. It is not necessary to state it, because it is clear to
everyone, he says: some ethnic activists are in fact in the service of
the Bahuns, they eat the *jutho* (leftovers) of their rice meals and they
use *janajati*s as a ladder for their personal promotion (ibid.: 59). For
this reason, the *janajati*s should join together with the oppressed
people to construct Mao's supreme unity. In which case, we may
wonder why the Magars should be granted a specific autonomous
territory and why Lok Bahadur Thapa Magar is not fighting for the
autonomy of a kind of 'oppressed land'?

Prachanda recently stated:[37] 'It is not essential that a person be-
longs to a *jat*, what is essential is his thinking [*bichar*].'[38] This recalls

[37] The leader gave this talk during the first meeting of the Madheshi Mukti Morcha
(Madesi Liberation Front) held in Sarlahi in August 2001. Representatives of several
organisations were present, among them Suresh Ale Magar (chairman of the
Magarant Liberation Front).

[38] This kind of statement recalls the fate of the autonomous territories created for
the minorities of Northern Vietnam. During the First National Congress in 1935,
minorities were granted the right to create separate states, but when inaugurating the

the story of the cat pretending to become an ascetic in order to catch and eat mice more easily, which is popular among the Magars.

A member of the Nepal Magar Sangh interviewed by Li Onesto (1999) expressed it thus:

> If a New Democratic government gives Magars equality and opportunity in every aspect, they will not demand a separate autonomy but will participate in the New Democratic government. They are hopeful that the Maoists will give the Magar people equality…and will not be compelled to make a separate nation.

This 'new democratic' government refers to the Maoist government. Thus it seems that the demand for autonomy is conditional on complete equality and participation in the government, but the only formation mentioned as capable of giving this is the CPN (Maoist). This would partially explain why the project of an autonomous Magar territory has been so vague until now, and somehow contradictory.

In the same way that Sanskritisation created or reinforced a split among the Magars of the Gulmi area, resulting in the contrasting status and attitudes of the *bhaisi khane* and the *bhaisi nakhane* (buffalo-meat eaters and non-buffalo-meat eaters), the powerful Maoist ideology, based on terror, seems to have had a strong effect on the group. I gained an impression of the operative dimension of Maoism when one of my Magar friends from Gulmi told me that he had left his first wife because she had become a Maoist. Although this was far from being the true reason, it was revealing that this argument could be presented as a justification of the breaking of an alliance.[39] This may indicate that supporting or rejecting Maoism can have the same effect, on marital alliances for instance, to those of Hinduisation inside the Magar group: in the past, the breaking of an alliance could be explained in terms of the breaking of Hindu rules. In the same way, it

---

creation of the first autonomous region in 1955, Ho Chi Minh specified: 'The Thai-Meo Autonomous Region…will always enjoy the education and the leadership of the Party' (Michaud 2000: 357–8).

[39] Another more striking example of the operative aspect of Maoist ideology on the behaviour of Magar guerrillas can be read in Uma Bhujel's account of her escape from a jail in Gorkha: 'We started digging the tunnel on Mao's anniversary on Paush 11, and we planned to finish it on the anniversary of the People's War' ('Kamyunist andolanma', *Janajati Manch*, 5, 1, n.d., p. 18).

appeared to me that the first signs of internal dissension among Magar ethnic activists and intellectuals were linked to Maoism.

For an external observer, Magar written production showed very strong group solidarity at the beginning of the 1990s. At that time, the demand for an autonomous Magar territory appeared as a pleasing but totally unrealistic idea and its main demands were religious and linguistic. Operation Romeo in Rolpa, followed by the initiation of the people's war and its promise of autonomy for the nationalities, politicised the Magar ethnic activists and shattered their unity, dividing them into two wings: the unitarists and the autonomists. I have presented the available written production of the latter, who are openly affiliated to the Maoists, and I have shown how they try to reconcile ethnicity with class ideology. This dilemma, which parallels the more general Magar irresolution between criticising and endorsing the Maoist movement, is in fact apparent in most recent Magar writings. There is a balance between the contradictions apparent among the two wings of Magar activists: one is fighting against communalism while demanding ethnic territorial autonomy, which is itself a fulfilment of communalism; and the other views communalism as a kind of self-defence of the oppressed groups (the *janajati*), and considers a specific Magar action to be legitimate, but is none the less unitarist. Both wings are engaged in a kind of 'freedom' movement, but while this is conceived as a physical decolonisation of a specific territory for the former, as shown by the first slogan of the Magar Liberation Front ('Hindus leave the Magarat'), it is idealistic and institutional for the latter, who aim at an equal treatment of all groups within the present Nepali state.

This relationship between social activism and the Maoist movement is certainly not unique to the group studied here. Each social group has experienced a different history and has responded to the advent of the people's war in its own way. For a numerous, heterogeneous and scattered group like the Magars, ethnic autonomy is fundamentally utopian in nature and thus much more revolutionary than it would be in other contexts. The elaboration of its ideal realisation implies the acceptance of revolutionary ideas and actions, such as huge forced population displacement and the appropriation of land, and avoids mention of the internal problems of the composite group thus unified.

POSTSCRIPT

Since this article was written in November 2001, two major events relating to the Magars have taken place: on 11 October 2002, Gore Bahadur Khapangi, the president of the Nepal Magar Sangh, was appointed by the king as minister of women, children and social welfare, and on 1 January 2003 the Maoist activist and founder of the Magarant National Liberation Front surrendered to the authorities: two signs of the reinforced role of the Magars in formal politics.

DEMOCRACY AND DUPLICITY

THE MAOISTS AND THEIR INTERLOCUTORS IN NEPAL*

Pratyoush Onta

'*Duplicity*: The quality of being deceitful in manner or conduct; the practice of being two-faced, of dishonestly acting in two opposing ways; deceitfulness; double-dealing' (*The New Shorter Oxford English Dictionary*, 1993).

Some time in the early 1990s, some graduates of the 1981 class (to which I belong) from St Xavier's High School, Jawalakhel, met for a reunion in Kathmandu. One of my closest friends in school had in the meantime become a medical doctor. While his achievements in high school had been rather modest, he had surprised himself and the rest of us with some notable successes in medical school. Most of the get-together was taken up by his sermons to us lesser mortals who had chosen to specialise in subjects other than physiology. Among his long monologue, one bit stuck in my memory: 'If you can figure out the causes and consequences of diabetes in a patient,' he said, 'you will have mastered medical science to a large extent.' As we discuss the Maoist movement in Nepal, I am reminded of his words.

It is not clear if knowledge of the aetiology and pathological consequences of diabetes is central to one's grasp of human medical science. My friend's saying is appropriate not because he might have been right; but because it can be customised for another context: 'If you can figure out the full causes, career and consequences of the

* I am grateful to David Gellner, Michael Hutt and other participants of the SOAS conference in early November 2001 for constructive feedback on an earlier version of this chapter. The ideas here were developed during conversations with many people. While all of them cannot be individually thanked, I must mention Krishna Hachhethu, C. K. Lal, Rama Parajuli, Ramesh Parajuli, Hari Roka, Khagendra Sangraula, Sudheer Sharma and Deepak Thapa. Any shortcomings are mine alone.

Maoist movement in Nepal, you have mastered knowledge about contemporary Nepali history and society.' Personally, I cannot claim such expertise. The Maoist movement almost seems beyond comprehension in terms of its details. This lack of understanding partially derives from the nature of the movement, which draws strength from guarding its own information, while strategically using propaganda to obfuscate. Hence, only some of its broad contours are within the grasp of analysts.

This chapter has a modest aim. It provides a somewhat personal reading of the linkages between some noteworthy features of post-1990 Nepali politics and society and the growth of the Maoist movement in Nepal. In particular, the first section, by extending a line of argument first proposed by Shah (2001a), argues that pervasive conditions of duplicity provided fertile ground for the growth of the Maoist movement as a determined, dictatorial and violent one. Brief details of the political, commercial and 'civil society' worlds in Nepal are provided as ethnographic contexts for this argument. The duplicity present in the operational dynamics of these separate but connected worlds of social Nepal impeded democratic growth and facilitated the triumph of the Maoists. The second section examines the work of two of the major non-Maoist interpretive communities of the Maoist movement. In particular, I consider the interlocution between the Maoists on the one hand and the mainstream Nepali media and left intellectuals on the other, to show how the Maoists and their others fought over representations of Nepali realities.

Written in my capacity as a Nepali social commentator and discussion programme host, the intent of this chapter is more to generate an informed and engaging discussion of the themes explored here than to be academically proper. In contrast to my earlier work in the discipline of history, the present arguments are made at a general level, and are documented less obsessively. It must be stressed that the examples presented below are from personal experiences in Kathmandu. Whereas the tendencies outlined are the dominant ones, exceptions to them do exist as scattered fragments of hope. This analysis pertains to the period prior to the State of Emergency, which was imposed in Nepal in late November 2001.

PERVASIVE DUPLICITY AND MAOIST GROWTH

Political Sector Duplicity

The view that if minor legal transgressions are ignored in a new democracy they eventually grow to paralyse the entire society finds resonance in Nepal's experience since 1990. When the movement-oriented political groups of the Panchayat era turned themselves into political parties, they failed to build their institutions in democratic ways. While almost all of them mouthed democratic slogans, none built mechanisms whereby the small illegalities of party leaders, ideologues and members could be disciplined through transparent, credible but decisive sets of intra-party rules and procedures. Small political misdemeanours were allowed to occur with impunity in each of the big parties—Nepali Congress (NC), Communist Party of Nepal (Unified Marxist-Leninist) (CPN [UML]) and Rastriya Prajatantra Party (RPP)—while personal aggrandisement, often in the name of helping the party, was overlooked. Although opposition parties often indulged in moral posturing, they too failed to come up with effective laws to tame the excesses of the ruling party. The CPN (UML), which led the opposition for most of this period, was unable to create a social environment in which laws that would govern party finances—said to be the single most important source of political corruption in Nepal—could be passed. This kind of deceit on the part of the political parties contributed directly to a widespread disenchantment with the multi-party democratic set-up, and facilitated the political arrival and growth of the Maoists.

Notable non-Maoist left parties that did not have significant representation in parliament (the CPN [Marxist-Leninist], CPN [Masal], CPN [Unity Centre], and the Nepal Workers and Peasants Party [NWPP]) engaged in their own version of double-dealing when it came to the Maoist movement. They were envious of the kind of publicity and influence that Prachanda and his party had managed to garner through their recourse to arms. All of these small left parties, or, more specifically, certain factions within them, wanted to turn a friendly face to the Maoists while simultaneously denouncing them for resorting to armed revolution before the 'objective conditions were ready'. By engaging in this double talk, the parties led by Bamdev Gautam (CPN [ML]), Mohan Bikram Singh (Masal), Prakash (Unity

Centre) and Rohit (NWPP) not only relinquished most of their 'nationalist' agenda to the Maoists but also succumbed to their tantalising seductions. Two examples will suffice to establish this.

After representatives from Masal and Unity Centre had spent months working out the unification modules of their respective parties, the Maoists declared the Prakash-led Unity Centre to be their 'closest friend'. This coincided with the disciplining of Mohan Bikram Singh within his Masal party for his marriage to a party cadre who was much younger than himself, and a heightening of animosity between the Maoists and the CPN (Masal). All talk of unification had been relegated to the margins by the autumn of 2001. Another example is Prachanda's extended conversations with Bamdev Gautam in the Indian town of Siliguri (where he also met other Nepali left leaders): these were enough to scuttle the 2001 round of CPN (UML) and CPN (ML) unification efforts. The voluminous articles in weeklies such as *Samadrishti* (close to CPN [ML]), *Jana Ekata* (close to CPN [Unity Centre]), and *Hank* (close to CPN [Masal]) in relation to the duplicitous characteristics of the small left parties vis-à-vis the Maoists stand as testimony to one of the greatest tragedies of the Nepali left movement. Scattered in their separate camps, these splintered left parties were unable to challenge the Maoists in terms of their ideology and party activities. In other words, they could not stop the recruitment of left cadres into the Maoist camp, especially after the attack on the Dolpa district headquarters of Dunai in September 2000.

On the question of political duplicity, the late King Birendra is also culpable. Although often described as a perfect constitutional monarch by Nepali and foreign commentators, he was unable to curb the personal excesses of certain members of the royal family (including his son and nephew) and thus discipline the institutional paraphernalia of monarchy. In addition, his vagueness regarding the location of the army in post-1990 Nepal helped the Maoists. As one who held the title of Supreme Commander of the Royal Nepalese Army, the king failed to make clear that he was only its symbolic head, as intended by the spirit of the Constitution of Nepal, 1990. In effect, elected governments felt that the army was not really under their command. Given this ambiguity, the Maoists had only to overcome the poorly-armed, poorly-paid, not-trained-for-combat police personnel of the home ministry. This they did with a thoroughness that was staggering. These weaknesses of the politicians and the former monarch, evident in the duplicitous manner in which they have run their own institutions, have come back to haunt Nepalis in the form of the Maoist movement.

Commercial Sector Duplicity

In June 1999, the Kathmandu-based forum Martin Chautari organised a public discussion on the topic of 'Boarding Schools, Government Schools: Leading to a Two-Class Oriented Nepal?' Many interested participants spoke with anger about the way in which private schools had been overcharging students. Computer and lab fees had been taken from infants, library fees had been charged even when the school did not have a functioning library, and admission fees were being collected from every student every year. In other words, the participants felt that the private schools were fleecing guardians in the guise of providing 'quality education'.

Some months later, in October 1999, this writer held a discussion on the same topic on the Radio Sagarmatha talk show, *Dabali*. One of my guests, the political scientist Krishna Hachhethu, stated that sixty-five per cent of his monthly salary from the Centre for Nepal and Asian Studies was dedicated to the school fees of his three children. Highlighting the fact that his own father had to spend no more than five per cent of his salary on the education of his offspring, Hachhethu discussed how the rising fees charged by the schools had 'corrupted' him academically, as he was forced to take up consultancies that did not contribute to his research. He said, 'If the practice of charging exorbitant fees from their wards cannot be monitored by the schools themselves, it will lead to a full-fledged two-class and corrupt Nepali society.'

These discussions took place when the two associations of private and boarding schools—the Private and Boarding Schools Organization of Nepal (PABSON) and the National Private and Boarding Schools Association of Nepal (NPABSAN)—were busy bickering with each other over the organisational spoils, and with the government to extract more facilities for their own trade. Establishing a fair, transparent and robust mechanism for the self-regulation of the fee regime and for the punishment of those members who violated guidelines was far from their programme. The parents' sane and modest demands for a fair fee regime went unheard. The teachers' justifiable demands for more secure working conditions under proper contracts were ignored. Instead of building a collective institutional and moral force that could withstand scrutiny from other legitimate sources and oppose the extortion by weapon-carrying groups, these associations of private schools made the ground fertile for haphazard fee structures, unmonitored curricula and general duplicity in school management. They did all this while trumpeting their own contribution to the national educational scene and economy, not to mention the cause of Nepali nationalism.

Hence, when the Maoists attacked private schools, the latter had none to blame but themselves. The Maoists have taken advantage of the duplicity present in every sector of Nepali society to develop their campaign, and the private schools proved to be no exception. Because of their duplicitous character, private schools have managed to alienate parents, who have therefore not come to their support *en masse*. That is why when the Maoists forced many private schools to close, the associations of private schools could do nothing but watch their members shut up their shops. Those that remained open, it was said, were paying 'donations' to the Maoists. After a week-long private school *bandh* called in 2001 by *krantikari* (revolutionary) students affiliated to the Maoists, some people hoped that perhaps a collective resistance to the coercive denial of school children's access to education would emerge. That did not happen. Instead, anecdotal evidence suggested that some big Kathmandu schools were paying 'protection' money to the Maoists. That payment, unfortunately, showed up indirectly in the bills received by parents such as Hachhethu.

Similar developments took place in other sections of the private or commercial sector in Nepal. Take for instance, the alcohol industry, very much in the news in 2001. Saubhagya Shah (2001b) analysed the ban on alcohol demanded by the women's wing of the Maoist party, the All Nepal Women's Association (Revolutionary). According to the author, when local communities protested against the seamy side of the 'culture' of alcohol consumption in the early and mid-1990s (i.e. before the Maoists took up the issue), the 'government and the industry either ignored or brutally suppressed' them. The current backlash against alcohol 'is a result of the complete success of the

liquor lobby in dismantling all state and social supervision and regu-
lation in the production and promotion of alcohol in Nepal'. 'Liquor
capitalists given free reign' ignored sane voices calling for modera-
tion and failed to self-monitor their industry. As Shah observes, it
was sad that there could be '"talks" on the alcohol issue only when it
came with the fire and brimstone of the Maoist women'. Examples
from other sections of the private sector, including the tourism and
carpet industries, could also be provided, but more evidence is not
needed to argue that when duplicity is combined with commercial
avarice, and mechanisms for self-monitoring are not developed, the
private sector cannot protect itself from the extortion demands of
groups such as the Maoists.

'Civil Society' Sector Duplicity

For some years now, the term 'civil society' has been in currency in
Nepal. 'Civil society' has become a politically correct term that has become synonymous with the non-governmental sector in Nepal. Liberal theory recognises, in broad terms, the triangle-like relationship
between the state, the market and civil society. In this framework,
'civil society' is said to encompass all institutions and individuals that
constitute that part of a society which monitors and checks the
excesses of the state and the market. When the state fell into relative
disfavour among the powerful development set some years ago, the
non-governmental sector and the market were touted as magical
options. That is when the term 'civil society' began to be bandied
about among development experts, although it has been in use in
social theory—of both liberal and Marxist persuasion—for a much
longer period.

In Nepal, native *bikas* (development) experts quickly indigenised
the mantra of 'civil society' by translating it as *nagarik samaj* (literally, 'citizens' society'). Its domestication inaugurated its overuse.
Over the past five years, many seminar papers have been presented
with titles such as 'The Role of Civil Society in X: Y Perspective'.
Unfortunately, experts have not defined in precise terms what constitutes civil society in the Nepali context. It is implied that modern
NGOs are the chief agents of civil society, although customary volun-
tary associations could equally be a part of it. By extension, even an
obscurantist, regressive 'traditional' collective cannot be excluded
from this ambiguous 'civil society'.

Definitions offered in the realm of theoretical categories contain little merit in a country where many influential NGOs and newspapers—essential elements of civil society elsewhere—are merely the appendages of political parties and the occupants of offices of state. In addition, it remains the case that the question of whether or not civil society is capable of performing the function ascribed to it in the theoretical terrain has not been given adequate attention in Nepal. If professionals from various walks of life and their institutions (such as academics, journalists, auditors and lawyers) are members of Nepali civil society, there is need to question their ability as active checks and balances. They must possess, among other things, professional competence, financial independence from the state, and moral and intellectual integrity. While in each of the professions listed above there are several individuals who fulfil these criteria, their professional societies, through which many civil society initiatives are pushed ahead, cannot be said to be competent in the same way. Currently, many Nepali professional societies are highly partisan and organisationally debilitated by politically fractious squabbling. Many of these societies either exist to provide a respectable garb for otherwise mediocre professionals or as fun-time forums. Were they not repositories of international hope in their capacity as 'civil society institutions', they may have been above comment. In actual fact, there is nothing to be optimistic about here. These organisations are functionally incapable of performing civil society duties (see also Onta 2000).[1]

Thus seen the political and commercial sectors are not the only parts of Nepali society that are corrupt and duplicitous. Nepali civil society is also corrupt—financially, intellectually and morally—and demonstrates the same kind of duplicitous character that is found in the two sectors discussed above. While this truth is abomination for most brokers of development in Nepal, it is a lived reality for the rest of society. Hence Nepal has human rights activists, including those in the team that went to Nuwagaon in Rolpa in July 2001 to supposedly 'mediate' between the army and the Maoists, who not only give a *lal salam* (red salutation) to the Maoists[2] but also have colleagues in

[1] For scrutiny of the concept of civil society and its relation to the donor community and democratic space in Nepal see Tamang (2003).

[2] See the *Kantipur* of 20 July 2001 for a photograph by journalist Khim Ghale that captures the mutual exchange of *lal salam* between Dr Mathura Prasad Shrestha, a

Kathmandu who run organisations in which staff are denied access to project documents and the accounts of donor-funded projects. While the *lal salam* may in itself not be cause for comment, association with selectively reticent organisations certainly is.

The so-called 'modern NGO' sector is not the only one that thrives on duplicity. Other non-governmental entities seem to be afflicted by the same malady. The Nepali literary organisations that supposedly prop up Nepali national culture built around the Nepali language could be taken as an example. These organisations are in the business of granting awards to various people for their 'contributions to Nepali literature.' Awards there are aplenty, but a search for a comprehensive list of criteria of eligibility, the names of the people in the selection committee, or details of the decision-making process, yields no results. The award presenters choose to maintain a stoic silence on these issues. I do not know of many literary awards that make the award-granting process transparent. Secrecy is even celebrated, and award-presenters privately acknowledge that fixing and swapping are common (see Onta 1999a).

Steeped in pervasive duplicity and corruption, the civil society sector has failed to provide a strong collective resistance to the Maoists, be it ideological or organisational. Inadequately worked-out critiques of Nepali Maoism, stray protest rallies, lists of individuals killed or missing since the beginning of the Maoist movement—these are all there is to show. In the meantime, some human rights organisations have worked as fronts to facilitate the Maoist cause.

To summarise: duplicity in the political, commercial and social sectors in Nepal made it possible for the Maoists to advance their political agenda with relative ease. The duplicity of the late monarch ensured that the military was never a serious threat to the Maoists. Collective resistance in the contexts outlined above was too expensive an option for representatives of various Nepali sectors. Instead, individuals and businesses preferred to strike their own private deals with the Maoists. The tragic situation is encapsulated in the glee of the owner of a two-star hotel in Kathmandu who was only too happy to part with Rs 10,000 as a 'donation' during the Maoist *chanda atanka* ('donation' campaign) in the late summer of 2001. The Maoists had

---

member of the team of human rights activists that visited Nuwagaon, and Sijal, described as the district secretary of the CPN (Maoist).

failed to properly assess his *chanda*-worthiness, a fact that the hotelier recounted with no small pleasure to his friends.

THE BATTLE OVER REPRESENTATION

The Maoists' ability to use the duplicity of the other sectors of Nepali society to their own advantage, and their dominance over the Nepali police forces, guaranteed that they would capture Nepal's mainstream political agenda. *Chanda* campaigns ensured that Maoist resources were constantly replenished. If the Maoists won the war to seize the political agenda and feed the stomachs of their cadres in these ways, how did they fight the battle for the representation of Nepali realities? Two non-Maoist interpretive communities are examined in this connection.

Media

How have the mainstream Nepali media interpreted the Maoist movement and how have the Maoists, in turn, used the media? Overall, the mainstream media have demonised the Maoists to a certain extent. When the Maoists began their campaign in 1996, the Nepali political establishment was quick to condemn their acts (such as murders of political workers and other individuals, looting of banks and arson) while offering little serious political analysis of the forty-point demand that Baburam Bhattarai had placed in front of the then prime minister, Sher Bahadur Deuba. As the mainstream political leaders debated the nature of Maoist violence—whether it was 'political' in nature or just simply 'criminal'—while still disagreeing on how to solve the problem, the Nepali media began to report incidents of murder and excesses by the Maoists. As the insurgency grew and the government responded with brutal police repression in some areas of mid-west Nepal, the Nepali media could not adequately cover ground-level events (Thapa 2001). Instead, they began to criticise successive governments for allowing the Maoist problem to fester. No matter what the objective conditions claimed for a 'revolution' might be, the Nepali mainstream media consistently avoided any serious analysis of the links between socio-economic conditions and the rise of armed insurgency in the early days of the Maoist campaign. This happened partly because of the poor state of social

science research on this linkage in Nepal. As advocates of what the
Maoists would call the *sudharbadi* (reformist, gradualist or revision-
ist) school of social change, it is no surprise that, in the beginning, the
Nepali media deprecated the Maoists.

But, as Rajendra Dahal (2000/1) has argued, this type of coverage
slowly gave way to more sympathetic reporting on the Maoists, for
several reasons. As the Maoist campaign grew, media personnel began to be more directly affected by the violence and the simultaneous
inefficacy of successive governments. The latter state of affairs, according to Dahal, engendered a resigned attitude on the part of the
media ('if the government can't do anything to check the Maoists,
why should the media take any risks?'). This feeling was heightened
by the explicit and implicit threats the Maoist ideologues and cadres
started to deliver to media personnel, either in direct messages or
through general public utterances. Under these circumstances, the
Nepali mainstream media felt safe to report on government ineffi-
ciency and to appear 'soft' on the Maoists. Going soft included providing unwarranted coverage to Maoist activities such as their open
meetings (*janasabha*s), although one journalist has also defended
this possibly excessive coverage as a by-product of the curiosity
regarding Maoist activities, unprecedented as they were on Nepali
soil, on the part of the media people (Luitel 2002: 43). Going soft
also meant providing ample space in the op-ed pages for long essays
by Maoist leaders and ideologues about party activities and positions,
and commentaries on other events and processes in Nepal. Such col-
umn space was often not forthcoming for other less-celebrated political commentators.

Following the Maoist attack on Dunai in September 2000, the
mainstream media capitulated even further. As the morale and the
recruitment drive of the Maoists increased, members of the mainstream press initiated a new genre of 'travel reportage' based on
their Maoist-sponsored visits (Aryal 2002). Except for one or two
write-ups, most of these reports of Maoist 'guided tours' were overtly
sympathetic to the Maoists. The journalists mentioned being met by
tour guides who later turned out to be Maoists of various ranks. They
described long walks through unfamiliar territories, some with several 'martyrs' gates'. They narrated conversations with Maoists in
some Maoist 'shelters' or 'restricted areas' and the performance of

'revolutionary' cultural programmes that, more often than not, lasted through the night. These writings, often accompanied by photographs showing Maoist guerrillas posing with their weapons, generally failed to inform the reading public about new developments within the Maoist movement and their immediate impact on specific localities and communities. Nevertheless, they provided generous publicity to the Maoists.[3] The Maoist leaders who participated in the talks with the Nepal government during the second half of 2001 recognised this aspect. At the conclusion of the second round of talks, the Maoist leader Krishna Bahadur Mahara publicly stated that media persons had acted as an *utprerak shakti* (inspirational force) for the erstwhile success of the movement and thanked journalist 'friends' for the 'help they had rendered to the movement' (Luitel 2002: 45).

But even before Mahara's appreciation of the mainstream press had become public, reportage on the Maoists changed after most of the mainstream newspapers printed photographs of the Maoist-induced carnage at Naumule, Dailekh in early April 2001. In particular, the photo of the wife of a policeman killed in that attack weeping over her husband's body, taken by Chandrasekhar Karki,[4] generated a mood in which tame travel reportage could no longer make good copy. Instead, the *swajanko bilap* (lamentation of the victims' relatives) genre of reporting, stories on the bereaved victims of Maoist violence, which already existed, took off after Naumule. Subsequently, as disruptions in Kathmandu schools by Maoist-backed students became routine, mainstream newspapers again began to assume a more aggressive stance towards the Maoists (Aryal 2002).

The detention of a group of journalists in Rolpa in early September 2001 (Y. Shahi 2001) indicates that the Maoists have been wary of independent reporting. Such reporting could possibly unearth information that would challenge Maoist claims of achievements in the areas under their *jan sarkar*s. Are schools functioning better in Maoist-controlled territories? Do people have access to better primary health care? Are 'cultural changes' (such as a ban on alcohol) sustainable without the backing of arms? Independent reporters could seek answers to these and other related questions. These findings

[3] My assessment of this kind of travel reportage by journalists is based on a reading of about 20 such accounts including Pathak (2000), Bista (2001) and Sapkota (2001/2).

[4] *Kantipur*, 8 April 2001.

could better inform the Nepali public about the ethos of the Maoists and the capacity of their institutions beyond the threat of armed violence. The Maoists fear this possibility and would probably do everything to make the work of independent reporters impossible in the areas under their control.

During the tame reporting phase, the Maoists took advantage of the mainstream press, and at other times they have been generally able to put their agenda on the front pages of Nepali newspapers. As mentioned, they have had almost unlimited access to the op-ed pages of mainstream newspapers and magazines both before and after Baburam Bhattarai's famous article about the royal massacre appeared in *Kantipur* on 6 June 2001 (2001a). However, the mainstream Nepali media has also been able to resist Maoist lollipops, when they have shown their determination to expose Maoist excesses (see Aryal 2002). But one must add that such determination has not been consistent. On the other hand, one should not underestimate the ability of the Maoist press—pamphlets, newspapers and magazines—to accost readers with propaganda and rebuttals of anti-Maoist arguments. While the state has made some botched attempts to clamp down on the Maoist press,[5] party cadres have taken good advantage of Nepal's press freedoms to foster their own cause.

Left Intellectuals

As elsewhere, in Nepal, the most strident critique of the 'ultra-left' has come from within the left tradition.[6] The ranks of the harsh critics from within the left include Hari Roka (formerly with CPN [ML], now an independent leftist), Narayan Dhakal (formerly with CPN [UML], then CPN [ML], then retired from politics, now CPN [UML] again), and Khagendra Sangraula (an independent left writer). These writers have taken issue with the Maoists on several counts (such as wrong understanding of Nepali present, non-sustainable revolutionary methods, use of extreme violence and destruction, callousness shown towards victims and relatives of their own violence

---

[5] All newspapers considered 'pro-Maoist' were shut down by the security forces, and their staff arrested on 26 November 2001, just hours before the announcement of the emergency (editor's note).

[6] For a Maoist reading of diverse literary responses to Maoism in Nepal see Baral (2000/1).

and that of the state). Here, only the Maoist response to these three intellectuals is mentioned.

When Roka moved away from the CPN (ML) and became one of the chief proponents of the so-called *tesro dhar* (third way) of the Nepali left in the year 1999–2000, the Maoists tried to recruit him into their relatively thin middle ranks. Their efforts were redoubled when the *tesro dhar* movement failed to take off. Instead of joining the Maoists, Roka chose to become a student of economics at Jawaharlal Nehru University in New Delhi. From what I know, the Maoists have never felt the need to respond to Narayan Dhakal in any serious manner. Perhaps Dhakal's frequent shifts of position made him suspect in the eyes of the Maoist leaders. Going by these instances, it appears that two of the Maoists' tactics in dealing with left intellectuals have been to try and incorporate some while ignoring others.

The third tactic involves the measured delegitimisation of other left intellectuals through repeated attacks on them in Maoist views-papers and journals. The person who has been the most visible target of such attacks is the Marxist writer Khagendra Sangraula, who, along with others such as the commentator C. K. Lal, has been one of the most vocal and consistent critics of the Maoists in Nepal. The vilification of Sangraula has happened via both the political and literary registers of the Maoists. The supreme Maoist leader Prachanda has proclaimed that Sangraula, whose erstwhile criticisms of left party culture (for their lack of intra-party democracy and their use of mantras as analysis, among other things) were well known, has even abandoned ideological commitment to the cause of the left in his novel *Junkiriko Sangit* (The Music of Fireflies; Sangraula 1999). According to Prachanda, Sangraula's novel reeks of 'imperialist dollars' and it 'seems to have been written to make fun of Marxism, the communist party, class struggle, people's resistance and revolution'. He concluded, 'Other than to present the conspiracy of the imperialists in a fanciful way, I saw no other objective in the book' (Prachanda 2000/1: 40).[7]

[7] These statements have been extracted from a longer interview the Maoist leader gave to the journal *Kalam* on the theme of people's cultural movement, in which he also issued a veiled warning to those such as Sangraula by saying that cultural imperialism must also be dealt with through physical retaliation if necessary.

Prachanda's criticisms of Sangraula were elaborated upon by a member of the Maoist party politburo and the party's chief literary aesthetician, 'Kiran' alias Chaitanya (2000/1), and the Maoist literary 'expert' Dr Rishi Raj Baral (in many places, including Baral 2000/1). Like Prachanda, these two criticised Sangraula by associating him with imperialism. They concluded that Nepali NGOs made up of Nepali citizens are 'imperialist tools' that try to derail 'the revolution in progress'. Baral, for instance, tried to 'prove' this point by repetition. Writers who have opposed Maoist violence and shown an interest in critically examining the life of non-governmental entities in the present conjuncture of Nepali society—including Sangraula in *Junkiriko Sangit*—become 'NGO litterateurs' in Baral's lexicon.[8] Non-governmental entities and persons who might be involved in them in any capacity, whether institutional or conceptual, become 'enemies of the revolution'. Their lives and work are denigrated in the crudest of terms, and this is a central strategy in the culture of Maoist political discourse.

Baral, who once worked as a spy for the Nepali government (a fact which he has publicly acknowledged and for which he has 'apologised') practises a mode of analysis that does not adhere to logic. Nor does it exhibit the humility of a social analyst trying to examine a complex social scenario. But that would be expecting too much from a person who in the dubious capacity of a literary critic often describes his own work as the cutting edge of progressive writing in Nepal (see, for example, Baral 2000/1). Baral and his Maoist comrades can only imagine a society where the state is in the hands of the Maoist Party and the rest of Nepal has to follow its dictates. Baral's idea of democracy is locked within armed violence. There is an assumption that other means of social revolution are not feasible (see Bhattarai 2003). Accustomed to eliminating people who question the appropriateness of Maoist tactics and who pose a problem to the 'forward march of the Maoist revolution', it is within the scheme of things for Baral and his literary and military superiors to dismiss Sangraula and issue indirect threats of a physical *saphaya* (elimination).

Individual critical left intellectuals have been constrained by the lack of organisational backing, and hence have been ineffective in

---

[8] For a discussion of Sangraula's novel and some predictions of how different sectors of Nepali society will respond to it see Onta (1999b).

countering the Maoist cultural and literary onslaught. The Pragati-shil Lekhak Sangh (Progressive Writers Association), the largest such organisation, has been more or less moribund for the last five or so years (first under the leadership of Govinda Bhatta, who is close to CPN [UML], and now under Ninu Chapagain, who is close to CPN [Unity Centre]). While raising the occasional protest against the government, it has not taken a firm stand against the Maoists and their excesses. That possibility, to a large extent, has been scuttled by the presence of Baral in the present executive committee of the Sangh. Hence the Sangh has been unable to act as a force multiplier of criticisms of the Maoists offered by individuals such as Sangraula. Having developed no organisational autonomy and democracy of its own, the Sangh exists more as a historical entity whose members fight rhetorical battles with straw enemies of their own creation, in shrill or turgid language, rather than as a forum for critical dialogue on the present realities of Nepal.

While I do not suggest that duplicity is the cause of the Maoist movement in Nepal, I have argued that the duplicitous character of the political, commercial and civil society sectors has left open adequate space for Maoist expansion. On their side, the Maoists have not turned down the opportunities so presented. They have largely been able to place their own agenda in the mainstream Nepali media and marginalise perspectives critical of them through repetitious rhetorical exercises. Given the context elaborated above, a purely military-led solution of the sort that seems to resurface periodically may not be adequate to counter Maoist domination over Nepal's politics.

GENDER DIMENSIONS
OF THE PEOPLE'S WAR

SOME REFLECTIONS ON THE EXPERIENCES
OF RURAL WOMEN*

Mandira Sharma and Dinesh Prasain

BACKGROUND

The active involvement of women has been one of the most discussed aspects of the Maoist insurgency in Nepal. Between 1998 and
November 2001, the Maoists organised guided tours for Nepali and
foreign journalists through the rural areas under their control. What
the journalists invariably brought back for public consumption were
reports and photographs of women constituting a large proportion
of the participants in Maoist processions, many of them dressed in
combat fatigues or wearing red scarves and carrying guns in a casual
manner. It was reported that women constituted anywhere between
thirty to forty per cent of the Maoist cadres: they had assumed roles
ranging from nurses, messengers and organisers to fully-fledged
guerrilla fighters.

Such images and stories have forced analysts to ask certain new
questions about gender relations in Nepali society. Why have so many
rural Nepali women taken part in the insurgency, even to the extent
of becoming guerrilla fighters, many of whom have been killed by the
state's security forces in battle or in custody? What specific life experiences convinced or compelled the women to take part in Maoist
activities? How does this relate to dominant cultural narratives in
Nepal which portray women as weak and submissive? What impact

* This chapter is a revised version of a study conducted for DFID Nepal in May 2002.
The authors designed the study with support from Liz Philipson of the London School
of Economics. Mandira Sharma visited prisons and conflict-affected villages to interview women. Mandira Sharma and Dinesh Prasain jointly analysed data and wrote
the text.

will it have on power relations between men and women in Nepal, both locally and nationally? These are important questions for students of gender relations in contemporary Nepal, although it is difficult for the present study to do justice to these issues. It must be mentioned here that this chapter does not examine gender relations between Maoists, especially in the light of criticism that some women have left the party disappointed with the gap between rhetoric and practice.[1]

Here, we try to reflect on some aspects of women's relationship to the Maoist movement, basing our discussion on our analysis of the experiences and perspectives of women who have at one time or another been involved in the party's activities. Interviews were conducted in May 2002 with a number of women (and also some men) in villages in Bardiya and Banke districts in the western tarai, as well as with women from western and eastern Nepal who were in prison at the time. The State of Emergency was still in force during our first visits to these villages and prisons.

This chapter also draws on field visits to Rolpa, Dang, Bardiya, Salyan and Udayapur districts in December 2002, and follow-up visits to some of the respondents in the May 2002 interviews. We were very distressed to discover that a few of the women interviewed in May had since been killed by the security forces.[2] One such woman had surrendered herself, intending to resume life outside the party. However, after some time she was arrested by a group of security personnel and her whereabouts are still unknown. Her neighbours and relatives suspect she has been killed. Some of those interviewed in prison eight months earlier were still languishing there.

WOMEN WITHIN THE CPN (MAOIST) ORGANISATIONAL STRUCTURE

Women can support and take part in the Maoist insurgency either through sister organisations or directly through the party. The All

---

[1] Shova Gautam et al. (2001) discuss gender relations within the CPN (Maoist). The Maoist perspective is available in Com. Parvati (2003), though the piece does not defend the party from its detractors on this count. A critique from the left on the women's question and the Maoists is available in Shakya (2003). Shakya is a member of the All Nepal Women's Association (ANWA), the women's wing of the CPN (UML).

[2] These incidents, however, were not the consequences of the study or interviews.

Nepal Women's Association (Revolutionary), (ANWA [R]), is the women's wing of the CPN (Maoist). The other affiliated mass organisations include the All Nepal National Free Students Union (Revolutionary), various ethnic liberation fronts and people's cultural forums. As members of these related organisations, women perform various roles for the party. They raise 'awareness' in the social groups they represent in order to persuade more people to support the Maoist cause, and they provide information, care of the wounded, shelter, and other logistical support to party members. The ANWA (R)'s most publicised work has been its militant anti-alcohol campaign, but women members of Maoist sister organisations have also actively participated as jury members and judges in the people's courts that have been set up to resolve local disputes.

There are two ways in which a woman, or indeed a man, can be involved directly in the party. One is through its organisational political wing and the other through its military wing. The main function of the organisational wing is organisation building and the recruitment and indoctrination of members and prospective members. The military wing is obviously involved in defensive and offensive military tasks, and has two broad categories: the people's militia and the people's army. Those involved in the people's militia receive basic military training and use rudimentary weapons. They are called into action when needed but engage in their regular agricultural work for most of the time. They do not wear uniform. Those who are enlisted in the people's army are 'professional' military persons, with a formal hierarchy and chain of command, and are subject to general military organisational rules such as transfers, promotions and prosecutions.

Although this is very difficult to verify, as mentioned, it is reported that women constitute anywhere between thirty and forty per cent of the Maoists' military force, which, according to conservative estimates, totals at least 10,000 people. Among the women military personnel, it is reported that most come from ethnic and Dalit groups, but there are also women from the Bahun-Chetri castes. Again, their exact distribution is hard to ascertain. During a visit in December 2002 to Rolpa, one of the strongest Maoist support bases in the midwestern hills, the Maoist cadres claimed that women's participation in the people's war had been increasing even further more recently. They claimed that women now constituted about fifty per cent of the

Maoist cadres in Rolpa. They had created a new women-only platoon comprising forty-six persons, which they said had been very active in military offensives in Rolpa and elsewhere. During informal discussions, one such woman guerrilla said that they had also formed such women-only platoons in a few other districts, including Dang and Bardiya.

Ideologically, the Maoists claim to favour an end to the patriarchal organisation of society. In the Nepali context, it appears that this position is exemplified by their demand for equal rights for women to inherit ancestral property. In the well-known forty-point demand submitted to the government just before the declaration of the people's war, one point deals exclusively with this: 'patriarchal exploitation and discrimination against women should be stopped. Daughters should be allowed access to paternal property'. However, the full liberation of women and gender equality are to be achieved only in a classless or communist society. Hence, there is all the more reason for women to take part in the revolution. Such positions are explained to Maoist women, and also more generally, through political classes, 'cultural' programmes, the party media and the mass print media. Is it because of such statements and official positions that the Maoists have succeeded in garnering the support of rural women? There must also be something else that has attracted or forced women to support the Maoists, because similar statements have been made and similar positions adopted by many other political parties and civil society groups for a long time in Nepal. Let us look at the perspectives of women involved in the Maoist movement. (We have changed the names of the women, and of the villages in some cases, to protect the women's security.)

EXPERIENCES OF WOMEN INVOLVED IN THE MAOIST MOVEMENT

Domestic Violence and Alcohol Abuse

'My father is an alcoholic. After taking alcohol he assaults me and my mother. Every day we are scared when he goes out for a drink. Two of my brothers left home for India to escape this situation. It is embarrassing for me too. I joined the women's organisation to join the anti-alcohol campaign' (Saraswati B. K, prisoner).

'They came to my house, talked about my suffering, warned my husband who used to beat me every day. I had heard that we were supposed to go to the chairperson of the Village Development Committee [VDC], but I did not go there. I do not think he can provide justice to women since he himself beats his wife all the time. Since they [the Maoists] have become active in this village, they have taken actions against many abusive husbands. Since they were people from the same village I did not need to tell them the story, they knew it themselves. So I support them, they provide real justice for women' (a woman from Purandhara VDC, Dang).

Although severely tortured by the police for her support for the Maoists, and still in prison, Saraswati openly admits that she is still an ardent Maoist supporter. The main reason she cites for supporting the Maoists is the anti-alcohol movement launched by ANWA (R). She explains that her whole family has suffered the abuse of her alcoholic father, and that she has experienced violence at home since her childhood. Her alcoholic father used to beat her mother and every member of the family when he had been drinking, and she and her siblings were ashamed of their father's behaviour when they met friends in school and the wider community. Her brothers left for India for the same reason. So she strongly believes that her family has been ruined by alcohol and domestic violence.

Although violence against women is rooted in the asymmetrical power relations that exist between men and women in society, the Maoists' anti-alcohol movement has appealed strongly to women in village Nepal, especially as they see that it is directly linked to the possibility of ending domestic violence. The majority of village women have experienced some kind of violence in their family or community. Wife battering after alcohol abuse is a common practice in many parts of rural Nepal. Men spend many hours of the day playing cards, drinking and gossiping with other men in local teashops. It is the women who work in the fields, go to the forest to collect firewood and fodder, tend the cattle, take care of the children and cook for the family. This generalisation seems to hold despite the differences in gender relations in the variegated and numerous social groups in Nepal.[3]

There are no public forums to which the women victims of violence can turn for support. The Village Development Committee, or

[3] Tamang (2002) questions the existing, a-political and problematic 'gender' analysis that informs much development discourse in Nepal, particularly in its flattening of the variety of gender norms extant in Nepal.

any public institution for that matter, is dominated by men who view violence against women as normal and a private family matter. Such institutions are so unfriendly to women that the victims of violence are effectively discouraged from reporting to them. The whole justice system has somehow failed to respond to the problems that women face in Nepal. The patriarchal mindset of individuals such as judges and VDC chairmen has made justice inaccessible to women. One study reveals that fifty-seven per cent of sitting judges take the view that a husband is fully entitled to administer a slap to his wife to 'correct her attitude' and sixty-six per cent are of the opinion that women should share the blame for violence committed against them (see also Bennett 1983, Belbase and Pyakuryal 2000). This situation is different in places where the Maoists are present. The Maoists are receptive to the complaints of gender-based violence against women. They warn and beat abusive husbands. They have even forced some abusive husbands to perform household chores they traditionally never touched.

State Violence

'The police arrested my husband from the room. I was sleeping next to him when they came to arrest my husband. I asked for the reason and they told me that they were taking him for interrogation and would release him after some days, but next day they killed him. I lost the hope that I could get any justice from this system' (Maya Chaudhary, Udayapur).

'All the male family members left home. I used to go to my neighbours' house to sleep at night, fearing police search and atrocities. Life was neither safe nor easy. So I support the Maoist party in the hope of getting free of such a life' (Uma Chaudhary, Udayapur).

'Whenever the army enters the village, we get a few new women joining the militia...Whenever the army enters the village they don't just eat and take away the chickens and food the villagers have, they also torture women and even rape them. They burn the houses and terrify the people. Those poor people do not have any place to go to seek justice. So they come and join the party, in order to retaliate' (a woman Maoist cadre, Rolpa).

One woman said that she started carrying a gun as a guerrilla fighter in order to get even. Her husband was a supporter of the CPN (UML), but was very supportive of women's struggles against injustices in the village. The police suspected him of supporting the Maoists, and came to the house many times to arrest him. During such visits, the police beat and harassed her. In addition they took away chickens, goats and whatever they had in the house. Her husband eventually joined the Maoists after such continued harassment, which only led to further harassment for the whole family. She had to go to other villagers' houses to escape police brutality and threats to her life. She also witnessed the police torturing and killing innocent villagers, which she said made her feel that there could be no justice for the poor in the village. Finally, she also decided to join the party to fight back against such suppression. Later, her husband was arrested from the village and was subsequently killed by the police. Killing is a brutal act. But the manner of this particular killing was heinous. This indeed reveals the dynamics motivating many other women as well as men to join the Maoist movement, as has been pointed by several other commentators (see Gautam 2001, Maharjan 2000). This is a classic case of violence breeding more violence.

When the government initiated Operation Romeo, hundreds of people were arrested, including many women. During the period a number of cases of rape by police personnel were also reported. Many of the arrested were taken to court on false charges. For instance, a sixteen-year-old named Buji Maya was imprisoned without any knowledge of the charges against her (Gautam 2001). Female members of families whose male members had run away were threatened and abused physically and psychologically. Seventeen-year-old Purna Budha also fled to the 'jungle' when her father and brother escaped because they could not cope with the harassment and threats of the police. The state's operations against women involved in ANWA (R) have been very brutal. In 1998, when ANWA (R) organised a programme in Kathmandu, some 168 women were arrested, including radical left political leaders, teachers, student and women. Many of them were severely tortured and abused by the police.

Rural Nepali women have also experienced an indirect form of violence in the form of bad governance.[4] The policies made at the national level are not responsive to the perspectives, needs and aspirations of the vast majority of rural women. At the local level, the

[4] Violence needs to be described in its broadest possible sense and not reduced to its dictionary definition (see also Bhattarai 2003). In a comprehensive study of 'violence', the state is perhaps no less liable to be criticised for its use of violence against the women of Nepal than any extra-constitutional force.

women interviewed said they had become disillusioned with democracy because the Nepali Congress government provided patronage to the people who had oppressed them as Panchas for a long time. The women started supporting the Maoists, providing them with shelter, cooking food for them, and so on, because they were very responsive to women's issues and encouraged their participation in public affairs. The legitimacy of the government was further eroded when men and women were prevented from registering court cases, and when the government launched ruthless police operations instead of trying to win the confidence of the people by addressing the root causes of their discontent.

Aspirations for Cultural Change

'I feel I am free to some extent. I am given the responsibility of making people aware of our culture and uniting them to protect our culture. Singing and dancing is my hobby, which I can do now. I have found a forum in the Maoist party' (Shanti Chaudhary, Dang).

'There are so many atrocities committed by the police in our village. The Maoists do not harm us. They are the people of our own village. These days they visit door to door and conduct classes on many issues for us. We now know how to talk to people, why the Maoists are against the government and why it is important to support the Maoists' (woman from Panchakule VDC, Dang).

'I fell in love with a Muslim boy. I got married to him. However, our parents on both sides did not accept our marriage because my family are Hindu. We were socially ostracised. The landlord in our village ordered us to leave the village. We were treated as untouchable. They [the Maoists] approached us, knowing our problem. They understood us. They accepted us. So we also supported them. Then, my husband was killed by the security forces on the allegation that he had supported the Maoists by providing them with food. I was left behind; I did not have any means to survive. I was pregnant at the time my husband was killed. Again, the Maoists came and assisted me. They are the ones I can turn to in my need. I will never get this support from government people. So why should I not support them? They bring food, I cook for them' (a woman in Bardiya).

Another woman who supports the Maoists tried to explain why she does so despite the fact that her husband is strongly opposed to it. She was forced to marry a man when she was eighteen years old, although she wanted to marry another man, whom she loved. Later she discovered that her husband was an alcoholic. He constantly blamed her for everything that went wrong in the house, and abused her both physically and psychologically. She is still living with her husband: she clearly dislikes this but she does not have much choice because she fears that village opinion would be unsupportive if she decided to leave him. On top of that, it would be very difficult for her to find an alternative means of survival if she left her husband, and she has to support her two children. She has developed an intense dislike for the culture which sanctions every behaviour of men, however unjust and illogical it may be, but treats women very cruelly. 'I have heard that the Maoists are fighting such injustices,' she says.

Young women, even schoolgirls, are joining the people's war in increasing numbers. When we talked to some young women in the villages in Dang they said that because of the Maoists they now had access to public forums to express their ideas and interests as never before. They said that women, and especially young girls, have long been treated as the property of men. They did not like the attitude towards women held by their families and communities, such as restrictions on their mobility, and visible and invisible discrimination. They had been forced to accept options in their lives that had been determined by someone else. Men had captured all of the public institutions, and women faced harassment in all of them. Especially for the young girls, there were no places for entertainment. After the arrival of the Maoists, they said, they had access to public forums and entertainment in the form of cultural programmes, in which they could participate without fearing harassment from men. Some young women said, 'We are now more free because of the Maoists. Therefore, we support them, even in physical actions against the class enemies in the village.'

Women have joined the party irrespective of their caste and rank. The villagers who have not joined the party as full-time workers, and are not carrying guns, also say that Maoist women and men come door to door, provide literacy programmes, make them aware of their rights, roles and contribution. The Maoists also talk about how women have been suppressed in the present society, and make them aware that theirs is the only party working for their liberation.

Economic and Cultural Effects of the War

Many women tell of how their husbands or male members of their family were either killed or joined the Maoists during the initial stage of the state's anti-insurgency operations. Moreover, as the male members of the family either fled to the jungle or to India to escape from the state's oppression all the responsibilities of the family fell upon the women's shoulders.[5] Mirule, a mainly Magar village of Rolpa, became a village without men (see Gautam et al. 2001). As a result the women were forced to plough the land. This is considered an exclusively male task, and there is a strong belief that a woman will invite disaster if she touches the plough. However, without touching the plough they could not plant the crops, so they ploughed their fields themselves, and roofed their houses as well.

In the absence of men, women had to assume the roles traditionally occupied by men. This had a dual impact. First, the myth that women could not do men's jobs was shattered, and the absence of men also gave women opportunities to take part in public life. Helping each other, exchanging labour, debating the issues and taking decisions provided them with a sense of confidence. During village development committee elections, because there were no men to contest them, women came forward and were elected. Thus, illiterate peasant women become active in politics. Second, the feminisation of the rural economy also led to frustration among women. As one woman described it, they were forced to suffer so much difficulty that they decided their hardships would be more worthwhile if they contributed to the liberation of the oppressed people from such suffering.

The Anti-terrorist Legislation and Lack of Rule of Law

'What is wrong if I join the Maoists to overthrow this system?' asked a woman during one of our follow-up visits to a prison. She had been arrested a year earlier, detained in police custody and severely tortured for three months, and then sent to prison under preventive detention. She reported that she was blindfolded and kept in a room with a bare floor for three months. Describing the methods of torture,

---

[5] It should be made clear that, in the aggregate, Nepali rural male out-migration was not triggered by Maoist activity and the state's reaction to it; it was merely exacerbated. Contrary to the currently fashionable analysis that blames all of Nepal's ills on the Maoists, there is a long-standing and respectable tradition of rural male out-migration from Nepal.

she said her hands were tied together, she was forced to lie down on the floor and was beaten with sticks on the soles of her feet. She also said that water with chilli powder was poured into her nose, so that she would confess to her involvement in Maoist activities.

The new Terrorist and Destructive Activities (Control and Prevention) Act (TADA) (passed by parliament in April 2002) provides for preventive detention for a maximum period of three months. But this woman had been in preventive detention under the TADA for nearly a year. The provision for preventive detention has been grossly misused. In one of the prisons in Kathmandu, forty women with similar stories were under preventive detention in December 2002. Theoretically, habeas corpus writs could be filed to challenge such prolonged illegal detention. However, there were two problems. First, the security forces would 'release' the detainee for a few hours at the end of the three months, and then instantly re-arrest and detain him/her for another three months. This could be repeated several times. Second, the political environment was not favourable. Lawyers who filed or tried to file habeas corpus writs immediately after the declaration of the State of Emergency were and continue to be threatened with death by the security forces. There have been cases in which the state security forces have reportedly killed detainees on whose behalf such writs have been filed. Family members were too afraid to go to the detention centres to seek information on the whereabouts of detained relatives, even when they had seen them being arrested by the security forces. They were too frightened even to ask for the dead bodies of their family members for cremation or post-mortem examination. They feared being labelled as Maoist supporters and being arrested themselves.

Numerous instances of arbitrary arrest, illegal detention, disappearance and extra-judicial killing by the security forces with a *de facto* guarantee of impunity have been reported by Amnesty International (Amnesty International 2002a and b). Similarly, the National Human Rights Commission of Nepal disclosed a summary report on the human rights situation in the country, based on visits to thirty-five of the seventy-five districts of Nepal, in October 2002. The report highlights the problems of illegal detention, extra-judicial killing, and killing of innocent people in fake encounters. It also mentions a number of problems related to people's lack of access to justice.

Intimidation by the Maoists and the Logic of War

It would be a gross misrepresentation of the situation if we gave the impression that all the women in rural Nepal supported the Maoists. The women interviewed in jail were imprisoned for their involvement in Maoist activities. Also, the villages we visited were known to have some Maoist influence. Therefore, it is obvious that the views expressed by our interviewees would be supportive of the Maoists. In the communities we visited, especially in Dang, there was virtually no presence of the state institutions, including the security forces. The people who did not support the Maoists would find it difficult to speak their minds, because of fear. Nevertheless, we were able to interview a few people in the villages who were not supporters of the Maoists, though it was clear that they were in the minority.

One man, a staunch Nepali Congress supporter with a twelve-year-old daughter, was apparently in great distress. The Maoists had visited his family three times to tell him that his daughter had to join their cultural group because she is a good dancer. He said he had so far succeeded in finding excuses for not letting them take her with them, but believed he could not do that forever. He said he might leave the village for good when he had the means to do so. He said similar things had happened to one of his neighbours who had a sixteen-year-old daughter. This seems to support allegations that the Maoists had abducted women in other parts of the country.

Despite the Maoists' rhetoric on gender equality, the gender-based division of labour in the village seemed to be persisting. For instance, only women were fetching water from public taps. In a house where we stayed the night, it was the women who worked in the kitchen. When we discussed such issues with a 'responsible' Maoist official in the village, he said we could expect complete gender equality only after the class struggle was successful. Women's liberation is a much-used phrase in the Maoist-influenced villages, but there seemed to be little clarity on what exactly constitutes such liberation.

The logic of war had resulted in many women and men in villages supporting the Maoists. There is clearly a history of resistance to the powerful in many villages, just as there is also a history of avoiding conflict with them and complying with their orders. Because the state forces have withdrawn from many rural areas, the Maoists remain the only force with coercive powers. Apart from the national radio, the Maoists exclusively control the other means of propaganda. Moreover, people have very little to gain, and indeed much to lose, from not supporting the Maoists.

Conclusion

The present conflict is not a product of just the past few years. It has behind it a long history of bad governance, oppression, corruption and marginalisation of people, especially women. Therefore, the conflict should prompt a review of the functioning of the state, and strategies should be adjusted accordingly. The Maoists have capital-ised on the widespread and legitimate discontent among rural women. That Nepali women suffer discrimination in the social (Bhattachan 2001, Manandhar and Bhattachan 2001), cultural (ibid. and Bennett 1983), legal (FWLD 2001) and political spheres (Shrestha 2001/2a) is an established fact. As well as gender-based discrimination, rural Nepali women have also suffered class-based and caste/ethnicity-based violence. It has been possible for the Maoists to capitalise on the longstanding grievances among women for a number of reasons: (a) the Maoists have systematic and effective campaign strategies that are based on detailed local knowledge and conducted with locally comprehensible methodologies; (b) they have increasingly had coercive powers to silence alternative views, helped by the de-creasing presence of the government, political parties and civil soci-ety; and (c) they are creative and willing to relate the broader issues to the concrete situation of local rural women, especially through the organisation of people's courts which address women's immediate need for justice quickly, efficiently and transparently.

Bad governance has helped to delegitimise the state and legitimise the Maoists. The government has been at best a remote entity for most rural women, and its programmes have not been responsive to their needs and aspirations. They have had little access to and much less control over the decision-making processes that affect their life. At its worst, their contact with the government has been harmful to them, especially since 1996. Many rural women have either been abused themselves or have seen their family members, relatives or neighbours victimised by the security forces.

War and direct violence have obviously done great damage to women in rural Nepal, individually and collectively. The Maoist movement, on the other hand, has also set precedents for alternative experiences, practices and discourses on gender equality. It is surprising that the policy makers and other political parties do not seem to have learned any lessons from the Maoists' success in mobilising women's support. They have done very little to address gender issues, either within their organisations or more generally. It is also interesting to note that the Maoists themselves have not as yet publicly produced an agenda setting out how they would seek to address gender issues more meaningfully in the immediate future—before the utopia of a classless society is achieved. In the last round of (failed) talks between the government and the Maoists in 2001, women were conspicuous by their absence in the negotiating teams on both sides, not to mention the facilitators and mediators. Besides the absent women, even the women's issue was marked by its absence. Talks about talks are, again, in the air. Apparently, the negotiators, facilitators and mediators are again going to be a men-only team. Will such negotiations take into account the day-to-day experiences and aspirations of rural women who have flocked to the Maoists in the expectation of concrete changes in the asymmetrical gender (and class and caste) relations? Will they address in a meaningful way the suffering and injustice perpetrated against women by the armed forces?

Part III. Geopolitical and Comparative Perspectives

HIGH EXPECTATIONS, DEEP DISAPPOINTMENT

POLITICS, STATE AND SOCIETY IN NEPAL AFTER 1990*

Joanna Pfaff-Czarnecka

The Maoist movement has been gaining momentum in Nepal since 1996, and in early 2002 nobody could deny its saliency or its far-reaching impact upon people's lives there. Indeed, the Maoist movement had been setting the political agenda to a very large extent for some years, and it remained uncertain how a satisfactory settlement could be reached when the political stakeholders' positions and aims clashed so severely. Inside and outside Nepal, many different views, perspectives and positions have been taken on the Maoists' goals and their impact upon Nepal's future development and well-being. Obviously, visions of where Nepali society is heading and how to get there differ significantly, according to political allegiance. Very shortly after the successful implementation of a multi-party system in 1990, the Maoist leaders decided that their goals could not be pursued within the parliamentary process. The bulk of the population, on the other hand, expressed great hopes and expectations in the immediate aftermath of this 'spring awakening'.

* The author wishes to express her thanks to participants in the SOAS-Maoism Conference in November 2001 for their comments and queries. The comments formulated by Andrew Hall, who acted as discussant of this essay, were especially valuable. Needless to say, all limitations are the author's own.

The majority of the Nepali people have not joined the Maoist movement. However, there is no doubt that its popularity grew during the 1990s, while the formal legitimacy of the political system and its office holders suffered severe losses. Most Nepalis do not regard the Maoist movement as an alternative to the current multi-party political system. However, the nature of the democratic transition in Nepal may have induced disappointed citizens to seek other political options. This essay is an attempt to reflect upon the democratic transition in Nepal over the last decade. Rather than investigating the disruptive impact of the Maoist movement upon this process, another perspective is being adopted here. It is argued that the existence of popular support for the movement (although not the impetus for its formation) needs to be seen in the rather unsatisfactory path of democratisation in Nepal, as perceived by the preponderance of the population.

I suggest that one major reason for the existence of popular support for the Maoists is the widely discernible disillusionment with current political structures and processes, and therefore it is crucial to highlight the main features of this ailment. I am not suggesting that great hopes are being placed in the Maoist movement, but an openness to political alternatives is discernible. The path of the political transition in Nepal has been all the more criticised and deeply regretted by the Nepali people because in the aftermath of the 1990 'spring awakening' expectations regarding the transformation of the state, politics and societal forces were very high and the disappointment was, subsequently, very deep.

THE 'SPRING AWAKENING' AND A TURBULENT DECADE

After the political changes of 1951, the question of whether liberal democracy was an adequate political form in view of Nepal's historical legacy was extensively debated. By 1990, however, the great majority of Nepalis had endorsed the idea that a multi-party democracy was the most suitable form for the country and had joined forces in a struggle for its realisation. Very soon a discussion was taking place in public about how democratic transformations were to be designed, and how their goals would be realised once they had been set in motion. Everybody acknowledged that the odds against success were severe, given the adverse political forms and positions which were firmly established within Nepali society, the slow pace of economic growth, and the disruptive nature of the changes generally known as 'modernisation'. The obstacles have been numerous, without doubt. The fragile economy was under great strain following the 1989–90 dispute with India, and severe floods in 1993 augmented these hardships. Besides, administrative and political reforms did not bring the expected results. To name just a few elements: the political parties, especially the Nepali Congress, were severely affected by internal disputes and autocratic tendencies; the relationship between the government and the opposition remained precarious; and policies such as decentralisation, liberalisation and governmental reform had not yet brought the expected results.

Nepal's experiments with democratic reform, and their rhetoric and representation, have taken several turns since the overthrow of the Rana regime in 1951. It is not difficult to demonstrate how complex and even paradoxical the political changes have been: one needs only to remember how fundamental and radical the democratic transition was, in view of the nature of the former political structure, the old political culture, and the social order. Among the paradoxes that come to mind were the attempts under King Mahendra's rule to depict democratic institutions through recourse to religious concepts (Burghart 1984). It is also not self-evident that it is possible to elect a communist government through general elections in the last Hindu kingdom on earth—as was the case during the 1990s.

From the late 1970s onwards there were ebbs and flows of civil discontent with regard to so-called 'Panchayat democracy'. In November 1989, news of the momentous events surrounding the fall of the Berlin Wall reached Nepal. I was sitting in the house of a Congress opposition leader in Dolakha district when I heard a report on this international milestone on Radio Nepal. In spring 1990, Nepal too was overwhelmed by the new democratisation wave (Hachhethu 1992) and, as everybody recalls, the king gave in to persistent protests, in the course of which at least forty persons had lost their lives. His Majesty agreed to form a government based upon a multi-party system, and to install one of his fiercest political opponents, K. P. Bhattarai, as the prime minister *ad interim*. Many people remember the live transmission of 9 November 1990, when King Birendra read out the text of the new Constitution. This was the moment when a new political form was promulgated within which sovereignty no longer belonged to the king but to the people; which guaranteed the division of judicial and executive powers and the multi-party system; and which conferred far-reaching civic and political rights on Nepali citizens, who were no longer subjects.

'We want democracy'—this slogan was heard all over the country at that time, in countless villages and cities. And today? Most of my conversational partners would probably subscribe to Parry and Moran's (1994: 15) statement, based on observations in many other countries around the world: 'Notwithstanding its triumph as an ideology of this era, democracy is an uncertain stage and democratisation an uncertain process.' Nevertheless, it can be assumed that most Nepali people view democratisation—along with economic growth—as a central societal goal, and only a few wish to see the former system return. Nor does it seem that the Maoist option has wide public appeal. However, in view of the disappointing performance of the short-lived governments elected after 1991, it is not surprising that the movement has gained momentum.

The 'third wave of democratisation' (Huntington 1991) which swept over Nepal, along with other countries, has not only mobilised people at the political centre in Kathmandu. On the contrary: all over Nepal, even in the remotest valleys of the Himalaya, political change has been clearly visible. A new generation of activists and leaders emerged, promoting and debating new visions of the social order and forging new coalitions. The formal guarantees of a democracy—universal franchise, the separation of powers, rights to information and organisation—have been established, and they do not exist merely on paper. A number of very successful reforms and developments occurred, among which the king's acceptance of his new status as a constitutional monarch was crucial. Furthermore, the new constitutional provisions were realised in many important respects: Supreme Court verdicts, such as those on elections, were upheld; elections were conducted in a free and fair manner; the rights to organisation and to information were realised; and the army stayed out of politics.

However, efforts to realise further goals were impeded by many different barriers. These included, to name just a few: the organisational weakness of state agencies, a lack of political will, a lack of efficiency, almost non-existent systems of accountability, far-reaching centralisation, power abuses, and autocratic, hierarchic and fatalistic orientations. These weaknesses will be examined in more detail below. Since this analysis is intended to support the thesis that there is a link between people's disappointment with their government's political performance and the popularity of the Maoist movement, but does not claim that the Maoists' visions provide a plausible alternative, it is necessary to establish that many other reasons underlie the movement's emergence and the dynamics of its escalation.

EXCURSION: WHY HAS A MAOIST MOVEMENT EMERGED IN NEPAL?

No simple explanation can be given for the emergence of the Maoist movement in Nepal, or for its success. First, we need to consider the regional (i.e. South Asian) repertoires of leftist ideologies and modes of action underlying protest movements, including armed conflicts. Over the last five decades, South Asia has seen various stages of left-wing mobilisation, disparate forms of civil disobedience, and armed conflict. The Naxalite movement was the most prominent early influence on the political agenda, but it was by no means unique. Previous movements have left a rich legacy behind: this provides guidance on how to organise and suggests discourses on injustice and appealing modes of self-representation. Moreover, the Nepali Maoist movement fits not only into a South Asian pattern of how to conduct and represent armed conflicts: global ebbs and flows of mobilisation and insurgency have built up a pattern of action which can be 'read' and 'understood' in all parts of the world.

Second, there is the impressive ability of the movement's leaders to mobilise, organise and maintain the involvement of their followers. The strong linkages to a local base that Baburam Bhattarai was able to establish in west Nepal during his prolonged stay in Rolpa and Rukum districts are especially worthy of mention. In my view, the ability of the leaders to traverse geographical and social distances while mobilising local people must be seen as a lesson for many persons in elevated formal political and administrative positions. The inability of state officials, especially politicians, to bridge their social distance from the vast majority of the population has impeded the democratisation process.

Nepal's rugged terrain is the third condition privileging this type of action, and comparisons with Peru and Afghanistan come immediately to mind. Given the precarious economic situation in the country, joining the Maoist movement became an attractive option for young men and women in a growing number of districts. Some of these districts are not really remote, but the ability to maintain control and to shift quickly between places is severely impeded in Nepal. The fourth reason lies, as has repeatedly been stressed, in the low level of societal development, especially economic development, which could provide a venue for the incorporation of capable young people into the labour market. Whereas literacy rates had increased over preceding decades, more school leavers failed the School Leaving Certificate examinations (to be taken at the end of the tenth year of school) than passed. If the Maoists are a young people's movement, then they appear to be an alternative or 'outfall' option (Elwert 2001) for those who consider themselves unable to gain access to the formal system. The option to join the Maoists is most probably additionally supported by the very high degree of failures in the SLC, so that the failed pupils cannot hope to enter positions within the government or within (the very few) enterprises. Being thoroughly concentrated upon the state as service provider and as employer, it is not possible to use the market as another option, for it is almost nonexistent in the hill areas.

Finally, and this will be the main focus of this essay, such alternative options cannot be explained simply in terms of a lack of opportunity in the labour market. It is obvious that the persistent stagnation of development in the field of production and consumption has been combined with deficiencies in political development, hence the inability of the vast majority of Nepal's people to participate in political processes and institutions. Because deficiencies in various fields reinforce each other, people's disappointment with the lack of democratic innovation in politics and administration has increased their readiness at least to consider other political options. This is why I perceive the appeal the Maoist movement has acquired in Nepal to lie in, among other things, the disenchantment of many people all over the country with the path Nepali politics is taking. The weak performance of the governmental bodies and political leaders has enhanced the readiness of some stakeholders to follow the Maoists and to embark upon an alternative line of political transition. This trend may not be apparent among the inhabitants of the Kathmandu valley, but it shows up in less accessible areas of the country. Therefore, it is important to analyse the current crisis systematically, and from different (e.g. top-down and bottom-up) perspectives (Panday 1994).

NEPAL'S LACK OF 'DEEP DEMOCRATIC' INSTITUTIONS

Several leading Nepali political scientists, as well as their colleagues in neighbouring fields of research, have analysed the current crisis in the democratic transition in Nepal (e.g. Kumar 1995, Hachhethu 1995, Kumar 1995a), and have provided in-depth results regarding the deficiencies in politics and institutions at national level (e.g. Dahal 1996). In my view, these findings need to be supplemented with contributions from yet another perspective, i.e. by investigations of discontinuities in political and governmental processes, as observed at the sub-national level, in villages and towns all over the country. A democratic transition which fulfils the formal criteria of a polyarchy (Dahl) is a very substantial move in the process of political reform, but it does not suffice. 'Deep' reforms, to borrow Diamond's term (1997), must occur, in order to avoid what Claude Aké (1995) has aptly characterised as the 'democratisation of disempowerment', a condition in which formal rules and regulations exist only on paper. Either the rhetorical depictions of the power holders cover up substantial civil, political and other human rights abuses, or else democratic forms enter into an uneasy co-existence with the autocratic and particularist institutions of a former era.

Nepal conforms to a widespread pattern of transitional situations all over the world, in which reforms have been undertaken, but have not been successfully implemented. Very often, formal rules and regulations are not being realised or institutionalised, and, rather than lose their former prerogatives, resourceful strongmen manage to gain ground within the new system (Migdal 1994). Especially when viewed from a local-level perspective, a range of inconsistencies becomes apparent when democratic reforms are confronted with pre-existing coalitions, forms of particularist incorporation (O'Donnell

1997) and autocratic attitudes, which bring the reforming forces to a halt (see Hagopian 1994). Uneasy compromises emerge unintentionally, or they can be forged on purpose. For instance, in the West African context Bierschenk and Olivier de Sardan (1999) discern 'parallel structures': formal state institutions, designed according to democratic patterns, continue a precarious co-existence with previous political structures, dominated by local leaders. Migdal (1988) has proposed a 'triangle-of-accommodation' model, suggesting that formal office holders come to negotiate with strongmen who strive to retain their power enclaves, and that all eventually come to accommodate one another. In the Nepali context, such accommodations result in a formation I call a 'distributional coalition' (see below).

The main indicators of the national crisis in Nepal become especially accentuated when they are viewed from a local perspective. The problems of Nepal's democratic transition become apparent in three distinct but interrelated areas. First, the persistent problem of the lack of systems of accountability in Nepal needs to be highlighted: this problem prevails not only at the centre, but all over the country. This deficit shows up, first and foremost, in the performance of many civil servants who are the key persons in their respective districts, though it is not confined to their actions. Second, many examples from all over Nepal indicate that quite a few elected politicians are inclined to seek autonomy from their constituencies. It is important, therefore, to establish how politicians represent their constituencies and through what means the followers can make their leaders support common goals and objectives. Third, a clash of values, attitudes and representations needs to be detected. In a world where new modes of interaction overcome spatial distances, the role of verbal representations in the creation of images becomes crucial. Since local societies in even the most remote parts of the world are increasingly drawn into global streams—in the case of Nepal, especially through links established in the course of development cooperation—handling representations becomes a strategic resource. Handling powerful rhetoric can be socially extremely effective nowadays, when the harmonising depictions of social relations offered by local leaders cover up persisting social cleavages. By using such egalitarian rhetoric, the élites create grey zones of power.

This discussion is intended to demonstrate that in situations where a 'democratisation of disempowerment' obtains, the strategic use of democratisation rhetoric can bring about social effects that are contrary to the stated goals—i.e., it can reinforce autocratic structures rather than bring about their end. Early Western debate on participation models has already highlighted the élite bias inherent in participatory forms. Currently, at a time when 'participation' has established itself as a powerful rhetoric, those people (and there are many of them) who experience their leaders as unjust, corrupt and acting independently of their constituencies, resent the gap that exists between the egalitarian rhetoric employed by local élites on the one hand and the power differentials experienced in everyday life on the other.

This chapter deliberately adopts a local level perspective. It is only through knowing about everyday forms of conflict and disappointment that we can become fully cognisant of the disenchantment with the political system, and especially of the ways in which high-flying plans and rhetoric are realised in practice. However, we still know little about local level politics and the continuous negotiations that take place over institutions and values. Therefore, my hidden agenda here is to suggest that scholars who work in Nepal expand this crucial field of research. It is essential to combine the efforts of scholars of various disciplines if we are to grasp the discontinuous nature of exchanges between the state, society, and the international organisations that have been intervening in Nepal for many decades (Shrestha 1996, Poudyal 1994) and have significantly affected the direction of the political process. It is most especially when they are observed from the 'local level' perspective that the transitions, changing potentials and problems of Nepal's young democracy come to light. From this perspective, the extremely discontinuous nature of the on-going incorporation of local societies into state and global structures becomes clearly apparent.

THE EXPANSION OF GOVERNMENTAL SPHERES OF INFLUENCE

During the last few decades, the Nepali state has expanded significantly and (at least until 1996, when the Maoist movement started to gain momentum) it has managed to incorporate the major political forces into its formal structure. Until recently, it was able to maintain law and order throughout the country. Since 2000, however, several districts have been brought under Maoist rule. All over Nepal, governmental agencies and their representatives have been involved in the distribution of goods and expertise, aimed, as has been repeatedly stated at official level, at the enhancement of production and consumption. The governmental practice of (re)distributing resources is by and large a new phenomenon in Nepal. For centuries, the state had been extracting goods and money from its subjects through different kinds of revenue collection (M. C. Regmi 1972, 1978), and only granting exemptions from or reductions of the prescribed contributions when subjects were clearing land, building terraces or constructing irrigation channels, and thus paying their dues with their labour instead. Currently, although it continues to collect revenue, the state either redistributes part of the revenue, or channels down the resources that flow into Nepal from abroad as foreign aid.

Through its distributive practices—or, to be precise, through its potential to provide financial resources and services to the people— the state's expansion and its grip upon its citizens has increased significantly. The functionaries of state agencies, from the highest civil servant down to the peon, have established a focal position for themselves within Nepali society. Because they dispense goods and services which are badly needed by almost everyone, they have come into focus as potential distributors. In most parts of Nepal, the governmental agencies remain the only providers of such resources. It is only in the central districts and in the tarai that *exit*-options (Paul 1992, using Hirschman's concept) are available.[1] The option of acquiring goods and services through market mechanisms is lacking in most other parts of the country. In view of this fact, state offices and officers—be they the local district officer or the peon—acquire the role of *gatekeepers*. Being in charge of goods and services to which the population holds a legitimate right but has no means of claiming, they can deliberately create scarcities or delays in provision, so that their services acquire the nature of scarce goods. A myriad examples come to mind: issuing licences, registering land, allotting

---

[1] According to A. O. Hirschman, customers or members of organisations select the exit-option by ceasing to buy a firm's product or leaving the organisation. In the present case, being thoroughly concentrated upon the state as service provider and as employer, it is not possible to use the market as another option, for it is almost nonexistent in the hill areas.

credit, paying out money through the cashier's desk, providing ferti-lisers on time, selling food-stuffs allotted to regions prone to food scarcity, or piling up court cases in order of precedence.

Obviously, the state has something to give in contemporary Nepal. However, it has often been the case that governmental bodies have functioned on principles which are very different from those laid down in the formal rules and regulations. As in many other coun-tries, numerous state officials impede the functioning of their offices while exploiting their positions to put their private interests first. By creating scarcities and obstacles, they deliberately create a gap bet-ween state and society, and subsequently act as mediators, helping those people who are willing to make a private contribution, while letting the others wait. In many countries (and Nepal is no exception here), parallel structures emerge—in a different sense from that dis-cussed above—because individual civil servants use their positions to establish informal horizontal and vertical networks within and out-side their organisations. When a civil servant uses resources provided by his own office, such informal networks tend to become institution-alised. Michael Lipton (1989) suggests that this kind of parallel struc-ture brings about true 'shadow configurations'. Therefore, following Long (1993), Handelman (1995) and others, we need to distinguish between organisational logic on one hand and individual action on the other. Dynamics within the formal structures of state agencies and the individual actions of their functionaries tend to impinge on one another, with consequences that are partially unintended.

Through their (potential) distributive practices, state bodies and officials tighten their grip on and extend their influence over society, while only a few people are able to gain access to goods that are legit-imately theirs, scarce though they may be. In view of the tremendous obstacles that are put in front of most people in Nepal in order to prevent them from getting hold of goods they have been promised, they are unlikely even to receive such basic welfare services as health treatment or drinking water. While the official rhetoric stresses the on-going decentralisation process as a means of enhancing people's participation in order to strengthen development efforts, it is striking that the amount of responsibility allotted to local people in these new designs far exceeds their competence and their chance to claim their rights (see e.g. Gilmour and Fisher 1989).

Zygmunt Bauman's thesis of 'seduction' (Bauman 1993), established in the context of Western societies, holds true for Nepal as well. This maintains that when the state has something to give to its people it is less compelled to display any ideological manifestations. In official rhetoric, state officials stress that their major concern is to enhance the productive base of the country and to contribute to people's well-being through investment in the consumer sector: hence this new emphasis on the provision of financial resources, goods and services. There is no doubt that some efforts (carried out both with and without foreign assistance) have borne fruit. However, we must not overlook the hidden agendas that accompany these laudable endeavours. 'Giving something' to people strengthens the state's position because there is less incentive for the state to use force or the threat of force. The political scientist Jonathan Fox maintains that with the increase of distributive practices 'carrots' acquire a more important role than 'sticks'. Given the privileged position of state officials as gatekeepers, they are able to establish themselves in focus and hence to strengthen their standing vis-à-vis the population whose 'servants' they are supposed to be. While 'the state' as provider reinforces its focal role, the officials tend to create—or at least to reinforce—semi-clientelist structures (Fox 1994), in which informal networks bind clients to them.

While a state's legitimacy is enhanced for as long as it continues to strengthen its citizens' life-chances as producers and consumers, it may lose legitimacy when its plans and rhetoric are not matched by practice. It is bad enough when it fails to provide the goods; it is all the worse when the scarce goods listed in the Five-Year Plans do not reach the public, but are captured by those responsible for their distribution. The lack of accountability systems relates directly to the topic of democratisation. With the division of executive and judicial powers, various means emerge which possess the potential to guarantee the rule of law and good governance. Public accountability obtains through diverse means (see e.g. Paul 1992), and professional standards within governmental agencies that should rule out misuse are but one option. 'Horizontal systems of accountability' (O'Donnell 1997) are an important element of democratic institutions. The existence of governmental agencies exerting control over each other is simultaneously an indicator of democratisation and an important

base for strengthening it. Another potential means is judicial practice, through which abuses can be brought to court. However, the
design of Nepali decentralisation does not foresee the provision of
either of these two types of control at district level. Whatever controlling mechanisms obtain, they are vertical in character, conform-
ing to the overall centralised pattern. Citizens cannot assert their
social and economic rights in a district court against persons who
abuse their power, nor are there established mechanisms to control
corruption horizontally, i.e. between and through independent state
agencies at district level. Finally, there are no provisions to fight
abuses through the political process.

POLITICAL PARTICIPATION

The re-establishment of a multi-party system in Nepal has been a
decisive step towards creating a base to strengthen people's participation. Elections in multi-party democracies open up diverse possibilities for political participation: the freedom to exert political will,
the equality of all to give their votes, the opening up of spaces in
which deliberations can be carried out. As a consequence, the legitimacy of political procedures and confidence in the system tend to be
enhanced. When one remembers the political cultural climate before 1990, it is clear that decisive changes have taken place: where
harmonising rhetoric formerly abounded, nowadays there is wide
scope for critical dispute. Admittedly, the pronounced hierarchical
orientations still persist, and tend to impede the expansion of popular political will. Nevertheless, it seems that the process of opening
up the public sphere for controversial debate and for critical examination of the élites is now irreversible. This has not always been the
case: formerly, the norm was subordination and subservience to the
superior, and avoidance of any public critique of those in power.

However, it cannot be denied that the development of democratic
institutions continues to be impeded. The disappointed electors have
the option of not re-electing their representatives after the latter
have failed to perform, and they make use of it. But the far-reaching
'autonomy' (Fox 1992) that many politicians enjoy vis-à-vis their voters is striking in Nepal, especially when the only political opponents
have already disappointed their constituencies in equal measure in

former legislatures. Additionally, there is the problem that local politics is embedded in a larger political system which is dominated by hierarchic, centralised and nepotistic orientations. Politicians who strive to live up to egalitarian standards may not be able to gain the necessary support from their political superiors or other powerful personalities. In Nepal, as in many other developing countries, the notion is widespread that all public contributions, including development projects, have to be mobilised through private channels of access. As a result, weak networks may render dedicated leaders powerless, despite their righteous moral standing.

Since most local electorates have been repeatedly disappointed by the performance of their leaders, and tend not to believe the political candidates anymore, their expectations are likely to diminish. Often, out of two unpleasant options—a corrupt leader, or a weak leader—people may opt for a leader of lower moral standing who is however more likely to acquire badly-needed goods and services by mobilising his own patrons. In the continuous power game, different undesirable options obtain. While private networks and semi-clientelist structures prevail, the political leaders in villages and districts tend to extend their autonomy from their local supporters when they can demonstrate strength through external networking. As a consequence, those leaders who can present themselves as skilful providers of goods and services acquire at the same time the ability to withdraw from the control of the electorate. Their elevated political and social standing is by no means incidental. On the contrary, in at least some parts of rural Nepal there is a strong tendency for distributional coalitions to form between civil servants, politicians and entrepreneurs.

The term 'distributional coalition', coined by Mancur Olson (1982), was developed from the rent-seeking approach, focusing on forms of collective action within organisations involved in the redistribution of societal produce. While Olson's analysis identifies distributional coalitions as formal structures (trades unions, lobbies, cartels), this notion will be used in relation to Nepal to depict informal structures in the first place; that is, distributional coalitions will be analysed as they are formed by office holders within and between organisations. Olson's model provides a basis for this analysis in many respects. First, it identifies a drive to coalition formation in the course of

distributive practices, i.e. the many governmental and non-governmental activities usually depicted as 'development'. Second, Olson's
very influential thesis on the logic of collective action holds true for
Nepal as well. The smaller the co-operative units, the higher the likelihood that they will be efficient. The more efficient they are, the
greater the gratification of those involved. To be a member of a
coalition means receiving a reward which exceeds the individual
losses of those excluded from the coalition, who receive less due to
the practices of its members. Members of distributional coalitions
who act as gatekeepers are much smaller in number than the persons
who are entitled to the goods that are being misappropriated. These
are the great majority: the tax-payers, the consumers, those who are
especially needy.

The main reason for the formation of distributional coalitions is
the state's role in channelling down goods, funds and services, and its
weakness in the sense that accountability mechanisms do not function properly. Members of distributional coalitions who benefit from
this deficiency can be seen as strategic groups (see Evers and Schiel
1988). Within the coalitions, the main objective is to maintain and
augment opportunities for the appropriation of state-managed resources by persons in public positions, who take advantage of these
positions by participating in 'capture', and benefiting individually.

In many districts of Nepal, the value of the goods allotted to the
population and redistributed by state organs far exceeds the sum
which is brought together through taxation locally. Clarke (2000) has
even suggested that external funds are locally considered as 'manna
from heaven', in the sense that they happen to come 'from nowhere'.
This may be the reason why people do not openly remonstrate that
resources allotted to them have been misappropriated—the idea of
ownership or entitlement has not been generated. Further research
is necessary in order to establish whether the population is more
ready to protest against such misuse when the goods that are being
redistributed are regarded as self-generated. Also, it remains to be
seen whether distributional coalitions are less likely to form in those
parts of Nepal where markets provide an exit-option vis-à-vis the
state, or at least whether they are less successful and, if so, why.

The distributional coalitions are formed and operate through the
pooling of various resources, brought together by a variety of partners.

This is where the role of the politicians becomes crucial, whether they are themselves entrepreneurs, especially contractors, or not. While there is a strong tendency to restrain access, coalition partnership is open to those who bring in new resources. Three types of actors prevail, however. They have been identified in other countries by authors such as Paul (1992), Migdal (1988) and Hart (1992), where they form perennially shifting but basically similar constellations. In Nepal, state employees, politicians and entrepreneurs pool their resources, while remaining in accommodation processes that are always difficult. It goes without saying that they are all involved in the capture of societal resources. At this juncture, the critical role of many politicians comes to light. Rather than controlling capture and acting on behalf of their own constituencies, they are accused of persistent power abuses. The allegations are not necessarily made with anger. Minor cases of corruption and nepotism are taken for granted as a rule, and occasionally even narrated with a smile. However, all over Nepal the 'clients' within the population increasingly consider themselves to be the legitimate recipients of goods and services provided by 'the state'. Therefore, disappointment, if not anger, is more and more often expressed.

Distributional coalitions are small units consisting of persons occupying different positions and charged with different functions, who channel resources away from their rightful recipients. The partners differ in their relation to the local population. While Nepali civil servants circulate between districts, politicians and entrepreneurs are 'local people' in the sense that they have usually been born in the area and have spent most of their lives there. The local élites, especially the elected politicians, need to manoeuvre between different groups of people. They are involved in dense webs of relationships with the local population, established through kinship, friendship and patron-client relations, as well as through less personal relations which come about through the electoral process. Simultaneously, they form alliances with their political superiors as well as with officials, i.e. with persons who are in different ways external to the local context. External ties and external support are an important resource for the politicians. On the one hand, goods and services that are badly needed locally can be procured through these channels, and this provides a good basis for re-election. Frequently, chances of re-election are enhanced when the local electorates expect their leaders to be good 'providers' of resources. On the other hand, of course, the electorate seeks to commit its leaders, to make them accountable, publicly and privately, whereas the politicians are keen to use their external support to gain as much autonomy from the local basis as possible (see Fox 1992).

The role of civil servants in the distributional coalitions is obvious: they manage the goods allotted to the public. Despite continuous efforts to decentralise, the civil servants continue to operate within highly centralised and hierarchical structures. It also seems (but thorough research is needed in this field) that in view of the highly unstable political situation the role of the bureaucracy has strengthened and the state has expanded all the more. Acting as gatekeepers to the resources they are supposed to allot, many civil servants tend to present themselves as unreachable to their 'clients', while the clients seek to gain access to them and to establish personal relationships with them. But those civil servants and employees who come as strangers to new districts are usually unable to extricate themselves from the relations and commitments already established by their predecessors. Again, more research is required to establish how widespread the existence is of distributional coalitions in districts all over Nepal. Where they have been established, they function because participation in such networks pays.

The question of why the individual stakeholders join in is not difficult to answer. Civil servants need politicians who are ready to misuse funds, because they can control their constituencies. If politicians were not co-opted (though there is a question about who co-opts whom), people would be more likely to protest. Also, it is essential to implement a *part* of a project and disburse a *part* of the funds; in order to do so, they require the co-operation of politicians and contractors. When it comes to misappropriating funds and allotting them to their rightful recipients, there must be a balance between 'retain' and 'take', because the prospect of being allotted further funds must keep open criticism at bay. If too many resources are misappropriated, protest is more likely. All over Nepal, there is a tremendous need for funds and projects, and as aid organisations provide not only resources that can easily be captured, but also nondifferentiable goods such as bridges or schools, local people can expect to benefit in future. Additionally, successful results must be displayed whenever superiors or the representatives of development agencies come to evaluate progress. Here, the entrepreneurs play a crucial role because they are in charge of attracting a labour force.[2] It is also their task to produce presentable results. Implementers and donors need to be shown successful projects: schools, irrigation channels, health posts; and they want to see 'the proper attitude': progressive farmers, co-operating user groups and functioning local communities.

Nevertheless, in view of frequent abuses of power and misappropriations of funds, the question arises immediately: why has there not been more protest? The answer lies, first, in the lack of such a tradition in many parts of Nepal. Second, the distributional coalitions, as much as they strive to keep their size small, are unable to close their boundaries. Numerous aspirants are able, as a consequence, to gain access to key partners among the political leaders, and at times, especially before elections, they become indispensable. On the other hand, of course, the politicians and their allies have an interest in not sharing the resources they misappropriate with this 'middle field'. The bargaining results in political patronage and in promises that need to be fulfilled, one day.

The precarious character of the Nepali democratic transition and administrative innovations comes to light in the bargains reached between key members of distributional coalitions and the 'middle field'. Formally, democratic institutions, in the form of adult franchise, multi-party elections, right to information and freedom of speech, as well as far-reaching administrative measures aimed at decentralisation and enhanced accountability systems, have been established. However, the persistent paternalist networks and very rational clientelist attitudes (to gain access to strong leaders and benefit from these relations while leaving the bulk of the local population behind) bring the reforms to a halt. The mounting disappointment with the system comes from two directions. First, not many members of local societies manage to gain access to these networks, and, having tried for a while, they look for other options. Additionally, those members of the middle field who have been hoping

---

[2] Especially in remote areas of Nepal, labour is a scarce resource due to seasonal labour migration.

for benefits in exchange for their loyalty may not be inclined to wait any longer. In their case, the option of 'voice', to use Albert Hirschman's term, may gain more and more appeal.

THE GROWING GAP BETWEEN PUBLIC RHETORIC AND THE REALISATION OF PLANS AND PROMISES

The actions of all the stakeholders involved in distributional coalitions have had a detrimental impact on the success of development co-operation in recent decades. In their actions, they have been supported by their external 'partners'. Or at least, according to villagers in several parts of the country, they have not been prevented from conducting harmful action by the external partners, and especially by the donors. The villagers' criticisms stress that donors are not really willing to evaluate results, and they claim all too quickly that a project is successful. Hence, in the assessment of many people among the local population, foreign donors have been repeatedly, though unintentionally, providing backing to persons involved in capture and misuse. This unintended support is identified especially in the fact that the culprits are not taken to task when projects fail.

Various reasons are given for this ambiguous situation: first, many failures are not evaluated as failures, but are instead interpreted as successes. Hence, an irrigation channel that has never been put into use can be seen as a failure, but an alternative assessment can claim that now that all the important preparations have been completed, it will be put into operation shortly. This kind of explanation is rather common: 'what is not completed will be finalised in due course', whatever 'in due course' may imply. The second argument runs as follows: because development aid organisations need to rely upon local allies who are capable of mediating between the local society and their partners from development agencies, the implementers are prepared to tolerate some aloofness and minor failures by these focal figures. Bierschenk and Olivier de Sardan (1999) have coined the term 'development broker' ('*Entwicklungsmakler*') to denote a special category of person who is capable of maintaining interaction with the donors, who knows their language (i.e. key categories) and who proves to be an efficient partner, as a successful organiser of fellow villagers in various development activities. They suggest, and observations from Nepal confirm this view, that a fair deal of toler-ance, and even support, is accorded to persons who are capable of fulfilling the donors' objectives.

Over the last few decades, a large number of important develop-ment activities have been carried out by His Majesty's Government and non-governmental organisations with foreign assistance. The whole country has benefited, albeit unevenly, from roads, bridges, power stations, schools, health posts, environmental protection de-vices, savings schemes, loans to farmers and entrepreneurs, and drinking water schemes, and this list could go on. However, severe criticism has been formulated, repeatedly and by a variety of actors, of the extent to which resources allotted to the beneficiaries have been captured and have never reached them.

The related problems are many and various. Above all, members of local societies are deprived of crucial resources that would enhance their production and consumption. However, other prob-lems are no less dramatic. Currently, even in the most remote areas of Nepal, villagers are well aware that the success of development cooperation has to rely upon representations of its success. What the villagers observe is that enthusiastic depictions of development interventions do not necessarily correspond with assessments at the grassroots. Moreover, the villagers' experience is that their leaders often benefit from aid at their expense, regardless of the outcome.

Success is no longer measured purely by results, but also in the forms of local co-operation, internally as well as between the villag-ers and their various 'partners'. This means that the process also plays an important role, and not solely the outcome. Especially in recent years, development co-operation has been shaped, very rightly, as a process that entails learning, in such a way that new capacities can be developed in terms of political awareness and democratic atti-tudes. Democratisation is a value as such, and the notions it carries—especially 'participation' and 'civil society'—have been repeatedly portrayed as desirable. As a result, they have been furnished with positive connotations in the national and international public spheres where development co-operation is scrutinised. The local and national audiences debating the direction, efficiency and merits of such inter-ventions, as well as the international audiences that provide support and money, are particularly important examples of such public arenas.

Hence, those persons who use these terms are likely to gain in legitimacy, as has been observed all over Nepal in different situations in the course of development interventions (see Pfaff-Czarnecka 1998).

The high legitimacy of the term 'participation' stems from the fact that those persons who argue that popular participation has become an important element of public-political life simultaneously imply that they have played an important role in this process. Public images can be manipulated in many different ways. However it is one thing to make this claim and quite another to provide evidence that the local power structures have been altered in such a way that an increasing number of people, especially those formerly excluded from the formulation of the political will, can formulate their goals and undertake measures in order to achieve them.

Unfortunately, there is a strong tendency for local élites to deploy the rhetoric cherished by international donors very successfully. It seems that members of élites who pursue their private interests, and also many donors, have an interest in creating grey zones or smoke-screens that use rhetoric to cover up deficiencies in project implementation. Those members of élite groups who manage to manipulate fashionable values and categories tend to expand their resources at the expense of their fellow villagers. This is because egalitarian rhetoric does not only tend to conceal persistent inequalities within local societies, it can even exacerbate them. Viewed from the perspective of oppressed and marginalised people, this type of new coalition is yet another instance of inequality, which contributes to a diminution of confidence in the functioning of the national and international orders.

By referring to one case study, it can be demonstrated how this postulated discrepancy becomes socially effective when members of a local society learn how they are being represented by donors, and how they can manipulate the idealising images that have been attributed to them to their own advantage (see also ibid.). The following account of a development intervention in a village in far west Nepal shows how members of this local society have learned to use and manipulate the value-loaded notion of 'local community'. I intend to show what some of them gain by playing this game, and to identify the interests that have made this representation so central to negotiations.

The village in question provides a good example of the ways in which members of a local society react to the notions carried into their lives by those who come as development experts. While looking mainly, if not only, for its own benefit, and as it appropriates common resources for itself, the local élite has managed to create an egalitarian image of the village and to communicate it to outside observers. It goes without saying that the élite is successful in presenting itself as especially dedicated to the general well-being. Even though the bulk of the villagers resent the discrepancy between the outward appearance and the selfishness of their leaders, they remain silent.

The story can be summarised very briefly. The village is known for being very successful in implementing development projects, and especially for the ways in which these are carried out through collective action. There are two functioning drinking water faucets and several kitchen gardens—a rarity by the standards of far-west Nepal. The village also has three well-maintained latrines that are a novelty in the area, and, when asked, the village headman is always ready to demonstrate the weaving skills he acquired in a government-sponsored training programme. Everything seems to work, and the local leaders dispel any possible objections in advance. To give an example: originally, five water taps and eight latrines were planned. If they are asked when the remaining items will be completed, the leaders state that so far all of these objects have been built collectively, and that the project will be completed in due course. What they fail to mention is that so far the village collectivity has contributed its labour to building structures only in the immediate vicinity of the leaders' dwellings. They are also silent about the fact that the rest of the villagers have been waiting for their facilities to be completed for the last three years.

In the meantime, a film team organised by the donors visits the village and produces a documentary film to record these successes. The communal spirit of the village is beautifully illustrated in footage of colourful feasts and picturesque terraced houses. Although most of the villagers readily join in the filming, in private discussions their criticism grows. Many of the villagers feel that they have been made fools of. Hardly anybody expects to have water taps built in his part of the village through collective effort. The resentment and the distrust of future development interventions are strong.

On the other hand, the enterprising leaders (so skilled in creating positive public images) have been rewarded for their skills. They have received money to pay the workers' wages, and for materials and the necessary equipment for building a village library lit by solar energy. The library reflects the leaders' progressive and communal spirit all the more. It symbolises learning and a predilection for appropriate technologies (solar energy is rarely used in this area; the equipment is too expensive). Furthermore, a library implies common access. But this is not the case: the building is primarily reserved as a meeting place for the leaders, who all belong to the same political party.

I hope to have indicated the main dimensions of the discrepancy. The village élite is able to display the communal spirit which it and its villagers have demonstrated to the outside world. However, it feigns this spirit, and by doing so profits from it. As a sort of distributional coalition, the leaders benefit most from the external support while contributing no more work than their fellow villagers. One of their major resources is their ability to manage the public image that is externally attributed to them. Of course, it is an achievement to be aware of the existence of such a highly valued image. Furthermore, it requires an ability to create—or rather to take advantage of—the grey zone which exists in global representation patterns. The ability to manage a public image is a strategic resource: it extends the local leaders' external contacts and enhances their prestige. Consequently, they are able to fortify their own position in relation to the other villagers.

Nowadays, development interventions involve a variety of actors: international aid organisations, transnational NGO networks, local politicians, civil servants and élites, as well as other interest groups from among the local society. Hence, people who belong to different cultures (including professional and organisational cultures) are brought together by development interventions. Furthermore, in these arenas different scales of social organisation come together, and these could hardly be more disparate. Since they dispose of forceful means, development interventions provide direct links with and channels of access into local societies. The development discourse, combining two impossibly different levels of social organisation (figuratively speaking, the 'think-tanks' in Washington and local villages) is only possible because development practice has in fact created such a link: it has enhanced access to remote societies through institutional arrangements. Additionally, one important field of development practice appears to overcome societal cleavages by creating public images that are well-suited to the negation of physical distances and power differentials. Positive terms such as 'solidarity' and 'communal forms' are the most salient images in this process.

Hence, I repeat, development agencies emphasise participatory forms: terms such as 'people's participation' and 'community involvement' are considered to be especially effective ways of stressing the active role of the local population in solving their problems. We should not overlook the political correctness inherent in such programmes: the highly esteemed notion of 'community' implies equality and co-operation—and hence norms of reciprocity—as well as the beneficial role played by the foreign expert, the national expert, the village leader, for the sake of local societies integrated by common values and norms. Seen in this way, the villagers are portrayed as the principal agents seeking to enhance their own well-being, while the civil servants and the development experts assume the role of partners. Obviously, this terminology bears a high legitimating potential for those who claim that they are facilitating the process.

To some extent, these dynamics within local societies reflect the processes that are taking place on the international aid scene. Generally, 'images of villages and village life accompany the promotion of development ideals' (Pigg 1992: 491). As has been repeatedly pointed out by scholars, two important factors accompany aid cooperation. First, there is 'an asymmetry of power that no amount of well-intentioned dialogue can remove' (Elliott 1987: 65); and second,

Many local institutions have developed a capacity to absorb the pressures from the donor... This is not only a question of dressing up project applications in the language the donors are known to like: it is much more a question of creating the impression of movement in directions which the donor is thought to be demanding...a smokescreen of pseudo-participation will be put down which will leave the real distribution of power unchanged (ibid.).

Just as local élites find ways to avoid being made accountable to their fellow villagers, development experts can also avoid close scrutiny. Grey zones which impede the flow of information protect at least some of those concerned with promoting global images of solidarity from losing their legitimacy. While representing others, they can take advantage of existing spatial and social distances: 'the effects of human action reach far beyond the 'vanishing point' of moral visibility' (Bauman 1993: 193). Legitimacy is maintained by present-ing harmonious pictures of solidarity. However, under these condi-tions, while postulating partnership (unless partnership has really occurred), the distance between the putative partners is increasing.

CONCLUSION: THE STRENGTHENING OF HIERARCHIC
AND AUTOCRATIC POWER STRUCTURES

All the ambivalences, paradoxes and discontinuities discussed in this essay indicate that political transitions cannot be conceived of as lin-ear processes. The Nepali experience confirms the findings of re-search in political science, sociology and anthropology. All those naïve-sounding but nevertheless well-received prognoses which state that everything is getting better and better are being confronted with models which conceptualise cyclical dynamics in power constella-tions; with approaches on the 'Iron Law of Oligarchy' (Fox 1992), as well as with the concept of political reaction (Hirschman 1992). In many countries the 'democratisation of disempowerment' (Aké 1995) has occurred, instead of a linear process of democratisation. This state of affairs is particularly likely in situations where the offi-cial rhetoric paints a picture of popular participation, while polaris-ation continues.

It is not only the politics and processes of state expansion that are prone to significant drawbacks. Also, the widely discussed and highly valued 'civil society', or that which represents itself as such, displays significant discontinuities when élite members expand their auto-cratic rule while presenting themselves in an egalitarian garb. It is important to be cautious of promising representations, such as those which proclaim the potential benefits of networking 'from below', in case they conceal the élite capture of such endeavours. We do not know the extent to which these political, social and cultural disconti-nuities impede people's willingness and potential to pursue their own goals. The less confidence there is in the existing structures, the greater the likelihood is that people will be amenable to political alternatives. Precisely because there are strong civil society poten-tials in Nepal, it is important to distinguish between the 'desirable' and the 'given'.

Nepal's political transition can be seen as an ambivalent process. The political take-off has been significant, but a strong headwind impedes efforts to democratise. Despite tremendous gains, such as the right to information, free expression and free association, the voices of many concerned citizens, or of those who seek to counter-act abuses of power, have not resulted in measures which counteract the obstructive forces. Moreover, there are no functioning systems of accountability. Political leaders quite often achieve a fair deal of autonomy from their electors, all the while elaborating their clientelist bastions and maintaining their hierarchical attitudes, but successfully hiding these endeavours. Furthermore, we must not overlook the globalising forces that contribute to the potential for conflict, especially by exacerbating the on-going polarisation of Nepali society. The deficiencies of the Nepali democratisation process have their roots in, among other things, the nature of external interven-tions, which needs to be understood through further research, and altered. At the moment, little confidence may be derived from the fact that the on-going efforts to pursue democratic reform fail to reduce opportunities for autocratic take over. This is the area in which new options—i.e., more radical efforts to pursue democratic reform, but not the Maoist vision—are desirable.

A HIMALAYAN RED HERRING?

MAOIST REVOLUTION IN THE SHADOW OF
THE LEGACY RAJ

Saubhagya Shah

'If the impetus for conflict develops externally, if the strategists, supplies, and grounding ideologies come from outside the country, and if
all of these are structured principally to benefit foreign goals, what is
the relevance of the concept of internal war?' (Nordstrom 1999)

'What if these theorists are so intent on combating the remnants of a
past form of domination that they fail to recognize the new form that
is looming over them in the present?' (Hardt and Negri 2000)

The notion that the armed campaign launched by the Communist
Party of Nepal (Maoist) in 1996 is a reaction to chronic poverty,
inequality, lack of development, corruption and general neglect by
the government has assumed the status of a truism among the Maoists' apologists and critics alike. As general descriptions, these characteristics certainly hold true, and to a large extent they help to
legitimise and rationalise the rebels' actions. Such generalisations,
however, do not explain why the present insurgency chose a particular time-space coordinate or a specific form for its manifestation.
Nor does the argument that destitution and underdevelopment were
causal factors explain why Rolpa, Rukum, Salyan, Dang and Pyuthan
districts of Rapti zone became ground zero for the Maoist insurgency. If social and economic marginalisation alone were responsible for the emergence of the communist revolt, the hill districts of
Karnali, Seti and Mahakali zones would be far more likely candidates, not only because of their grinding poverty and chronic food
shortage, but also because of the nature of their terrain and their
inaccessibility from state centres. By national standards, Rapti zone
displays average developmental indicators: most of the district head-

quarters are linked by a road network, the area is traversed by the all important east-west Mahendra highway, and it enjoys a network of basic rural telecommunication facilities (Gurung 1998: 171). Rapti zone also boasts a relatively prosperous agricultural countryside. In recent years, Rapti hill districts have even achieved a small measure of commercial success in exporting cash crops such as fruits, spices and vegetables.[1] It is therefore apparent that the epicentre of the Maoist uprising is by no means the most marginal region in Nepal. A holistic analysis of the Maoist insurgency must therefore move beyond simplistic economic causality and engage with the other processes and forces that are at work: the economic context can only be a point of departure, not the analytical conclusion. I suggest that the factors that led to the rapid growth of the insurgency include: acute disunity within the ruling parliamentary parties; the ideological and structural weakness of the Nepali state; the rapid ethnicisation of the Maoist movement; a long-standing culture of recruitment into foreign armies in the Maoist heartland; extra-territorial linkages; and, most significantly, the general retreat of the Nepali state during the initial phase of the conflict (Shah 2002).

The immediacy of the Maoist crisis has caused many to forget that this is not the first time that Nepal has experienced an armed rebellion in its hinterlands. Similar disturbances in the past were quickly defused when the state displayed sufficient determination and coherence in its response. A decisive stance on the part of the state prevented minor uprisings from developing into protracted guerrilla wars. In contrast, the reaction of the state to the Maoist insurgency has been characterised by utter confusion, to the extent that even after six years of particularly destructive violence the government in Kathmandu had yet even to define the nature of the threat. Official pronouncements continued to describe the Maoist insurgency variously as a simple law and order problem; as a socio-economic malaise; as terrorism; or as just another 'political issue'. In the absence of any conceptual clarity among the ruling élites, public security deteriorated rapidly, even as the Maoists consolidated their organisation and military assets at a brisk pace between 1996 and 2001.

Rather than seeing the people's war as a phenomenon unto itself, I will argue that the present conflict does not merely exhibit strong

---

[1] It may be recalled here that Rapti zone was the beneficiary of a USAID-funded integrated rural development project during the 1970s and 1980s.

parallels with the oppositional politics of the past century in Nepal, but is in fact a continuation of that tradition—a tradition that is sustained by the particular nature of South Asian inter-state relations and wider global opportunities and constraints. The recourse to history and geopolitics not only makes familiar what otherwise appears unique, but also offers a tentative trajectory for the current conflict in Nepal. We are, after all, enjoined by Mao himself to 'Look at its past, and you can tell its present; look at its past and present, and you can tell its future' (Mao Zedong 1967: 11).

In linking the Maoist movement to the wider regional context, the unit of analysis must always extend beyond the national borders, especially those of a nation characterised as a 'periphery of a periphery' (Cameron 1994). What happens across the porous boundary often has more influence on events than what goes on inside. Therefore, I argue for a historically linear and geopolitically horizontal frame of reference for the people's war. Furthermore, the notion of national security as the sum total of internal and external determinants implies that any examination of the Maoist issue in Nepal must be attentive not only to the internal dynamics but also to the external forces that shape the present conflict (Thomas 1986, Gordon 1992). Theoretically and empirically, the challenge is to recognise the internal and external sources of the war and trace the specific pathways of their intersection.

Methodologically, the topic of Maoism in Nepal is still highly problematic for a scholarly assessment because the complexities of the guerrilla conflict expose the limitations of both anthropological and social-scientific approaches. On the one hand, the arbitrary violence and physical risks of a war zone make a sustained ethnographic rendering of the insurgency impossible.[2] On the other hand, the sudden twists and turns, public posturing, hidden agendas, and a shifting nexus of clandestine alliances at both national and regional levels overwhelm standard social science tools. Any attempt at drawing a coherent picture of the on-going war has to rely largely on newspaper reports, the elliptical public utterances of the protagonists, party

---

[2] Conducting research on conflict issues or contested arenas is never risk free, but the sheer violence of guerrilla war is likely to distort the direction and focus of research, or simply make it impossible. These risks are particularly severe for local scholars, intellectuals and journalists. For a pertinent discussion of research methodology in dangerous contexts see Jipson and Litton (2000).

political literature, and cryptic pronouncements from various government sources. In the fog and din of war, hazarding meaning in the
silences and absences of the propaganda campaign often rests on a
creative deployment of Max Weber's notion of *verstehen* and Paul
Ricoeur's suggestion of a 'hermeneutics of suspicion'.

I have found 'oppositional politics' to be a much more useful conceptual tool in explicating the Maoists' motives and actions than splitting hairs over the semantics of 'terrorism' or 'people's war', which
are overburdened with ideological and moral expediencies. When
shorn of its rhetorical posture, the CPN (Maoist) seeks quite simply
to overthrow the present regime and monopolise state power. The
means employed to achieve this goal will be seen as 'terrorism' or
as 'people's war', depending upon the sympathies of the evaluator.
Moreover, by examining the present conflict as a form of oppositional politics geared primarily to capturing the whole or a part of
state power, it becomes possible to establish explanatory connections
and continuities with earlier forms of oppositional politics in Nepal
and their external implications.

THE COERCIVE ENVIRONMENT

Considering the numerous wars, ethnic and secessionist conflicts,
nuclear stand-offs and foreign military interventions of the last five
decades, the description of the post-colonial settlement in South
Asia as 'intrinsically unstable' comes across as an understatement
(Gordon 1992: 19, see also Ramana and Nayyar 2001, Ganguly 2001,
Kothari and Mian 2001, Sisson and Rose 1990). A combustible mix
of colonial legacy, imperial ambitions and religious extremism en-
sures that the whole region, home to a fifth of all humanity, is never
far from Armageddon. At the heart of the subcontinental maelstrom
is the Legacy Raj Syndrome: a regional milieu characterised by a
high level of inter-state depredation and bad faith. The core tensions
of the Legacy Raj are sustained by the polymorphous character of
the post-independence power élites, whose conception of self and
mission oscillates between that of anti-colonial heroes on the one
hand and heirs to the British Raj on the other. It is this contradictory
impulse that generates cycles of destabilisation outwards into the
regional system in the form of economic pressures, political sub-

version, proxy wars and military adventures. Independence, which bequeathed the greater part of the British Raj to the Indian republic, also left it with a split personality. Ashis Nandy's examination of the post-colonial mind is apposite in this context:

It is not an accident that the specific variants of the concepts with which many anti-colonial movements in our times have worked have often been the products of the imperial culture itself; even in opposition, these movements have paid homage to their respective cultural origins. I have in mind not only the overt Apollonian codes of Western liberalism that have often motivated the elites of the colonized societies but also their covert Dionysian counterparts in the concepts of statecraft, everyday politics, effective political methods and utopias (Nandy 1982: 198).

While India's representation of itself as the 'largest democracy', its anti-colonial legacy and its Gandhian profile offer a certain moral high ground on the world stage, New Delhi's ability to shake things up in the immediate neighbourhood provides the masters of the Legacy Raj with experiential proof of their imperial inheritance and a direct measure of their self-worth. Because the history of empires in recent centuries has been dominated by white Euro-American expansion and hegemony, even the most astute observers have failed to recognise the derivative imperial practices of black and brown sahibs, even when their impact is no less consequential for millions (Ahmad 1983, Ludden 2002, Hardt and Negri 2000). The 'pathological urge to dominate' (Mannoni 1990: 102) apparently transcends racial and territorial discontinuities. The chasm between India's international persona and its regional practices has led some to the 'sobering thought that colonial powers such as Britain, France and USA should display greater respect for UN principles than democratic India' (Datta-Ray 1984: 60). Thus, the lived experience at the regional margins is out of line with the two dominant tropes of South Asian scholarship and discourse: 'post-colonialism' and 'independence'.

Following their anti-colonial struggle, the Indian élites cultivated a progressive internationalist identity by subscribing to the principles of Panchasheel (the five principles of peaceful coexistence in interstate relations), non-alignment, and the United Nations. Nehru and his generation of Indians claimed the moral leadership of the Third World in a discourse of de-colonisation and Afro-Asian solidarity. This was projected in moral opposition to the Western powers, which were seen as tainted by colonialism and slavery. Paradoxically, how-

ever, within South Asia the Indian nationalists mimicked and consolidated the British colonial worldview and practices (cf. Rose and Scholz
1980, Jayawardena 1992, Jalal 1995, Werake 1992). Consequently:

> The long anti-colonial struggle left the Congress party with a hybrid security
> policy. It was a policy that was shaped both by the nature of the predomi-
> nantly non-violent struggle and by British colonial attitudes to security. The
> two made uneasy bedfellows. Generally, this innate tension was resolved
> through application of the Gandhian doctrine of non-violent conflict resolu-
> tion in India's dealings on the world stage and adherence to the colonial
> inheritance in its actions on the subcontinent (Gordon 1992:6).

The duality was apparent in many of the Indian leaders. Even as
they chased the British out of the subcontinent, Nehru and others
'...sought to have India recognized as the rightful successor to the
British Raj' in the region (Wriggins 1992: 97). Accordingly, India's
goal of 'quarantining the subcontinent from what it would regard as
outside interference' has remained the basic foreign policy objective
since independence (Gordon 1992: 172–3). India made its propri-
etary claim to the quarantine zone in January 2002, when Colin
Powell, the US secretary of state, visited Nepal to offer support to
the government in its fight against the Maoist rebels. The *Times of
India*,[3] a mainstream newspaper that consistently reflects the Indian
government's thinking on regional matters, expressed its objection
to Powell's visit thus: 'If Pakistan-based cross-border terrorism violates Indian sovereignty, the same sovereignty is no less transgressed
when, despite the 1950 treaty with Nepal, Indian sensibilities are
ignored by Mr Powell's explicit offer of military aid to the Himalayan
kingdom' (22 January 2002).

Independent India came to nurture great power ambitions and
was not satisfied with merely maintaining the level of influence the
British had exercised over the Himalayan kingdoms (Khadka 1997:
76–8, Dhanalaxmi 1981). While the British had largely limited themselves to defining the Himalayan states' foreign policy options, India
sought to control their domestic politics as well. According to one
assessment, New Delhi's primary goal has been to 'obtain both
regional and external acceptance of India's hegemonic status in the
subcontinent' (Rose 1978: 60). While reinforcing the basic tenets of

---

[3] For a discussion of the role played by the mainstream Indian media in projecting
the Indian government's views on Nepal see Bhusal (2001).

British imperial policies, 'Indian hegemony over the subcontinent has been modulated in a number of phases that involved the integration of the princely states, the forcible absorption of Hyderabad, Kashmir, and Goa, the annexation of Sikkim, an imposed protectorate over Bhutan, a dominant presence in Nepal and Bangladesh, and finally the humbling of Pakistan' (Ziring 1978: vii).[4] In the eastern Himalayas, a treaty concluded in 1950 turned Sikkim into an Indian 'protectorate'. As it turned out, the danger to Sikkim did not come from any adversary, but from the protector itself: twenty-five years after Sikkim signed the treaty of friendship, India annexed it through a two-stage process of destabilisation and military occupation (see Datta-Ray 1984). A similar treaty concluded with Bhutan obliged the latter to be 'guided' by India on foreign affairs and defence (Rahul 1971). It can be argued that the inner contradictions of India's regional policies have contributed much to making South Asia one of the world's most volatile and violent regions, and that Indian officialdom tends to regard its actions as both righteous and successful.

Nepal's relationship with postcolonial India posed different problems. Because of its older national roots and a monarchical line that pre-dated the British consolidation of India, New Delhi could not convert Nepal into a formal dependency through treaty instruments as it did with Sikkim and Bhutan. Nepal was described as 'a wholly sovereign state' and India had 'no legal title to interfere in its affairs. The treaty of friendship concluded by the two countries in 1950 provides only for consultations in the event of a threat to the security or independence of either party' (Myrdal 1968: 194). Even though the last Rana prime minister, Mohan Shamsher, had made significant concessions to India in the 1950 treaty in a desperate bid to prolong the Ranas' rule, this was apparently not enough to satisfy New Delhi's ambitions in Nepal.

Precisely because India lacks formal treaty rights commensurate with its ambitions in Nepal, New Delhi has undertaken a range of diplomatic and covert manoeuvres to 'mold the political evolution of

[4] After the departure of the British from South Asia, the Americans sought to fill the power vacuum in the region after the onset of the Cold War and China's involvement in Tibet and the Korean war. During this phase the Indians courted US influence, but they also resented the US presence in the region at times. For a brief discussion of the Indo-American relationship in the Himalayan region see McMahon (2002) and Goldstein (1997).

Nepal in its own image and to establish some kind of de facto protectorate' (Myrdal 1968: 195). These initiatives have yielded mixed results for India, and have had profound consequences for Nepal. One of the most consistent features of this policy has been the covert and overt support India has provided to various oppositional outfits fighting the Nepali state, in order to exert leverage over the latter. Indian goals in South Asia and the means employed to achieve them are best framed in terms of the closely linked concepts of '*compellene*' (Schelling 1966), 'coercive diplomacy' (George 1994), or 'strategic coercion' (Freedman 1998). 'Strategic coercion' refers to the 'deliberate and purposive' use of threats to 'influence another's strategic choices' in inter-state relations (ibid.: 15): 'The distinguishing feature of coercion is that the target is never denied choice, but must weigh the choices between the costs of compliance and non-compliance' with some room for bargaining as well (ibid.: 36).

Examining the linkage between terrorism and the concept of strategic coercion, Lepgold observes that in recent decades there has been an 'increase in politically motivated, state-sponsored or state-assisted violence against citizens and governments of other states' (Lepgold 1998: 135). This form of coercion can include active participation in specific terrorist acts across the border, or a more passive tolerance where a 'government is looking the other way while terrorists or drug traffickers are operating on its territory' (Lepgold 1998: 145).

Syed Ali brings the framework of 'strategic coercion' to bear on India's strategic policies towards Tibet, Kashmir and Sri Lanka, and argues that India is characterised by its use of 'covert coercion' as an instrument of regional policy. The major advantage of this form of coercion is its plausible deniability:

Those engaged in coercion have tended to be reluctant to spell out their specific demands and deadlines. Instead they have appeared to rely on the target interpreting their activities as establishing the parameters of acceptable behavior (Ali 1998: 249).

The concept of strategic coercion in interstate relations illuminates and complements Blackstock's earlier notion of 'subversion' as a foreign policy tool which falls between open diplomacy and covert military action. A state which is pursuing subversion against another can utilise local 'counter-élites', which can be either political or ethnic formations. These elements are deployed in a variety of ways in order to cause the 'splitting of the political and social structure of a victimized state until the fabric of national morale disintegrates... These tensions or vulnerabilities may be exploited by setting such groups against each other in hostile, uncompromising opposition' (Blackstock 1964: 50). A subversive strategy leads finally to:

...the undermining or detachment of the loyalties of significant political and social groups within the victimized state, and their transference, under ideal conditions, to the symbols and institutions of the aggressor. The assumption behind the manipulative use of subversion is that public morale and the will to resist intervention are the products of combined political and social or class loyalties which are usually attached to national symbols, such as the flag, constitution, crown, or even the persons of the chief of state or other national leaders (Blackstock 1964: 56).

If they are viewed in terms of Blackstock's framework, the past five decades of Nepal–India ties stand as a classically subversive relationship. The overall thrust of New Delhi's policies towards Nepal has been inspired by narrow national interests and not universal values, even if concerns about democracy, human rights and progress are occasionally raised to legitimise aggressive pursuits. A brief survey of Nepali oppositional politics and its interface with Indian strategic interests is necessary to further clarify and concretise these concepts and processes.

CO-OPTED OPPOSITION

After Jang Bahadur's bloody coup in 1846, a motley opposition began to coalesce around the exiled monarch, Rajendra, in Banaras. Unfortunately for Jang Bahadur's opponents, the British had already made a pact with Nepal's new ruler by this time. As a result, the East India Company firmly discouraged the opposition groups from organising any resistance to the usurper from Indian territory. The first serious opposition to Jang Bahadur dissipated after a brief battle in the Alau plains near present-day Birganj. King Rajendra was subsequently captured by Jang Bahadur's troops and imprisoned for the rest of his life. The defeat of the purely domestic opposition stabilised Rana autocracy for another hundred years (Bhandari 1970/1: 115, Tyagi 1974).

Nepali oppositional groups would find favour in the Indian plains only after the departure of the British from the subcontinent in 1947.

With Nehru's barely concealed support, the Nepali Congress was able to quickly dislodge the 104-year-old Anglophile Rana autocracy in 1950 after a few skirmishes in the tarai towns (Nath 1975, Rowland 1967). New Delhi helped to install the first democratic government in Nepal, in the expectation that it would remain dependent upon India for its policies as well as its security. 'As much as we stand for the independence of Nepal,' Nehru made it known, 'we cannot allow anything to go wrong in Nepal or permit that barrier [the Himalayas] to be... weakened because that would be a risk to our own security' (Gordon 1992: 7–8). However, when China attacked India in 1962, it pushed across its long and disputed border with India: Beijing had no need to detour through Nepal's mountainous terrain to get to India. Even though Nehru's concerns about the security of Nepal's northern frontier were thus proved to be largely unfounded, successive generations of Indian leaders and bureaucrats continue to use the issue of Himalayan security to place conditions on Nepal's independence.

Along with the imperial prerogative of 'security', India has used its democratic credentials to give a moral colouring to its acts of economic and political manipulation in Nepal. India's decision to oust the Ranas and install a Nepali Congress Party government has accordingly been interpreted as a strategic response to the new threat posed by communist China's arrival in Tibet, or as a logical extension of India's democratic mission in the Third World. But if India was motivated by an urge to spread democracy in South Asia, why would it exclude Bhutan—a country that is under treaty obligations to abide by New Delhi's advice—from its democratic mission and instead support a non-democratic regime there? As one of the more insightful writers on power illustrates, various ideological claims 'have furnished explanations and warrants for imperialist domination and resistance to it, for communism and anticommunism, for fascism and antifascism, for holy wars and the immolation of infidels' (Wolf 1999:1). It is an irony of democracy that great powers have tended to buttress authoritarianism among useful clients while wishing democracy on non-acquiescent states. South Asia is no exception to this global paradox.

Having been ousted from power by King Mahendra in 1960, the Nepali Congress was in the midst of an armed revolt in the early

1970s. After strong protests from Kathmandu, the then Indian foreign minister Swaran Singh issued a statement assuring the Nepal government that India would not allow its territory to be used for anti-Nepal activity (Gaige 1975: 187). Later, when the Indian prime minister, Indira Gandhi, further curtailed his political activities, the Nepali Congress leader B. P. Koirala gave up the path of armed rebellion and returned from exile with a new policy of 'national reconciliation'. As a consequence there was a cessation of India-based violence in Nepal for the next decade or so.

A cursory review of the fate of oppositional politics in Nepal shows that there is a high probability of success when there is sufficient foreign support. When such patronage is lacking, political opposition has had to compromise with the Nepali state. 'You can't be victorious in an armed struggle,' reminisces K. P. Bhattarai, the former prime minister and one of the founding members of the Nepali Congress Party, 'unless you have a false border'.[5] Like a flirtatious wink, Bhattarai's 'false border' is more than the unregulated frontier between the two countries: the wink is, rather, an allegory for the furtive affair with the alien. Frederick Gaige had come to the same conclusion from an academic standpoint almost a quarter of a century earlier when he concluded: 'Although the terai is a natural base of operations for the Nepali Congress or the Communist party...it is unlikely that without the blessing of the Indian government, opposition parties will be able to mount another serious campaign against the government' (1975: 193). Some of the notable examples of failed insurrections include Dr K. I. Singh's revolt against the agreement reached in New Delhi in 1950 between India, the Ranas, the Nepali Congress and King Tribhuvan; and the violent campaign launched by the Marxist-Leninist faction of the Communist Party in Jhapa in the early seventies. Both of these uprisings lacked external backing. In the former case, Indian troops actually intervened to capture K. I. Singh from within Nepal (Rowland 1967: 147, Sharma 1970).

Following King Mahendra's royal coup in 1960, the Nepali Congress began its second armed rebellion from bases in India. These attacks, organised by Subarna Shamsher, were developing into major threats to the regime when the Indo-China war broke out in 1962. Distracted and demoralised by the Chinese invasion on its northern

5 From K. P. Bhattarai's autobiography *Atma Katha*, quoted in *Spotlight*, September 2001.

frontier, the Indian government abruptly suspended its proxy campaign against the Nepali government (see also Jha 1977 and
Chatterji 1980). Thus, the newly introduced Panchayat system
received a reprieve that lasted for thirty years.

Although this is denied by the new orthodoxy in Nepal, New Delhi
contributed significantly to the eventual dismantling of the Panchayat system in 1990. The bold proclamation made by the Indian
leader Chandra Shekhar during the initiation of the people's movement in Kathmandu 1990 was not very different from Nehru's ration-
alisation of the ejection of the Ranas, which he issued in an expansive
moment in the Indian parliament almost four decades earlier. Nehru
declared, '...we have accordingly advised the government of Nepal
...to bring themselves into line with democratic forces that are stirring the world today and that there can be no peace and stability in
Nepal by going back to the old order' (Rowland 1967: 146–47).
Addressing an opposition rally less than a kilometre from the royal
palace in Kathmandu, Chandra Shekhar, who later became India's
prime minister, invoked the same moral sanctimony in attacking
King Birendra and the Panchayat regime: '...no man should consider
himself god, and... they [the people of Nepal] should take courage
from the overthrow of tyrants like Ceausescu, Marcos and the Shah
of Iran' (Khanna and Sudarshan 1998: 53). One unalloyed acknowl-
edgment provides a rough estimate of the extent of external collaboration in the 1990 oppositional project:

The pro-democracy movement in Nepal can never be too grateful to all
Indian political parties and leaders who have supported it. Chandra Shekhar-
jee's involvement in our movement deserves a special mention because he
not only helped to organize support for it on such a wide scale in India but
has also inspired the people of Nepal themselves to take part in the peaceful
struggle for the restoration of their freedom and rights through his historic
speech at the Nepali Congress conference in Kathmandu on 18 January 1990
(ibid.: 58–9).

Although India extracted a number of favourable treaties after 1990
and has since enjoyed the convenience of dealing with a more com-
pliant government in Kathmandu, underlying bilateral irritants such
as territorial occupation, unequal sharing of water resources, trade
and transit hurdles, issues of immigration and citizenship rights for
Indian nationals, and the Bhutanese refugee problem have become
even more acute between the two countries since 1990. Vir Sanghvi,

an Indian intellectual, acknowledges that New Delhi has played different forces off against each other in the past, and that India is now having second thoughts about what it achieved in 1990. Bilateral issues have soured such that 'Today, we are actually much worse off in terms of India–Nepal relations than we were at any point in the 1980s' (Sanghvi 2001). So, has the less than full satisfaction with the post-1990 status quo in Nepal led India to contemplate alternative possibilities? The shifting regional patronages and expedient alliances necessitate a scrutiny of the transition from the people's movement of 1990 to the present people's war.

If New Delhi's strategic goal is to exert a *de facto* dominance over Nepal which it does not enjoy through *de jure* means, a condition of perpetual disruption serves this end. Frequent shifts in alliances and regimes keep the clients on their toes, forcing them to concede more to retain regional patronage. Insecure, transient rulers in Nepal are more likely to acquiesce to Indian demands than those who do not owe anything to India for their survival. It is no surprise that many of the most controversial treaties and accords with India have been concluded by insecure Nepali rulers threatened by an externally-backed opposition, or immediately after a regime change when the new élites are burdened with gratitude for the external patronage they have received. For example, all of the controversial Indo-Nepal treaties on the exploitation of Nepal's natural resources were enacted immediately after a change of regime in Nepal: the Gandak and Koshi treaties after the ousting of the Ranas in 1950, and the Tanakpur and Mahakali treaties after the overthrow of the Panchayat in 1990. Indeed, Mohan Shamsher signed the Treaty of Peace and Friendship of 1950 at his weakest moment, when his regime was already beginning to crumble.

In 1990, the Panchayat government had been similarly disabled by the mutually reinforcing actions of opposition demonstrations and the year-long Indian trade embargo. At a moment of extreme vulnerability, New Delhi sent a new treaty proposal on 31 March 1990 for the king to sign in return for the possibility of relieving the pressure on his beleaguered government. The terms of the new proposal were so harsh that they 'virtually put the clock four decades back to July 31, 1950' (Kumar 1992: 18). The crux of the treaty proposal rested on four restrictions on Nepal: 1) Nepal would not import arms or raise additional military units without Indian approval; 2) Nepal would not enter into a military alliance with any other country; 3) Indian companies would be given first preference in any economic or industrial projects in Nepal; 4) India's exclusive involvement would be ensured in the exploitation of 'commonly shared rivers' in Nepal.[6] Rather than sign the treaty with India in the hope of saving the Panchayat regime, King Birendra instead pre-empted New Delhi's calculations by abruptly handing over power to the alliance of the Nepali Congress and the United Left Front without seeking Indian assistance or mediation. While some of the Indian demands contained in the proposal were later fulfilled in the Joint Communiqué of 10 June 1990 signed by the interim prime minister Krishna Prasad Bhattarai in New Delhi, and other secret agreements entered into by the newly-elected prime minister Girija Prasad Koirala in 1991, many of the demands still remain unmet.[7] Viewed from this perspective, the Maoist insurgency now provides a convenient leverage against the Nepali state to assist the Indian government in its pursuit of the strategic objectives contained in the treaty proposal of 1990. Moreover, the unresolved territorial dispute between the two countries, the efforts to grant Nepali citizenship to Indian immigrants, the lingering Bhutanese refugee issue and the controversial trade and transit treaty are other Indian interests that would be directly affected by the duration and direction of the Maoist insurgency.

[6] The monarchy faced a range of daunting options when the oppositional movement got underway after the Indian embargo. 'Conjecturally, had the democratic movement in Nepal been prolonged at this juncture, the monarchy would have been confronted with a difficult choice. It would have been imperative for the monarchy and the Panchayat System either to cave in to Indian demands in exchange for (at least) India's critical restraint on the democratic forces in Nepal or order increased repression and bloodshed by further alienating the people' (Kumar 1992: 7). Kumar reproduces the text and a detailed discussion of the controversial treaty proposal.

[7] When Nepal's interim government took power in 1990, India ended its year-long embargo on Nepal as a gesture of goodwill. Unfortunately, the democratic transition did not bring substantial changes to the bilateral relationship. Despite its profession of support for the new government, New Delhi paradoxically insisted on retaining the bilateral regime that had existed during the Panchayat era (diplomatically, it was referred to as the '*status quo ante*'). Many of the political and economic challenges that have confounded bilateral relations since 1990 are a consequence of this contradiction between the profession of democratic endorsement and the practice of coercion.

THE RELUCTANT RULERS

During the first two years of the Maoist insurgency it became clear that the government's half-hearted, directionless approach to fending off the rebellion was failing. Instead of taking the necessary measures to contain the Maoist threat, successive governments chose the easier path of simply vacating the areas contested by the rebels. As more and more districts were lost, the Nepali police, the government's mainstay against the Maoist guerrillas, began to suffer crushing defeats, even in its defensive retreats. The gravity of the military situation aroused calls in various quarters for the deployment of the Royal Nepalese Army (RNA) against the guerrillas. However, an outcry against army deployment from within and without the ruling party weakened the leaders' political resolve and they backed away from taking the hard decisions.[8] After causing sensations on several occasions by making public statements in support of deploying the army against the Maoists, Prime Minister Girija Prasad Koirala performed a famous *volte face* when he reportedly said 'What if the army also fails like the police, do we then invite the Indian army?'

Why was the Nepali government so loathe to employ the legitimate force at its disposal in order to contain an armed rebellion that was clearly spinning out of the control of the demoralised police force? The absence of the political will and vision necessary to defeat a growing insurgency not only provided the Maoists with spectacular morale-boosting victories and battle experience against the civil police, but also enabled them to amass significant quantities of arms, ammunition and communication equipment from government armouries. Furthermore, the rebels superbly exploited the chronic infighting between and among the government, parliament and the political parties as they played one side off against the other (Shah 2001). The extreme disunity within the ruling circles prevented the Nepali state from articulating a clear, consistent and convincing response during the most critical phase in Nepal's history. The ambivalent attitude of the leadership towards the armed rebellion during its formative years enabled a small fringe outfit to grow into a fearsome military machine within a few years. Had political will and unity been

---

[8] *Himal Khabarpatrika* 10, 2, 2000 (16 Kartik 2057 v.s.), and various postings on *stratfor.com* (2001) analyse the debate on army deployment against the Maoists.

present, the initial disturbances would have been contained with minimal loss of life and property in 1996 and 1997 when the Maoists were still testing the political waters. Instead, the problem was allowed to fester and develop into a full-blown war that is now shaking the very foundations of the Nepali nation. In this sense, the Maoist crisis reflects a spectacular failure of leadership and governance at the highest level.

One reason for this reluctance could be the political culture of the new ruling class. Having been so recently engaged in a long struggle against the Nepali state from both within and without the country, there is still some residual discomfort and ambivalence among the new political élites in identifying with the core responsibilities of the Nepali state. The progressive, anti-establishment image cultivated during long periods of exile and opposition has not entirely worn off, nor has the romance of populist identification. It is not unusual for such politicians to experience a degree of ambivalence about employing the ultimate state power against those who happen to employ the same anti-establishment discourse, using similar populist idioms. The public perception of corruption and incompetence amongst the politicians also undermined the new élites' moral authority to take up the Maoist challenge with sincerity. Besides these personal dilemmas, there was perhaps a structural element which fostered inertia and a sense of futility among the ruling circles and prevented them from taking up the Maoist threat with a sense of conviction and purpose. Some inkling of the broader sources and inspirations behind the Maoist movement, the politicians' own experiences during the long years in opposition, and some appreciation of the nature and fate of previous oppositional movements in Nepal could have had a significant impact on the will and morale of the post-1990 democratic regime as it pondered the Maoist hazard.

DIAGNOSTIC EVENTS

An important part of the Maoists' mystique rested on their aura of being rooted in the red hills of Rukum and Rolpa. This provided them with unassailable political authenticity and moral legitimacy. It is from this moral high ground that the Maoists could label everyone else as anti-national stooges of Indian and imperialist masters.

However, the sheer pace of a number of 'diagnostic events' (Moore 1994) in the recent past has chipped away at this well crafted aura of authenticity and unassailability.

The first of these ruptures in the Maoist narrative was brought about by the murders of King Birendra and his family on 1 June 2001, which came as both an unexpected bonanza and a potential pitfall for the CPN (Maoist). Prior to the regicide, the Maoists had maintained a theoretical opposition to the monarchy, but had refrained from any direct attack on the institution as they systematically isolated and eliminated the police, local critics, and lower echelon workers of other political parties. It appears that the Maoists too were momentarily taken aback by the sudden turn of events in the palace. They nevertheless came to a tactical decision to seize the moment of fear, sorrow, and confusion to fast-forward their plan for a general urban uprising.

The Maoists portrayed the dead king as a patriotic figure who had been slain by the American and Indian intelligence agencies and local reactionary elements for standing up to oppose hegemonic designs on Nepal, and for refusing to participate in the larger imperialistic strategy of encircling China. The top Maoist ideologue, Baburam Bhattarai, stated in an article in a Kathmandu paper that the massacre was the handiwork of 'reactionaries', 'expansionists', 'fascists' and 'imperialists'. The Maoist leader declared that 'anyone crowned king will only be a puppet in their [the imperialists'] hands' and added, 'from any point of view, traditional, feudal monarchy is dead and the birth of the republic has already taken place' (Bhattarai 2001b). The Maoists accused the 'Gyanendra-Girija clique' (the new king, Gyanendra, and the Nepali Congress government headed by Girija Prasad Koirala) of being part of a larger external conspiracy. Claiming to be the only nationalist force left standing in the illustrious patriotic lineage of Prithvi Narayan, Mahendra and Birendra, the Maoists implied that they were the rightful inheritors of the dead king's patrimony and legitimacy. The rebels called on the RNA to desert and urged the public to join a general insurrection.

In order to spark off a general uprising against the new king, the Maoists unleashed an unprecedented series of attacks across the country in an attempt to destroy the morale of the government forces. Dozens of policemen were killed in these well-coordinated attacks, and numerous barracks were destroyed. On the night of 12 July 2001, the Maoist forces captured the Holeri garrison in Rolpa without much fighting and took more than seventy policemen hostage. At this point the government finally ordered the army to rescue the captured police personnel from the Maoists. Although many details of the army's operation in Holeri remain obscure, and none of the captives were rescued as a result of it, the Maoists suddenly ceased their offensive and entered into talks with the government. The army's entry into Rolpa was not a battleground defeat for the rebels, nor was it a tactical success for the government, yet it succeeded in abruptly shifting the focus of the Maoist campaign.[9] It is probable that a number of considerations encouraged the Maoist high command to retreat from armed confrontation with the army at the time. First, the intensified military campaign had failed to spark the expected general insurrection from the public. A journalist commented on the failed putsch:

There just wasn't enough critical mass in the protests for the Maoists to instigate an urban uprising by piggy-backing on public anger and shock, and the spontaneous outpouring of public grief indicated that deep down Nepalis believed, even respected, the institution of monarchy (Sharma 2001).

Clearly, the Maoist republicans had over-estimated the level of anti-monarchy sentiment among the urban populace, and especially in the army and other state organs. Without the synergy of a popular uprising, the heightened military campaign made unsustainable demands on the rebels' capabilities. Similarly, despite its rhetoric, the Maoist high command might also have come to the conclusion that it was not yet ready to take on the army. Thus came the classic tactic from Mao's book: 'one step backward'. Even though what happened in

---

[9] The Holeri debacle, however, led to the resignation of Prime Minister Girija Prasad Koirala. A number of military officials, including the chief of staff, have indicated in subsequent interviews that the civilian authorities had failed to give the military due orders and specify the rules of engagement to take on the rebels (see *Nepali Times*, 21–7 December 2001). It is likely that the prime minister issued an equivocal order that left him with enough room for denial should the operation go wrong. The army's reluctance to proceed into combat without full backing from the political leadership and a clear operational mandate was also interpreted in various quarters as a secret plot between the king and the Maoists to discredit the multi-party system. After the CPN (Maoist) made monarchy its sole target following the royal massacre, conspiracy theories that saw a royal hand behind the Maoist rebellion have largely subsided.

Holeri was not the Nepali army's finest hour by any stretch of the imagination, the prospect of a face-off with the army seems to have momentarily dampened the Maoist leaders' euphoria (see S. J. Shahi 2001).

The next turning point came in the form of a dramatic revelation in August 2001 that the Maoists were operating from bases in India: this cast them in an entirely new light (see Onta 2001, Lal 2001, Regmi 2002). The damning exposé not only shattered the Maoists' virtuous image of being rooted in Nepal, but also raised the spectre of sinister political duplicity. Numerous intellectuals in Kathmandu pointed out the Maoists' doublespeak on India—public defiance, secret complicity—the false coin of Nepali nationalism. The columnist Puskar Gautam asked why the Maoists had chosen India as a base and why India was hosting them on its territory, and wondered if the 'People's War and the republic thereof will turn out to be the result of Indian generosity as well' (Gautam 2001/2). Given India's political interest in Nepal and the open border between the two countries, it must be considered a considerable feat for the Maoists to have concealed their Indian ties for so long.

The revelation of the Maoists' secret links with India would have been less damaging were it not for their initial shrill opposition to India. Having identified New Delhi as the hegemonic power which presided over Nepal's semi-colonial condition, the Maoists had fed the masses for years on strident anti-India rhetoric. In a leaflet distributed throughout the country on 13 February 1996, the CPN (Maoist) denounced the Nepali government for 'prostrating itself before the foreign imperialists and expansionists and repeatedly mortgaging Nepal's national honour and sovereignty to them. The present state has been shamelessly permitting the foreign plunderers to grab the natural water resources of Nepal and to trample upon our motherland' (CPN [Maoist] 1996a: 18). In one interview, Prachanda asserted that his army would ultimately fight and defeat the Indian army in Nepal. However, such strident anti-India rhetoric was not accompanied by any tangible anti-Indian action. Apart from burning a few buses belonging to schools owned by Indians, the revolutionaries fastidiously avoided touching any of the substantial Indian economic interests in Nepal, even as they systematically destroyed the national infrastructure.[10] In fact, the Maoist insurgency coincided

[10] Newspapers have reported that the Maoists inflicted 12 billion rupees worth of damage on airports, hydropower stations, schools, hospitals, roads, bridges and

with a quickening in the pace of New Delhi's encroachment upon Nepali territory and the unilateral damming of border rivers (see Gautam 2001/2). While the Maoists intimidated Nepali citizens who wished to join Nepali military and police forces, they displayed a remarkable tolerance of the continued recruitment of Nepali youth into the armed forces of India and Britain. This was despite the fact that in the ultimatum they served on the government in 1996 the Maoists had demanded an immediate end to the recruitment of soldiers into foreign armed forces.

The secret ties with the Delhi Durbar proved to be a costly embarrassment to the Maoists, to the extent that their 'nationalist credentials are currently in tatters' (Gyawali 2002: 37). The paradox of receiving Delhi's patronage is that while it invariably leads to power and privilege in Kathmandu, the tie itself is a great drain on moral legitimacy. That is why the Nepali élites and counter-élites continue to marshal much intellectual and political labour to deny, mystify and glorify their Indian connections, deploying the circular logic of cultural kinship, geographical proximity, and historical inevitability. The Maoists likewise gained a decisive military edge from their collaboration with the Indian state. The military advantage, however, came at a significant loss of political authorship and moral autonomy as the collaboration quickly degenerated into an asymmetric client-patron dependency.

Before the Maoists could recover from this exposé, the 11 September attacks on the United States pummelled them further onto the defensive. The United States' sudden military presence in South Asia prompted Pakistan and India to try to outbid each other in their anti-terrorism credentials. Pakistan took the difficult decision to sacrifice the Taliban it had nurtured for a decade, in the futile hope that it could rescue its Kashmir front. The retreat from Afghanistan brought Pakistan's long quest for 'strategic depth' vis-à-vis India to an abrupt end. The intrusion of an external power in such a violent fashion was also a different kind of setback for India's strategic goal of quarantining the subcontinent from external forces. India knew better than to oppose the US military expedition at this juncture of

---

telecommunication facilities. During the same period, the rebels captured 330 million rupees worth of cash and bullion from public banks (Yogi 2002; *Nepali Times*, 94, 17–24 May 2002).

world history. Instead, it sought to capitalise on the new regional equation in two ways: first, by having the US lean heavily on Pakistan to rein in the militants fighting against Indian rule in Kashmir, and, second, by bringing Pakistan to submission by emulating the new American posture on terrorism.

Despite India's efforts to project Islamabad as the 'epicentre of terrorism', Pakistan does not enjoy a monopoly on state-sanctioned terrorism and proxy wars in South Asia. External subversion, despite its redefinition as 'terrorism' in the new political lexicon, remains a standard foreign policy instrument in South Asia (see Singh 1992, Little 1994, Ali 1998, Sardeshpande 1992, Piyasena and Senadheera 1986). The use of proxy wars and subversion as instruments of foreign policy is so pervasive that when the Indian Prime Minister Atal Bihari Vajpayee exhorted the nations of South Asia to desist from all types of terrorism at the eleventh summit conference of the South Asian Association for Regional Cooperation (SAARC), Chandrika Kumaratunga, the Sri Lankan President, who has lost an eye to bombs planted by terrorists, reminded the regional dignitaries that 'We can't encourage and finance friendly terrorist organizations in one place and attempt to defeat the others [elsewhere]'[11]

Outside the region, Western nations had all along been urging the Nepal government not to seek a military solution, and to solve the Maoist issue through peaceful negotiations. After the attacks on New York and Washington DC, the West became less willing to counsel peace. The sudden turn in global events is likely to prove unfavourable for the Maoists in the short run. The Maoists reacted to the new US war on terrorism with their usual defiance. They accused the United States of being the biggest terrorist and even threatened to fly planes into Singha Durbar (the government secretariat) and Narayanhiti royal palace to fulfil their objectives.[12] However, this public bravado was belied by a discernible and urgent desire for peace among some Maoist leaders. Kathmandu observers spoke of a

...completely changed Prachanda at the moment from what he used to be or the manner he used to serve ultimatums to the government...this changed stance of Comrade Prachanda could be due to the September 11 events in America which has tentatively vowed to wipe out the menace of terrorism

[11] *Telegraph*, 25 January 2002.
[12] *Kathmandu Post*, 24 September 2001.

from the world's map. Secondly, and most importantly perhaps, Comrade Prachanda and his insurgency got a major jolt the day the Indian leadership branded their organization as terrorist.[13]

Just as the sudden Chinese attack on India's northern defences caused Nehru to halt the Nepali Congress armed operations in 1962, the attacks on the United States in September are likely to strengthen the hand of the Nepali state against the Maoists. At the very least, the events of 2001 forced some of the main contradictions of the Maoist movement into sharp relief. As the diagnostic events discussed above indicate, the Maoists found themselves looking at a potentially adverse external environment, a more cohesive Nepali state that was gradually becoming less responsive to their intimidations, and their own ideological front that was cracking under the pace of events largely out of their control.

THE NOVEMBER 2001 OFFENSIVE

Taking everyone by surprise, the CPN (Maoist) gambled on a bold military exit from the political stalemate of late 2001. On 21 November Prachanda announced that his party was walking out of the peace talks. Immediately, the guerrillas launched a well-coordinated series of attacks across the country, destroying government headquarters in Dang, Syangja, Makwanpur and Solukhumbu districts. Dozens of security personnel and civil servants were killed and the guerrillas made off with a huge quantity of weaponry from government armouries and millions of rupees from the banks. It became clear that the rebels had used the four-month long ceasefire to strengthen their organisational base, improve their logistics, rearm, and get hundreds of their battle-hardened comrades released from detention. Up to this point the Maoists had carefully avoided confrontation with the army as they mauled the police force at will, but on 23 November they attacked the army camp in Ghorahi in western Nepal, and on the same night the government headquarters in Dang and Syangja were destroyed. The large amount of army ordnance looted from the Ghorahi army camp added automatic weaponry to the Maoists' arsenal and raised their morale enormously.

[13] *Telegraph*, 10 October 2001.

Historians will debate whether the Maoists were too successful for their own good in this offensive. The rebels probably intended to inflict quick, crushing military defeats to force the government to accede to more of their demands, a tactic that had worked in the past. However, the scale of the devastation shook the government from its slumber of denial and appeasement and caused it to muster the political will to finally face up to the aggression. On 26 November a State of Emergency was declared and the RNA was ordered to fight the Maoists, now officially described as terrorists.

For the first time in the six-year-old war, the Maoists were facing a credible resistance internally and growing isolation externally, especially in the West. In their decision to resume their violence, the rebel commanders seem to have underestimated the resolve of the government and the capability of the RNA, which had not seen sustained action since the Nepal-Tibet war during the 1850s except for brief skirmishes with Tibetan guerrillas in the early 1970s (see McGranahan 2002). The Maoist gamble to take on the *ultima ratio regis* at this point was no doubt, among other things, influenced by the often dismissive assessment of the RNA as nothing more than a 'ceremonial' and 'token' force lacking substantive purpose or potency. Despite the terrible body blows it received in the battles of Ghorahi, Achcham, Gam, Sandhikharka and Jumla, the RNA did not simply crumble, as was the case with the police force. What the army lacked in terms of tactical brilliance and offensive flair was partially offset by its ability to absorb Maoist poundings without organisational collapse. During its first year of deployment the army not only checked the further growth of the Maoist military but also reoccupied some of the positions earlier vacated by the police. In all this, the army proved its critics wrong, at least for the time being. Even though the RNA lacks an advanced arsenal or adequate logistics, it has substantial historical depth and an institutional coherence that is absent in some other organs of the Nepali state. Indeed, some of the core regiments of the army predate the founding of the Nepali nation and as such they were directly involved in the national unification campaign that began from Gorkha in the 1740s. As a consequence, the army is under a greater ideological imperative to resist the Maoists than other, younger state organs.

THE COSTS OF LIBERATION

The sequence of events since 11 September 2001 and its impact on the Maoist war in Nepal makes one acutely aware of how significantly the fate of the peasant eking out a subsistence in Jumla is tied to that of a broker working in the World Trade Centre in New York or a clerk at the Pentagon in Washington DC, even if the connection is not of any consequence in the reverse direction. The most interesting realisation, however, is not that soft states like Nepal are buffeted strongly by regional and international currents, but that even an avowedly revolutionary opposition often subsists by colluding with the same hegemonic structure it claims to resist.

To what degree can an autonomous resistance movement subsist in a vulnerable nation-state? Paradoxically, movements that promise liberation may deepen dependency when the intensification of the struggle causes the protagonists to raise their bids for external support in order to vanquish internal foes. After fighting Nepal's rulers for over three decades from India, B. P. Koirala wrote, 'If the struggle is dependent on someone else's support, that person will later impose his interests and we too become ingratiated to him' (Baniya 1997/8: 40). It is too early to predict which specific demands New Delhi might seek to project through the Maoists, but it is clear that it will want to strengthen its bargaining position on several of the outstanding bilateral issues discussed earlier against a government which is internally distracted and weakened. Such motives will be disavowed, but that is the nature of 'strategic coercion':

It may also be in the interests of both parties to deny that coercion has played a role even when it has: the coercer may not wish to appear a bully while the coerced may wish to dispel any idea that he is a weakling. What is at issue here is the way in which the actor constructs reality: the quality of that construction is a separate issue (Freedman 1998: 16).

The costs of acquiring foreign patronage add up on both sides of the present conflict. If he did not have the Maoists to vanquish at home, Sher Bahadur Deuba would not have rushed to put Nepali airspace and airports at the disposal of the United States in its war on Afghanistan. The immediate cost of this was the sacrifice of the principle of non-alignment which had been the hallmark of Nepal's foreign policy for four decades. Even though non-alignment appears anachro-

nistic in the aftermath of the collapse of the Soviet Union, it had
nevertheless been one of the few avenues in which Nepal had
asserted its independent identity after it emerged from the shadow
of the Ranas and their British patrons. Indeed, the quest for an
autonomous existence within the nation-state system had been a
major part of the Nepali nation-building project since the 1950s.[14]

Non-alignment was not only of ornamental value for Nepal, it had
real material consequences as well. From the Indian sepoy mutiny to
the two world wars, the Nepali government contributed men and
material to the British war effort. Such tributary practices continued
even after Indian independence, when Mohan Shamsher dispatched
a Nepali military contingent to assist Indian forces during the Hyderabad crisis. After it joined the non-aligned movement, Nepal did not
feel compelled to send troops to any of India's many wars in the
region. It is no surprise that a section of the Indian ruling circle had
been rather cool towards Nepal's bid for non-aligned status.[15]

The enduring frustrations in the bilateral relationship emanate
from a silent struggle between Nepal's post-colonial aspirations and
the neo-colonial ambitions of the Legacy Raj. The bilateral stress has
also served to neatly bisect the Nepali political landscape into two
antagonistic camps since the 1950s. The successors to the Ranas, the
Nepali Congress Party and King Tribhuvan, were content with the
new political order at home and with India's assumption of the British suzerain role. After King Tribhuvan's death, an alternative political formation soon coalesced around King Mahendra and other
nationalists which sought to take the emancipation from the Ranas
to its logical conclusion by seeking not only an internal transfer of

[14] There might be little substantive difference between Jang Bahadur's march to
Lucknow to relieve the British and Sher Bahadur's offers of assistance during the
Afghan war. Both were presented as civilisational wars of their times, and the services
rendered can be read as tributary obligations of a dependent condition.

[15] A typical view on this issue argues rather condescendingly that, 'Though not
impracticable, the conduct of a non-aligned policy in this geopolitical setting posed
concrete difficulties. For instance, if Nepal wanted to seek co-existence with communist China, it inevitably implied a dislocation of the intimate socio-economic bonds
subsisting between its people and India' (Nath 1975: 308). See Myrdal (1968), Jha
(1977), Khanal (1977), Muni (1977) and Rose (1977) among others for a discussion of
Nepal's struggle for non-alignment and neutrality in foreign relations. King Birendra's
proposal to have Nepal recognised as a Zone of Peace was rejected by India on similar
grounds (Jayawardena 1992: 300).

power but also liberation from India's external domination. The crown's ideological shift has caused New Delhi to maintain a rather critical, and occasionally hostile, attitude towards the Nepali monarchy since the 1960s.[16] S. D. Muni, a prominent Indian academic whose views help articulate New Delhi's policies on Nepal, represents the dominant Indian position when he argues, in his recent comments on the Nepali Maoists, that 'The constitutional monarchy in the Nepali context is an inherently incompatible arrangement' which poses '*the one real obstacle*' in synchronising Nepal's 'developmental interests vis-à-vis India' (Muni 2003, emphasis added). By implication, it would appear that the Indian ruling establishment finds all other political forces in Nepal, including the Maoists, to be amenable to its interests.

The underlying contest between the two ideological forces in Nepal (broadly characterised as the Indo-centric and the proto-liberational formations) has largely determined the contours of Nepali political life over the past fifty years, and will continue do so. The schism is a double bind for Nepal: on the one hand the ideological fault-line disables the articulation of a internally cohesive polity, on the other hand the same fissure continues to offer a convenient point of ingress for Indian political and economic manipulation.

FLEXIBLE IDEOLOGIES, ETHNIC REALPOLITIK

Despite their appropriation of Mao's legitimating brand name, the Nepali Maoists have displayed little fidelity to the Great Helmsman's economic and political programmatic.[17] Seven years into their people's war, they have yet to articulate a coherent economic, political and social vision for the country. The forty-point ultimatum issued to the prime minister in 1996 (see Appendix A) was a listing of

[16] Perhaps the most overt manifestation of this antagonism occurred when the Jain Commission, constituted by the Indian government to investigate the murder of former Indian Prime Minister Rajiv Gandhi, implicated the late Queen Aishwarya as a conspirator in the assassination. Many in Nepal saw the commission's report as a tactic employed to shame and intimidate Nepal's monarchy after the fall of the Panchayat (*Samakaleen*, 11 Dec. 1997; *India Today*, 8 Dec. 1997).

[17] The Chinese foreign ministry and its diplomats in Kathmandu have gone to great lengths to distance themselves from the Nepali Maoists. The Chinese ambassador to Nepal stated that the Nepali rebels were soiling Chairman Mao's name by their terrorist activities (*People's Review*, 16–22 May 2002).

individual grievances rather than a cogent revolutionary reordering of the economy, state and society. After entering into peace negotiations in July 2001, the Maoists put forth three substantive demands: the abolition of the monarchy, the formation of a interim government, and the election of a constituent assembly. By the third round of peace talks in November 2001, the rebels were insisting only on the constituent assembly. In light of the fact that the Maoists had not spelled out what is wrong with the present Constitution or what they would like to replace it with, the insistence on electing a constituent assembly to frame a new Constitution seems like the proverbial cart before the horse.

There does indeed exist a disjuncture between Maoism as a legitimating ideological discourse and the CPN (Maoist) as its practitioner in Nepal. The core thrust of Mao's programmatic was two-pronged: liberation from foreign domination and the reordering of internal class relations were two sides of the same revolutionary struggle. So far, the Nepali Maoists have displayed no real appreciation of Nepal's neo-colonial position in the region or any commitment to the dual thrust of Mao's strategy. Internally, they have moved decisively away from their vaguely defined 'semi-feudal' and 'semi-colonial' mode of class rhetoric to the mobilisation of a militant ethnic constituency (see Lecomte-Tilouine in this volume, Magar 2001).[18] Theoretically, Maoist publications still continue to represent ethno-national liberation as contingent on the resolution of the class conflict. Tactically, however, the Maoists' proposals for ethno-religious and regional mobilisation are far better articulated than their formulations on economy, class, or state. The CPN (Maoist) has declared the right to self-determination for all 'nationalities', 'oppressed' and regional groups (CPN [Maoist] 2001: 538). The process of ethnic polarisation and mobilisation calls the claims of the Nepali state to represent the diversity of the Nepali population into question, and wins the Maoists recruits and bases among the ethnic minorities.

---

[18] The Maoists continue to analyse and represent the Nepali political economy largely as a feudal enterprise. For instance, Baburam Bhattarai recently described Nepal as being within 'precapitalist socioeconomic relations' (Bhattarai 2002a). However, some economists have argued that the 'Nepali state is no longer ruled by feudals: it has long passed, especially since the 1980s, into the hands of the trading class comprador bourgeoisie' (Gyawali 2002: 37). The Maoists are, in effect, 'trying to overthrow feudalism in a country already ruled by merchants' (ibid.).

With this objective in mind, the Maoists have created or aligned themselves with ethnic and regionalist outfits such as the Limbuwan Liberation Front, the Khambuwan National Liberation Front, the Magarat Liberation Front, the Tharuwan National Liberation Front, the Tarai Liberation Front, and the Newa Khala. Analysing the relationship between the Magar ethnic revival and the Maoist war, Marie Lecomte-Tilouine (forthcoming) finds a strong convergence between the growth of the Maoist movement and ethnic assertiveness among various groups during the past decade. Even though the Maoist leadership is predominantly Bahun, Chetri and Newar, the rank and file, and especially the fighting units, are reported to contain a higher concentration of ethnic groups (Onesto 1999: 3). The selection of Rapti as the Maoist core zone is no coincidence: Magars are the largest ethnic group in the area and have contributed significantly to the Maoist guerrilla units. In an interview, Prachanda is quoting as saying, '...these nationalities are so sincere and such brave fighters—historically they have had this kind of culture' (Onesto 2000: 6). The paternalistic homology thus established by the Maoist leader between race, culture, honesty and bravery is reminiscent of the colonial discourse on martial races.

The Maoist declaration of the 'right to self-determination' for ethnic groups no doubt follows the precedent set by Mao in China and Lenin in the former USSR. Following Sun Yat Sen, Mao proclaimed the right to 'self-determination' for minorities and the need to protect their 'spoken and written languages, their manners and customs and their religious beliefs' (Mao Zedong 1965: 306). Once the communists had taken over China, however, the promise of self-determination amounted to little more than costumed affairs at state pageantries, while in the former USSR forced relocations and assimilations were the order of the day during most of the Soviet Raj.

There is a certain sophistry involved in establishing equivalence between the Chinese and Soviet notion of a 'minority' and Nepal's closely interspersed and interlocking fields of castes and ethnicities. Unlike the former USSR and China, Nepal has no clear majorities or minorities, nor are there clearly delineated ethnic territories. It was basically due to this absolute power differential between the majority and the minorities that the Soviet and Chinese communists could promise the right to secession and later deny it, with few repercussions.

If the Nepali Maoists are earnestly committed to the project of creating multiple ethnically homogeneous states out of present-day Nepal, they will clearly be deviating from the precedent set by Mao, who made an expedient use of the minority constituency during the revolutionary war. But if instead the CPN (Maoist) is seeking to fully emulate Mao by taking the ethnic fronts for a power ride, the experiment could be entirely different in Nepal. After the Maoists attain their political goals and seek to demobilise, the ethnic genie, raised on ambitions of secession and separate statehood, may not wish to go back into the bottle so quietly: ethnic chauvinism has a tendency to take on a life of its own. Unlike Mao and Stalin, the Nepali Maoists would not have the wherewithal to contain the ethnic firestorm they had ignited.

Even as the CPN (Maoist) continues to promise the ethnic fronts a self-determination that would, in theory, re-establish the pre-unification *baise* and *chaubise* principalities, in the same breath they also speak of being the true guardians of unified Nepali nationalism as founded and expounded by the House of Gorkha (Bhattarai 2001b). The Maoists have been very critical of all other political forces for their alleged anti-national credentials, and they have asserted with puritanical zeal that they alone stand for the territorial integrity of a single country.

As if its diametrically opposed positions on the nation and multiple 'nationalities' were not confusing enough, the CPN (Maoist) passed an even more intriguing resolution at its second national convention in early 2001, calling for Nepal to enter a soviet-style federation of South Asian republics (Wagle 2001, also see Sharma in this volume). Short of a military conquest, the prospect of such a regional union emerging in South Asia through mutual consensus is highly unlikely. Despite the serious political and historical obstacles which stand in its way, it is interesting that the leaders of the ruling Bharatiya Janata Party (BJP) in India have also aired their hopes for the realisation of a subcontinent-wide 'Akhand Bharat' nation, basing these hopes on brahmanic assumptions about the religious and cultural unity of South Asia.[19] The apparent convergence in the world view (or regional view, to be more precise) of India's far right and the Nepali far left is quite interesting.[20] All three of the Maoist propositions

[19] *timesofindia.com*, 22 Jan. 2002.
[20] Even as the CPN (Maoist) indulges in the systematic destruction of the Hindu religious and cultural edifice in Nepal, senior Maoist leaders have upheld the right of

reviewed here—the promise of self-determination which, when taken to its logical conclusion, would entail dividing present-day Nepal into multiple ethno-states; the nationalistic pledge to consolidate the existing nation-state; and immersion into a sub-continental federation—cannot be true at the same time. In fact they stand as mutually exclusive. Despite being often accused of dogmatism by their detractors, the Nepali Maoists display a remarkable degree of ideological mobility and deliberate ambiguity, and have proved to be particularly dexterous in maintaining contradictory positions. The drift from both Maoist and Marxian doctrine was officially institutionalised in early 2001, when the party's second national conference declared its governing ideology to be 'Prachanda Path', appropriately conveying the double meaning of 'extreme path' and 'path of Prachanda', after their party's powerful chairman.

While the Maoists are shifting internally from the rhetoric of class conflict to that of ethnic polarisation, externally, their rhetoric on imperialism and hegemony notwithstanding, they have so far exhibited little interest in undoing Nepal's subordination in the regional or global matrix. On the contrary, the rebels have adopted a Machiavellian pragmatic to turn the Nepali state's historic external limitations into potent assets. These strategies, while conveying the appearance of novel breaks with the past, invoke historical precedents at several levels. Karl Marx's sense of *déjà vu* is particularly illuminating here:

…just when they seem engaged in revolutionizing themselves and things, in creating something entirely new, precisely in such epochs of revolutionary crisis they anxiously conjure up the spirits of the past to their service and borrow from them names, battle slogans and costumes in order to present the new scene of world history in this time-honored disguise and this borrowed language (Marx 1978: 595).

The familiar historical terrain the Maoists have traversed over the past seven years en route to their final rendezvous with the Legacy Raj provides a basis for identifying the Maoist war as a replication of the conventional form of oppositional politics, rather than a revolutionary break from it. All successful oppositional engagements have so far entailed a coupling with Indian interests in order to

Hindu fundamentalists to build the Rama temple on the disputed Babri Masjid site in Ayodhya. Maoists have also sought to win favours from New Delhi by giving credence to Indian accusations that Nepal has become a launching ground for Pakistani subversion against India (*Spotlight*, 24–30 May 2002).

encircle, coerce and compromise the Nepali state, and it appears that the Maoists have also opted for this proven strategy, albeit in a different guise.

A cursory survey of the fate of recent communist insurgencies in the Third World provides us with some possible scenarios for Nepal. Under favourable external circumstances, it is conceivable that the state will defeat the Maoists, as was the case in Thailand, Malaysia and Sri Lanka. Alternatively, if the regional milieu continues to favour the Maoists, the present strife could degenerate into a long war of attrition as in Colombia at present, and Guatemala and El Salvador in the past, before the rebels finally made peace with the state. Although the CPN (Maoist) models itself on the Shining Path movement and takes much inspiration from its Andean comrades, the Peruvian state under President Fujimori largely destroyed the Peruvian Maoists. Unless the prevailing international context alters radically, the Maoists are unlikely to replicate the classic communist victories once seen in Vietnam, Cambodia, Cuba, Korea and China.[21]

Although it is a relatively weak state, Nepal has in the past displayed a remarkable ability to defuse, co-opt or neutralise armed rebellions when the rebels have lacked sustained foreign backing. If the Maoists are denied Indian support and Western governments continue to back the Nepal government in the present conflict, the Maoists will find it hard to repeat their spectacular successes. On the other hand, whenever there has been adequate extra-territorial support for Nepali oppositional forces, the Nepali state has had to concede not only to them but also to their foreign patrons. Sensing the lack of enthusiasm for orthodox communist doctrine among important constituencies both within and outside the country, the CPN (Maoist) leadership in 2002 began to quietly back-pedal on its revolutionary goal of a Maoist one-party state and a communist economy.

---

[21] Comparing extreme left politics in Peru and Nepal, Andrew Nickson suggests that a transition from authoritarian rule to a non-performing democratic regime is a fertile space for Maoist revolutionaries. 'In the case of Peru, the early years of the armed struggle launched by Sendero Luminoso went largely unreported in the euphoria created by the return to democracy. There was general disbelief that a tiny faction of the communist movement which had been quiescent during the military regime, would choose this moment in time to launch its revolutionary war' (Nickson 1992: 382). While there are some commonalties in the evolution of the CPN (Maoist) and the Shining Path Maoists of Peru, there are also significant differences, especially in their regional and ethno-religious contexts, which Nickson did not take into account.

The only revolutionary objective now retained is the destruction of the 'feudal' monarchy (RW 2002, MIM 2002).[22] The latest ideological repositioning is seen as a tactical manoeuvre to check the growing isolation from the middle classes and to make the insurgency more acceptable to a Western audience which might be opposed to communism but sympathetic to a republican cause arrayed against a 'feudal monarchy'. The ideological dissimulation from the dictatorship of the proletariat to what Maoist leader Baburam Bhattarai describes as a 'bourgeois democratic republic' has already contributed to a vertical split within the Nepali Congress in 2002. If the ruling party fissure becomes a catalyst for a wider realignment in the underlying bipolarity of Nepali politics, the process will produce strategic military and political options and assets for the CPN (Maoist).

It is interesting that even as the Indian government stepped forward to condemn the Maoists and offer the Nepali army some military hardware,[23] newspaper reports suggested that the Maoists continued to receive supplies and shelter in India.[24] By supporting and supplying both sides of the civil war in Nepal, New Delhi has perfected the imperial art of divide and rule. This is not the first time it has done so. Before Mohan Shamsher signed the controversial treaty with India in 1950, Nehru went on assuring the Nepali prime minister that India would come to his aid even as New Delhi was readying the Nepali Congress for the eventual assault against the Ranas (K. C. 1976: 12). As B. P. Koirala put it, 'It seems that India always had two opposing jaws; one would direct [us] to stay with the king while the other would encourage [us] not to be afraid of going against the king' (Koirala 1998: 305).[25] The clashing of jaws is a powerful metaphor

[22] These ideological shifts were first reflected in two articles posted on the web by Baburam Bhattarai during the first half of 2002. The first of these is addressed to a Western audience, while the second one is aimed at the Nepali middle classes and Nepali migrants working in the West.

[23] After 11 September 2001, the Indian prime minister and foreign minister publicly announced that India would help the Nepali government in its fight against the Maoists, whom they now identified as terrorists. India was the first country to do so (*People's Review*, 17 Oct. 2001).

[24] These contradictory moves from India, especially after 11 September 2001, can perhaps be explained by the possibility that the various organs of the Indian state, viz. the foreign ministry, defence establishment and the intelligence agencies, were pursuing different sets of objectives within the same policy framework towards Nepal, and not necessarily working at cross-purposes.

[25] A month after the Indian foreign minister had labelled Nepali Maoists 'terrorists' and publicly pledged support to the Nepali government in the conflict, the senior

for the internecine conflict that is violently churning up the entrails of the divided Nepali polity today.

The editorial in the *Times of India* which sought to chastise US secretary of state Colin Powell for offering the Nepal government some support against the Maoists also gave an indication of India's relationship with the Nepali rebels by contrasting them favourably with Osama bin Laden. 'Unlike the Taliban and many outfits inspired by Osama bin Laden, the Maoists of Nepal, for all their violence, represent a progressive protest movement which is neither anti-modern nor exclusivist in ethnic and religious terms,' the paper argued.[26] In a cogent critique of the various hegemonic discourses of civilisation, enlightenment and order the British employed to justify their domination over the Indians, Jawaharlal Nehru noted: 'Thus hypocrisy pays its tribute to virtue and a false and sickening piety allies itself to evil deeds' (Nehru 1966: 63). While it might be too early to judge whether this advocacy of the 'progressive, modern and inclusive' Maoists is inspired by Nehru's 'sickening piety' or by something noble, the message from India's fourth estate was quite clear: one country's terrorists are another's progressive agents. Given the disposition of the Legacy Raj and the oppositional imperative in Nepali politics outlined in this chapter, the contours as well as the final outcome of the present war will depend largely on the manner in which the opaque relationship between the Delhi Durbar and the Nepali Maoists matures in the months ahead.

Maoist leader Krishna Bahadur Mahara flew in from New Delhi on an Indian Airlines flight to lead the Maoist delegation in the third round of talks with the government held in Kathmandu. Subsequently, many of the Maoist leaders continued to provide regular statements and interviews to various media from different Indian cities.

[26] 'Terror Error' (editorial), *Times of India*, 22 Jan. 2002.

MAOISM IN NEPAL

TOWARDS A COMPARATIVE PERSPECTIVE*

Philippe Ramirez

Although Nepal's mainstream press has carried an abundance of commentary on the Maoist movement, much of it subtle and well-informed, it is striking that the non-Nepali and earlier forms of Maoism have seldom been discussed.[1] An insight into these aspects could contribute greatly to understanding the contemporary Maoist movement in Nepal. In fact, while the development of the movement itself has been strongly influenced by the context in Nepal, the identity its promoters explicitly claim, their phraseology and the empirical features of the conflict, refer directly to a 'Maoist' model. This chapter offers a few examples that show what a comparison with similar phenomena elsewhere could bring to an anthropological approach to Nepali Maoism, as well as the methodological difficulties that such comparisons can entail.

Comparisons can be drawn on several grounds, and can adopt several approaches: geopolitical, sociological, historical, or economic. My main perspective here will be anthropological and sociological or, to be more precise, I will focus mainly on the relationship between ideology—in the broad sense, as a set of representations and discourses—and social processes. To what extent can other Maoist phenomena be compared with what happens in Nepal, in terms of the social groups and ideologies involved?

Of the numerous courses that are open to it, this comparison will follow two main axes. These correspond to two basic questions, which, in the long term, could help to delineate the specificities and general-

* I thank Krishna Hachhethu, Hari Roka and Marie Lecomte-Tilouine for their comments on this chapter.

[1] As an exception to this generalisation see the 'Red Alert' issue of *Himal South Asia*, Sept.–Oct. 1997.

ities of the Maoist movement in Nepal. These questions pertain to
the conditions and conceptions of the people's war:

(1) Which factors determine the location of the 'base areas', the
     cradles of all instances of people's war? What are the relative
     weights of local grievances and tactical issues?
(2) What do different Maoist ideologies have to say on the subject
     of violence? How can discourses on violence be interpreted in
     terms of political culture?

THE GENESIS: WHY HERE AND NOT THERE?

Political movements professing Maoism have not met with the same
success everywhere, neither in different countries on the same conti-
nent, nor in different areas of the same country. Though a truism,
this assertion has some far-reaching sociological implications. Geopolitical and socio-economic factors are the most commonly invoked
causes of Maoist insurgencies. The geopolitical context, i.e. external
interference, or at least external influence, may be decisive at the
national level. In Cambodia, Ho Chi Minh's original scheme for an
'Indochinese federation' of socialist states gave the first impetus to
the creation of a Cambodian communist movement in the fifties;
later on, the combined interference of Hanoi, Beijing and Washington in Cambodia were crucial ingredients in the emergence of the
Khmer Rouge (Kiernan 1982, 1985). Similarly, the Sino-Indian crisis
was one major component of the Naxalite phenomenon (Banerjee
1984: 89) and, according to some, Indian interference has played a
central part in the growth of Maoism in Nepal. International interference is less obvious elsewhere—in the Philippines or in Peru, for
instance. As for the socio-economic thesis, it is so widespread that it
does not need to be set out in detail here. Without evoking the Maoist theory itself, the most prevalent version of this thesis identifies the
state's failure to address the economic grievances of deprived populations as the primary causative factor. Obviously, it can hardly be
denied that, in the most general terms, Maoist insurgencies spring
from materially distressed areas. If we descend to the local level,
however, these two factors seem to me to fall short of a full explanation of why a movement appears in a particular district, and not in

neighbouring ones. Furthermore, the important question of how an alien political entity, Maoism, has been introduced and possibly adopted also remains unanswered. This is a central issue, because it is concerned with the elementary processes through which, at a very local and concrete level, an external or isolated initiative encounters a society.

How was it, for example, that Naxalism developed in a well-demarcated and compact area of India, stretching from the Darjeeling tarai to northern Andhra Pradesh, but was almost totally absent elsewhere? While the proximity of China could be a possible explanation for the northern origins of Naxalism, China's influence on the later evolution of the movement is less easily discerned. As for the socio-economic explanation, it is barely admissible in this case: are agrarian relations more egalitarian in the Indian states of Maharashtra and Uttar Pradesh than they are in West Bengal? Similarly, southwest and east Cambodia, the strongholds of the Communist Party of Cambodia before 1970, experienced neither the poorest economic conditions nor the most strained social relations (Vickery 1984: 140). And the province of Ayacucho, the cradle of Sendero Luminoso, was not during the eighties the most depressed region of Peru (Marks 1996: 258).

As we are dealing with insurgencies here, and more particularly with Maoist insurgencies, military tactics are of great importance. An armed struggle will naturally be launched in mountainous and forested tracts where, according to Mao Zedong himself, 'base areas' will be more securely established and defended (Mao Zedong 1938: 94–6). As a matter of fact, almost all of the Naxalite areas were situated in the least populated belts of eastern India, and this had immediate implications for the social environment in which the movement would evolve: these regions were those inhabited by so-called 'tribals' (to use the anthropological jargon on India) i.e., by politically and culturally 'peripheral' groups. The three main centres of the Naxalbari uprising in 1967 were situated around Santhal, Oraon and Rajbansi villages (Banerjee 1984: 86). Parallels can be drawn with the Indian-populated zones of eastern Peru in the 1980s (Degregori 1989). In the Philippines, the New People's Army tried to establish its initial 'base areas' in central Luzon, but had to shift to the more unapproachable sectors of northern Luzon and the islands of Samar and

Mindanao when it came under military pressure in 1974 (Marks 1996: 98). The first base areas in Cambodia present a more complex picture: all were situated in geographically peripheral and thinly populated zones, but some were inhabited by the dominant Khmer ethnic group.[2] The JVP (Janata Vimukhti Peramuna) insurgency of 1971 in Sri Lanka was launched in relatively central and populated areas of the island, and its brevity provides a very telling example: it was checked by the state within six months (Marks 1996: 179–82). According to the documents at our disposal, no ethnic revolt preceded the commencement of Maoist activities in any of these areas, whether in Peru, India or the Philippines. Similarly, it should be emphasised that the initiation of a people's war has never provoked a general ethnic uprising—and to date this has also been the case in Nepal.

Thus, although revolutionary activity can benefit from discontentment with the centre among peripheral ethnic groups, it benefits first of all from the military advantages of their natural environment. This was acknowledged by the Communist Party of Nepal (Maoist) itself: '...for waging war in Nepal it has neither large area, nor any possibility of using any sea; neither there is wide forest, nor there is any possibility of direct help or support from any other neighbouring country. However, the geographical situation [i.e. mountainous terrain] is most favourable for waging guerrilla war' (CPN [Maoist] 1996).

Assuming that the sites of original Maoist insurgencies are distinguished first and foremost by their tactical assets presumes that they are outcomes of a rational choice made at an early stage, rather than of spontaneous insurrection. This leads us directly to the question of the identity of those who instigate people's wars. An essential factor in the geographical setting of Maoist insurgencies seems to be the individual backgrounds of their leaders. This is particularly apparent in South Asia. The Naxalbari leaders had been active in local CPI committees well before the revolt occurred in May 1967. Charu Mazumdar was from a *zamindari* (landowning) family, his own father being a lawyer. He grew up and established peasant organisations in Siliguri and Jalpaiguri, a few dozen kilometres north of the Naxalbari area (Banerjee 1984: 86, 319–22). Jangal Santhal, a peasant member of the Darjeeling district committee of the CPI (M), played a role in

---

[2] The Khmer Rouge later enforced an artificial ethnic cleavage between the rurals ('the old people') and the urbans ('the new people') (Vickery 1984: 87).

promoting committee policies among Santhal villages before 1967. Babulal Biswakarma, another Naxalbari leader, was from a landless family of the same region. Vempatapu Sathyanarayana ('Sathyam'), the colourful leader of the Srikakulam movement in Andhra Pradesh (1968), was part of a group of communist teachers who had been mobilising local minorities since the 1950s, and he married two women from the Savaru and Jatapu ethnic groups (Banerjee 1984: 101). His closest assistant, Adibhalta Kailasham, also a school teacher, was the son of a Srikakulam landlord. And when in the early 1980s the Andhra insurgency spread to the northwest of the state it was a result of the creation of the 'People's War Group' by Kondapalli Seetharamiah, another school teacher, who lived in nearby Warangal.

The following model could be proposed: the Naxalite movements were launched by literate individuals who hailed from areas close to the hearth of the uprising, and relied upon networks which went down to the village level. The leading figures in the Shining Path movement came mainly from the educated gentry of provincial towns such as Ayacucho, in the Peruvian hinterland, who developed contacts with the surrounding Indian communities. It seems that in Peru, as well as in India, activists from ethnic minorities, while not barred from leadership positions, were confined to secondary levels. In fact, most connections between Sendero Luminoso and the Indians were built by Osman and Martinez, two anthropologist members of the Central Committee. The original Khmer Rouge strongholds in east and southwest Cambodia were established in the early 1960s by former anti-French rule activists with a communist background, who reactivated their local cells.[3] Originating from the local bourgeoisie, generally moderately educated, and including several Buddhist monks, they were subsequently (1963–67) joined by Phnom Penh 'intellectuals' such as Hou Youn, Khieu Samphan and Pol Pot. These had been born to leading families, had received a university education in France, and were mostly top-level bureaucrats.

Thus it may be suggested that the most favourable terrain for Maoist insurgencies appears to exist at the interface between individual-centred networks and peripheral areas and groups. This is

[3] The archetype of the provincial leaders is undoubtedly the famous Ta Mok 'the Butcher', who strengthened his already powerful southwestern network by giving his numerous daughters in marriage to rising communist cadres (ibid.: 106).

particularly true in the initial phases of an insurgency, when the insurgents depend heavily on the human environment to guarantee secrecy and supplies. Later on, when the movement's authority and autonomy have been established, the willing support of the local population becomes a less crucial factor. To what extent does this pattern conform to the Nepali reality? The Nepali insurgency sprang up and built its main stronghold (and until 1999 almost its only one) in the isolated and peripheral mid-western districts of Rolpa and Rukum. Obviously, from the very beginning of the insurgency in February 1996, violent raids were launched in less remote districts too, for example in Gorkha and Kavre. However, it was in Rolpa and Rukum that the guerrilla movement openly established its authority. Two particular features of this region may be pointed out: the existence of 'autonomous' political networks, and the presence of fairly numerous ethnic minorities.[4] Taken separately, neither is peculiar to mid-western Nepal: it was their convergence that was decisive.

Throughout Nepal, the strength of personal networks plays a crucial role in the shaping of the local political landscape. This particular part of Nepal, situated broadly between the Rapti and Karnali rivers, is the home of networks which broke away from the political forces that were dominant at the national level. West Nepal as a whole had shown a tendency to reject the authority of Kathmandu on several occasions. To give just two examples: Doti and Jumla revolted against the Gorkhali authorities after the eighteenth-century unification of Nepal and, after the fall of the Ranas, Bhim Datta Pant, a provincial governor installed by the Congress liberation army in the far west, refused to lay down his arms, and organised peasant rebellions against slave owners (Ojha 2000/1, Pokhrel and Vasyal 1998/9). However, Rolpa and Rukum do not seem to have followed such tendencies until more recently. To understand what happened there, one must consider the next district to the east, Pyuthan. In 1954, half a dozen activists calling themselves the 'Progressive Study Group' provided a three-month political and physical training to 150 local youths. Subsequently, armed clashes with the 'local feudals' occurred in Narikot (Pokhrel and Vasyal 1998/9: 10–12). One of these activists was Mohan Bikram Singh Gharti, who made his way onto the Central

---

[4] On the Magars and the Nepali Maoist movement see de Sales (2000: 56–7) and Lecomte-Tilouine (this volume).

Committee of the Nepal Communist Party as early as the second convention of 1957, and secured second place for it in the Pyuthan constituency in the 1959 general elections.[5]

Although many details of Mohan Bikram Singh's biography remain obscure, the dramatic course followed by this central leader within the Nepali left is important for an understanding of the political history of this area of Nepal. After the abolition of the multi-party system in December 1960, Mohan Bikram Singh managed to keep communist cells active in east Pyuthan, thereby weakening the influence of the local Nepali Congress Party and extending links to localities just across the district borders in Argha-Khanchi, Gulmi and Baglung. Throughout his career in the party, Mohan Bikram followed a confrontational line, systematically challenging the dominant one, and this led him to form a separate organisation under his own leadership, the CPN (Fourth Convention) in September 1974. The Fourth Convention adopted a so-called 'hard line' and formulated plans for an armed insurrection. It called for a boycott of all state-organised polls, and the results of the 1980 referendum on multi-partyism clearly showed the nature and extent of Mohan Bikram's regional influence: the rate of abstention was very high in a zone which extended from Argha-Khanchi and Pyuthan to Salyan, and included Rolpa and Rukum. The radical programme of the Fourth Convention was not translated into noticeable violence at the local level. Individually, workers of the party had to face tough repression by the police, including both arrest and torture. However, during both the pre-referendum period and the 1990 movement for the restoration of democracy, Pyuthan itself does not seem to have experienced the kind of major agitation which occurred in Kathmandu, the tarai, Myagdi or neighbouring Argha-Khanchi. Nevertheless, this zone was clearly moving away from the direct influence of the CPN (Marxist-Leninist), which was gradually becoming the mainstream CPN faction.

The process of fragmentation, which took place at an organisational level in the extreme left in the 1980s, had direct repercussions at the local level. The ideological separation in 1983 between Nirmal Lama and Mohan Bikram Singh, the two main leaders of the Fourth Convention, did not cause a split in the party's western strongholds,

[5] On the history of the Nepal Communist Party see Rawal (1990/1) and Surendra K. C. (1999/2000).

where its leaders were under the direct authority of Mohan Bikram Singh. As a result, all former Fourth Convention workers and supporters in Pyuthan, western Argha-Khanchi and Gulmi—and possibly in Rolpa as well—adopted the new label 'CPN (Masal)'. Mohan Vaidya's rupture from Masal in 1985 and the creation of his 'Mashal' party had more serious consequences: Masal's outer zones suffered a crack, particularly in Dang (Vaidya's birthplace) and in Rolpa. In the latter district, oppositional activities against the Panchayat regime had become especially strong in the pre-referendum period, under the leadership of Barman Budha. The Nepali army's intervention in Thabang-Rolpa in 1981 helped to radicalise Budha's audience.[6] Masal's residual influence suffered a further blow in November 1990: while Mohan Bikram Singh remained underground even after the restoration of multi-party democracy and stuck to his plans for an armed struggle aimed at the establishment of a Nepali republic, other Masal leaders were contemplating positions of power within the new regime. Consequently, the faction led by Baburam Bhattarai left CPN (Masal) and joined the CPN (Mashal) and the Fourth Convention to form the Unity Centre, presided over by Prachanda (CPN-Mashal), in order to contest the upcoming elections under the banner of the 'United People's Front' (Samyukta Jan Morcha).

The results of the 1991 general election in the mid-west gave a clear picture of the realignment of local political forces. The UML had to acknowledge its weakness in Rolpa, Rukum, Pyuthan, Jajarkot and Kalikot, and it withdrew almost all of its candidates in favour of the United People's Front (UPF) and the Nepal Workers and Peasants Party (NWPP). Rolpa and Rukum confirmed the growing grip of Mashal on the area at the expense of Masal, with the UPF winning in three constituencies and securing second place in a fourth. In these two districts, Masal's call for a boycott was heeded only in a few localities of Rolpa. In contrast, Pyuthan proved its obedience to Mohan Bikram Singh with the country's highest rate of abstention (sixty per cent).

Thus, personal antagonisms and organisational splits at senior levels of the communist movement resulted in very concrete differentiations at district level, reflecting the strength of personal networks in

[6] The 1952 peasant agitation led by Kami Budha (mentioned in CPN [UML] 2001/2: 2 but not in Pokhrel and Vasyal 1998/9) would have to be documented to explore the possibility of links between it and the subsequent striking of communist roots in Rolpa.

the political system. When the CPN (Maoist) was preparing for armed struggle in the months leading up to February 1996, it did as other Maoist movements had done elsewhere: it relied on old, well-entrenched local networks. And no other region combined the advantage of providing not only these networks, unchallenged by other components of the left as they were in eastern Nepal, but also a population in a geographically marginal position. The split between the eastern zone (Pyuthan, west Argha-Khanchi) and western zone (Rolpa) of Mohan Bikram Singh's former domain resulted in significantly different political histories. Ironically, the roles of these two factions were inverted when Masal contested the 1999 elections: three local Masal leaders (Navaraj Subedi, Hari Acharya and Dilaram Acharya) were elected in the eastern sector (Pyuthan-2, Pyuthan-1 and Argha-Khanchi-1), while in the west Barman Budha and Krishna Bahadur Mahara, who had been UPF MPs in 1991 (Rolpa-1, Rolpa-2), became senior leaders of the Maoist insurgency.

Neither the brutality of state repression in the Rolpa-Rukum area during the 1990s nor the deep resentment it aroused in the local population should be underestimated, but they have to be placed in their proper historical and sociological context. As in most of the other cases given here, the political leadership that was in the vanguard of the insurgency did not follow or spring out of a peasant upheaval: it preceded it.

THE ANNIHILATION OF CLASS ENEMIES

The other domain in which a comparison of the Nepali Maoist movement with similar phenomena elsewhere may prove enlightening is that of ideology. Here I will address only certain components of the worldview of Maoism as they are reflected in the leaders' writings. At first glance, Nepali Maoist literature, like other Maoist literatures, may seem so stereotypical and abstracted that one might reject it as having no heuristic value at all. Do Maoist texts have any link with actual practice, other than in the military field? My opinion is that an attempt to answer this question may in itself contribute to a better understanding of the political culture of Nepal's Maoist phenomenon. At the very least, one should attempt to trace the genealogy of the Nepali Maoist texts.

Take, as an example, the justifications offered for violence. In March 1995, a year before the commencement of the people's war, the third plenum of the CPN (Maoist) stated:

The aim of the armed struggle is to solve the basic contradictions between feudalism and the Nepali people, imperialism—mainly the Indian expansionism—and the Nepali people, comprador and bureaucratic capitalism and the Nepali people, and in the immediate term the contradiction between domestic reaction which is made up of a combination of feudal and comprador and bureaucratic capitalist classes and backed by Indian expansionism and the Nepali people. This way it is clear, the target of armed struggle will be confiscating the lands of feudals and landlords and distributing them amongst the landless and poor peasants on the basis of land-to-the-tiller theory and to attack them for the purpose...(CPN [Maoist] 1997a).

Thus, 'solving contradictions' was the final aim, but what about the means, 'armed struggle'? Was it necessary simply because no alternative existed, or does violence possess an inherent value? In fact we find here that violence is not justified in terms of need, but is instead asserted to be an essential quality of the Nepali people.

The reactionary propaganda that the Nepali people are peace-loving and that they don't like violence is absolutely false. It is an incontrovertible fact that the Nepali people have been waging violent struggle for their rights since the historical times...The domestic and foreign reactionaries including the revisionist elements have been time and again ditching and conspiring against the fighting tendency of the Nepali people. Today the greatest responsibility has fallen upon the revolutionaries to initiate armed struggle methodically and consciously against feudalism and imperialism and to complete the New Democratic Revolution by representing that great historical legacy (CPN [Maoist] 1997a).

The political project that one might ingenuously attribute to a socialist party, i.e., enhancing the fate of the poor, seems here to be pushed into the background in favour of a mission of a very different nature. According to a messianic logic, the party is conceived as the revealer of an inherent violence that has to be unleashed. Who or what, precisely, is the target of this violence? Baburam Bhattarai, responding during the same period to a question put to him by a 'reactionary' paper, insisted on drawing a distinction between aiming at a 'position' or 'class' and aiming at individuals, an argument possibly inspired by Stalin (1930):

Class struggle led by revolutionary communists, i.e. those upholding Marxism-Leninism-Maoism, is never aimed at eliminating 'non-communists', as you charge. The aim of revolutionary class struggle in the current phase of New Democratic Revolution is to eliminate feudalism and bureaucratic capitalism. Please do note the difference—we want to eliminate the 'class position' of these parasitic classes and not necessarily eliminate the class enemy physically (Bhattarai 1995).[7]

Nepali Maoist ideologues have typically been unforthcoming about their justification for eliminating individuals. This feature of Nepali Maoist discourse will have to be addressed in the future, because the 'annihilation of class enemies' is one of the main, and in fact chronologically the first, forms of action in contemporary Maoist insurgencies. The main theoretician of early Nepali Maoism, Pushpa Lal Shrestha, did not advocate the annihilation of individuals.[8] The annihilations (*khatam karbahi*) enacted in Jhapa district in May 1971 by the district committee of the CPN (later on called the 'Jhapalis') was a revealing event in the history of the Nepali communist movement, because it forced its actors to clarify their position on the timing and concrete form of the armed struggle. Most leaders with a Maoist leaning (and also the Nepali Congress leader B. P. Koirala [Rawal 1990/1: 82]) praised the symbolic value of the initiative, but condemned the physical assaults on individuals. Hence, Pushpa Lal himself declared that 'the assassination of individuals will not topple the Panchayat system' (ibid.: 82).[9] As a matter of fact, the ideological debate on the adequacy of such methods covered up a reshaping of allegiances within the party. Nevertheless, targeting individuals was still, as a doctrinal standpoint, marginal within the communist movement.

The Jhapalis were inspired mainly by the Naxalbari actions, which consisted almost entirely of landlord eliminations. Although violent encounters with police patrols occurred from the very beginning in India's Maoist movements, concerted attacks on police posts and government infrastructure did not occur during the Naxalbari insurgency itself. In the Nepali people's war, the official stance of the CPN (Maoist) was that no annihilations would take place in the 'first stage' of the people's war, i.e. 'the initiation', which lasted for eight

---

[7] However, Stalin assumes that 'ousting capitalist elements' is an inevitable result of 'restricting' them.

[8] Most of the writings of Pushpa Lal Shrestha have been published by the Pushpa Lal Smriti Pratisthan.

[9] Mohan Bikram Singh was the only one to utterly condemn these acts, speaking of 'individual terrorism' which he attributed to 'pro-Chinese reaction' (Rawal 1990/1: 83).

months from February 1996:[10] 'The forms of actions resorted to in this initiation process are clearly seen to include guerrilla actions, sabotage and propaganda action and the form of annihilation is seen to be purposely avoided' (CPN [Maoist] 1996), although the reason for this avoidance was not clear. However, whether they were planned or not, such actions did take place from the very beginning. As explained in the *Worker*, one of the mouthpieces of the CPN (Maoist): 'Although the Party had appealed not to resort to annihilation at this stage, several cases of annihilation have also occurred due to unavoidable circumstances' (CPN [Maoist] 1996). Another official position was that these actions were necessary due to government oppression ('Dosro Yojana...' 1996).

After the second plan of the first stage of the people's war was launched, annihilation was openly assumed, although precise definitions of actions and targets varied from one text to the next. While a review published in the *Worker* in February 1997 announced that 'during this plan period selected annihilations of local tyrants, police informers and policemen were carried out', another article published the same month in *Jana Yuddha* stated that 'corporal punishment [*sharirik danda*] and annihilation' were applied to 'corrupt elements, local tyrants [*gunda*] and CID [intelligence officers]' (CPN [Maoist] 1997b; see also 'Dosro Yojana...' 1996). In sharp contrast with the first plan, where no details of such operations were given, full reports of armed squads performing annihilations during the second plan were published. Targets were systematically described as 'babblers' (*phataha*) and 'informants' (*suraki*).[11] An evaluation published in Phagun 2053 (February–March 1997) assumes 'more than 25 *khatam*' for the first four months of the second plan, and forty for the whole of 2053 (1996/7), thereby admitting at least fifteen 'unplanned' annihilations in the last six months of the first plan ('Dosro Yojana...' 1996).

It is noticeable that after the war had begun the initial purpose of the annihilations ('facilitating the seizure and redistribution of land')

[10] The attack on the Holeri police post on the first day of the people's war (13 Feb. 1996) constituted the model for initial stage actions: 'Ultimately bound by the policy of not killing any policemen at this initial stage, the militants ransacked the office, seized the store and took hold of a substantial amount of high explosives and other utilities and escaped to safety' (CPN [Maoist] 1996).
[11] See *Jana Yuddha* (2: 9–11) for illuminating accounts of *khatam*s carried out between the months of Asadh and Phagun 2053 v.s. (late 1996 to early 1997).

seemed to give way to different aims: tactical suppression, reprisals against enemy agents, and 'punishment'. The different motives seem to be interchangeable: for example, an attack on a civilian and the seizure of a *tamasuk* (debt bond) was described as 'sabotage' (*Jana Yuddha* 2: 9–11). Similarly, actions against police officers as well as mere constables were justified both on moral grounds and/or as retaliations. Further investigations of the semantic structures of Nepali Maoist discourse may shed more light on concepts such as 'people's enemy' (*dushman*), and on the distinction between *khatam* ('annihilation') and *saphaya* ('cleansing') on the one hand and *hatya* ('murder') on the other. The term *hatya* is never used to denote actions undertaken by Maoist squads: they are labelled as *khatam*, which somehow has the neutral value of 'putting an end to', or as *saphaya*, which may be understood in a military-practical sense ('cleaning up') or in a moral sense ('purifying'). However, actions involving the deaths of Maoists are systematically labelled *hatya*. Thus, it is the nature of the victim, or of the 'target' (*nishana*) to use the exact Nepali Maoist term, that qualifies the nature of the act. 'Suppression' is the killing of the people's enemies, while 'murder' is the killing of the 'people' (*janata*). Another possible interpretation would place the actor at the centre of the paradigm, with the 'people' effecting *khatam* and their enemies effecting *hatya*.

The changing character of the Nepali Maoist discourse that attempts to justify annihilations must surely reflect pragmatic pressures. The perception of this type of action by both domestic and international opinion may be one consideration: attacks on individuals that are described as 'tactical', i.e, as a necessity of war, may be more acceptable. Another reason may well be that the Nepali Maoists encountered a gap between their original elimination programme and the social realities that confronted them. The policy of attacking local landlords, in particular, took it for granted that there was a severe concentration of land ownership in the hill regions of Nepal, similar to the situation in North Bengal and Jhapa. However, even the documents quoted by Baburam Bhattarai himself in his 'Politico-Economic Rationale of People's War' show that more than eighty per cent of Nepal's agricultural population in 1971 was made up of owner-cultivators who owned sixty-five per cent of the total cultivated area, with even higher figures for the hills (Bhattarai 1998). More recent official data confirm this picture, revealing a scarcity of land which is

suffered more or less evenly by all, rather than a blatant alienation of
land by a minority. In this respect, the contrast between conditions in
the eastern tarai region, with ten per cent tenant-only households in
1991, and the western hill region, with only two per cent, is noticeable (HMG Nepal 1994: 11–20). Without denying that the hill peasant is facing very harsh living conditions in present-day Nepal, it may
none the less be suggested that the representation of a mass of landless cultivators working for large absentee landlords is either 'constructed', or at least imported. The fact is not peculiar to Nepal's
Maoists. The Khmer Rouge faced similar problems when they tried
to identify land alienation in provinces where neither large landlords
nor landless peasants could easily be found. Hou Yuon and Hu
Nim, Khmer Rouge economists, acknowledged this situation at an
early stage, and had to create the concept of 'disguised big property'
(Kiernan 1982: 34–86.)

Compared to events in Bengal between 1968 and 1970 and in
Jhapa in 1971, Maoist crop seizures are strikingly rare in what is presented as a peasant-oriented struggle. One of the very few Naxalbari-
type operations was undertaken in Gorkha to mark Mao's birthday
on 26 December 1997 when 'several dozens armed guerrillas occupied about 30 hectares of rice-yielding land of notorious absentee
landlord and seized a major chunk of the crop ready for harvest'
(*Worker* 4 May 1998). Here, the programmatic motive of land redistribution clearly met the need for symbolic actions. Similarly, a Maoist report on the annihilation of several police officers and civilians in
1997 stated that such an action possessed an 'immense political significance' and was 'highly appreciated by the people' (CPN [Maoist]
1997b). It seems that the performance of the act may in itself be as
important as its concrete outcome. This point requires deeper scrutiny. Nevertheless, once the insurgency was launched, the concern
for popular mobilisation became a higher priority than long-term
social reform. In fact, 'determining working policies according to
actual conditions' is in line with the principles proclaimed by Mao
himself (Mao Zedong 1948a: 229). In this case, the evolution of the
discourse points either to changes in the conditions, or to the discov-
ery of the 'actual conditions'.

An investigation of the relationship between Nepali Maoist discourse and practice and Nepali cultural patterns may also benefit
from a comparative perspective. In fact, Maoist representations

involve an assemblage of ideological developments derived from several other national experiences. For example, there would be a difference between the patterns of behaviour in West Bengal which are assumed in Mazumdar's theory and the social reality upon which the Nepali Maoists wanted to impose their model. Trying to detect clear relationships between the different versions of Maoism and the cultures in which they have evolved is not without serious methodological problems. These have to do with the interpretation of the texts themselves, with the picture of the society which emanates from the texts, with the representativeness of the texts, and with the distinction between individual and collective conceptions. However, this is the fate of all reflections on the role of imported ideologies and literatures (in the religious field for example), although the novelty of Maoism in Nepal adds to the difficulty. This must not prevent us from setting Maoist materials of different origins side by side, in order to identify differences and determine whether any such divergences proceed from cultural or sociological variations.

In 2000, Prachanda insisted that 'from the ideological point of view the greatest influence on the communist revolutionaries of this region has been that of the historic Naxalbari movement...' (Prachanda 2000/1).[12] The functions of violence in Mazumdar's writings are in line with the necessity of struggle, as defined first by Lenin and then by Mao. The idea that violent struggle is a founding act, because it means emancipation, is a classical notion in Marxism-Leninism: it may also be related to universal conceptions of sacrifice.[13] For Mazumdar, emancipation is obtained simultaneously in two ways: by the 'annihilation' of the enemy, which removes oppression, and by the psychological mutation it provokes among the actor, who becomes full of 'contempt for death'. Mazumdar relays this idea profusely, introducing the notion (which is not found in Lenin, so far as I know) that contempt for death marks the emancipation towards egoism:

[12] Most of Prachanda's writings have been published in Prachanda (1995/6) and Prachanda (2000/1).

[13] In 1906, Lenin wrote, 'The masses must know that they are entering upon an armed, bloody and desperate struggle. Contempt for death must become widespread among them and will ensure victory. The onslaught on the enemy must be pressed with the greatest vigour; attack, not defence, must be the slogan of the masses; the ruthless extermination of the enemy will be their task; the organisation of the struggle will become mobile and flexible; the wavering elements among the troops will be drawn into active participation' (Lenin 1965, vol. 11: 534).

Without class struggle—without the battle of annihilation—the doors of the initiative of the poor peasant masses can never be opened, the political consciousness of the fighters can never be increased, the new man never emerges, the people's army can never be built. Only through carrying on the class struggle, the battle of annihilation, can the new man be born—the man who will defy death, and will be free of all self-interests. And with this contempt for death, he will move up to the enemy, will snatch away his rifle, will avenge the murder of martyrs, and in this way the people's army will emerge' (Mazumdar, 'Hate, Brand and Smash Revisionism' [1970], quoted in Banerjee 1984: 112–113; see also Sanyal 1969).

This millennialist role of violence, which is linked elsewhere in Mazumdar's writings with the restoration of pride to the oppressed, might usefully be contrasted with the functions of violence against individuals in Mao's thought. Mao's ideas on this specific point did evolve considerably, particularly after the end of the Second World War, when he wrote, 'it should be seen that they [the rich landlords] do not become targets of mass struggle'. While the rectification campaigns of 1954–6 were being launched, he insisted that eliminations should be decided above all on pragmatic grounds: 'We don't have them executed, not because their crimes don't deserve capital punishment but because such executions would yield no advantage' (Mao Zedong 1948b: 184 and 1956: 299). However, the period which can be more pertinently compared with Naxalbari and present-day Nepal is that of the 'Report of an Investigation of the Peasant Movement in Hunan' (1927). Commenting on the peasants' attacks on 'local tyrants', and on the peasants 'lolling for a minute on the ivory-inlaid beds belonging to the young ladies', Mao emphasised the humiliating and punitive functions of these outbursts, force being the only way to 'overthrow the deep-rooted authority' (Mao Zedong 1927). These behaviours cannot be said to correspond to dominant Chinese norms in the early twentieth century, and especially not to the Confucian ethic of restraint. Mao used them purposefully as examples of 'exceeding the limits', stating that 'proper limits have to be exceeded in order to right a wrong, or else the wrong cannot be righted'. But they illustrate a conception of annihilation which is specific to the 'Chinese Maoism' of the 1930s, and which differs both from the 1940s notion of 'purification' (Mao Zedong 1948a) and from the almost sacrificial logic of Mazumdar.

Maoism cannot be considered as a static doctrine. To use Maoist terms, the 'universal truths' have to be applied to 'concrete conditions'.

Following Mao, different ideologies have opened up different ways. Peru's Shining Path articulated Maoism in terms of more locally specific Amerindian conceptions: the well-entrenched millennialism, which viewed destruction as a condition for change and which had been theorised by Mariategui before Mao's ideas ever reached Latin America, offered a fertile ground for the imported ideology, as local populations had been waiting for a salving upheaval for a long time (Degregori 1989). And, beyond ideology, the practices of the Shining Path took specific shapes which point to the cultural dimension of violence; for instance, the heads of annihilated persons were crushed, in order to prevent the return of their souls (Hertogue 1989: 105).

What I hope to have conveyed in the two comparisons above is the value of approaching Maoist phenomena from within, i.e. of paying particular attention to the people involved, and to their conceptions. To return to our original questions: we have seen first how the emergence of Maoist insurgencies cannot be explained with reference only to the state of socio-economic relationships. The relationship of an individual to a particular network and a particular territory are also essential in the appearance and development of such movements. The Nepali case is strikingly similar to others in this regard. Similarities are less obvious on the second point, pertaining to conceptions of violence. In fact, while the more doctrinal parts of the various Maoist ideologies display a stereotypical character, their other components are more open to adaptation. Discourses on annihilation seem to be particularly sensitive to their immersion in specific environments, although it remains difficult to determine the respective roles of the individual ideologue and the collective culture in this process. Nevertheless, sketching the features of Nepali Maoist political culture will definitely require us to collect and analyse the discourses of local actors, a task which for the moment remains to be done.

This field of study is much more extensive than the present discussion might suggest. The centrality of violence in all versions of Maoism is bound up with fundamental sectors of the cultures in which they have appeared, such as conceptions relating to death, blood and flesh. Marxist writers have always made an intensive use of corporal patterns: Prachanda has described dead enemies as 'stinking worms' (*Worker* 3 [1996]); Lenin compared the death of the old society with a disintegrating body full of miasmas, and Guzman evoked the

'reactionary fleshes'. It remains to be seen how far such ideas penetrate or reflect the cultures concerned. How, for instance, should the
anthropologist consider metaphors such as the following, used by
Abimael Guzman: 'The people's blood ascends like furious wings
and the stricken flesh converts itself into a powerful vengeful lash'
(Guzman 1980: 312)? Should they be treated as purely lyrical formu-
lae, invented by an isolated writer, or do they mirror pre-existing cultural patterns? More generally, relationships between Maoist dialectics
and local societies are a vast area of research if we seek a clearer view
of what happens in Nepal. Maoist dialectics is a powerful tool of
opposition. It is highly 'political'. It sets up a fundamental cleavage—
between 'the people' and 'the people's enemy'—and explains that
they have to be 'resolved' through the most radical means. Local political and cultural structures can hardly remain unaffected.[14]

[14] In many Nepali villages this logic encountered a political structure which in fact
was organised along a rift between two opposing factions, but in a state of relative
balance. For an example at the village level see Ramirez (2000). For a discussion of a
similar rift at national level see Roka and Thapa (1999).

Part IV. Afterwords

THE EMERGENCY AND NEPAL'S POLITICAL FUTURE*

Hari Roka

BACKGROUND TO THE EMERGENCY

Eight months have passed since the emergency was imposed on this country. Its duration will depend upon the wishes both of the Maoist army that is waging a people's war and the Royal Nepalese Army (RNA) that is fighting a counter-war. Both sides are intent upon making the present liberal democracy as weak as possible, but each is also making full use of liberal democracy to attract the individuals and forces, both political and non-political, that operate within it. Each has its own basic objectives. The conservatives (the palace and the upper class that relies upon it) want to retrieve in legal form the political power that was snatched from them by the 1990 people's movement. To this end, they not only want to bring an end to the Maoist people's war, they also want to demoralise the supporters of liberal democracy, mentally and physically. They created pressure to extend the initial six-month emergency by another three months, and thus killed two birds with one stone. Similarly, the Maoists believe that power will only be captured when the present democratic structure has been dismantled, that the people's war should be fought to this end, and that the war is the only means of success (CPN [Maoist] 2000/1: 29). To make this strategy succeed, the Maoists have in the past adopted the tactic of playing on internal conflicts within other political parties, both large and small. For a certain period, this proved

* This chapter was written by Hari Roka in Nepali in July–August 2002, and subsequently translated and edited by Michael Hutt.

243

very successful in splitting the UML and preventing its subsequent reunification, in sowing the seeds of the current split in the Nepali Congress, and in preventing the unification of Masal and the Unity Centre: the splits within these parties provided the Maoists with an opportunity to strengthen their grip on the grassroots. In order to counter those parties which remain politically effective, the CPN (Maoist) has continued its policy of violent attacks, abductions and political murders.

In the beginning, the liberal democratic parties adopted a clear strategy of using the Maoists, who occupied a weak and limited area, to weaken one another. Secretly, government ministers provided the Maoists in their own constituencies with annual donations. The parties that formed the parliamentary opposition said that because the Maoists were a political party the problem required a political solution. They turned a blind eye and did not protest even when funds were diverted from local institutions and development works and handed over to the Maoist people's war, and so the Maoists were able to show the people that they were powerful and well-established, and this helped them to extend their power all the more.

It was natural for the aristocracy of the old order to be angered by the fact that its power had been ended, making it powerless, voiceless and stationary, and to desire an end to democracy. As soon as the people's war was announced as a struggle for an alternative to liberal democracy, it believed it had been granted a great opportunity. Therefore, it spread exaggerated accounts of the Maoist people's war, secretly provided it with economic assistance, identified every weakness of liberal democracy as a root cause of the problem, and declared that democracy had proved a failure. Because of the continuing nature of their assistance and the fact that they stood for the liberal capitalist option, Comrade Prachanda gave clear assurances to his secret helpers in an interview given to the *Kantipur* daily: 'There is no need for people who once trusted the king and the monarchical system to fear the Maoist movement.'[1]

The liberal market economy authorised by liberal democracy provides no means of economic or social redistribution; nor does it promote activity directed towards social reform. Those on the receiving end of the so-called 'free market' economy have not perceived there

[1] *Kantipur*, 28 Jyesth 2058 v.s. (10 June 2001).

to be any options for them within liberal democracy. It is not unnatural for them to despair of the effects of corruption, black marketeering, privatisation, nepotism, favouritism and injustice, and the oppositional movements that always ended in compromise. Nor has it been unusual for the people to take up the Maoist people's war as the only reliable option when the three main forces of liberal democracy (constitutional monarchy, the ruling Nepali Congress and the main opposition, the CPN [UML]) were engaged only in a struggle for power and took different views of the people's war. In particular, it was understandable for the people to become disenchanted with the repulsive political spectacle of the Nepali Congress trying to hold on to power indefinitely, the main opposition trying to get into government by any means at all, and the palace trying to regain the power it had lost.[2] Thus, in case the Maoists' efforts were not enough to ensure that the Maoist people's war would flourish in the people's minds, they also received the full assistance of these other forces.

In the early years, the Maoist strategy of killing Congress workers and destroying the police infrastructure enabled the palace and the CPN (UML) to delude themselves that the people's war was centred on opposing the ruling Congress government and attacking its organisational infrastructure. Similarly, the Nepali Congress believed that it was the only democratic force in the country and that the people's war had been designed merely to destroy it. Therefore it deployed the police, who were loyal to it and under its control, to oppose and suppress the Maoists. While the palace looked on as the struggle for power between the Congress and the UML continued and internal conflict within both parties escalated, the opposition parties, including the UML, began to search for a political solution, or to create political pressure for a solution through negotiations. Unsure of what it should do, the Congress divided the police into two and began to supply one with small arms and training, in order to provide a military option. Over the past three years the Congress government has increased spending on the police for security purposes in the name of suppressing the Maoists, and provided the army, commanded by the king, with less in comparison. Therefore it is not unnatural for the army to feel that it has been insulted, and to resent the 'force' that has been established to take its place (Roka 2002: 36).

[2] 'The palace' does not mean only the king and the royal family; it should also be taken to include the nobility and the Royal Nepalese Army.

This development upset Nepal's balance of political power substantially. In the palace, the old king's lineage was destroyed. The palace massacre took place at a time when it was felt that the palace-aligned forces had not received support for their own class since the re-establishment of democracy. After the massacre a new royal leadership was established. The new king was exhorted to be more active and assertive of his class interests than the old king had been, and this he is proving to be.

The pace of events in the politics of Nepal has quickened since the palace massacre, and the curtain of delusion that hung over many of the forces involved is being torn aside. The Maoists' assumption that the present king, Gyanendra, and the Congress leader and erstwhile prime minister, Girija Prasad Koirala, colluded with one another has turned out to be false. The confusion in the UML about whether the palace massacre would signal a new change or a revival of the old ways has ended. Similarly, the uncertainty over whether the Maoists were standing on their own feet or were relying on help from somewhere else has been dispelled. And in the same way the palace has acquired the facts on whether the Maoists are simply anti-Congress, are merely bent on seizing power for themselves, or are truly fighting for a genuine republic. Similarly, the powerful imperialist countries have reached a decision on whether the Maoists are a movement that is fighting to redress economic, social, ethnic and regional imbalances, or whether they are terrorists. The Holeri incident of July 2001, the meeting of all left parties held by the Maoists in Siliguri, the four months of negotiations between the Maoists and the government (July–November 2001), and the Maoist attack on the Dang barracks in November 2001, gave everyone the opportunity to recognise everyone else.

After the emergency was imposed on 26 November 2001 it was inevitable that the schism between 'friends' and 'foes' would widen. There could have been no more golden opportunity for the palace, which had been trying for a long time to play a decisive role, to achieve peace, in the sense that all liberal democrats in the country were united in their will to assist the palace against the Maoists. Three months after the emergency was first imposed, it was approved again in constitutional form. This meant that liberal democrats became powerless, and power came to be polarised in two centres: the palace and the Maoist army.

In one of the two Congress camps, the mistaken notion that the army, controlled by the king, would destroy the Maoists, and that in the meantime the liberal democrats would continue to conduct democratic politics comfortably, both in government and in opposition, has come to an end. The UML still believes this, but the illusion will end soon. Thus, the Maoists appear to be increasingly dependent upon militarisation. They believe that because they have an army they can do whatever they like and the people will accept whatever orders they are given: this kind of militaristic tendency is widespread in the Maoists' ranks (Shrestha 2001/2b: 22). But the foreign assistance given since November 2001 to the army and the army-backed government, and the killing of thousands of innocent citizens and Maoist guerrillas over this period, have shattered that illusion.

Within the parliamentary political parties, the struggle for power has been characterised by strife, division, immorality, corruption and programmatic deficit, and the sequence of events they themselves have set in motion by their inability to go among the people with any moral courage has given birth to a deep crisis for liberal democracy. The Maoists' campaign of murdering individuals pitilessly and destroying the physical development infrastructure is ensuring that the emergency, whether formally promulgated or not, will continue.[3] Thus both of these forces (the Maoists and the democrats) have helped to prolong an emergency that was imposed in accordance with the wishes of the palace.

THE BACKGROUND TO THE PEOPLE'S WAR

Ideological and Organisational Background

The Central Nucleus was established around 1970, after Comrade Mohan Bikram Singh and late Comrade Nirmal Lama were released from the central jail (see Thapa, this volume), and it was at this time that ideological preparations were made for an armed people's war. The Nucleus decided that the Nepali people's revolution and armed struggle would be a mixture of the Russian model of armed popular

---

[3] In fact, the emergency lapsed on 28 August 2002, but because on 4 October the whole Constitution was effectively suspended, the 'emergency' can now be said to have been deepened and extended indefinitely.

revolt and the Chinese model of the protracted people's war (CPN [Maoist] 2000/1: 39). After the other communist parties, which were divided at that time, had decided to struggle for 'total revolution' (*mulrupma purnaprapti*) these leaders emerged from jail and proposed a second option. Before a decade had passed in the process of establishing an organisation, the Fourth Convention began to split into three factions. These were Masal, led by Mohan Bikram Singh; the Fourth Convention, led by Nirmal Lama; and Mashal, led by Bhakta Bahadur Shrestha. After a few years, Mashal, which had established a grip on the younger generation of activists, embraced and gave expression to the guiding philosophy of the Fourth Convention, in the form of Marxism-Leninism-Maoism. It also committed itself to changing the reformist line on the question of political power, looking at the question of elections in conjunction with the need for a people's war, and prioritising preparations for a people's war and all activities of organisation and struggle (ibid.: 44). The Sector Incident of March 1986 can be cited as an example of this being brought into both tactics and strategy. A large number of small booths, constructed of glass and steel, had been installed at strategic points all across Kathmandu, to provide vantage points from which police officials could monitor public activity and movement, traffic flow, and so on. The student wing of Mashal, led by Pushpa Kamal Dahal ('Prachanda'), attacked and destroyed most of these installations, using stones and bottles. This incident led to fifty or sixty student activists going to jail on suspicion of involvement.

After 1988, the Panchayat system was in a very critical condition, with the country undergoing economic crisis and the political situation running out of control. The relationship between Nepal and India deteriorated in 1989 and India imposed an economic blockade in violation of international conventions. When the political parties[4] reached a consensus on the need to launch a struggle for the re-establishment of democracy, the violent Maoist campaign, which remained latent at that time, disappeared from sight. After the people's movement of 1990, Masal, led by Mohan Bikram Singh, took membership of the Revolutionary Internationalist Movement (RIM) and boycotted the first general elections in 1991. This prompted the Mashal

---

[4] These parties were the Nepali Congress and various communist factions, some of which are now within the CPN (UML), and others which are not.

Party, led at that time by the present Maoist leader Prachanda, to join forces with the Fourth Convention (led by Nirmal Lama) and form the CPN (Unity Centre). During the first general elections this remained underground but established a political front organisation, the United People's Front (UPF), which took part in the elections. Baburam Bhattarai, who had defected to the Unity Centre from Mohan Bikram's Masal, was entrusted with the leadership of the UPF. But although he took part in the general elections under the cloak of the UPF, Prachanda gave a higher priority to the people's war in the circular he issued to ordinary party members after the elections, in which he wrote of 'trying to advance the current movement to the highest point, trying to become involved in campaigns that are going on independently in their own areas against the dishonest babblers (*phatahas*)'[5] and so on. Against this background, it is clear that preparations for the people's war began well before 1996 and were not merely a consequence of the emergence of a parliamentary system, the policies and programmes adopted by the government, or the failure of those programmes and policies. A long-term view taking into account the political history of the left shows that the people's war was not a revolution of 'rising expectations' as is often assumed.

Popular Consciousness, the Movement and Polarisation

In primarily economic terms, but also in terms of its politics and society, the Nepali state is dependent upon others. But in modern Nepal (since 1950), education and the information culture have made popular consciousness much more influential. Primary school enrolment, which was only twenty per cent in 1965, increased dramatically to eighty-two per cent in 1987 and in 2000 it amounted to 5.3 million. At secondary school level, it increased during the same period from five per cent to twenty-six per cent. In 1990 there were 24,000 schools, but by 2000 that number had increased to 37,000. Looked at in another way, in 1965 secondary school enrolment was only 21,000, rising to 120,000 in 1971, 497,000 in 1986 and nearly 1 million, roughly twice the 1986 figure, in 2000. This kind of increase in education would necessarily bring about a radical change in the way the public

[5] Circular issued by CPN (Unity Centre) on 21 Saun 2050 v.s. (5 August 1993).

thought (Nickson 1992, Roka 2000). But a country that was economically dependent did not have the ability to provide its educated people with employment. Also, the pre-1990 Panchayat system and the policies it implemented did not offer much hope of generating new kinds of employment. Even after the political parties that came to power in 1990 installed a liberal market economy on a permanent basis, there was no question of this being possible. In previous decades the achievements of the agricultural sector remained extremely depressing. The primary sector has the greatest number of people dependent upon it (over seventy-five per cent), but amounts to less than thirty per cent of the national gross domestic product. Being neglected, agriculture remained backward, provided only minimal income and has not been in any condition to attract educated young people.

Nepal was unified 233 years ago, but it is only during the past twelve years that there has been an atmosphere in which the people could make their voices heard. Because of liberal democracy, minority ethnic groups, Dalits, and women, all of whom have long been oppressed, realised the extent to which they had been ignored in religious, social, political, economic and also psychological terms. Thus, they began to call for the beginning of a struggle for their rightful place in the state. But in the liberal democratic economic and social structure, which gave quarter to favouritism and allowed only those with power and resources to gain access to the state machinery, these amounted to little more than slogans for the political parties, which could not really implement them in practice, even within their own parties—which continued to be dominated by upper caste males. Thus, only dissatisfaction and discontent were created. The political parties should have addressed the discontent which appeared in the economic and social spheres with a process of re-distribution through land reform and appropriate land management. To reform the electoral system they should have changed the structure of parliament to ensure that the electorate was properly represented. In order to bring Dalits, ethnic minorities and women into the national mainstream, they should have established a new distribution process in these spheres, but because of selfishness and a lack of planning this did not prove possible. Those in power were unable to understand that Nepal is basically a country of minorities. Besides which, dominant groups do not relinquish or share power from philanthropic

intent. As a consequence, discontent arose among a substantial por-
tion of the population and democracy provided an opportunity for
this to be easily revealed.

In a liberal capitalist democratic society, there is always an opposition which counters those who are in power. In economic, social and
ideological terms, the opposition maintains a political difference,
over and above certain democratic norms, and it represents a legitimate voice for the people. In the case of Nepal, however, there did
not appear to be any great philosophical or practical difference between the policies of the main opposition and those in power. This is
explained by the lack of fundamental difference in the class basis and
therefore orientation of the two major political parties, the Congress
and the UML. Due to this, the people began to lose faith in the opposition. A policy vacuum was opening up inside the political structure,
and this is achieving a certain permanence even now. In this sense, it
is not surprising that the educated sectors of the minority ethnic and
Dalit communities, who were experiencing great frustration, came to
regard the Maoists' promise of equality, a republic and a rethinking
of democracy as an attractive option (Nickson 1992: 381). After the
CPN (Maoist) began the people's war in 1996, a rapid process of
polarisation began and the political foundations of the old order began to collapse. In particular, those who understand the Nepali communist movement see the whole process of its development since 1949
as one of proscription after proscription (*nisedhka nisedh*). Pushpa
Lal proscribed and displaced Rayamajhi as leader, Mohan Bikram
Singh proscribed and displaced Pushpalal, then he was proscribed
and displaced by the CPN (ML) of that time, and now by the Maoists.

Since the onset of the people's war, great changes have begun to
take place in Nepal's politics, and a great wave has been generated in
a society which has in reality remained frozen for several centuries.
This has overtaken the ordinary changes that were taking place through
an evolutionary process, and has increased the pace of the changes
that determine the coherence or dissolution of society. Of course,
this development began alongside the changes of 1990, but the increase
in the ability to understand, organise and lead it has been more recent.

At a time when an internal realignment is taking place, changes in
international politics cannot but have an influence in Nepal. The
events that took place in America on 11 September 2001 and the

United States' so-called 'war on terrorism' began to affect this rapid polarisation. While in the past it was principally India and China who had an influence in Nepal's politics, the interest taken by the United States and Britain has now increased. The suddenly amplified American activity in Nepal, and India's and China's surprising silence, have increased support for the Maoists. The Maoists had often claimed that as their movement gathered pace India would intervene and that they would have to fight India. But instead it is American security experts who have kept both India and China quiet, who have created an environment which is conducive to them assisting the Indian army, and who have arrived in the villages of Rolpa bringing with them money, technical assistance and military hardware with which to pat the RNA on the back (Sharma 2002: 15–21). Thus, Nepal's internal politics, complete with a monarchy shorn of its liberal democratic camouflage, have come not only to be economically and politically tied up with external politics, but also increasingly articulated to the worldwide imperialist political economy.

The United States' and Britain's apparent interest in Nepal's politics has laid bare the political polarisation that had remained confused in the past. In today's American-led world, questions arise about people's support for or opposition to globalisation, and support for or opposition to terrorism. Because of the war that the United States is driving forward in the name of controlling terrorism, autocracies and partyless regimes have begun to take rebirth in many countries, instead of liberal democracies. The rise of the military ruler Pervez Musharraf in Pakistan can be taken as one example of this. Because of the regional political balance and its deteriorating relations with Pakistan, India's central politics is compelled to kneel before the United States. India's rightwing Bharatiya Janata Party has begun to show the imprint of Pax America in its domestic and external affairs. On top of this is the idea, widespread among Indian policymakers, that Nepal, which is weak and disorganised in socio-economic and political terms, may be the only country that will remain dependent upon and obedient to India. From this perspective, it is conceivable that the palace and pro-palace forces will become the dominant power, and the Maoists the opposition. Similarly, it has begun to seem that the role of liberal capitalists will become extremely irrelevant, and lacking in popular and international support.

The presence of the Western powers, especially the United States and Britain, are givens, not just for Nepal, but for most developing countries of the world. Likewise, the presence of the 'big neighbour' India, with its expansionist designs, is also a given. Their power can only be exercised with the connivance of the dominant sections in Nepal's polity, be they the palace and its advisers or the parliamentary parties. Here a conjuncture of interests comes into play, so it is difficult to simply lay the onus of interference on either the 'foreign hand' or on its home-grown clients.

THE FUTURE OF THE MAOISTS AND OTHER LEFT PARTIES

There are striking similarities between contemporary Nepal and pre-Second World War Europe. In Europe, Finland's Admiral Horthy and Marshal Mannerhein, Poland's Marshal Pilsudski, Serbia's King Alexander and Spain's Francisco Franco had no definite ideological plans for how they would run their respective countries. They were anti-communist, and the class character of their social base accounted for this (Hobsbawm 1996: 113). Therefore, as they went about seeking a suitable rightwing image, they found that it was close to Hitler's and Mussolini's, but to be like that was not possible for them. The thinking and posturing of those who hold power in Nepal at present are just like those of pre-war Europe. Those in power have only one agenda: to crush the Maoists by any means—to finish off those with different views and ideas, while calling them Maoists. They do not think of seeking the reasons for the origins of the people's war, or of using any other constitutional means. Therefore, ever since the emergency was imposed the army has been killing thousands of innocent citizens—Tharus killed in Dang at the beginning of the emergency; travellers in a truck in Salyan; peasants from Dhading who had gone to dig out an airstrip at Kalikot; peasants fishing in a river in Khotang: none of these were Maoists (Shrestha 2001/2b, Mainali 2002, Dixit 2002b). Many army soldiers with no field experience were killing Maoist supporters and citizens who knew nothing at all about the Maoists, as well as Maoist guerrillas. The problem for other soldiers is that they cannot distinguish between villagers, left-leaning citizens, Maoist citizens, and Maoists (Dixit 2002b: 33). Thus, it has become normal to kill any Maoist supporter or well-wisher who has been arrested, but who refuses to surrender and act as an infor-mer for the army. The killing in custody of the writer and journalist Krishna Sen proves that people who have been arrested are being killed. The practice of announcing a reward through the government media to anyone who can locate a named person, whether living or dead, has come to be understood as an admission that the disap-peared person has already died. It must be mentioned that the death penalty is outlawed in Nepal so any killing by the state is by definition extra-constitutional.

There seem to be three reasons for killing an arrested person. First, this cuts down government expenditure on the person and also reduces rumours. Second, in the future the person could otherwise be a witness to the army's killing of ordinary citizens. Third, and most important, if someone is released from prison tomorrow, he could become an opponent of the autocratic government and permanently active against the establishment. No one is opposing these continu-ing murders, not even the UML leadership, which is a supporter of liberal democracy but can be seen sitting in silence, because it lacks the resolve and courage to speak out. Additionally, it senses that if the Maoists are destroyed its own future will be secured. There is no indication of any resolve to keep open a democratic space, no matter who the political enemy is, or of any foresight that today's silent bystanders could be tomorrow's victims.

The Maoists' Politics

In the early days, when they were beginning their guerrilla war, the Maoists adopted three main strategies: (1) to organise in the villages and wage a guerrilla war to encircle the towns; (2) not to attack the army, led by the king, until they were powerful, but attack only the police and police posts; (3) to attack the Congress, but not the other left parties. The first of these aimed to establish base areas, the second aimed to create hostility between liberal democrats and the conservative forces of the palace, and the third aimed at creating contradictions among the liberal democrats. As the people's war entered its third year the Maoists had more or less achieved all three of these objectives. Before it entered its fourth year, after a split oc-curred in the UML over the question of nationalism and the Mahakali Treaty, they had succeeded in creating a nationwide organisation and had taken the revolutionary and romantic activists under their control. After this they changed their third strategy and applied their rule of proscription. In other words, Maoism can only find its place with the fall of the UML and Masal, after which it can climb the staircase of success. So next the Maoists began to attack the UML and Masal as well as the Congress.

With the attack on Dunai in Dolpa, the Maoists achieved success over the police. The army remained a mute onlooker, and this convinced the Maoists that their strategy had succeeded in creating huge divisions among the enemy. The ruthless attack on the police at Naumule in Dailekh caused great concern to the still silent Western forces and the human rights activists reared under their protection. After the army refused to act on its behalf, the Nepali Congress government pushed its proposal for an armed police force even more vigorously. This provoked the palace to become forceful; and that this new assertiveness was also the result of the royal massacre and the coronation of a new king has already been mentioned above.

After the palace massacre, the effectiveness of the Maoists' strategies began to be reduced. The Maoists' praise for the late king and declaration of a working unity with him made the middle-class intelligentsia that had been attracted to the Maoists by the romance of republicanism realise that the Maoists were not really for a republic: instead, they were opposed to liberal democracy and wanted an end to it. Second, the village, district and central *jan sarkar*s they had established and were trying to establish were appointed, rather than elected. Even in their so-called base areas the Maoists were able to secure only between twenty-five and thirty-five per cent of the votes for their own activists when they conducted a village-level election exercise some three years ago (the majority of seats was won by UML and Nepali Congress candidates.) For this reason they chose to select and appoint, rather than elect, and had come to burden the people with military policy more than with politics, with the result that they had introduced not unity with the ordinary people, but barbarism. Third, the opportunity they had envisioned for the creation of a united people's front had been denied them by all of the activities mentioned above. Fourth, their strategy, based on the belief that after the royal massacre power could be accumulated by creating divisions within the Nepali Congress, turned out to be a failure when a government was formed under Sher Bahadur Deuba's leadership. The massacre succeeded in strengthening the palace, uniting it with its army, and enabling it to garner international support. An environment was created in which all the forces would assemble in the same place to crush the Maoists, and also, if the opportunity arose, to bring about the end of liberal democracy.

The CPN (Maoist) isolated itself: it had bypassed the CPN (UML) and Masal, which were forces it would need if it was to create the first united people's front. Because of the Maoists, these parties were obliged to reach an accommodation with the traditional forces, and 11 September put an end to an atmosphere in which regional political forces could not intervene, so that India was obliged to join with Nepal's constitutional forces. Because the Maoist leadership had strayed outside class-based politics, and had adopted a politics of internal autonomy on regional or ethnic bases, its central grip on the organisation loosened and it began to get out of control. This created the environment in which the talks broke up and the Maoist attacks in Achham and Dang took place. Even as they were saying that the mistakes made by Peru's Shining Path movement would not be repeated, they began to demolish the development infrastructure: bridges, micro-hydels, telecommunications towers and drinking water supply pipes. They started campaigns to demolish and burn postal and forest offices and health posts and shut down schools, and this reduced ordinary citizens' faith in them.

Seven years of people's war have turned the Nepali public mind upside down. It has kindled a flame of rebellion in people, but those in charge of the people's war have shown such a lack of principle and order, and such intolerance towards the people, that they have shoved the left movement as a whole onto a kind of directionless path. Callous deeds such as using defenceless people as a human shield during their attacks, killing detainees and police personnel in heinous ways, and meting out death sentences to ordinary people suspected of informing on them gives some inkling of the kind of tyranny the Maoists might bring if they won tomorrow. That is why the CPN (Maoist) has come to be extremely isolated from national and international politics. And now that India, which it had made its place of refuge, has begun to implement the extradition treaty of 1953, one wonders whether perhaps their failure is coming closer.

The UML

The economic, social and cultural policies adopted by the UML (which until a few years ago was considered to represent the people-based mainstream) could not even maintain it in the centre left. Once it achieved power, it had to leave its past behind to dedicate itself to liberal democracy. Nor could it embrace the Scandinavian model of the welfare state in modern politics by changing its name and flag. All of its contradictions have separated it from the old traditional left parties, but it has not been able to secure credibility as a western-style liberal democratic party. This theoretical and ideological dilemma, coupled with its indecisiveness, has isolated it from the political mainstream.

It is not only that the UML has clearly displayed its opportunistic character by removing itself from the commission set up to investigate the royal massacre, rejecting the Maoists' proposal to fight for a republic, supporting the emergency, and accepting the dissolution of parliament and the announcement of elections unconditionally, it has also shown itself to be devoid of policies and unsure of what it should do. The thinking it has adopted, which says that it will be able to engage more successfully in politics in its own right once the army has defeated the Maoists, suggests that it does not understand the generally-accepted concept of class contradiction. It supports neither the Maoists' demand for a republic nor the return of an unfettered monarchy, and accepts the policies imposed by the IMF and the World Bank such as structural adjustment. Thus, the UML has rejected republicanism and refused to fight against feudal forces: in this sense, it is now disinterested, and outside the political mainstream.

The other small left parties suffer from their extremely narrow, traditional nature, in other words their extreme orthodoxy. The main barrier to their progress is that they have not had the opportunity to move beyond an analysis of Mao Zedong's concept of 'new people's democracy' (*naya janvad*), which dates from about 1935/6. In this sense it is not just that they have not engaged with globalisation and the changes wrought in public consciousness by the revolution in the world of communications, they have not even understood the changes that have taken place in the economic and social framework over the past half century, or if they have understood them they have chosen to ignore them. For this reason, their politics sometimes runs into an extreme form of Maoism, and they place great hope in it. Alternatively, they become inspired by the objective of sharing in the fortunes of the UML as it moves ever further right, and finding their salvation in that. Looked at in these terms, the current polarisation has rendered the whole left movement insipid and extremely weak in the face of the extreme rightist establishment. None the less, about sixty-five per cent of the electoral public continues to place its faith in the left parties.

THE COUNTRY'S POLITICAL FUTURE AND THE DEMISE OF LIBERAL CAPITALISM

With regard to the existence and permanence of the palace, the present political situation in Nepal appears to be very unpredictable. Many have forecast that with the assistance of the army and with active international support the palace will become strong. They have come to believe that a 'popular Musharraf' can occupy the space vacated by the murdered dissenters and replace liberal capitalist democracy with a popular autocratic leadership like that of Lee Kuan Yew in Singapore. As the process of polarisation continues and politics becomes increasingly a case of the Maoists versus the palace, not only the unarmed ordinary people but also the so-called intellectuals and civil society can be seen taking up positions on one side or the other. But what they do not understand is that the emergency cannot be imposed on the country forever, and the dissenters will emerge even stronger.

The palace has not been able to progress beyond its old concept of a city-state—in terms of investment, empowerment of the people, provision of social justice and decentralisation. The issues that concern the palace at present are very distinct ones, and they do not include questions about ethnic minorities, religion and language, caste-based and gender discrimination, and so on. The palace will remain faithful to and under the protection of the international powers based on globalised liberalism, which support it and ensure its future, but which cannot create policies that bear any responsibility to ordinary citizens. There is an internal domestic reason for this too, which is that the palace's traditional forces are possessed of an extremely feudal mentality, and in terms of their use of power they are very conservative and partial to a centralised system. They cannot breach the four walls of the palace and enter the people's domestic sphere. Since the royal massacre the palace has become extremely displaced among the people. Because the present crown prince is implicated in several killings and associated with certain disreputable youths, he and his father remain distrusted and disliked. In these circumstances, one cannot envisage a centralised political permanence for the palace in Nepali politics. Even if it is established in the current political situation, it will not achieve permanence.

Friederich von Hayek (1944) has pleaded that a liberal democracy and a liberal economy should be regarded as indivisible, and over the past two decades the world's biggest capitalist countries have been practising just that. Hayek's argument is that a free market is equated with the freedom of the individual, who should be left alone if he is to achieve his full potential. Markets and governments should not be linked; that is, the government should not intervene in the market. Nepal, more than any other third world nation, has had to suffer the consequences of the literal application of this definition to a country that is extremely backward in societal and political terms (Hobsbawm 1996: 270–1). Because liberal economics was adopted, wealth could not be redistributed fully among an economically deprived people, and a large proportion of the population, already disadvantaged by its class status, fell even further behind. Because the influence of economics fell directly upon politics too, it was impossible for them to compete politically or run in the mainstream.

Liberal capitalist democracy expurgated the need for the state to save and foster, to establish social justice and generate means of employment, albeit through capitalist means. Over the past ten years or so, the centralised accumulation of capital and the connection with its international institutions has deprived Nepal of investment, production and employment. Those who had a strong grasp in the political and economic fields became stronger, and their international reputations grew. The ordinary people became emaciated and inert. Thus, the country began to suffer poverty, malnutrition and hunger. After the discontent that arose from this was suppressed as anti-democratic and stopped being attended to, the Maoists drew it to themselves.

Individualism is the first value of liberalism. It was only natural that its influence should penetrate not only the country but also the political parties themselves, so that sleaze became synonymous with 'politics' for the average Nepali. It was routine for quarrels to break out between those who were in power, those who were not, and those who had been displaced from power: the first victim of this was the UML, and in the subsequent war the Congress. Now, both of these forces are sometimes the palace's toys, sometimes the Maoists', and sometimes the tools of external forces. Thus, because they do not know how to use the constitutional people's rights attained in 1990, these too are being lost. It seems clear that in the country's present politics these parties have lost their decisive role.

After twelve years of liberal democracy, the majority in Nepal does not want a system that resembles the Panchayat autocracy of the past, nor the watered down version of liberal democracy that the state has failed to protect. Nor does it wish to absorb the pointless suicidal politics of the Maoists. If such a situation is not understood in all its seriousness, and if without seeking anyone's consent each of the political forces remains bent on achieving its own objectives, then the future of an underdeveloped country like Nepal will disappear in darkness. The politics of proscription could again break Nepal, after its 233 years of existence, into pieces. Once ethnic, religious and communal activities have diverged from their ideological track, Nepal could become a country that can be compared with Yugoslavia, Burundi or Congo.

How will a country that is unable to stop the present war stop the conflicts of later days? So let each side ponder all of these matters and enter into talks. These talks should be more than mere occasions for ceasefire. 'Peace' should be seen as more than the cessation of armed hostility. The only option seems to be peace talks, a common minimum programme that can include all the people in the political and economic spheres, a redistribution of property, a programme of political reform and a new model of democracy which includes healthy competition, and in which there is room for everyone. Otherwise, it will be as if the country has ceased to exist as it is engulfed by even greater conflict.

LIVING BETWEEN THE MAOISTS AND THE ARMY IN RURAL NEPAL*

Judith Pettigrew

Despite recent interest in the anthropology of war, relatively little attention has been paid to the analysis of how conflict is lived or represented by the people caught in its midst (Zur 1998: 18). This chapter—based on fieldwork carried out in rural Nepal in 2002[1]—contributes to the anthropology of political violence by addressing three issues. First, it examines villagers'[2] interpretations and representations of combatants and villager-combatant relationships in Maurigaun,[3] a village in what was considered to be a less active[4] area of the Maoist insurgency at the time of writing. It considers how the presence of Maoists and army personnel and their activities impinge on villagers' lives and the surrounding landscape of trails, fields and forests. Second, the discussion examines villagers' fears by exploring the 'culture of terror' that has developed in the village. Third, it considers villagers' survival strategies and asks which cultural practices become meaningful in the face of ongoing fear and what creative strategies come into play to resist the vicissitudes of armed violence.

One of the main anthropological contributions to the study of political violence has been the development of the concept of 'cultures of terror' (Taussig 1987, 1992; Green 1995; Suárez-Orozco 1987).

* For comments on earlier versions of this chapter I am grateful to Sandra Rouse, Sara Shneiderman, Chetana Lokshum and Sharon Hepburn. I am especially indebted to my informants and to those who assisted me in conducting the research on which this chapter is based. A British Academy Small Grant provided financial support.

[1] The ethnographic present described in this chapter is mid- and late 2002.

[2] My closest informants are middle-aged women and the perspectives contained within this piece are primarily those of members of this group.

[3] Maurigaun is a pseudonym, as are all other names. Certain ethnographic details have been disguised in this piece in an attempt to protect the identity of my informants.

[4] Maurigaun is, however, close to an area that was badly affected by the conflict.

261

Michael Taussig—whose early ideas have been further developed by writers such as Green, Sluka and Suárez-Orozco—states that where political torture and murder become endemic, 'cultures of terror' flourish. Jeffrey Sluka, the editor of the first edited volume on the anthropology of state terror, suggests that:

A culture of terror is an institutionalised system of permanent intimidation of the masses or subordinated communities by the elite, characterized by the use of torture and disappearances and other forms of extrajudicial 'death squad' killings as standard practice. A culture of terror establishes 'collective fear' as a brutal means of social control...When fear becomes a way of life...a culture of terror has emerged (Sluka 2000: 22–3).

'Cultures of terror', Suárez-Orozco states, have their 'own vocabulary and grammar, cultural facts and artefacts'. In Argentina, where he conducted his research, this vocabulary included words such as 'disappeared', 'torture centres', 'torture rooms', and 'electric prods' (1992: 240). A central aim of this chapter is to elucidate the cultural facts and artefacts of the 'culture of terror'[5] in Maurigaun, and to draw attention to its vocabulary.

While the mundane experiences of everyday life, such as working in the fields, walking to town, visiting friends, eating or sleeping, continue to dominate most people's lives on a daily basis in many parts of rural Nepal, at any moment a familiar routine can be pierced by unexpected terror and violence. Violence, as one of Linda Green's Guatemalan informants explained is '...like fire, it can flare up suddenly and burn you' (Green 1995: 109).

Green suggests that '...with repetitiveness and familiarity people learn to accommodate themselves to terror and fear'. Fear becomes routinised. Many Nepalis I have spoken to over the last year claimed they were getting used to their unusual circumstances. Curfews, army check posts, the militarisation of life in Nepal and even living with the Maoists are all becoming habitual. As Green notes, the routinisation of terror '...allows people to live in a chronic state of fear with a façade of normalcy at the same time that terror permeates and shreds the social fabric' (ibid: 108). The socialisation to terror does not stop the fear but rather allows people to get on with

---

[5] I critically distance myself from the term 'culture of terror' because I consider it to be imprecise and requiring further definition. Despite my reservations, I retain the term as I feel that it provides a useful framework within which to consider my work.

what they have to do to survive in an extreme situation. Since it is not possible to live in a constant state of alertness, feelings of chaos are diffused throughout the body but surface frequently in dreams and chronic illness. A veneer of normality masks the terror that is never far away. In this chapter I apply Green's model to Maurigaun and investigate whether fear is becoming routinised in people's lives.[6]

Carolyn Nordstrom (1995, 1997, 1998) draws attention to the inter-relationship between creativity and political violence. Violence, she suggests, is '…about the destruction of culture and identity in a bid to control (or crush) political will' (1997: 4). People at the epicentres of violence, however, resist it and '…it is in creativity, in the fashioning of self and world, that people find their most potent weapon against war' (ibid.). Her work on the Mozambican civil war highlights the creative resources that people use in times of conflict to survive and 'un-make war'. She argues that:

Self, culture and reality are (re)generative. People ultimately control the production of reality and their place in it. This is an interactive process. They produce themselves, and equally, they are produced within, and by, these cultural processes. As much as terror warfare tries to dismantle the viable person, people fight back (Nordstrom 1998: 110).

Using ethnographic data from Maurigaun, I explore the fear that pervades the lives of rural Nepalis and the survival strategies and cre-ativity that villagers bring to bear on the extraordinary situations they are forced to encounter. This chapter is thus concerned with how conflict-related violence[7] dismantles the social world and how peo-ple actively attempt to re-create their world within a context of on-going war.

A distinction between the terms 'terror' and 'fear' is not usually made in the literature on 'cultures of terror' and frequently the words are used interchangeably. Fear and terror are, however, different. According to Oltmanns and Emery, 'Fear is experienced in the face

---

[6] This exploration is preliminary and further research is required before more con-clusive statements can be made about the routinisation of fear in Nepal.

[7] Violence has a long history in Nepal, which includes, for example, the violence of exclusion on the basis of caste, gender, class or ethnicity and state-perpetrated vio-lence such as the use of torture. What is new is community-wide conflict-related vio-lence, which 'un-makes' the social world in a particular way.

of real, immediate danger…and helps to organize the person's behavioural responses to threats from the environment…' (1995: 198). Terror, according to Rothschild, is the 'most extreme form of fear…the result of the (perception of) threat to life' (2000: 61). While villagers in Maurigaun live in fear of their lives on an ongoing basis, their day-to-day experience is predominantly that of chronic fear which is interspersed with periods of terror. The discussion below is thus concerned with the impact of long-term fear and periodic terror.

BACKGROUND

When I arrived in Maurigaun in the summer of 2002, it had been two years since I had last visited the village. At the time of my previous visit in 2000, forest-based Maoists were coming into the villages for 'donations' and guns and to give propaganda speeches and cultural programmes. By 2001 there was a Maoist training camp established in the vicinity of the village and stories abounded about the comings and goings of the Maoists who operated openly in the area.

In November 2001 a nationwide ceasefire and the accompanying talks between the government and the Maoists broke down when the insurgents withdrew from the talks and launched a series of attacks on military and civilian targets in Dang, Surkhet, Syangja and other parts of the country. For the first time the guerrillas attacked the Royal Nepalese Army. On 26 November 2001, the Government of Nepal imposed a State of Emergency, called out the army and put into place an Ordinance granting the state wide powers to arrest people involved in 'terrorist' activities. Under the Ordinance (which became an Act in the spring of 2002) the CPN (Maoist) was declared a 'terrorist organisation' and the insurgents labelled as 'terrorists'. With the institution of the State of Emergency, some fundamental rights guaranteed in the Nepali Constitution, including freedom of expression, freedom of the press, freedom of movement and assembly and the right to constitutional remedy, were suspended.

The introduction of an emergency marked the escalation of the conflict and turned it from a low-intensity conflict to a high-intensity one.[8] Seddon (2002: 2) estimates that 250 people (Maoists and

---

[8] 'Low intensity armed conflict: at least 25 battle-related deaths per year and fewer than 1,000 battle-related deaths during the course of the conflict. Medium intensity

security personnel) were killed in the days between 23 and 26 November 2001 alone. During the first month and a half of the emergency the Nepali human rights organisation INSEC (Informal Sector Service Centre 2002: 65, 67) reported that 687 people were killed by the security forces, with a further 184 killed by Maoists. In the following months, the conflict continued to spiral with the Maoists launching several large-scale attacks on the security personnel.

In April 2002, Amnesty International (2002a: 2) stated that according to official sources more than 3,300 people had been arrested on suspicion of being members or sympathisers of the CPN (Maoist) in the first month after the State of Emergency was declared. By the end of February 2002 the number had risen to over 5,000. By August, 9,900 'Maoists' had been arrested, of whom 1,722 remained in custody (ibid.). Many people were being held in army camps without access to their relatives, lawyers, or doctors and with virtually no prospect of their cases being brought to court. Amnesty International has repeatedly appealed to both the government and the Maoists to stop extra-judicial killings and other human rights violations.

LIVING WITH THE MAOISTS

I returned to Mauriguan on a hot monsoon afternoon in July 2002. At first glimpse, things looked very much as before: children playing by the buffalo pond, women washing at the tap, a group of people clustered in the teashop. As I approached I was surprised to see so many unfamiliar faces: young men and women whom I had never seen in the village before. This is hardly surprising, I told myself, as I have been away for some time and as the first teashop in the village this particular place tends to attract visitors. I called out a greeting and the three casually dressed young men standing at the door replied. As I rounded the corner into the main street the usual collection of teenage boys was playing basketball, watched by a group of younger children standing on the sidelines, too little to be allowed to

---

armed conflict: at least 25 battle-related deaths per year and an accumulated total of at least 1,000 deaths, but fewer than 1000 deaths per year. High intensity armed conflict: at least 1,000 battle-related deaths per year' (DFID 2002: 11, based on a definition from Wallensteen and Sollenberg 2000).

join in. 'You've come,' someone shouted out. 'I have come,' I replied. I continued my journey through the village, stopping briefly for greetings at water taps and across the walls of courtyards. I noticed that Krishna Maya's teashop was boarded up but otherwise things looked much as they did when I first visited twelve years before.

Several hours after arriving in the village I sat on the opposite side of the hearth from a friend. Over a cup of tea I told her that I was thinking of visiting nearby villages to get details of army killings, which I knew from a meeting with a human rights organisation had not been fully documented. Gita looked horrified; she did a quick scan of the veranda and courtyard and told me in a hushed and hurried voice:

'You cannot go there, it is terribly dangerous, and you cannot talk about the killings. They are secret things. It is very dangerous to talk about what the army does. Do you not know that the Maoists are here nearly every day? They come and force villagers to feed them, there is no choice. And then the army comes and they blame people because they fed the Maoists. It is a very dangerous time now...'[9]

She stopped abruptly and tensed as we heard footsteps outside. 'Stop talking,' she said. 'I don't know who it is.' Gita was visibly relieved when she discovered that it was a young neighbour. 'Where are they? How many are there?' she asked him. 'There are five,' he replied. 'Three men and two women—they have forced the women's committee to open the committee house and that is where they are going to sleep tonight.' Gita turned to me and commented:

'They don't all sleep at once; they take turns to sleep and turns to guard. At least one or two of them are always awake. Sometimes a woman from our ethnic group comes, she speaks our language. She is from a far-off village

---

[9] While based primarily on fieldwork undertaken in the summer of 2002, this chapter also incorporates material from a second period of fieldwork conducted at the end of the year. During the first period of fieldwork Maoists were coming into the village on a regular basis but in relatively small groups of between five and fifty. At the time of the second period of fieldwork large groups of Maoists totalling between 300 and 450 were regularly entering the village.

Quotes contained in the text were reconstructed from memory. In some cases the words are verbatim but in other cases they are approximations which capture the meaning of the statement but are not the exact words. I am responsible for translating them from the local language into English.

and she is pregnant. We haven't seen her for a while and we wonder if she has been killed in a skirmish as she couldn't run fast enough.'

On the second morning of my stay I visited one of the teashops to have a chat with the proprietor, a young woman who is originally from a village two days' walk away in a neighbouring district. It was midday and as most people were out in the fields we were alone except for her youngest daughter who was playing on the ground in front of us making a 'teashop' out of stones, sweet wrappings and match sticks. In hushed tones, Durga told me about the visit of the Maoists to her shop last week.

'In the early evening a group arrived. They were heavily armed and they wore belts with bullets around their waists. One of the girls was very young— she couldn't have been more than thirteen. It upset me to look at her as she was about the same age as my eldest daughter. I am so glad that I sent Nani to live with my friend in the town so there is no chance that she will be forc- ibly recruited by the Maoists. The leader of the group told me that they wanted food and to stay the night. I told them that I could feed them but I pleaded with them not to sleep in the house. I said "If you stay here and the army arrives then all my family will be killed." One of them laughed and replied, "Then we'll die together." I begged them not to stay and they left after they had eaten.

'It is such a frightening time, things that we could never have imagined are now happening on a regular basis. Did you know that one of my best friend's relatives was killed by the Maoists? He was a teacher and one day last winter Maoists came to the school where he was the deputy headmaster and dragged him out of the classroom. They called all the villagers together and in front of them they accused my friend's relative of giving the police infor- mation about a Maoist who was captured some years ago, they also accused him of refusing to give money and of teaching Sanskrit which they had banned. Then they took him to a tree and secured him to it. They stabbed him in the shoulder and the stomach, and shot him in the head. The villagers were too frightened to help him or tell his family and it was only the next day that his body was removed by the police. Just before he was killed his friend visited him and pleaded with him to leave the village. He wouldn't go because he said that the school would close if he left because the headmaster had already gone. The teachers here are also very worried because this morning the Maoists told them that they have to give them two months sal- ary. They don't know what to do. It is such a lot of money but they know that the Maoists have killed and injured many teachers and so they will probably have to give it to them or leave the village.'

The following evening, villagers congregated in Gita's courtyard for a dance to raise funds for the repair of village paths. The event was conducted with the usual joking, flirting and teasing but the numbers in attendance were small. On past occasions people from all over the village would turn up in large noisy groups guided through the dark streets by flaming pieces of wood held aloft. I was disappointed not to see an old friend but a neighbour explained:

'Most nights Maoists come to her house as it is positioned at the top of the village, close to the forest, and has good views of the surrounding area. She would have liked to have come to see you but she had to stay at home and cook as a group arrived just before dark. Her life is difficult nowadays.'

'What does she do?' I asked. 'She is frightened but she just gets on with her housework and farm work, what else can she do?' replied her neighbour.

When I asked my informants what their feelings about the Maoists were they stated that they were 'frightened of them'. On several occasions people followed this statement with a non-verbal illustration of how Maoists forced them to do things at gunpoint. Villager-Maoist relationships, however, are complex. Sitting around the fire one evening, a group of middle-aged and elderly women told me some of the things they knew about the groups of Maoists who regularly visited. In a hushed voice an older woman explained, 'Two of the young Maoist women who come to the village are pregnant. Another woman recently gave birth in the forest but the baby died as it didn't have enough food.' When I asked how they knew these things, they replied, 'They tell us. They force us to feed them but they also talk to us and sometimes we ask questions and sometimes they answer us.' When I asked what type of people Maoists are, I was told, 'Some are very violent and like to kill and they do lots of killing but others are not like that. They have different ideas to the government but they don't like killing.'

THE ROYAL NEPALESE ARMY

Maurigaun has never had a police presence[10] and prior to the declaration of the emergency villagers could enumerate recent visits by

[10] Although Maurigaun has not had a police presence, many other areas have had extensive contact with the police. There is a long history of police-perpetrated violence in Nepal and it is clear that excessive police violence has often prompted people to join the Maoists.

the police or the army. Like many other rural Nepalis, the inhabitants of Maurigaun policed themselves. The only time the law enforcement agency entered the village was following the committal of a serious crime. In the past it was enough to state that 'the police came' to explain that a serious crime had been committed. The army rarely visited. The only time I saw an army patrol in Maurigaun prior to November 2001 was on polling day in 1991, and then the villagers that I was sitting with commented 'What are *they* doing here? There is no need for *them*.' The Royal Nepalese Army (RNA) is seen as an outside force made up primarily of people from other ethnic groups who share little in common with the inhabitants of Maurigaun.

On the day of my arrival in the village I discovered that the friend I was to stay with was out in the fields. 'Come and have tea at my house!' shouted a neighbour. When the social pleasantries were over I asked Sunita and her husband Kancha about life in the village. 'How are things? Are there Maoists around?' I asked. 'Yes, almost all the time,' replied Sunita. 'There is a group here today. They are sitting at the teashop with their guns beside them. You must have seen them but maybe you didn't notice their guns.' 'Does the army come?' I asked. 'Yes, they come' replied Sunita and continued,

'A couple of months ago Kancha and I were working in the fields below the village. We were alone, just the two of us. Suddenly I saw the helicopters coming, there were two of them. I watched them from the time they were like tiny moving ants in the distance until they landed. As they came closer and closer I nearly fainted with fear and I said to myself, "Maybe this will be the day I die." I was terrified that the soldiers would behave as they have behaved in other villages where they hit and killed people. The soldiers stayed one night and patrolled around the village and the surrounding area. They asked us if the Maoists come and if we feed them and we said that we hadn't seen the Maoists and that we don't feed them. We had no choice but to lie. We didn't want to be beaten and we didn't want to die. They left, we were lucky.

'Terrible things have happened in my friend's village. Some months ago Maoists killed an army officer. Shortly afterwards the army came to search the village and hit everyone with rifles. They hit old and young alike and they even hit people in the stomach. During the search a helicopter circled overhead and fired into the village and the nearby forest. The firing was aimed at houses where the soldiers thought they saw smoke. A few days later somebody told the army that Maoists were eating a meal in the next village. By the time the soldiers arrived the Maoists had left and only the family remained. The soldiers came in with their guns firing and killed the newly-married daughter and her husband who was home on leave from his job in Saudi Arabia. She died with her hand full of rice. The Maoists escaped but they were arrested the next day. I heard that when they were caught they were hiding among the children in the school. They were apprehended in the school grounds but they were not killed in front of the children, they were taken a little way into the forest and killed there. The radio said that they were killed during a fight but this wasn't true—they were killed after they were caught. One day shortly after that a *lato* [deaf-mute man with a learning difficulty] was shot dead by the army as he ran away when he saw them. He didn't understand and as he was frightened he ran and they killed him because they thought that he was a Maoist. The army killed a friend of my mother's when she was cutting grass for her buffalo in the forest. They heard something moving and they just shot, they didn't bother to check who it was and so my mother's friend died. Nowadays we are very frightened of going into the forest, we can be killed, looted or raped at any moment…there is nothing we can do…'

Shortly afterwards I left for the house I was to stay in. There the first fifteen minutes were taken up with greeting friends and neighbours. Once the welcomes were over, Gita turned to me and said:

'Take that *kurta* off [Punjabi style dress; *kurta* is an abbreviation of *kurta surwaal*] and put on one of your *lungis* [*sarongs*]. Don't wear a *kurta* around the village or when you are walking on the trail. You must always wear a *lungi*. You are wearing a *kurta*, you have no *tika* [vermillion powder] on your forehead, and you are not wearing glass bangles: you are dressed like a Maoist woman. It is very dangerous to dress like this nowadays. The army checks for three things. First of all they look to see if the woman is wearing a *kurta*, if she is, then they check for two further things—they look at her forehead to see if she is wearing *tika* and at her forearms to see if she is wearing glass bangles. They go like this: one for *kurta*, two for no *tika*, three for no bangles and four shoot. Many women have died in this way. Go and change into a *lungi* now, put your *kurta* in the bottom of your bag and do not bring it out again while you are here.'

The villagers I spoke with are very frightened of the army: although they personally have not been physically mistreated, neighbours and kin in nearby villages have. Those I encountered saw the army as distant, terrifying and unpredictable. The soldiers are marked out by the manner in which they arrive, move around the village and surrounding area and behave and interact with locals. As they usually visit the village by helicopter, they arrive unannounced. Unlike those who walk, there is little opportunity for people to be forewarned of their imminent visit. They bring an intimidating array of military hardware that has never before been seen in the village—helicopters, automatic and semi-automatic weapons, military radios and other equipment. They maintain a physical and spatial distance as 'they keep to themselves', 'eat alone' and do not engage in conversation. Informants commented, 'It is impossible to converse with them; they only ask questions and give orders.' The movement of army patrols through the forest is seen as particularly frightening because people feel that they shoot randomly. Consequently, individuals working in the forest at that time are at risk of being targeted as Maoists regardless of what they are doing or who they are. As an informant stated, 'They could easily have checked the identity of the *lato* in my friend's village but they didn't, they just shot him.' While the security forces are in the village people fear that they will learn about their interactions with the Maoists. When the army leaves, villagers worry that the Maoists will interpret their interactions with the army as traitorous. Although no one in Maurigaun has been denounced as a spy, several people in the locality have been punished by the Maoists for allegedly spying. Villagers are particularly fearful of the deaths of Maoist leaders because they feel that they will be accused of betraying the Maoists to the security forces and will be severely punished. What is important is not actual guilt but the perception of culpability. An informant explained, 'It doesn't matter if you are guilty or innocent, what is important is that people believe you are guilty. If a commander was killed around here then terrible things would happen to people in the village and nobody could save us.'

LIVING BETWEEN THE MAOISTS AND THE ARMY

At first glance Maurigaun looks much as it did before, and in many ways it *is* much as before. Each day villagers get up, work in the fields, eat, visit each other's homes, plan weddings and funerals, visit the health post, and walk to town. In the public spaces of the village the talk is of everyday matters: people meet and discuss who has got married, who has got a job overseas, who has died, arrangements are made to work together, the cost of the building of the new nursery school is discussed. The women chatting and washing the mud off their legs at the village tap after a day of fieldwork pay no outward attention to the armed Maoists sitting listening to the radio just yards away. The small crowd of villagers sitting at the shop do not stop their conversation when a young Maoist comes to request supplies from the shopkeeper. It would appear that the people of Maurigaun have become used to living with the insurgents.

Yet this show of normality is a façade. There is another side of Maurigaun where fear and terror find expression and where people struggle to use whatever strategies they can to cope with their changed environment. In the private space of the home people talk together in hushed tones. They discuss which part of the village the Maoists are staying in and wonder about the possibility of future visits to their hamlet. They question why certain parts of the village are frequently targeted and others not—which is likely to do with geographical proximity to potential escape routes. Throughout my visits this 'tracking' of the Maoists continued, with villagers quietly passing information on to family, friends and neighbours about the presence and movements or expected movements of the insurgents.

Several times as I walked around the village, villagers checked which path I intended to take and indicated their approval or disapproval of a particular route without explaining further. To the outsider this would have appeared to be a casual interaction—similar to many others that villagers in this area engage in concerning people's movements—but it was not. While villagers frequently talk about movements in space they do not talk in *quite* this way. In an attempt to regain a degree of control over their environment, villagers engage in a series of sophisticated communications which mimic their usual patterns but in reality are different. Such interactions allow information about the presence and movements of their uninvited guests to be safely conveyed in public places. In the privacy of homes and when people feel relatively safe the discussions are more expansive and more direct as they talk about the best way to communicate or negotiate with the Maoists. Stories and experiences from other villages are recalled and comparisons made. The next visit of the RNA is wondered about and its movements in the area commented upon. While negotiation is considered an option with the Maoists it is perceived to be less useful with the security forces. At the sound of footsteps in the courtyard, a deadly and tense silence falls over those gathered around the hearth. It is only when it is clear who has arrived that people relax and there are often a few moments of silence before conversation is resumed.

I could detect the changes best in those to whom I am closest. My friend Gita sat in her place by the side of the hearth and stirred the lentils with her usual deft hand movements, but her quiet and self-assured presence had a different edge to it. She was at times visibly jumpy and some of her movements were jerky. She laughed and joked but sometimes I caught a look that I had never seen on her face before—fear. My self-assured, confident, outspoken friend was deeply fearful. When questioned she did not deny her feelings but rather said, 'Yes, I am very, very frightened.' She then went back to stirring the pot and changed the subject.

I noticed a new alertness in others also. Small bits of information that might have been disregarded in the past are now carefully noted in case they might provide some information about the movements or behaviour of either side. Visits to town and, more importantly, the return journey are carefully planned so that the travellers will be home before nightfall. People are extra careful about what they say and to whom they say it. Silence is an important coping strategy and widely deployed when interacting with both sides. For children who started learning accepted norms of interaction in a different time and who have had to re-learn them, it is confusing.

Raju is eight and I have known him all his life. He is a shy, obedient little boy who is rarely punished by his elders. As his mother and I prepared vegetables for the evening meal we talked in vague terms about the recent arrival of two groups of Maoists in the village when suddenly Raju asked, 'Are you talking about the Maoists?' With barely a break in her conversation his mother turned to him and said, 'Do not talk about these things' and then slapped him hard on his leg. Tearful, he retreated into the corner. When I later questioned Sita about her actions she explained to me that Raju had not yet learnt to be silent. 'He must learn not to speak about certain things. It is hard for him but he must learn as it could be a matter of life or death. Nowadays you cannot be sure of whom you are talking to and so you must know when to be silent.' Raju is becoming socialised to the realities of living in a war zone.

Whether it is on the basis of ethnicity, caste, gender or class, villagers have long categorised people by dress. Nowadays this reading of attire has taken on new meaning with the potential for dire consequences. As stated above, villagers in Maurigaun note that Maoist women wear *kurta*s, no *tika*, no glass bangles and Gold Star trainers; therefore it is believed that to dress like this is to place oneself at great risk of being killed by the security forces. At first examination the categorisations appear simplistic: if you are wearing a *kurta* you could be killed as a Maoist. People, however, have no faith in the army's ability to make distinctions between people or its interest in doing so. If the army cannot or will not differentiate between Sunita's mother's friend—an elderly woman cutting grass for her buffalo in the forest—and armed insurgents, then how can it be trusted to make subtle distinctions based on the idiosyncrasies of dress? In a world of rumour and counter-rumour, anxious villagers try to make some sense of a concrete piece of guidance with which they are presented. For Gita 'the wearing of a *kurta*' and 'death as a suspected Maoist' are inextricably interlinked. In a time of horrible and unpredictable uncertainties, knowing what combination of clothing to avoid is a concrete piece of information that can be acted upon and passed on to others in an attempt to make them safe. That it might be somewhat outdated—because Maoist women's 'fashions' change, as was subsequently pointed out to me by a colleague—is irrelevant because this information both accurately reflects recent experience and gives villagers a small sense of control over the chaos that surrounds them.[11]

For villagers the reading of people's bodies and their apparel is a primary strategy in the process of identification. Maoist men, however, dress like most other Nepali men, so there are endless rumours about how you can identify one. It is said, for example, that they 'carry large packs', 'wear Gold Star trainers', and 'look extra alert.' Villagers know that these descriptions apply to a significant proportion of the young male population, so in the end, when a new face appears, people resort to some combination of the above criteria. My research assistant was initially thought by locals to be a Maoist because he was a young, unknown male in casual clothing. It was only after he was seen with me that people realised that he was my new assistant. A shopkeeper who spoke to him after she discovered his

---

[11] It is widely believed that female members of the Maoist People's Liberation Army wear either *kurta surwaal* or combat dress. During the second half of 2002 I was told that because the *kurta surwaal* had become identified as Maoist female dress, some Maoist women who formerly dressed like this had begun wearing saris, *tika* and bangles when not on active combat duty to distract attention from themselves.

identity told him that while she had looked at him as calmly and impassively as she could, she had been worrying to herself about who he was and what he might do.

Villagers know the local Maoist supporters. Several informants mentioned to me that a local leader 'Does not give *dukha* [hardship] to people in this area as he knows them. Instead he gives his *dukha* elsewhere.' As this individual is not often in the locality the fear is of those leaders who visit and who are 'not local and bring their *dukha* with them to give out here'. Villagers hope that their pre-existing networks with local Maoists will be protective. However, as everyone is differently positioned in relation to the Maoists and has different inter-relational histories with them, it is not certain whether previous relationships will be protective or destructive. A villager told me that his '…brother had been to school with a local leader'; a fact that he hoped would protect him and his family from Maoist aggression.

Most Maoists who visit the village are not from the vicinity and thus villagers cannot count on pre-existing relationships to protect them. The basis of their interaction with these 'visitors' revolves around the forced provision of food and shelter. Here the interactions are complex because local norms of hospitality demand that guests—depending on their status—be afforded great respect. Guests, while honoured, are also indebted and are expected to behave with propriety and to respect the possessions and spatial arrangements of their hosts' homes. They are also expected to reciprocate and provide hospitality to their hosts at a later date. But what about forced 'guests'? Maoists do not partake in the usual guest-host cycle of reciprocity and they are not welcome visitors.

During a subsequent visit to Maurigaun I had an opportunity to observe villager-Maoist relationships when a group of insurgents suddenly appeared in a house I was visiting. While entry was politely negotiated it was quite clear that the householder had no choice but to host the rebels, and while she was not required to feed them on this occasion she was required to provide tea and accommodation. Interactions between the householder and the Maoists drew on a range of cultural norms including pre-existing Nepali notions of age and seniority whereby the hostess scolded her 'guests' as she would village teenagers.[12] For example, shortly after their arrival she said to

[12] With one exception the members of the group billeted in this house were teenagers.

the leader, 'Move that gun away from my shawl, we villagers don't like guns' which he subsequently did. On another occasion she scolded him for drinking too much hot water and complained when a young woman placed a stick for cleaning her gun in the fire. Their visit, she muttered to me quietly, was 'like a bazaar, too much noise and too many goings on'. At other times, however, she was wary and after mildly teasing two young men who were drinking tea beside the hearth she commented that they should not take offence as she was 'only joking', a pattern that repeated itself several times during the day. The explanation of why I was in the village ('visiting during her holidays') was carefully backed up with details of my history of staying in the area and attention drawn to the fact that there are photographs of me in some village houses. Later in the day, when the Maoists were carrying out small domestic tasks such as sewing on buttons and washing clothes, she and several other female neighbours engaged in mild put-downs. She commented, for example, that the combat dress of a young man was smart but that his shoes 'did not match'. Another woman stated that the Maoist uniform was 'rather thin' compared to the uniform of her relative who is in the British Army. A third woman turned to a young Maoist and forcefully stated, 'You speak our language, don't you? You are just pretending that you don't.' His embarrassed reaction confirmed her suspicion.

It is difficult to ascertain how much support for the Maoists currently exists among villagers. When I asked my closest informants, they were adamant: 'We are not Maoists and we do not support them. They have made life very dangerous and difficult for us. No one in this village has joined them.'[13] It is, however, difficult to judge who has left the village for employment and who has left on the pretext of seeking employment and instead joined the Maoists or was forcibly recruited. Despite their assurances, villagers would not necessarily know who has joined, as Maoists are usually posted to locations outside their home area.[14] In addition, villagers have good reason to conceal any connection their families may have with the guerrillas.

Many people are very disillusioned with the arena of formal politics, which they see as having little relevance for them. When I asked what the government does for them, people commented, 'They give

[13] During a subsequent visit I met Maoists from nearby hamlets.

[14] See Pettigrew (2003) for a discussion concerning the attraction of the Maoists for young people and their involvement in the movement.

the village a little bit of money each year and do nothing else.' The disdain in which the government is held is increasing as villagers now have detailed experience of the security forces and are horrified by what they and their neighbours have seen. As is known from other areas, human rights violations committed by the security forces play a role in increasing support for the Maoists. In Maurigaun the Maoists have not yet physically harmed villagers,[15] but they are fully aware of the brutality with which the Maoists have treated people in other areas. Because of the abuses of the army in the area it is possible that support for the Maoists may have increased among certain sectors of society. Without detailed information, however, it is impossible to assess this, and my informants all adamantly denied it.

The presence of the Maoists and the security forces has changed the way people move around the village and the surrounding countryside. In the past women worked alone in close-by fields and sometimes even in more distant ones if they knew that others were in the vicinity. This has now changed. Women stated that they no longer work alone, fearing that if they do they may be raped by either side. When I questioned them further my informants admitted that while they are frightened of both sides they feel that they are more at risk from the security forces as they have heard stories of the mistreatment of civilian women by the army. People also fear being caught in the crossfire or being mistaken for insurgents while working in the forest. By choice villagers prefer to go into the forest in groups as the jungle has always been seen as a potentially dangerous place. While the fears of the past related mainly to concerns about the presence of malevolent supernatural entities, the fears of the present relate primarily to who else is in the jungle. Local forest landmarks used to be mnemonic cues recalling stories of people and events of the past. Now, in new and disturbing ways, they prompt memories of places where people have been killed.

FEAR, TERROR AND HEALTH

On my last afternoon I went to the health post to visit a friend who works there and to find out if the changed circumstances are having

[15] Villagers did, however, report that three young men from a distant district who were working in the area were badly beaten by Maoists who wrongly accused them of being thieves.

an impact on people's health. The health worker I spoke to confirmed that people are experiencing high levels of fear. 'Everyone is frightened and no one knows what will happen next,' he commented. He is trained in mental health care and has some basic medications available. However, he added, 'Most people do not seek treatment for these problems as they don't realise that they can be treated. Instead people come with headaches and stomach aches and some people come because they are having trouble sleeping.'

When I asked villagers if there were new healing rituals for the changed situation, people replied that there were not. I talked to a local healer who explained, 'We can do protective rituals for people, for hamlets of the village or even for the whole village but we don't have any special rituals against the Maoists or the army.' I asked him about the effects of the violence on villagers, the surrounding landscape, and the Otherworld:

'It is a bad situation now. People are frightened and so they don't feel very well. There are many violent deaths. The souls of people who have died in this way and not had the required rituals are wandering round and can cause problems for the living. Many people who travel through the forests nowadays do not respect the local gods and they do not ask permission to enter their areas and so the gods become angry and give *dukha* to the living.'

On my last afternoon in the village I decided to administer an anxiety questionnaire[16] to a small sample of people. Out of twelve people surveyed, only two had anything like normal anxiety and even those had scores at the higher end of the normal range. Of particular note were the almost hundred per cent affirmative responses to three questions: those about fearing death, being frightened and fearing the worst.[17] I was particularly struck, as these are new worries. The concerns of the past revolved around obtaining overseas employment for family members, the frequency and size of remittances, securing quality education for the young, obtaining health care, and

[16] The Beck Anxiety Inventory which has been validated for use in Nepal (see Kohrt et al. n.d.)

[17] 'Anxiety' in contrast to 'fear' is defined by Oltmanns and Emery as '...a more general or diffuse emotional reaction—beyond simple fear—that is out of proportion to threats from the environment' (ibid.). Although I administered an anxiety inventory because I had it to hand, what it identified, particularly in relation to the three stated questions, was fear rather than anxiety. I do not consider the responses that I obtained to be 'out of proportion to threats from the environment'. People in Maurigaun are frightened rather than anxious.

building a new school. People felt safe in the village in contrast to the town, which they considered to be unsafe and morally degenerate. Ironically, villagers in search of safety must nowadays relocate to the urban centres for security.

When I asked people how they were sleeping some replied that they had no problems but others reported sleep disturbances. Friends and neighbours recounted the fears of the night, of being awakened by voices outside or by footsteps on the village paths. Others spoke of frightening dreams in which themes of violence and death played a prominent role.

There are similarities between the situation in Maurigaun and that described by Green in Guatemala (Green 1995), where fear is a chronic condition to which people have become socialised. According to Green, the routinisation of fear does not imply conformity or acquiescence to the *status quo* but rather it allows people to live in a chronically fearful state with a veneer of normalcy. In Maurigaun the ability to maintain the façade of normalcy is important as it provides a measure of reassurance—if the normal daily activities can be carried out then it cannot be too bad. However, in many cases people have moved so far down the line of adapting themselves to a new way of living that they no longer notice the endless small accommodations that they make on a daily basis. It was only when I drew her attention to it that Sita consciously acknowledged that she was teaching Raju a new way of communicating (or not communicating)—one that he may have to use one day in order to survive. The tension that pervades my friend's body when someone enters the courtyard has become normal to her. I noticed it because I had not seen it before. She has become so used to it that it is simply the way she is. The dance that is held in the village every year, which always attracted large crowds, was not performed this year. When I questioned people about this I was told that there were no volunteers to dance in it. What was not said was that it would have been impossible in the present climate to hold such a large public event.

Fear has changed residence patterns. Two years ago my friend Gita lived alone, although most nights a relative and her daughter joined her. Now the upstairs of her house is inhabited by a group of young men who are there explicitly to provide a measure of protection, or at the very least a sense of solidarity. In other parts of the village boarded-up houses stand empty, as their inhabitants have relocated to the town. The migration of young people in search of employment has increased as young men and women leave in fear of being accused by the security forces of being Maoists or of being forcibly recruited by the insurgents.[18]

The impact of chronic fear on consciousness and culture in rural Nepal is profound and requires further attention. Researchers must explore the mechanisms through which long-term fear operates. They need to take into account the specific socio-cultural context within which fear develops and is experienced, as well as to consider its local interpretations and representations. The analysis also needs to incorporate perspectives from comparative research conducted on communities in other countries, as well as insights from the literature on the psychology and physiology of fear and terror.

CREATIVITY AND THE VIOLATION OF INTIMATE SPACE

Despite the outward appearance of mundanity in Maurigaun, fear is widespread. People go to work, visit neighbours and kin, occasionally sing and dance, marry, have children, plan for the future, leave or decide to stay. Surface normality is maintained but at a deeper level the cracks reveal themselves in the embodied manifestations of chronic fear, the ever present vigilance, the disturbed sleep patterns, the violence-themed dreams, the adapted work patterns and in the emergence of new approaches to child socialisation. The impact of the conflict is embedded not only in the social landscape and in people's bodies but also in the geographical and spiritual landscape. Violent acts are inscribed in the land and the souls of those who have died bad deaths roam the valleys and forests scattering sorrow in their wake and bringing more *dukha* to those already unfortunate enough to live between the Maoists and the army.

The 'culture of terror'[19] that has developed in Maurigaun can be characterised primarily as a violation of intimate space. Neither the

[18] Out-migration of young people, especially men, from this area has a long history. Recent events are merely exacerbating a long-established pattern which predates the insurgency.

[19] Due to limitations of space, it is not possible to adequately address the vocabulary of fear and terror here. A preliminary review suggests that the following words and phrases, which I have translated into English from the local language, should be

security forces nor the Maoists respect village distinctions between public spaces (paths, water taps, meeting places) and the private space which intersects public space but which is marked by ever decreasing circles of intimacy from courtyard to veranda to house interior.[20] Public spaces are frequently seen as dangerous and polluting and so harmful influences must be stopped at the door. Demarcations, barriers, thresholds and spaces impede free movement and also symbolically transform people during their transition from one social sphere to another (Robben 1989, 2000, van Gennep 1960). According to Antonius Robben, who is writing about forced entry in Argentina,

... socio-spatial divisions reinforce the ego differentiation between inside and outside. A forced entry is thus experienced as an attack on the ego and violates the emotional, physical and cultural protection offered by the house (Robben 2000: 75–6).

While the security forces visit relatively rarely, their intrusion into intimate space is often deeply violating. They commit assaults by searching houses, going through possessions and entering sacred space by searching areas which contain shrines. As witnessed in nearby villages, they hit people, shoot at their houses from helicopters and turn their homes into battlefields. Maoists, on the other hand, visit Maurigaun frequently seeking food and shelter, and while they do not conduct searches or go through possessions, their penetration into intimate space is also deeply violating. While their entrée to a household may be conducted with courtesy, within minutes of their arrival they transform the household into a military camp. Guns are stacked alongside household and agricultural implements and bomb-making materials are placed next to weaving equipment. The courtyard, which only minutes earlier contained women weaving and children playing, is transformed into a gun-cleaning and bomb-making space. The veranda on which invited guests are welcomed and offered seats is turned into a place in which to transcribe revolutionary songs and sew revolutionary flags.[21] The most intimate space of house

included: 'frightened', 'terrified', 'forced to provide food', 'forced to give money', 'patrols', 'helicopters' and 'random firing'.

[20] Space is an important concept in shaping local culture in an area like Maurigaun (see Bickel and Gaenzsle 1999). The violation of space has extensive ramifications which warrant further investigation.

[21] While the presence of Maoist cadre in the village was seen to be invasive, at the same time it held its attractions. Although my informants stated categorically that they

interior and hearth is also violated as insurgents warm themselves by the fire, drink tea, place gun-cleaning equipment in the hearth and ignore village caste rules which dictate that those who are considered to be of low caste should not enter the homes of those considered to be of a higher caste. The Maoist assault thus extends into the most intimate core of the house and by extension is a symbolic assault on its inhabitants. The assault is exacerbated by the fact that the unwelcome guests position the house at the centre of a potential battlefield for the duration of their stay.

Villagers, however, not only endure but also creatively respond to the fear in their midst. One of the greatest resources that villagers draw on is local information. Local people 'track' the movement and numbers of Maoists in the village and convey this information to others. When Maoists arrived in the village during one of my visits, under the guise of making a visit to a shop a neighbour and her young son did a reconnaissance to estimate the numbers and possible destinations of the insurgents so that she and their neighbours could be prepared. Another woman went on a supposed errand to a different part of the village to acquire information about the movement of the insurgents there. These women could not prevent the visits to their homes but by anticipating them they acquired a measure of control over their immediate destiny. Once the Maoists have arrived in a house the owners can take small steps to enhance their security, such as checking that sentries have been posted or—as in the case of the shop keeper who pleaded with them not to stay the night—negotiate the duration of their visit. Villagers also engage with Maoists on the basis of commensality, and by sharing conversations and jokes—albeit warily—they attempt to gain protection against insurgent-perpetrated violence. Through the process of social interaction villagers try to thwart the potential violence that Maoists bring into their homes. They attempt, in other words, to take the violence out of the insurgents. By drawing on cultural models such as the indebtedness of a guest and the right of an older person to maintain authority over a younger one, villagers challenge Maoist hegemony. By

---

are not Maoist supporters, many of them have attended and enjoyed Maoist cultural performances. Most of these performances took place in the village but some villagers also attended dancing and singing programmes in a nearby training camp which is now disbanded. People told me that they considered the performances to be 'good' and more impressive than the performances of local youth groups.

forcing themselves into people's homes, Maoists transgress and violate the intimate realm of courtyard, veranda and house and commit a deeply symbolic assault on its residents, but by appealing to the cultural boundaries of hierarchy and indebtedness, villagers can symbolically 'dis-arm' their youthful invaders. Fear remains a way of life but agency provides a possibility for creative resistance.

Part V. Appendixes

A. THE FORTY-POINT DEMAND OF THE UNITED PEOPLE'S FRONT (FEBRUARY 1996)

CONCERNING NATIONALITY

1 All discriminatory treaties, including the 1950 Nepal-India Treaty, should be abrogated.
2 The so-called Integrated Mahakali Treaty concluded on 29 January 1996 should be repealed immediately, as it is designed to conceal the disastrous Tanakpur Treaty and allows Indian imperialist monopoly over Nepal's water resources.
3 The open border between Nepal and India should be regulated, controlled and systematised. All vehicles with Indian licence plates should be banned from Nepal.
4 The Gurkha/Gorkha Recruitment Centres should be closed. Nepali citizens should be provided dignified employment in the country.
5 Nepali workers should be given priority in different sectors. A "work permit" system should be strictly implemented if foreign workers are required in the country.
6 The domination of foreign capital in Nepali industries, business and finance should be stopped.
7 An appropriate customs policy should be devised and implemented so that economic development helps the nation become self-reliant.
8 The invasion of imperialist and colonial culture should be banned. Vulgar Hindi films, videos and magazines should be immediately outlawed.
9 The invasion of colonial and imperial elements in the name of NGOs and INGOs should be stopped.

CONCERNING PEOPLE'S DEMOCRACY

10 A new Constitution should be drafted by representatives elected for the establishment of a people's democratic system.

11 All special privileges of the king and the royal family should be abolished.

12 The army, the police and the bureaucracy should be completely under people's control.

13 All repressive acts, including the Security Act, should be repealed.

14 Everyone arrested extra-judicially for political reasons or revenge in Rukum, Rolpa, Jajarkot, Gorkha, Kavre, Sindhupalchowk, Sindhuli, Dhanusa, Ramechhap, and so on, should be immediately released. All false cases should be immediately withdrawn.

15 The operation of armed police, repression and State-sponsored terror should be immediately stopped.

16 The whereabouts of citizens who disappeared in police custody at different times, namely Dilip Chaudhary, Bhuwan Thapa Magar, Prabhakar Subedi and others, should be investigated and those responsible brought to justice. The families of victims should be duly compensated.

17 All those killed during the People's Movement should be declared martyrs. The families of the martyrs and those injured and deformed should be duly compensated, and the murderers brought to justice.

18 Nepal should be declared a secular nation.

19 Patriarchal exploitation and discrimination against women should be stopped. Daughters should be allowed access to paternal property.

20 All racial exploitation and suppression should be stopped. Where ethnic communities are in the majority, they should be allowed to form their own autonomous governments.

21 Discrimination against downtrodden and backward people should be stopped. The system of untouchability should be eliminated.

22 All languages and dialects should be given equal opportunities to prosper. The right to education in the mother tongue up to higher levels should be guaranteed.

23 The right to expression and freedom of press and publication should be guaranteed. The government mass media should be completely autonomous.

24 Academic and professional freedom of scholars, writers, artists and cultural workers should be guaranteed.

25 Regional discrimination between the hills and the tarai should be eliminated. Backward areas should be given regional autonomy. Rural and urban areas should be treated at par.

26 Local bodies should be empowered and appropriately equipped.

CONCERNING LIVELIHOOD

27 Land should belong to "tenants". Land under the control of the feudal system should be confiscated and distributed to the landless and the homeless.

28 The property of middlemen and comprador capitalists should be confiscated and nationalised. Capital lying unproductive should be invested to promote industrialisation.

29 Employment should be guaranteed for all. Until such time as employment can be arranged, an unemployment allowance should be provided.

30 A minimum wage for workers in industries, agriculture and so on should be fixed and strictly implemented.

31 The homeless should be rehabilitated. No one should be relocated until alternative infrastructure is guaranteed.

32 Poor farmers should be exempt from loan repayments. Loans taken by small farmers from the Agricultural Development Bank should be written off. Appropriate provisions should be made to provide loans for small farmers.

33 Fertiliser and seed should be easily available and at a cheap rate. Farmers should be provided with appropriate prices and markets for their produce.

34 People in flood- and drought-affected areas should be provided with appropriate relief materials.

35 Free and scientific health services and education should be available to all. The commercialisation of education should be stopped.

36 Inflation should be checked. Wages should be increased proportionate to inflation. Essential goods should be easily and cheaply available to everyone.

37 Drinking water, roads and electricity should be provided to all villagers.

38 Domestic and cottage industries should be protected and promoted.

39 Corruption, smuggling, black marketing, bribery, and the practices of middlemen and so on should be eliminated.

40 Orphans, the disabled, the elderly and children should be duly honoured and protected.

B. FULL TEXT OF PRIME MINISTER SHER BAHADUR DEUBA'S MESSAGE TO THE NATION (27 NOVEMBER 2001)

Today our country is passing through a difficult situation. Terrorists by the name of Maoists have terrorised Nepalese life through killings, violence and bloodshed. Despite this, we invited them to the negotiating table for a peaceful resolution of our differences and the country's problems so as to give an outlet to the problem. In fact the talks with the Maoists and the efforts to find a peaceful solution were not only the desire of the government but also of the entire nation.

However, the Maoist group has taken to the path of causing serious setbacks to the fabric of national unity and security by means of violence, terrorism and killings. We showed the utmost flexibility to bring the Maoist group that was expanding its activities through violence for the past six years into the mainstream of politics. But the Maoist terrorists totally ignored our honest efforts and the people's wishes. At a time when our view that counter-violence cannot be an answer to violence has suffered a setback, the government has arrived at a decision to mobilise all its security agencies to control such activities.

We patiently discussed their demands and requests in the hope that we could bring them into the mainstream of Nepali politics and society through talks based on mutual trust. And we made efforts to give space to the possibilities of peace and the building of a violence free civilised society. In the course of facilitating and building a more congenial atmosphere for talks, we even fulfilled their many demands. Though they treated the Nepalese people and democracy as enemies, the government as a propagator of democratic culture did not treat them as an enemy. Efforts were made to bring those who had lost their way onto the right path. Even after an understanding was reached to enter into talks by halting violence and murder and even after the talks got off the ground, the Maoists continued to engage in different criminal activities. They looted food grains from farmers and indulged in violence. They made assaults on religious ceremonies and the people's faiths. They kept on attacking the institution of monarchy—the symbol of the faith of the Nepali people—the Constitution, multi-party democracy and basic human rights. They made attempts to disturb social goodwill and weaken national unity and integrity.

We were optimistic about the possibility of hammering out a peaceful solution. But the group called the Maoists perpetrated violence and a bloodbath unparalleled in the history of peaceful Nepal. The country was optimistic about arriving at a certain conclusion through peace talks. Three rounds of talks had already been held and we were in preparation for the fourth round of talks. But the Maoists unilaterally broke off the dialogue and peace efforts all of a sudden. Consequently, the nation once again has become bogged down in a vicious cycle of violence, killings and terrorism.

With utter disregard to the government's efforts and the people's goodwill, the Maoist terrorists carried out attacks on innocent people, political party workers, civil servants etc. They even attempted to hurt national integrity by assaulting the security personnel including the police and army.

His Majesty's Government has decided to declare a State of Emergency in the country to prevent the bad situation in the country from deteriorating further. The maintenance of peace and order by mobilising the security agencies has become our foremost duty and necessity. Though the declaration will cause some discomfort to the people, the inconvenience caused by it is minimal as compared to that caused by the terrorism that is widespread in the nation.

I am fully convinced that all Nepali people, political parties and the civic society are aware of the fact that a government accountable to the people won't take such a difficult decision if there was no unaffordable situation in the country.

I am also fully convinced that all political parties and every section of the civil society will extend their cooperation to the government in the present difficult situation. The government will be fully alert to civic liberties despite the declaration of an emergency. Necessary legal provisions will be made so that the civil society is least affected. But there may be still some inconvenience during the emergency. In the present situation, all Nepali people should be united for the sake of the public interest, monarchy, the present Constitution, multiparty democracy and the welfare of Nepal, and remain committed to rooting out terrorism.

I am of the belief that the attention of the nation and the people will be focused on peace and order rather than on discomfort, which is only for a short time. At a time when the country is confronting a great challenge, the government is with the people because it is not a separate entity aloof from the people. It is the foremost duty of the government to provide security to the life and property of the people.

I make an earnest appeal to all Nepalese brothers and sisters to focus our power and attention against terrorism so that we can shoulder the serious responsibility successfully. Encouraging terrorism under any pretext will be considered as a serious crime against the country, people and democracy.

All the persons, groups and institutions within and outside the country aiding and abetting terrorism through a supply of arms, money and information have to be brought under the purview of law and punished accordingly. I expect cooperation and guidance from all political parties, the entire mass media and civil society in this national campaign.

His Majesty's Government will bring the terrorists before the people and to book. I want to assure the nation and the people that the security agencies of the government are capable of materialising the people's desire and resolve to put an end to the violence and terror for good.

The government will move ahead by reaching an understanding with all political parties for social and economic reforms and development and for consolidating security arrangements. The cooperation of the civil society and the political parties in this endeavour is most crucial. I want to state here that all friendly countries and institutions having goodwill towards Nepali democracy in the country are with the Nepali people and His Majesty's Government in combating terrorism.

C. FULL TEXT OF KING GYANENDRA'S ADDRESS
   TO THE NATION, 4 OCTOBER 2002*

Beloved Countrymen,

The greater good of Nepal and the Nepalese people is our only goal. History is witness to the fact that the Institution of Monarchy in Nepal has always been guided by the wishes and aspirations of the people. We have, time and again, expressed our commitment to democracy and we would like to assure our countrymen that democratic ideals will always continue to guide us.

* From *Rising Nepal*, 27 November 2001.

It is known to all that in keeping with the tradition of the Shah dynasty to remain ever dedicated to the paramount welfare and progress of the Nepalese people, the democratic multiparty polity was reinstated in the Kingdom in 1990 in accordance with the wishes of the Nepalese people. It is also clear that during the 12 years since its reinstatement, a number of political exercises have been adopted for the consolidation of democracy. In this spirit, we had, at the recommendation of the Prime Minister, dissolved the House of Representatives on May 22 and set November 13 as the date for elections to the House of Representatives. The Prime Minister, who was entrusted with the task of conducting the general elections, had made a submission to us for the removal of difficulties under Article 127 of the Constitution of the Kingdom of Nepal, citing the current adverse situation prevailing in the country as the reason for not being able to hold the general elections on the stipulated date in accordance with Article 53 (4) of the Constitution. This led to a constitutional difficulty and void, creating a complicated situation in the country. As it is our responsibility to preserve nationalism, national unity and sovereignty, as well as to maintain peace and order in the country and also to ensure that the state of the nation does not deteriorate for any reason, a situation has arisen wherein, by virtue of the State Authority as exercised by us and in the spirit of the Constitution of the Kingdom of Nepal-1990, as well as, taking into consideration of Article 27 (3) of the Constitution, Prime Minister Sher Bahadur Deuba should be relieved of his office, owing to his incompetence to conduct the general elections on the stipulated date in accordance with the Constitution, and the Council of Ministers dissolved. Similarly, the general elections slated for November 13 also needs to be postponed. We, therefore, issue the following orders in accordance with Article 127 of the Constitution of the Kingdom of Nepal-1990.

1. Prime Minister Sher Bahadur Deuba has been relieved of his office as of today, October 4, 2002, for his incompetence in not being able to conduct the general elections on the stipulated date, and the Council of Ministers dissolved.
2. The general elections to the House of Representatives to be held on November 13 this year have been postponed.

As it will take some time to make new arrangements, we will exercise the executive powers of the Kingdom of Nepal until such arrangements are in place and we ourselves undertake the responsibility of governance in the country.

We are confident that the political parties will extend cooperation in constituting a new Council of Ministers by sending recommendations, within the next five days, of persons who have clean images and who will not be participating in the forthcoming general elections.

We will never allow the commitment and allegiance to Constitutional Monarchy and the multiparty democratic polity to be compromised. The government to be constituted will make adequate arrangements for peace and security as soon as possible and conduct the general elections.

There is no need for security personnel, civil servants or the countrymen to deviate from their responsibilities and duties. We are confident that everyone will fulfil their duties from their respective places and that, with the best wishes of the Nepalese people, all will be well.

May Lord Pashupatinath bless us all!
Jaya Nepal!

His Majesty the King has, in accordance with the Constitution of the Kingdom of Nepal 1990 and with the advice and consent of the Council of Ministers, promulgated the Terrorist and Destructive Activities (Control and Punishment) Ordinance 2001 as it had become necessary to make necessary legal provisions to control terrorist and disruptive activities so as to provide security to the general public and ensure peace and order in the Kingdom of Nepal and as Parliament is not in session at present.

BIBLIOGRAPHY

Acharya, Meena and Lynn Bennett 1981. *Rural Women of Nepal: An Aggregate Analysis and Summary of 8 Village Studies* 2 (9). Kathmandu: Center for Economic Development and Administration (CEDA), Tribhuvan University.

Adhikari, Bishnu P. 1999. *Democracy Watch: Annual Survey of Political Development in Nepal, 1997.* Kathmandu: Centre of Nepal and Asian Studies (CNAS).

Ahmad, Aijaz 1983. 'Imperialism and Progress' in Ronald H. Chilcote and Dale L. Johnson (eds) *Theories of Development: Mode of Production or Dependency?* Beverly Hills: Sage Publications.

Aké, Claude 1995. 'The Democratisation of Disempowerment in Africa' in J. Hippler (ed.) *The Democratisation of Disempowerment: The Problem of Democracy in the Third World*. London: Pluto Press (in collaboration with the Transnational Institute).

Ale Magar, Suresh 1993/4 (2050 v.s.). 'Nepal magar sangh: itihasdekhi vartamansamma' (The Nepal Magar Sangh: From History up to the Present) *Lapha* 1 (6).

———— 1997/8 (2054 v.s.). 'Magar samaj ra bahudaliya shasan pranali' (Magar Society and the Multi-party Ruling System) *Langhali* 6.

Ale Magar, Vijaya 1999 (2056 v.s.). 'Magar morcha kina?' (Why a Magar Front?) *Kanung lam* 5 (2) 19.

Ali, Syed 1998. 'South Asia: The Perils of Covert Coercion' in Lawrence Freedman (ed.) *Strategic Coercion: Concepts and Cases*. Oxford University Press.

Amnesty International 1997. *Nepal: Human Rights Violations in the Context of a Maoist 'People's War'*. London.

———— 2002a. *Nepal. A Deepening Human Rights Crisis: Time for International Action*. London

———— 2002b. *Nepal: A Spiralling Human Rights Crisis*. London.

Anon 1997. 'One Year of People's War in Nepal' *Revolutionary Worker* 911, 15 June.

———— 1998. 'Nepal: People's War is Sinking Roots' *Revolutionary Worker* 950, 29 March.

———— 2000. 'Red Flag Flying on the Roof of the World' *Revolutionary Worker* 1043, 20 February.

293

────── 2001a. 'Need for Development of Indigenous People Stressed During the Seventh Convention of the Nepal Magar Association' *Rising Nepal*, 5 March.

────── 2001b. 'Yasari ghoshana gariyo jilla janasarkar' (This is How the District People's Government was Announced) *Jana Bhavana National Weekly* 19 (41), 30 July.

────── 2001c. '700 Maoists Surrender in Four Districts' *Kathmandu Post*, 7 December.

────── n.d. 'Report on the International Seminar on the Nationality Question' (*www.revolutionarydemocracy.org*).

Aryal, Prashanta 2002. 'Nepali chapama dunai kandapachiko maobadi bidroha' (Maoist Rebellion in the Nepali Press after the Dunai Episode) in Pratyoush Onta, Ramesh Parajuli and Rama Parajuli (eds) *Mediako antarvastu: vividh vishleshan* (Media Content: Various Analyses). Kathmandu: Martin Chautari, Centre for Social Research and Development (CSRD).

Banerjee, Sumanta 1984. *India's Simmering Revolution: The Naxalite Uprising*. Calcutta: Subarnarekha.

Baniya, Balram 1997/8 (2054 v.s.). 'B. P. ko naya upahar' (B. P.'s New Gift) *Samanata* 1 (1) (A review article on B. P. Koirala's memoir *Jail Journal*).

Baral, Lok Raj 1977. *Oppositional Politics in Nepal*. Delhi: Abhinav.

────── 2000. *The Regional Paradox*. Delhi: Adroit.

────── 2001. 'Maoist Insurgency and Government' *Kathmandu Post*, 6 August.

──────, Krishna Hachhethu and Hari Sharma 2001. *Leadership in Nepal*. Delhi: Adroit.

Baral, Rishiraj 2000/1 (2057 v.s.) 'Yatharthako gatishil paksha: saundaryabodh ra sirjana' (The Active Aspect of Reality: Aesthetics and Creativity) *Kalam* 9 (1).

Bauman, Zygmunt 1993 (1989). *Modernity and the Holocaust*. Cambridge: Polity Press.

Belbase, Narayan and Sucheta Pyakuryal 2000. *A Study on Gender and Judges*. Kathmandu: Pro Public.

Bennett, Lynn 1983. *Dangerous Wives and Sacred Sisters: Social and Symbolic Roles of High-Caste Women in Nepal*. New York: Columbia University Press.

Bhandari, Dhundiraj 1970/1 (2027 v.s.). *Nepalko alochanatmak itihas* (Critical History of Nepal). Kathmandu: Prakash Prakashini.

Bhattachan, Krishna Bahadur 2001. 'Sociological Perspectives on Gender Issues in Changing Nepalese Society' in L. K. Manandhar and K. B. Bhattachan (eds) *Gender and Democracy in Nepal*. Kathmandu: Central

Department of Home Science, Women's Studies Programme and Friedrich Ebert Stiftung.

Bhattarai, Anil 2003. 'A Case for Radical Non-violent Politics' in Deepak Thapa (ed.) *Understanding the Maoist Movement of Nepal*. Kathmandu: Martin Chautari, CSRD.

Bhattarai, Baburam 1995. Interview in *Independent* 5 (41) (posted on *www.maoism.org*).

—— 1998. 'Politico-Economic Rationale of People's War in Nepal' *Worker* 4.

—— 1998/9 (2055 v.s.). *Rajnaitik arthashastrako ankhijhyalbata* (From the Lattice Window of Political Economy). Kathmandu: Utprerak Prakashan.

—— 2001a (2058 v.s.). 'Naya "Kotparba" lai manyata dinu hunna' (We Should Not Recognise the New 'Kot Massacre'), *Kantipur*, 24 Jeth (6 June).

—— 2001b (2058 v.s.). 'Akasmik dhangale ganatantra ko janma bhaekocha' (Suddenly a Republic has been Born) *Rajdhani*, 29 June (15 Asadh).

—— 2002a. 'Nepal: Triangular Balance of Forces' *Economic and Political Weekly*, 16 November.

—— 2002b. 'Maoists Seek a Democratic Nepal'. Interview given to Chitra Tiwari *Washington Post*, 14 November.

Bhusal, Puskar 2001. 'The Fourth Estate of the State' *Nepali Times*, 14–20 December.

Bickel, B. and Martin Gaenszle (eds) 1999. *Himalayan Space: Cultural Horizons and Practices*. Zürich: Völkerkundemuseum.

Bierschenk, Thomas and Jean-Pierre Olivier de Sardan 1999. 'Dezentralisierung und lokale Demokratie. Macht und Politik im ländlichen Benin in den 1980er Jahren' (Decentralisation and Local Democracy: Power and Politics in Rural Benin in the 1980s) in T. von Trotha and J. Rösel (eds), *Dezentralisierung, Demokratisierung und die lokale Repräsentation des Staates. Theoretische Kontroversen und empirische Forschungen* (Decentralisation, Democratisation and the Local Representation of the State: Theoretical Controversies and Empirical Research). Köln: Köppe.

Bishop, Peter 1989. *The Myth of Shangri-La: Tibet, Travel Writing and the Western Creation of Sacred Landscape*. Berkeley: University of California Press.

Bista, Pratap 2001. 'Sashastra amsabhako pahilo anubhav' (The First Experience of an Armed Assembly) *Kantipur*, 2 February.

Blackstock, Paul W. 1964. *The Strategy of Subversion: Manipulating the Politics of Other Nations*. Chicago: Quadrangle Books.

Borre, Ole, Sushil Raj Pandey and Chitra Krishna Tiwari 1994. *Nepalese Political Behaviour*. Delhi: Sterling.

Burghart, Richard 1984. 'The Formation of the Concept of Nation-State in Nepal' *Journal of Asian Studies* 44.

Cameron, John 1994. 'Nepal's Development Thinking: Twenty Years on in Theory and Practice' *The Economic Journal of Nepal* 17 (2).

Campbell, Ben 1997. 'The Heavy Loads of Tamang Identity' in David N. Gellner, Joanna Pfaff-Czarnecka, and John Whelpton (eds) *Nationalism and Ethnicity in a Hindu Kingdom: The Politics of Culture in Contemporary Nepal*. Amsterdam: Harwood Academic Publishers.

Central Bureau of Statistics 1999. *Statistical Yearbook of Nepal 1999*. Kathmandu.

Chaitanya 2000/1 (2057 v.s.) '*Junkiriko sangit* ma lamkhutteka swar ra shabdaharu' (The Voice and Words of a Mosquito in *The Music of Fireflies*) *Kalam* 8 (4).

Chatterji, Bhola 1980. *Palace, People and Politics*. Delhi: Ankur.

Chetri, Ananda Bahadur 1973/4 (2030 v.s.). *Gaddar Pushpa Lal* (Traitor Pushpa Lal). Nepal: Rato Talwar Prakashan.

Clarke, Graham, E. 2000. 'Development in Nepal' in Ram Pratap Thapa and Joachim Baaden (eds) *Nepal: Myths and Realities*. Delhi: Book Faith India.

CPI (ML-PW) 1995. '30 Years of Naxalbari: An Epic of Heroic Struggle and Sacrifice' (*www.maoism.org/india*).

CPN (Maoist) 1996a. 'March along the Path of People's War'. Special issue 'Nepal: Hoisting the Red Flag to the Roof of the World' *A World to Win* 1 (7).

—— 1996b. 'The Historic Initiation and After' *Worker* 2.

—— 1997a. 'Strategy and Tactics of Armed Struggle in Nepal: Document Adopted by the Third Plenum of the CC of CPN (Maoist) in March 1995' *Worker* 3.

—— 1997b. 'One Year of People's War in Nepal: A Review' *Worker* 3.

—— 2000/1. 'Mahan agragami chalang: itihasko apariharya avashyakta' (The Great Leap Forward: The Inevitable Necessity of History). (Historic Memorandum of the Second National Convention of the CPN [Maoist]).

—— 2001a. 'Maobadiko jatiya nitisambandhi prastabma ke cha' (What is in the Maoist Proposal Regarding Ethnic Policies?) in Pratyoush Onta, Kumar Yatru and Bhaskar Gautam (eds) *Chapama janajati* (Janajatis *in the Press*). Kathmandu: Ekta Books.

—— 2001b. Press Communique of the Second National Conference, 26 February.

CPN (UML) 2001/2 (2058 v.s.). 'Maobadi tatha rajyadwara hinsa ra atank sambandhi adhyayan karyadal prativedan' (Report of the Working Group to Study Violence and Terror by the Maoists and the State) (*www.cpnuml.org*).

Dahal, Dilli R. 1996. *The Challenge of Good Governance: Decentralization and Development in Nepal*. Kathmandu: Centre for Governance and Development Studies.

Dahal, Rajendra 2000/1 (2057 v.s.). 'Maobadi andolan, sarkar ra nepali press' (The Maoist Movement, the Government, and the Nepali Press) *Swatantra Abhivyakti*.

Datta-Ray, Sunanda 1984. *Smash and Grab: Annexation of Sikkim*. Delhi: Vikas.

Degregori, Carlos Ivan 1989. *Sendero luminoso. Les hondos y mortales desencuentros: lucha armada y utopia* (Shining Path. The Deep and Deadly Misunderstandings: Armed Struggle and Utopia). Lima: IEP.

DFID (Department for International Development) 2002. 'Economic Aspects of the Conflict in Nepal: A Background Paper' (Draft Version). Kathmandu: DFID.

Dhanalaxmi, Ravuri 1981. *British Attitude to Nepal's Relations with Tibet and China 1814–1914*. Delhi: Bihari Publications.

Dhungel, Surya, P. S., Bipin Adhikari, B. P. Bhandari and Chris Murgatroyd 1998. *Commentary on the Nepalese Constitution*. Kathmandu: DeLF Lawyers Inc.

Diamond, Larry J. 1997. 'Introduction: In Search of Consolidation' in L. Diamond, M. F. Plattner, Y. -H. Chu and H. -M. Tien (eds) *Consolidating the Third Wave Democracies: Themes and Perspectives*. Maryland, London: The Johns Hopkins University Press.

Dixit, Kanak Mani 2002a. 'A New King and the Challenge of Democracy' in Kanak Mani Dixit and Shastri Ramachandaran (eds) *State of Nepal*. Kathmandu: Himal Books.

—— 2002b. 'Innocents and Insurgents' *Himal South Asian* 15 (6) June.

—— and Shastri Ramachandaran (eds) 2002. *State of Nepal*. Kathmandu: Himal Books.

Dixit, Madan Mani 1984/5 (2041 v.s.). 'Nepalma leninbadko pravesh: prarambhik tipot' (The Advent of Leninism in Nepal: Preliminary Note) *Chintan* (quarterly) Baisakh.

'Dosro yojana avadhi: samkshipta ghatana-samiksha' (The Second Plan Period: A Short Review of Events) *Jana Yuddha* 2, Phagun 2053 v.s. (1996/7).

Elliott, Claud 1987. 'Some Aspects of Relations between the North and South in the NGO Sector' *World Development* 15 (supplement).

Elwert, Georg 2001. 'Kühl, hochvernünftig und lernfähig. Wie terroristische Gruppen unter dem Dach von Ideologiefirmen effizient arbeiten und Attentäter heranziehen' (Cool, Highly Rational and Eager to Learn: How Terrorist Groups Work Efficiently Under the Cover of Ideology and Enlist Assasins) *Frankfurter Rundschau* 244.

Evers, Hans-Dieter and Tilman Schiel 1988. *Strategische Gruppen* (Strategic Groups). Berlin: Reimer.

Fardon, Richard (ed.) 1990. *Localizing Strategies: Regional Traditions of Ethnographic Writing*. Edinburgh: Scottish Academic Press.

Forum for Women, Law and Development 2001. *Discriminatory Laws in Nepal and their Impact on Women: A Review of the Current Situation and Proposals for Changes*. Kathmandu: Author.

Fox, Jonathan 1992. 'Democratic Rural Development: Leadership Accountability in Regional Peasant Organizations' *Development and Change* 23 (2).

────── 1994. 'The Difficult Transition from Clientelism to Citizenship: Lessons from Mexico' *World Politics* 46 (2).

Freedman, Lawrence 1998. 'Strategic Coercion' in Lawrence Freedman (ed.) *Strategic Coercion: Concepts and Cases*. Oxford University Press.

Gaige, Frederick H. 1975. *Regionalism and National Unity in Nepal*. Berkeley: University of California Press.

Ganguly, Sumit 2001. *India–Pakistan Tensions Since 1947*. New York: Woodrow Wilson Press.

Gary, Romain 1979. *Les Clowns Lyriques* (The Lyrical Clowns). Paris: Gallimard.

Gautam, Puskar 2001/2 (2058 v.s.). 'Siligudi kina?' (Why Siligudi?) *Himal Khabarpatrika*, 16–31 Bhadra.

Gautam, Shova 2001. *Women and Children in the Periphery of People's War*. Kathmandu: IHRICON.

──────, Amrita Banskota and Rita Manchanda 2001. 'Where there are no Men! Women in the Maoist Insurgency in Nepal' in Rita Manchanda (ed.) *Women, War and Peace in South Asia: Beyond Victimhood to Agency*. Delhi: Sage.

Gellner, David N. 1986. 'Language, Caste, Religion and Territory: Newar Identity Ancient and Modern' *European Journal of Sociology* 27.

────── (ed.) 2003. *Resistance and the State: Nepalese Experiences*. Delhi: Social Science Press.

George, Alexander L. and William E. Simmions (eds) 1994. *The Limits of Coercive Diplomacy*. Boulder: Westview Press.

Ghimire, Krishna 1980. 'Janmat sangraha ra samsamayik bampanthi rajniti' (The National Referendum and Contemporary Left-wing Politics). Unpublished thesis, Tribhuvan University.

Gilmour, D. A. and R. J. Fisher 1991. *Villagers, Forests and Foresters: The Philosophy, Process and Practice of Community Forestry in Nepal*. Kathmandu: Sahayogi Press.

Goldstein, Melvyn C. 1997. *The Snow Lion and the Dragon: China, Tibet and the Dalai Lama*. Berkeley: University of California Press.

Gordon, Sandy 1992. 'Domestic Foundations of India's Security Policy' and 'Conclusion' in Ross Babbage and Sandy Gordon (eds) *India's Strategic Future: Regional State or Global Power?* New York: St Martin's Press.

Green, Linda 1995. 'Living in a State of Fear' in C. Nordstrom and A. Robben (eds) *Fieldwork Under Fire: Contemporary Studies of Violence and Survival*. Berkeley: University of California Press.

Gupta, Anirudha 1964. *Politics in Nepal: A Study of Post-Rana Political Development and Party Politics*. Bombay: Allied.

Gurung, Harka 1998. *Nepal: Social Demography and Expressions*. Kathmandu: New Era.

Guzman, Abimael 1995. 'We are the Initiators' in O. Starn, C. I. Degregori and R. Kirk (eds) *The Peru Reader*. Durham: Duke University Press.

Gyawali, Dipak 2002. 'Reflections on Contemporary Nepali Angst' *Himal South Asian* 15 (4).

Hachhethu, Krishna 1992. 'Mass Movement 1990' *Contributions to Nepalese Studies* 17 (2).

—— 1995. 'Executive and Authority Building in Nepal: A Study on Premiership of Girija P. Koirala' in Dhruba Kumar (ed.) *State, Leadership and Politics in Nepal*. Kathmandu: CNAS, Tribhuvan University.

—— 2000. 'Nepali Politics: Political Parties, Political Crisis and Problems of Governance' in Dhruba Kumar (ed.) *Domestic Conflict and Crisis of Governability in Nepal*. Kathmandu: CNAS, Tribhuvan University.

—— 2001. 'Rajparampara ra vidhima vyapak parivartan' (Extensive Changes in Royal Tradition and Practice) *Himal Khabarpatrika* 11 (6), 30 June–15 July.

Hagopian, Frances 1994. 'Traditional Politics against State Transformation in Brazil' in J. S. Migdal, A. Kohli and V. Shue (eds) *State Power and Social Forces: Domination and Transformation in the Third World*. Cambridge University Press.

Handelman, Don 1995. 'Kommentar zu Heyman' (Commentary on Heyman) *Current Anthropology* 36 (2).

Harding, Luke 2001. 'Maoists Lay Siege to Nepal' *Observer*, 8 April.

Hardt, Michael and Antonio Negri 2000. *Empire*. Cambridge: Harvard University Press.

Hart, Keith 1992 (1989). 'Agrarian Change in the Context of State Patronage' in G. Hart, A. Turton and B. White (eds) *Agrarian Transformations: Local Processes and the State in Southeast Asia*. Berkeley, Los Angeles: University of California Press.

Hertogue, Alain and Alain Labrousse 1989. *Le sentier lumineux, un nouvel intégrisme dans le tiers-monde* (The Shining Path, a New Fundamentalism in the Third World). Paris: La Découverte.

Himal Association 2001. *Political Opinion Survey Nepal*. Kathmandu.

Hirschman, Albert O. 1991. *The Rhetoric of Reaction: Perversity, Futility, Jeopardy*. Cambridge: Harvard University Press.

HMG Nepal 1994. *National Sample Census of Agriculture 1991–92: Analysis of Results*. Kathmandu: National Planning Commission and Central Bureau of Statistics.

Hobsbawn, Eric 1996. *The Age of Extremes: A History of the World 1914–1991*. Vintage Books.

Hoftun, Martin, William Raeper and John Whelpton 1999. *People Politics and Ideology: Democracy and Social Change in Nepal*. Kathmandu: Mandala Book Point.

Holmberg, David H. 1989. *Order in Paradox: Myth, Ritual, and Exchange Among Nepal's Tamang*. Ithaca: Cornell University Press.

———, Kathryn March, and Suryaman Tamang 1999. 'Local Production/ Local Knowledge: Forced Labour from Below' *Studies in Nepali History and Society* 4 (1).

Huntington, Samuel P. 1991. *The Third Wave*. London: University of Oklahoma Press.

Hutt, Michael (ed.) 1994. *Nepal in the Nineties: Versions of the Past, Visions of the Future*. Delhi: Oxford University Press.

IIDS 1994. *The Third Parliamentary Election: A Study of the Evolving Democratic Process in Nepal*. Kathmandu.

INSEC (Informal Sector Service Centre) 2001. *Human Rights Year Book*. Kathmandu.

——— 2002. *Forty-five Days of State of Emergency*. Kathmandu.

Jalal, Ayesha 1995. *Democracy and Authoritarianism in South Asia: A Comparative and Historical Perspective*. Cambridge University Press.

Jayawardena, Amal 1992. 'Changes in Power Structure and Security Perceptions in the South Asian Sub-System' in P. V. J. Jayasekera (ed.) *Security Dilemma of a Small Nation*. Part One: *Sri Lanka in the South Asian Context*. Delhi: South Asian Publishers.

Jha, S. K. 1977. 'Policy Towards India: Quest for Independence' in S. D. Muni (ed.) *Nepal: An Assertive Monarchy*. Delhi: Chetana.

Jipson, Arthur J. and Chad E. Litton 2000. 'Body, Career and Community: The Implications of Researching Dangerous Groups' in Geraldine Lee-Treweek and Stephanie Linkogle (eds) *Dangers in the Field: Risk and Ethics in Social Research*. London: Routledge.

Joshi, Bhuwan Lal and Leo E. Rose 1966. *Democratic Innovations in Nepal: A Case Study of Political Acculturation*. Berkeley: University of California Press.

Joshi, Sushma 2002. 'Waiting for Rain' in Deepak Thapa and Kesang Tseten (eds) *An Other Voice: English Literature from Nepal*. Kathmandu: Martin Chautari.

K. C., Kaisher Bahadur 1976. *Nepal After the Revolution of 1950*. Kathmandu: Sharada Prakashan Griha.

K. C., Surendra 1999/2000 (2056 v.s.). *Nepalma kamyunist andolanko itihas* (History of the Communist Movement in Nepal). Kathmandu: Bidyarthi Pustak Bhandar.

Karki, Arjun and David Seddon (eds) 2003. *The People's War in Nepal: Left Perspectives*. Delhi: Adroit.

Kaucha Magar, Balkrishna 1998/9 (2055 v.s.). 'Pratham shahid Lakhan Thapa Magarprati apaman ki irshya' (Jealousy of or Insult to the First Martyr Lakhan Thapa) *Janajati Manch* 4 (1).

——— 2000/1 (2057 v.s.). 'Janajati andolan: vikas ra samasya' (The *Janajati* Movement: Development and Problems) *Janajati Manch* 4 (3).

Khadka, Narayan 1997. *Foreign Aid and Foreign Policy: Major Powers and Nepal*. Delhi: Vikas.

Khanal, Krishna and Krishna Hachhethu 1999. *Amnirvachan 2056: sansad ra sarkarka chunautiharu* (General Elections 1999: Challenges to Parliament and Government). Kathmandu: CNAS, Tribhuvan University.

Khanal, Madan P. 2002. 'Feebleness of the Mighty' *The People's Review* 7–13 March.

Khanal, Yadunath 1977. *Nepal: Transition from Isolationism*. Kathmandu: Sajha Prakashan.

Khanna, S. K. and K. N. Sudarshan 1998. *Encyclopedia of South Asia: Nepal*. Delhi: A. P. H. Publishing.

Khapangi Magar, Gore Bahadur 1996/7 (2053 v.s.). 'Nepalma janajatiharu sattama pugna chahanchan' (The *Janajati* Want Access to Power in Nepal) *Janajati Manch* 2 (3).

Kiernan, Ben 1982. *Peasants and Politics in Kampuchea 1942–1981*. London: Zed Press.

——— 1985. *How Pol Pot Came to Power*. London: Verso.

Kloppenborg, R. 1997. 'Theravada Buddhism in Nepal' *Kailash* 4.

Kohrt, B., R. Kunz, N. Koirala, V. Sharma, and M. Nepal (n.d.). 'Validation of the Nepali Beck Depression Inventory and Nepali Beck Anxiety Inventory'. Unpublished paper.

Koirala, B. P. 1998/9 (2055 v.s.). *Bishweshwor Prasad Koiralako atmabrittanta*. Kathmandu: Jagadamba.

——— 2001. *Atmabrittanta: Late Life Recollections*. Translated by Kanak Mani Dixit. Kathmandu: Jagadamba.

Kothari, Smitu and Zia Mian (eds) 2001. *Out of the Nuclear Shadow*. London: Zed Books.

Kumar, Dhruba 1992. 'Asymmetrical Neighbors' in Dhruba Kumar (ed.) *Nepal's India Policy*. Kathmandu: CNAS, Tribhuvan University.

——— 1995. 'State, Leadership and Politics in Nepal: A Preliminary Note on Transition' in Dhruba Kumar (ed.) *State, Leadership and Politics in Nepal*.

——— (ed.) 2000. *Domestic Conflict and Crisis of Governability in Nepal.*

Lal Bahadur 1992/3 (2049 v.s.) 'Karnalima svayattashasan' (Autonomy in Karnali). Karnali Mukti Morcha.

Lal, C. K. 2001. 'The Chicken Neck' *Nepali Times*, 24–30 August.

Lecomte-Tilouine, Marie 1993. *Les dieux du pouvoir. Les Magar et l'hindouisme au Népal central* (The Gods of Power: The Magars and Hinduism in Central Nepal). Paris: CNRS Editions.

——— 2000. 'Utopia and Ideology Among the Magars: Lakhan Thapa versus Mao Zedong?' *European Bulletin of Himalayan Research* 19.

——— 2003. 'The History of Messianic and Rebel King Lakhan Thapa: Utopia and Ideology among the Magars' in Gellner (ed.) *Resistance and the State.*

——— forthcoming. 'La désanskritisation. Ethno-histoire d'un groupe sans histoire: les Magar' (Desanskritisation: An Ethno-history of a Group with No History—The Magar) in Marine Carrin und Christophe Jaffrelot (eds) *Purushartha* 23 *Castes et tribus. Résistance et autonomie dans la société indienne* (Castes and Tribes: Resistance and Autonomy in Indian Society).

Lenin, Vladimir Illich 1965. *Collected Works.* Moscow: Progress Publishers.

Lepgold, Joseph 1998. 'Hypotheses on Vulnerability: Are Terrorists and Drug Traffickers Coercible?' in Lawrence Freedman (ed.) *Strategic Coercion: Concepts and Cases.* Oxford University Press.

Licchavi Magar 1993/4 (2050 v.s.). 'Ojhelma pardai shabda "langhali"' (*Langhali*: A Word Kept in the Shadows) *Lapha.*

Lipton, Michael 1989. 'Agriculture, Rural People, the State and the Surplus in Some Asian Countries: Thoughts on Some Implications of Three Recent Approaches in Social Science' *World Development* 17 (10).

Little, David 1994. *Sri Lanka: The Invention of Enmity.* Washington DC: United States Institute of Peace.

Liu, Melinda and Patricia Roberts 2001. 'Nepal's Maoist Threat' *Newsweek*, 18 June.

Long, Norman 1993. 'Handlung, Struktur und Schnittstelle. Theoretische Reflektionen' (Action, Structure, Interface: Theoretical Reflections) in T. Bierschenk and G. Elwert (eds) *Entwicklungshilfe und ihre Folgen. Ergebnisse empirischer Untersuchungen in Afrika* (Development Cooperation and its Consequences: Results of Empirical Research in Africa). Frankfurt and New York: Campus.

Lopez, Donald 1998. *Prisoners of Shangri-La: Tibetan Buddhism and the West.* University of Chicago Press.

Ludden, David 2002. *India and South Asia: A Short History.* Oxford: One World.

Luitel, Gunaraj 2002. 'Maobadi ra press: utsukta ra bhayako sambandha' (The Maoists and the Press: Between Curiosity and Fear) in Onta, et al. (eds) *Mediako antarvastu*.

Lungeli Magar, Sala 1997/8 (2054 v.s.). 'Magar samajko adikavi Jit Bahadur Sijali Magar' (The First Poet of Magar Society, Jit Bahadur Sijali Magar) *Raha* 4 (3).

Magar, Ujir 2001. 'Maoists Declare Admn, Vow to Fight Army' *Kathmandu Post*, 20 May.

Maharjan, Pancha Narayan 2000. 'The Maoist Insurgency and Crisis of Governability in Nepal' in Dhruba Kumar (ed.) *Domestic Conflict and Crisis of Governability in Nepal*.

——— 2001. 'Nepalma maobadi janayuddha' (Maoist People's War in Nepal). Paper presented in a seminar on 'Nepalko prajatantrik andolanma dwanda byabasthapanka rananitiharu' (Strategies for Conflict Management in Nepal's Democratic Movement) organised by the Centre for Democracy and Good Governance, Kathmandu, 5 October.

Mainali, Mohan 2002. 'Mrityubhanda kathor sajay' (A Punishment Worse than Death) *Himal Khabarpatrika* 12 (7), 17–31 July.

Manandhar, Laxmi Keshari and Krishna B. Bhattachan (eds) 2001. *Gender and Democracy in Nepal*. Kathmandu: Central Department of Home Science, Women's Studies Programme and Friedrich Ebert Stiftung.

Mannoni, Octave 1990. *Prospero and Caliban: The Psychology of Colonization*. Translated by Pamella Powesland. Ann Arbor: University of Michigan Press.

Mao Zedong 1927 (1967). 'Report of an Investigation of the Peasant Movement in Hunan' in *Selected Works of Mao Tse-tung*, vol. 1. Peking: Foreign Languages Press.

——— 1938 (1967). 'Problems of Strategy in Guerrilla War Against Japan' in *Selected Works of Mao Tse-tung* vol. 2. Peking: Foreign Languages Press.

——— 1948a (1969). 'Speech at a Conference of Cadres in the Shansi-Suiyan Liberated Area' in *Selected Works of Mao Tse-tung* vol. 4. Peking: Foreign Languages Press.

——— 1948b (1969). 'On some Important Problems of the Party's Present Policy' in *Selected Works of Mao Tse-tung* vol. 4. Peking: Foreign Languages Press.

——— 1956 (1977). 'On the Ten Major Relationships' in *Selected Works of Mao Tse-tung* vol. 5. Peking: Foreign Languages Press.

——— 1965. *Selected Works of Mao Tse-Tung* vol. 3. Peking: Foreign Language Press.

——— 1967. *Selected Works of Mao Tse-Tung* vol. 4. Peking: Foreign Language Press.

Maobadi samasya samadhan uchhastariya sujhav samitiko pratibedan (Report of the High-level Recommendation Committee on the Resolution of the Maoist Problem) 2000/1.

Marks, Thomas A. 1996. *Maoist Insurgency Since Vietnam*. Portland: Frank Cass.

Marx, Karl 1978. 'The Eighteenth Brumaire of Louis Bonaparte' in Robert C. Tucker (ed.) *The Marx-Engels Reader*. New York: Norton.

McGranahan, Carole 2002. 'After Mustang: Contemporary Perspectives on the Tibetan Resistance'. Paper presented at the conference on the Cold War and its Legacy in Tibet: Great-Power Politics and Regional Security, 20–1 April. Harvard University.

McMahon, Robert J. 2002. 'U.S. Policy Towards South Asia and Tibet During the Early Cold War'. Paper presented at the conference on the Cold War and its Legacy in Tibet: Great-Power Politics and Regional Security, 20–1 April. Harvard University.

Mehta, Ashok K. 2000. 'Trouble in the World's Last Shangrila' (*www.rediff. com*) December.

―――― 2002. 'Shooting to Kill in Nepal' *Himal South Asian* 15 (7), 4–5 July.

Michaud, Jean 2000. 'The Montagnards and the State in Northern Vietnam from 1802 to 1975: A Historical Overview' *Ethnohistory* 47 (2).

Migdal, Joel S. 1994. 'The State in Society: An Approach to Struggles for Domination' in Migdal, Kohli and Shue (eds) *State Power and Social Forces*.

―――― 1988. *Strong Societies and Weak States: State–Society Relations and State Capabilities in the Third World*. Princeton University Press.

Mikesell, Stephen L. 1993. 'The Paradoxical Support of Nepal's Left for Comrade Gonzalo' *Himal*, March/April.

MIM 2002. 'Communists: Where Do You Stand on U.S.$ (*sic*) Aid to Nepal?' Maoist International Movement 262.

Moore, Sally Falk 1994. 'The Ethnography of the Present and the Analysis of the Process' in Robert Borofsky (ed.) *Assessing Cultural Anthropology*. New York: McGraw-Hill.

Moran, Peter K. 1998. 'Buddhism Observed: Western Travelers, Tibetan Exiles, and the Culture of Dharma in Kathmandu'. PhD, University of Washington.

Muni, S. D. 1977. 'The Dynamics of Foreign Policy' in Muni (ed.) *Nepal: An Assertive Monarchy*.

―――― 2003. 'Monarchy Matches the Military' *Himal South Asian*, January.

Myrdal, Gunnar 1968. *Asian Drama: An Inquiry into the Poverty of Nations*. New York: Pantheon.

Nandy, Ashis 1982. 'The Psychology of Colonialism' *Psychiatry* 45.

Nath, Tribhuvan 1975. *The Nepalese Dilemma 1960–1974*. Delhi: Sterling.

Nayar, Kuldip 1977. *India: The Critical Years*. Delhi: Vikas.

Nehru, Jawaharlal 1966 (1946). 'The Ideology of Empire: The New Caste' in Immanuel Wallerstein (ed.) *Social Change: The Colonial Situation*. New York: John Wiley & Sons.

Nepal National Intellectuals' Association (Nepal Rastriya Buddhijibi Sangathan) 1997/8 (2054 v.s.). *Nepalma janayuddha–bhag ek* (The People's War in Nepal—Part One). Kathmandu.

Nickson, R. Andrew 1992. 'Democratization and the Growth of Communism in Nepal: A Peruvian Scenario in the Making?' *The Journal of Commonwealth and Comparative Politics* 30 (3). Reprinted in Thapa (ed.) *Understanding the Maoist Movement of Nepal*.

Nordstrom, Carolyn 1995. 'War on the Front Lines' in Nordstrom and Robben (eds) *Fieldwork under Fire: Contemporary Studies of Violence and Survival*.

―――― 1997. *A Different Kind of War Story*. Philadelphia: University of Pennsylvania.

―――― 1998. 'Terror Warfare and the Medicine of Peace' *Medical Anthropology Quarterly* 12 (1).

―――― 1999. 'Requiem for the Rational War' in S. P. Reyna and R. E. Downs (eds) *Deadly Developments: Capitalism, State and War*. Amsterdam: Gordon and Breach Publishers.

―――― and Antonius C. G. M. Robben (eds) 1995. *Fieldwork Under Fire: Contemporary Studies of Violence and Survival*. Berkeley: University of California Press.

―――― and Joann Martin (eds) 1992. *The Paths to Domination, Resistance, and Terror*. Berkeley: University of California Press.

O'Donnell, Guillermo 1997. 'Illusions about Consolidation' in Diamond, et al. (eds) *Consolidating the Third Wave Democracies*.

Ojha, Deviprasad 2000/1 (2057 v.s.). *Sudur paschimma janachetanako vikas ra 2007 salko krantiko itihas* (History of the Development of People's Consciousness and the 2007 Revolution in the Far West). Mahendranagar: Sudur Paschimanchal Samajik Seva tatha Anusandhan Samiti.

Olson, Mancur 1982. *The Rise and Decline of Nations: Economic Growth, Stagflation, and Social Rigidities*. New Haven and London: Yale University Press.

Oltmanns, T. and R. Emery 1995. *Abnormal Psychology*. Englewood Cliffs: Prentice Hall.

Onesto, Li 1999. 'Magar Liberation' *Revolutionary Worker* 1034, 12 December.

―――― 2000. 'Inside the Revolution in Nepal: Interview with Comrade Prachanda' *rwor.org* (*Revolutionary Worker* website).

Onta, Pratyoush 1999a. 'Making Awards Count' *Kathmandu Post*, 21 May.

―――― 1999b. 'Upanyasma "dalit boli" nai nayak ho' (In this Novel 'Dalit Speech' is the Hero) *Bikas* 15.

———— 2000. 'Before Saying what Civil Society Can do to Help Nepal's Disadvantaged People, Spare a Minute for Critical Self-reflection' in Khadga K. C. (ed.) *The Institutionalization of Democratic Polity in Nepal*. Pokhara: Department of Political Science and Sociology, Prithvi Narayan Campus.

———— 2001. 'Neighbourly Interests in Nepali Troubles' *Kathmandu Post*, 7 September.

Panday, Devendra Raj 1994. 'Political Parties, Grassroots Democracy, and Local Development in Nepal' *Nepal Political Science and Politics: Annual Journal* 3.

Parry, Geraint and Michael Moran 1994. 'Introduction: Problems of Democracy and Democratization' in G. Parry and M. Moran (eds) *Democracy and Democratization*. London: Routledge.

Parvati 2003. 'Women's Participation in the People's War' in Karki and Seddon (eds) *People's War in Nepal*.

Pathak, Dilbhusan 2000. 'Gambhirko vastavik rup' (The Real Form of *Gambhir*) *Kantipur*, 30 December.

Paul, Samuel 1992. 'Accountability in Public Services: Exit, Voice and Control' *World Development* 20 (7).

Pettigrew, Judith 2003. 'Guns, Kinship and Fear: Maoists among the Tamumai' in Gellner (ed.) *Resistance and the State*.

Pfaff-Czarnecka, Joanna 1998. 'Complex Communities in Nepal-Himalaya: Solidarity as a Way of Life and as a Global Category' in I. Stellrecht (ed.) *Perspectives on History and Change in the Karakorum, Hindukush, and Himalaya*. Reinbek bei Hamburg: I. Wetzler (Culture Area Karakorum, Scientific Studies 3).

———— 1999. 'Verteilungskoalitionen in Bajhang. Zu einem besonderen Typus von Mittlerstrukturen zwischen Staat und Bürger in (Fernwest) Nepal' (Distributional Coalitions: Remarks on a Special Type of Intermediary Structure between State and Society in Farwest Nepal). *Peripherie* 73/4.

Pieke, Frank N. 1995. 'Accidental Anthropology: Witnessing the 1989 Chinese People's Movement' in Nordstrom and Robben (eds) *Fieldwork Under Fire*.

Pigg, Stacey Leigh 1992. 'Inventing Social Categories through Space: Social Representations and Development in Nepal' *Comparative Studies in Society and History* 34 (3).

Piyasena, S. and R. Y. Senadheera 1986. *India, 'We Tamils' and Sri Lanka*. Delhi: Sri Satguru Publications.

Pokhrel, Ganesh and Rakesh Vasyal 1998/9 (2055 v.s.). *Rapti paschimko prajatantrik andolan* (The Democratic Movement to the West of the Rapti). Gulariya: S. Pokhrel.

POLSAN 1992. *Political Parties and the Parliamentary Process in Nepal: A Study of the Transitional Phase*. Kathmandu: Political Science Association of Nepal.

Popham, Peter 2001. 'Nepal Year Zero' *Independent on Sunday* (with photographs by Stuart Freedman), 12 August.

Poudyal, S. R. 1994. 'Trends in Foreign Aid in Nepal' in H. Bongartz, M. K. Dahal, A. Aditya and D. R. Dahal (eds) *Foreign Aid and the Role of NGOs in the Development Process of Nepal*. Kathmandu: NEFAS.

Prachanda 1995/6 (2052 v.s.). *Nepali krantika samasyaharu* (Problems of the Nepali Revolution). CPN (Maoist).

———— 1996/7 (2053 v.s.). *Janayuddhako pahilo gaurabshali varsha* (The First Glorious Year of the People's War). Central Publicity Department, CPN (Maoist).

———— 1998/9a (2055 v.s.). 'Press Communiqué of the Central Military Commission, CPN (Maoist)' *Worker* 4.

———— 1998/9b (2055 v.s.). *Janayuddhako tesro andhimaya varsha: ek samanya avalokan* (The Third Storm-like Year of the People's War: An Ordinary Survey). Kathmandu: Utprerak Prakashan.

———— 1999/2000 or 2000/1 (2056/7 or 2058/9 v.s.) 'Netritvadayi panktiko krantikari rupantaranko samasya ahileko janasanskritik andolanko pramukh samasya ho' (The Problem of Turning the Ranks of the Leadership into Revolutionaries is the Foremost Problem of the Present People's Cultural Movement) (Interview) *Kalam* 8 (2/3).

———— 2000/1 (2057 v.s.). 'Nepali janayuddha ra vicharadharatmak samsleshanko prashna' (The Nepali People's War and the Question of Ideological Synthesis) (First Publication, *Dishabodh Masik* 3) *Nepali Krantika Samasyaharu* vol. 2, CPN (Maoist).

———— n.d. *Mahan agragami chalang: itihasko apariharya avashyakta* (The Great Leap Forward: The Inevitable Necessity of History). Central Publication Department, CPN (Maoist).

Pradhan, Suman 1999. 'Rights-Nepal: Marginalised Minorities Threaten Political Revolt' (*www.oneworld.org*), January.

Rahul, Ram 1971. *Modern Bhutan*. Delhi: Vikas.

Ramana, M. V. and A. H. Nayyar 2001. 'India, Pakistan and the Bomb' *Scientific American*, December.

Ramirez, Philippe 1997. 'Pour une anthropologie religieuse du maoïsme népalais' (Towards a Religious Anthropology of Nepali Maoism) *Archives des Sciences Sociales des Religions* 99.

———— 2000. *De la disparition des chefs. Une anthropologie politique népalaise* (On the Disappearance of Headmen: A Nepalese Anthropology). Paris: CNRS Edition.

Rana Magar, Dol Bahadur 1995/6 (2052 v.s.). 'Nepal Magar sanghko aiti-hasik ruparekha' (Historical Outline of the Nepal Magar Sangh) *Magar Jagaran* 1 (1).

Rana, B. K. 1999/2000 (2056 v.s.). *Janajati ra bahunvad* (The *Janajati* and the Brahmanocracy). Butval: K. B. Pun.

————— 2001a. 'Maoist Insurgency from Magar Perspective' *Kathmandu Post*, 29 March.

————— 2001b. 'Maoists, Magars and the Government' *People's Review*, 29 March–4 April (online edition).

Rawal, Bhim 1990/1 (2047 v.s.). *Nepalma samyavadi andolan: udbhav ra vikas* (The Communist Movement in Nepal: Emergence and Development). Kathmandu: Pairavi Prakashan.

Regmi, Madan 2002. 'India Holds Both Maoist, Government' *People's Review*, 7–13 February.

Regmi, Mahesh Chandra 1972 (1971). *A Study in Nepali Economic History 1768–1846*. Delhi: Manjushri Publishing House.

————— 1978. *Thatched Huts and Stucco Palaces*. Delhi: Vikas.

Robben, Antonius 1989. 'Habits of the Home, Spatial Hegemony and the Structuration of the House and Society in Brazil' *American Anthropologist* 91 (3).

————— 2000. 'Disappearance, Protest and Reburial in Argentina' in Antonius Robben and Marcelo M. Suárez-Orozco (eds) *Cultures under Siege: Collective Violence and Trauma*. Cambridge University Press.

Roka, Hari 2000 (2057 v.s.). 'Bahudalka das barsha' (Ten Years of Multi-partyism) *Mulyankan* 52, Mangsir.

————— 2002. 'Sainyakaran mohako parinam' (Militarisation is the Result of Delusion) *Himal Khabarpatrika* 12 (4).

————— 2003. 'Militarisation and Democratic Rule in Nepal' *Himal South Asian* 16 (11), November.

————— and M. Thapa 1999. 'Nepal: Politics of Fragmentation' *Economic and Political Weekly* 34.

Rose, Leo 1977. 'King Mahendra's China Policy' in Muni (ed.) *Nepal: An Assertive Monarchy*.

————— 1978. 'India's Frontiers: From the Himalayas to Sri Lanka' in Lawrence Ziring (ed.) *The Subcontinent in World Politics: India, its Neighbors and the Great Powers*. New York: Praeger Publishers.

Rose, Leo E. and John T. Scholz 1980. *Nepal: Profile of a Himalayan Kingdom*. Boulder: Westview Press.

Rothschild, B. 2000. *The Body Remembers: The Psychophysiology of Trauma and Trauma Treatment*. New York: W. W. Norton and Co.

Rowland, John 1967. *A History of Sino-Indian Relations: Hostile Co-Exist-ence*. Princeton: D. Van Nostrand Company, Inc.

RW 2002. 'To Our Friends in America: From the International Department of the Communist Party of Nepal (Maoist)' *Revolutionary Worker*, 19 May.

de Sales, Anne 2000. 'The Kham Magar Country, Nepal: Between Ethnic Claims and Maoism' *European Bulletin of Himalayan Research* 19.

Sangraula, Khagendra 1999. *Junkiriko Sangit* (The Music of Fireflies). Kathmandu: Bhundi-Puran Prakashan.

Sanyal, K. 1969. 'Report on Peasants' Armed Struggle in Srikakulam' *Liberation* II (7).

Sapkota, Revati 2001/2 (2058 v.s.) 'Kasailai jhukyayaum, kasailai vastavikata batayaum' (We Fooled Some, and Told the Truth to Others) *Madhumas* 8 (5).

Sardeshpande, Lt Gen. S. C. 1992. *Assignment Jaffna*. Delhi: Lancer.

Schelling, Thomas 1960. *Arms and Influence*. New Haven: Yale University Press.

Seddon, David 2002. 'The Maoist Insurgency in Nepal: Revolutionary Theory and Practice'. Paper presented at the 'Symposium on South Asia', University of East Anglia.

Shah, Saubhagya 2001a. 'Betrayed Victims of a Treacherous War' *Kathmandu Post*, 16 July.

—— 2001b. 'The Other Side of the Alcohol Economy' *Kathmandu Post*, 19 August.

—— 2002. 'From Evil State to Civil Society' in Dixit and Ramachandaran (eds) *State of Nepal*.

Shaha, Rishikesh 1982. *Essays in the Practice of Government in Nepal*. Delhi: Manohar.

—— 1996. *Modern Nepal: A Political History* 1769–1955. Delhi: Manohar.

Shahi, Satish Jung 2001. 'Army Defends its Role in Holeri Operation' *Kathmandu Post* 26 August.

Shahi, Yagyabikram 2001. 'Krantikariharule mageko "passport" kasto ho?' (What Kind of Passport do the Revolutionaries Demand?) *Kantipur*, 14 September.

Shakya, Sujita 2003. 'The Maoist Movement in Nepal: An Analysis from the Women's Perspective' in Karki and Seddon (eds) *People's War in Nepal*.

Sharma, Bal Chandra 1970/1 (2027 v.s.). *Nepalko aitihasik ruprekha* (An Outline of Nepali History). Banaras: Manohar.

Sharma, Sudheer 2001. 'How Many More Bodies?' *Nepali Times*, 6–12 July.

—— 2002. 'Maobadi kina chanchan yuddhaviram?' (Why Do the Maoists Want a Ceasefire?) *Himal Khabarpatrika* 12 (3), 15–29 May.

Sharma, Sudhindra and Pawan Kumar Sen 1999. *1999 General Election Opinion Poll: How Voters Assess Politics, Parties and Politicians*. Kathmandu: Himal Association.

Shneiderman, Sara 2003. 'The Formation of Political Consciousness in Rural Nepal: Lessons from Local History'. Conference paper presented at 'Agenda for Transformation: Inclusion in Nepali Democracy', 24–6 April, Kathmandu.

Shrestha, Bal Krishna 1996. 'Local Development Strategy in Nepal: Insensitive Government, Conflicting Donor Agenda, and Emergent NG Initiatives at the Grassroots' in M. K. Dahal and H. Mund (eds) *Social Economy and National Development: Lessons from Nepalese Experience*. Kathmandu: NEFAS.

Shrestha, Kapil 2001. 'Reconsidering the Women's Human Rights and Political Rights' in Manandhar and Bhattachan (eds) *Gender and Democracy in Nepal*.

Shrestha, Pushpa Lal 1974. *Nepali jan andolan: ek samiksha* (The Nepali People's Movement: A Review). Naya Janabadi Prakashan.

Shrestha, Shyam 2001/2a (2058 v.s.). Editorial in *Mulyankan* 18, 22 Asoj.

—— 2001/2b (2058 v.s.). Editorial in *Mulyankan* 19, Paush.

Singh, Depinder 1992. *The IPKF in Sri Lanka*. Delhi: Trishul.

Singh, Mohan Bikram 1994/5 (2051 v.s.). *Ugra bampanthi bichardharako khandan* (Denunciation of the Ultra-Leftist Viewpoint). Kathmandu.

Singhvi, Vir 2001. 'To Play the King: India and Nepal' (*www.hindustantimes.com*), 6 October.

Sisson, Richard and Leo E. Rose 1990. *War and Secession: Pakistan, India, and the Creation of Bangladesh*. Berkeley: University of California Press.

Skinner, Debra and Dorothy C. Holland 1996. 'Schools and the Cultural Production of the Educated Person in a Nepalese Hill Community' in Bradley A. Levinson, Douglas E. Foley and Dorothy C. Holland (eds) *The Cultural Production of the Educated Person: Critical Ethnographies of Schooling and Local Practice*. Albany: SUNY Press.

Sluka, Jeffery A. (ed.) 2000. *Death Squad: The Anthropology of State Terror*. Philadelphia: University of Pennsylvania.

Sris Magar, Resham 2000/1 (2057 v.s.). 'Nepalma janajatiya andolan ra vargasangharsha' (The *Janajati* Movement and the Class Struggle in Nepal) *Janajati Avaj* 4.

Stalin, Josef 1930 (1976). 'Concerning the Policy of Eliminating the Kulaks as a Class' in *Problems of Leninism*. Peking: Foreign Language Press.

Suárez-Orozco, Marcelo M. 1987. 'The Treatment of Children in the "Dirty War": Ideology, State Terrorism and the Abuse of Children in Argentina' in Nancy Scheper-Hughes (ed.) *Child Survival: Anthropological Perspectives on the Treatment and Maltreatment of Children*. Amsterdam: Reidel.

—— 1992. 'A Grammar of Terror: Psychocultural Responses to State Terrorism in the Dirty War and Post-dirty War Argentina' in Nordstrom and Martin (eds) *The Paths to Domination, Resistance and Terror*.

Tamang, Seira 2002. 'The Politics of "Developing Nepali Women"' in Dixit and Ramachandaran (eds) *State of Nepal*.

——— 2003. 'Civilising Civil Society: Donors and Democratic Space in Nepal'. *Himal South Asian* 16 (7), July.

Tambiah, S. 1992. *Buddhism Betrayed? Religion, Politics, and Violence in Sri Lanka*. University of Chicago Press.

Taussig, Michael 1987. *Colonialism, Shamanism and the Wild Man: A Study of Terror and Healing*. University of Chicago Press.

——— 1992. *The Nervous System*. London: Routledge.

Tewari, R. C. 1983. 'Socio-Cultural Aspects of Theravada Buddhism in Nepal' *Journal of the International Association of Buddhist Studies* 6 (2).

Thapa, Deepak 2001. 'Day of the Maoist' *Himal South Asian* 14 (5).

——— 2002. 'The Maobadi of Nepal' in Dixit and Ramachandaran (eds) *State of Nepal*.

——— (with Bandita Sijapati) 2003. *A Kingdom Under Siege: Nepal's Maoist Insurgency, 1996 to 2003*. Kathmandu: The Printhouse.

——— (ed.) 2003. *Understanding the Maoist Movement of Nepal*. Kathmandu: Martin Chautari, CSRD.

Thapa, Pari 1999. 'Janajatika adhikar khosera grihayuddha nimtyaune prayas bhaeko cha' (An Attempt has been Made to Invite Civil War, Having Snatched away the Rights of the *Janajati*) *Janajati Manch* 3 (2).

Thapa (Kham) Magar, Hit Bahadur 1993. *An Introduction to Kham Magaranti Language*. Sita Devi Thapa Magar.

——— 1994. *Magarant itihas* (History of Magarant). Magarant: Sorathi Prakashan.

——— 1999. 'Magar Homeland Magarant' *Lapha* 5 (18/19).

Thapa Magar, Lok Bahadur 1999/2000a (2056 v.s.). *Magarant svayattata bare, ek adhyayan* (Concerning the Autonomy of the Magarant: A Study). Pokhara: Magarant Rastriya Mukti Morcha.

——— 1999/2000b (2056 v.s.). *Andha-jativadko virodh garo* (Let us Fight Blind Casteism), Asoj. Pokhara: Magarant Rastriya Mukti Morcha.

Thapa Magar, Surendra 1999. 'Maobadi Janayuddha ra Magarharu' (The Maoist People's War and the Magars) *Janajati Manch* 3 (4).

——— 1999? 'Hami aphnai bhumima sharanarthi bhaeka chauum' (We have Become Refugees in our Own Land) *Janajati Manch* 3 (2).

——— 2000. 'Hami pani Maobadi bhae ke huncha?' (What Would Happen if We Too were Maoist?) *Janajati Manch* 4 (3).

Thomas, Raju G. C. 1986. *Indian Security Policy*. Princeton University Press.

Tiwari, Chitra K. (n.d.) 'Maoist Insurgency in Nepal: Internal Dimensions' *South Asia Analysis Group Papers* 187 (*www.saag.org*).

Tyagi, Shushila 1974. *Indo–Nepalese Relations 1858–1914*. Delhi: D. K. Publishing House.

Upadhaya, Sanjaya 2002. 'A Dozen Years of Democracy: The Games that Parties Play' in Dixit and Ramachandaran (eds) *State of Nepal.*

van Gennep, A. 1960. *The Rites of Passage.* University of Chicago Press.

Vickery, Michael 1984. *Cambodia: 1975–1982.* Chiang Mai: Silkworm Books.

von Hayek, Friederich 1944. *The Road to Serfdom.* London.

Wagle, Achyut 2001. 'Prachandapath: New Political Jargon' *Kathmandu Post*, 30 March.

Wallensteen, P. and M. Sollenberg 2000. 'Armed Conflict 1989–1999' *Journal of Peace Research* 37 (5).

Watson, G. 1991. 'Rewriting Culture' in Richard G. Fox (ed.) *Recapturing Anthropology: Working in the Present.* Santa Fe: School of American Research Press.

Werake, Mahindra 1992. 'Foreign Policy Perspectives of South Asian States' in Jayasekera (ed.) *Security Dilemma of a Small Nation*, Part One: *Sri Lanka in the South Asian Context.*

Whelpton, John 1994. 'The General Elections of 1991' in Hutt (ed.) *Nepal in the Nineties.*

Wolf, Eric 1999. *Envisioning Power: Ideologies of Dominance and Crisis.* Berkeley: University of California Press.

Wriggins, W. Howard 1992. 'South Asian Regional Politics: Asymmetrical Balance or One-State Dominance?' in W. Howard Wriggins, F. Gregory Gause III, Terrence R. Lyons and Evelyn Colbert (eds) *Dynamics of Regional Politics: Four Systems on the Indian Ocean Rim.* New York: Columbia University Press.

WW 1996. 'Nepal: Hoisting the Red Flag on the Roof of the World!' *A World to Win* 1 (7).

Yami, Hisila 1997/8 (2054 v.s.). 'Sthaniya sattako avadharana' (A Reflection on Local Power) *Nava Chetana* 3 (1).

——— and Baburam Bhattarai 2000/1 (2057 v.s.). *Marksbad ra mahila mukti* (Marxism and Women's Liberation). Kathmandu: Utprerak Prakashan.

Yogi, Bhagirath 2002. 'High Stakes' *Spotlight* 21.

Ziring, Lawrence (ed.) 1978. *The Subcontinent in World Politics: India, its Neighbors and the Great Powers.* New York: Praeger.

Zur, J. 1998. *Violent Memories: Mayan War Widows in Guatemala.* Oxford: Westview Press.

INDEX

Chand, Lokendra Bahadur, 14, 66, 69
Chetri, 2, 58, 219
children, 98–9, 156, 160, 265–6, 270, 273, 280–1
China: attitude to Maoist movement of, 55–6, 217n, 252; CPN's relationship with, 25, 30, 235n; Cultural Revolution in, 32–3; Maoism in, 25, 48, 51, 53, 93, 95, 219, 222, 240, 248; and Naxalites, 32–3, 227; Nepal's relations with, 23, 208, 216n, 252; and Tibet, 117n, 198n, 201; war between India and (1962), 201–3, 213, 226
civil society: corruption of, 143–5, 151, 190, 258; definition of, 142, 185; ethnography of, 85, 137; Koirala government alienated from, 72; Maoist policy towards, 59; organisations, 16, 155; weakness of, 142–5, 164
class: basis of parties, 251; and caste, 131; class-based exclusion, 164, 259, 263n; classless society, 155, 165; concerns, 102; CPN (UML) view of, 257; economic, 131; enemies, 33, 160, 233–5, 239–40; and ethnicity, 124, 128, 134, 218, 221; loyalties, 200; Maoist analysis of, 45, 102–3, 130–1, 218, 234–5, 256; middle class(es), 223, 255; organisations (in Panchayat system), 29; peasant-worker, 24; professional, 4, 42; ruling class(es), 115, 207, 243, 246; social, 17, 42, 131; struggle, 23, 103, 132, 149, 163, 218, 234–5, 240; working, 42
communalism, 131–2, 134
Communist Party of India, 22–3
Communist Party of Nepal (CPN): anti-Congress position of, 23; banning of (in 1952–6), 24; conventions of, 24, 25, 28, 30; Darbhanga Plenum, 28; election performance of (1959), 26–7, 231; formation of, 3, 21–2; history of, 21–4; ideology of, 24–5, 27–9; internal dissent within, 27, 28, 30, 231; *see also* Communist Party of Nepal (Maoist); Communist Party of Nepal (Unified Marxist-Leninist); Fourth Convention.
Communist Party of Nepal (Fourth Convention), *see* Fourth Convention

Communist Party of Nepal (Maoist): 61; central committee of, 39; conventions/conferences of, 39; formation of, 5, 20, 36; organisation of, 38–40, 57; politburo of, 39; position on nationalities, 116; *see also* Maoist(s)
Communist Party of Nepal (Marxist), 31n
Communist Party of Nepal (Marxist-Leninist) [CPN (ML)], 34–5, 66, 138–9, 148–9, 251
Communist Party of Nepal (Masal), 34–6, 116n, 138–9, 232–3, 244, 248–9, 255–6
Communist Party of Nepal (Mashal), 35–6, 66, 232, 248
Communist Party of Nepal (Unified Marxist-Leninist) [CPN (UML)]: 4, 14, 53, 61, 138–9, 148, 151, 157, 232, 245–8, 255, 260; attitude to Maoists of, 65–7, 76–7, 254; contact between Maoists and, 48, 139, 246; in government, 4; internal differences within, 254–5; policies of, 57, 61, 127, 251, 257–8; splits with CPN (ML), 139, 244; workers attacked, 47
Communist Party of Nepal (Unity Centre), 36, 56, 138–9, 151, 232, 244, 249
Congress, *see* Nepali Congress
constituent assembly, demands for, 10–11, 15, 26–8, 31, 35, 59, 76, 78, 218
Constitution: (1962), 3; (1990), 4, 10–11, 13–14, 69, 169; call for new, 16, 56, 59, 120, 218; effective suspension of, 247n; federal, 120; proposed amendments to, 8, 57, 78; provisions of, 1, 69, 169; rights guaranteed by, 260, 264; spirit of, 139; *see also* constituent assembly, demands for; monarchy, constitutional
corruption: as cause of Maoist movement, 164, 192, 245; of civil society, 142–5; control of, 178; in development organisations, 100; in justice system, 128; Koirala government accused of, 72; local, 90; addressed by Maoists, 236; in police, 94; in politics, 138, 174, 178–81, 207, 247; and power, 17
CPN (UML), *see* Communist Party of Nepal (Unified Marxist-Leninist)

Integrated Internal Security and Development Programme (IISDP), 44, 69, 71

interim government, demands for, 10, 56–7, 59, 218

Jajarkot, 18, 42–5, 47, 50, 68–9, 119–20, 232

jan andolan, *see* people's movement

jan sarkar, *see* people's government

jan yuddha, *see* people's war

janajati, 45, 114, 117n, 127–9, 131, 132, 134

jati, 121, 124, 130–2

Jhapa movement, 32–4, 202, 235, 237–8

Jirel, 102

Joshi, Govinda Raj, 71

journalists: 46, 80, 84–6, 101, 104, 115, 143, 146, 209; treatment of, 12, 146–7, 152, 194n, 254; *see also* media

Jumla, 43, 214, 230

justice system: 17, 156–8, 162; courts, 19, 61, 68, 128, 158–9, 176, 177–8, 265; Maoist, 93, 127–8, 156; Supreme Court, 13, 169; *see also* people's courts

Kalikot, 12n, 42–3, 51, 69, 232, 253

Kavre, 42–3, 230

Khadka, Khum Bahadur, 49

Khadka, Rit Bahadur, 94–5, 101

Kham (language), 122, *see also* Magaranti

Khambuwan National Liberation Front, 42, 219

Khapangi, Gore Bahadur, 113, 120, 129–30, 135

kinship, 92, 181, 211

Kirat National Liberation Front, 42

Koirala, B.P., 22, 202, 215, 223, 235

Koirala, Girija Prasad: attempts to deploy army, 9–10, 69–72, 206, 209n; involvement in Biratnagar strikes of (1950), 22; and palace massacre, 246; as prime minister, 50, 64, 66, 69, 71–2, 205, 208; resigns as prime minister, 9–10, 72, 209n; and split of Nepali Congress, 13

Lal, C.K., 149

Lama, Nirmal, 31–6, 231, 247–9

landlessness, 234, 238

landlords, 46, 87n, 89, 102, 159, 234, 235, 237–8, 240

language issues, 1, 114, 116, 119n, 121n, 122, 124n, 125, 130, 134, 144, 258, 266, 276

Latin America, 241

Lenin, V.I., 22n, 121, 219, 239, 241

liberalism, 196, 258–9

literature: ethnic, 112, 116, 124n; Maoist, 148n, 149, 151, 233, 239; Nepali, 144, 149–50; political, 195

local government: attitude to Maoists of, 80; control of goods and services by, 175–6; leaders of, 173–4, 180–2, 186–8; in Maoist areas, 6, 41, 43–5, 49, 52, 68, 76, 82, 99–100, 126; in Panchayat system, 32n; politics of, 178–81, 184–6, 230–3, 242; suspension of elected, 13; weakness of, 19, 244; *see also* elections, local; people's government; state; Village Development Committees (VDCs)

Magar: 102, 112–35; Kham Magar, 20, 88, 102, 103

Magarant: 118–22; Liberation Front (Magarant Mukti Morcha), 116–21, 125–7; National Liberation Front, 41, 118, 121, 125–7

Magaranti, 122

Mahara, Krishna Bahadur, 147, 224n, 233

Mainali, Radha Krishna, 33

Majhi Liberation Front, 41–2

Mao Zedong, 28n, 30, 37, 39, 93, 117n, 120, 121, 132, 133n, 194, 209, 217–20, 227, 238–41, 257

Maoist(s): activities in Kathmandu, 40, 53; brutality of, 95, 145, 148; causes of movement, 136, 170–2, 192–5, 226–33; Central Military Commission, 52; criticism of, 148–9; cultural policies, 45–6, 49, 97–8, 103, 123, 150–1, 219, 274; cultural groups/programmes, 103, 147, 155, 160, 163, 264, 281–2n; dissatisfaction with, 47–9, 169;